Official History of Operations

on the

N. W. FRONTIER
OF INDIA
1936-37

The Naval & Military Press Ltd

Published by
The Naval & Military Press Ltd
5 Riverside, Brambleside, Bellbrook
Industrial Estate, Uckfield, East Sussex,
TN22 1QQ England
Tel: +44 (0) 1825 749494
Fax: +44 (0) 1825 765701
www.naval-military-press.com

In reprinting in facsimile from the original, any imperfections are inevitably reproduced and the quality may fall short of modern type and cartographic standards.

CONTENTS OF VOL. 1936-37.

OFFICIAL HISTORY OF OPERATIONS ON N.-W. FRONTIER OF INDIA.

	PAGE.
Glossary of Tribal Terms	ii
Order of Battle of Wazirforce	iv
List of Maps and Sketches	xiii
List of Illustrations	xiv
Index to Chapters	xv

GLOSSARY OF TRIBAL TERMS.

The Student reading this history who is new to the North Western Frontier of India, or without knowledge of the everyday tribal terms that are commonly in use there, is recommended to study the following short glossary.

A frequent reference to it on meeting names of places, etc., in the text will repay the trouble taken and add to the interest and understanding of the operations described.

It is to be noted also in connection with tribal names of places, that on the Frontier the same names recur in different places. Thus there are more than one "Mir Ali", one "Datta Khel" or one "Manzai", etc.; and it is desirable therefore, to keep close touch with the maps in order to avoid confusion of such names.

Algad—water course.

Badragga—tribal escort.

Barampta—seizure of men, animals or property to enforce reparation for an offence.

Chagul—a canvas water vessel.

Chigha—a pursuit party.

China—a spring, fountain.

Dara—a pass.

Gasht—a patrol.

Ghar—a mountain peak.

Ghazi—a Mussalman who devotes his life to killing an infidel or fighting unbelievers.

    As a title it has long been disused officially and its assumption by fanatical murderers is disapproved by respectable Muhammadans.

Ghundai—A knoll.

Jihad—a Muhammadan religious war—equivalent to a crusade.

Jirga—an assembly of tribal representatives or elders (maliks).

Kach—an alluvial flat on the bank of a stream

Kafila—a caravan, Trading convoy.

Karez—an irrigation channel, frequently bored through hillsides.

Kats—see 'Kach'.

Kharif—the autumn crop.

Khassadar—a tribal levy who in return for certain responsibilities receives pay from Government.

Khwar or Khor—a ravine.

Kirri—an encampment of nomads.

Kot—a walled hamlet.

Lashkar—a tribal gathering (not usually applied to less than 200 men).

Malik—a tribal representative or elder.
Mullah—one learned (or reputed to be so) in the Muhammadan scripture.
Narai or Kotal—a pass.
Oba—water.
Pakhal—a metal water container.
Pir—a saint.
Powindah—a nomad.
Punga—an upland glade or a patch of grazing ground.
Raghza—a plateau on the edge of a valley.
Rogha—a plateau on the edge of a valley.
Sangar—a stone breastwork.
Sar—head, peak.
Shariat—Muhammadan law.
Shin or Shna—green.
Spin—white.
Sur or Sra—red.
Tangi—a defile, gorge.
Tauda—warm.
Toi—a stream.
Tor—black.
Wam—the same as 'Kach'.
Warsak—spur of a hill.
Wuch—dry.
Ziarat—a shrine.

ORDER OF BATTLE OF TROOPS IN WAZIRISTAN, 1936-37.

(Where units or formations have been referred to in the text by an abbreviated title, the abbreviation used is shown.)

Abbreviations used in text.

HEADQUARTERS—
- Headquarters Wazirforce . . . .
- Rear Headquarters Wazirforce . . . .
- Headquarters Waziristan Division . . . .
- Headquarters 1st Indian Division . . . .
- Headquarters Bannu sub area . . . .
- Headquarters Manzai sub area . . . .
- Headquarters Wana Brigade . . . .
- Headquarters Razmak Brigade . . . . H. Q. Razmak Bde.
- Headquarters Bannu Brigade . . . . H. Q. Bannu Bde.
- Headquarters 1st (Abbottabad) Infantry Brigade . . H. Q. 1 Inf. Bde.
- Headquarters 2nd (Rawalpindi) Infantry Brigade . . H. Q. 2 Inf. Bde.
- Headquarters 3rd (Jhelum) Infantry Brigade . . . H. Q. 3 Inf. Bde.
- Headquarters 9th (Jhansi) Infantry Brigade . . . H. Q. 9 Inf. Bde.
- Headquarters 2nd Echelon . . . .

CAVALRY—
- Probyn's Horse (5th King Edward VII's Own Lancers) . Probyn's Horse.
- 8th King George V's Own Light Cavalry . . . . 8th Light Cav.
- Detachment The Scinde Horse. (14th Prince of Wales's Own Cavalry) . . . . Scinde Horse.

ROYAL ARTILLERY—
- Headquarters Frontier Post Group, Royal Artillery, Waziristan . . . .
- Post Group Royal Artillery 4·5″ (Howitzer), (Mir Ali) . ....
- Post Group Royal Artillery 2·75″ guns (Manzai) . . ....
- Post Group Royal Artillery 18-pounder guns (Wana) . ....
- Post Group Royal Artillery 4·5″ (Howitzer) (Wana) . ....
- Headquarters 4th Field Brigade, Royal Artillery . . H. Q. 4 Fd. Bde. R. A.
- 4th Field Brigade Signal Section . . . . . . 4 Fd. Bde. Sig. Sec.
- 4th (Cole's Kop) Field Battery (Howitzer) . . . . 4 Fd. Bty. (H).
- 7th (Sandham's Company) Field Battery . . . . 7 Fd. Bty.
- 63rd Field Battery (Howitzer) . . . . 63 Fd. Bty. (H).
- 66th Field Battery (Howitzer) . . . . 66 Fd. Bty. (H).
- 81st (Sphinx) Field Battery (Howitzer) . . . . 81 Fd. Bty. (H).
- Section 20/21st Medium Battery (Howitzer) . . . Sec. 20/21 Med. Bty.
- Headquarters 22nd Mountain Brigade . . . . . H. Q. 22 Mtn. Bde.
- Headquarters 23rd Mountain Brigade . . . . . H. Q. 23 Mtn. Bde.
- Headquarters 25th Mountain Brigade . . . . . H. Q. 25 Mtn. Bde.
- Headquarters 22nd Mountain Brigade Signal Section . ....
- Headquarters 23rd Mountain Brigade Signal Section . ....
- Headquarters 25th Mountain Brigade Signal Section . ....
- 2nd Light Battery . . . . 2 L. Bty.
- 3rd Light Battery . . . . 3 L. Bty.
- 2nd (Derajat) Mountain Battery (Frontier Force) . . 2 Mtn. Bty.

v

Abbreviations used
in text.

ROYAL ARTILLERY—contd.

3rd (Peshawar) Mountain Battery (Frontier Force)	3 Mtn. Bty.
4th (Hazara) Mountain Battery (Frontier Force)	4 Mtn. Bty.
5th (Bombay) Mountain Battery	5 Mtn. Bty.
7th (Bengal) Mountain Battery	7 Mtn. Bty.
8th (Lahore) Mountain Battery	8 Mtn. Bty.
12th (Poonch) Mountain Battery	12 Mtn. Bty.
13th (Dardoni) Mountain Battery	13 Mtn. Bty.
15th (Jhelum) Mountain Battery	15 Mtn. Bty.
17th (Nowshera) Mountain Battery	17 Mtn. Bty.
19th (Maymyo) Mountain Battery	19 Mtn. Bty.
Detachment 23rd Mountain Brigade Ammunition Column	....
Detachment 25th Mountain Brigade Ammunition Column	....

ROYAL ENGINEERS—

Base Engineer Park Bannu	....
Base Engineer Park Mir Ali	....
Base Engineer Park Mari Indus	....
No. 2 Field Company King George V's Own Bengal Sappers and Miners	2 Fd. Coy. S. and M.
No. 3 Field Company King George V's Own Bengal Sappers and Miners	3 Fd. Coy. S. and M.
No. 4 Field Company King George V's Own Bengal Sappers and Miners	4 Fd. Coy. S. and M.
No. 5 Field Company King George V's Own Bengal Sappers and Miners	5 Fd. Coy. S. and M.
No. 12 Field Company Queen Victoria's Own Madras Sappers and Miners	12 Fd. Coy. S. and M.
No. 14 Field Company Queen Victoria's Own Madras Sappers and Miners	14 Fd. Coy. S. and M.
No. 15 Field Company Queen Victoria's Own Madras Sappers and Miners	15 Fd. Coy. S. and M.
No. 19 Field Company Royal Bombay Sappers and Miners	19 Fd. Coy. S. and M.
No. 20 Field Company Royal Bombay Sappers and Miners	20 Fd. Coy. S. and M.
No. 22 Field Company Royal Bombay Sappers and Miners	22 Fd. Coy. S. and M.
No. 43 Divisional Headquarters Company King George V's Own Bengal Sappers and Miners	....
No. 6 Army Troops Company King George V's Own Bengal Sappers and Miners	....
No. 8 Army Troops Company King George V's Own Bengal Sappers and Miners	....
Wazirforce Field Survey Section	....
No. 1 Road Construction Battalion	....
No. 2 Road Construction Battalion	....
No. 4 Road Construction Battalion	....
No. 5 Road Construction Battalion	....
Military Engineer Services personnel	....
Military Engineer Services Depot, Bannu	....

	Abbreviations used in text.

INDIAN SIGNAL CORPS—

"A" Corps Signals	'A' Corps Sigs.
Detachment "B" Corps Signals (Operating Section and Wireless Telegraphy Section)	....
Waziristan District Signals	Wazirdist. Sigs.
1st Indian Divisional Signals	1 Div. Sigs.
Detachment 3rd Indian Divisional Signals	Det. 3 Div. Sigs.
Detachment 2nd Indian Cavalry Brigade Signal Troop.	....
Detachment 3rd Indian Divisional Signals (9th Infantry Brigade Signal Section Wireless Telegraphy Section)	....
Detachment Kohat District Signals	....
Detachment Peshawar District Signals	....

INFANTRY BATTALIONS. (British)—

1st Battalion The Hampshire Regiment	1/Hampshire R.
1st Battalion The Royal Norfolk Regiment	1/R. Norfolk R.
1st Battalion The South Wales Borderers	1/S. Wales Bord.
1st Battalion The Northamptonshire Regiment	1/North'n R.
2nd Battalion The Argyll and Sutherland Highlanders (Princess Louise's)	2/A. and S. H.
2nd Battalion The Green Howards (Alexandra, Princess of Wales' Own Yorkshire Regiment)	2/Green Howards.

ROYAL TANK CORPS—

1st Light Tank Company	1 Lt. Tank Coy.
6th Light Tank Company	6 Lt. Tank Coy.
7th Light Tank Company	7 Lt. Tank Coy.
8th Light Tank Company	8 Lt. Tank Coy.
9th Light Tank Company	9 Lt. Tank Coy.
11th Light Tank Company	11 Lt. Tank Coy.

INFANTRY BATTALIONS. (Indian)—

2nd Battalion 1st Punjab Regiment	2/1 Punjab R.
3rd Battalion 1st Punjab Regiment	3/1 Punjab R.
2nd Battalion 2nd Punjab Regiment	2/2 Punjab R.
2nd Battalion (King Edward VII's Own) 4th Bombay Grenadiers	2 Bombay Grs.
3rd Battalion 5th Mahratta Light Infantry	3/5 Mahratta L. I.
2nd Battalion (Prince of Wales's Own) 6th Rajputana Rifles	2/6 Raj. Rif.
3rd Battalion 6th Rajputana Rifles	3/6 Raj. Rif.
4th Battalion (Outram's) 6th Rajputana Rifles	4/6 Raj. Rif.
2nd Battalion (Prince Albert Victor's) 7th Rajput Regiment	2/7 Rajput R.
3rd Battalion (Duke of Connaught's Own) 7th Rajput Regiment.	3/7 Rajput R.
2nd Battalion 8th Punjab Regiment	2/8 Punjab R.
4th Battalion (Prince of Wales's Own) 8th Punjab Regiment	4/8 Punjab R.
3rd Battalion 9th Jat Regiment	3/9 Jat R.
1st Battalion (Duchess of Connaught's Own) 10th Baluch Regiment	1/10 Baluch R.
1st Battalion (King George V's Own) (Ferozepore Sikhs) 11th Sikh Regiment	....

	Abbreviations used in text.
INFANTRY BATTALIONS. (Indian)—*contd.*	
2nd Royal Battalion (Ludhiana Sikhs) 11th Sikh Regiment	2/11 Sikh R.
3rd Royal Battalion (Sikhs) 12th Frontier Force Regiment	3/12 F. F. R.
5th Battalion (Queen Victoria's Own Corps of Guides) 12th Frontier Force Regiment	5/12 F. F. R.
1st Battalion (Coke's) 13th Frontier Force Rifles	1/13 F. F. Rif.
2nd Battalion 13th Frontier Force Rifles	2/13 F. F. Rif.
6th Royal Battalion (Scinde) 13th Frontier Force Rifles	6/13 F. F. Rif.
1st Battalion 14th Punjab Regiment	1/14 Punjab R.
2nd Battalion (Duke of Cambridge's Own) (Brownlow's) 14th Punjab Regiment	2/14 Punjab R.
3rd Battalion 15th Punjab Regiment	3/15 Punjab R.
1st Battalion 16th Punjab Regiment	1/16 Punjab R.
3rd Battalion 16th Punjab Regiment	3/16 Punjab R.
4th Battalion (Bhopal) 16th Punjab Regiment	4/16 Punjab R.
1st Battalion (Prince of Wales's Own) 17th Dogra Regiment	1/17 Dogra R.
2nd Battalion 17th Dogra Regiment	2/17 Dogra R.
1st Battalion 2nd King Edward VII's Own Gurkha Rifles. (The Sirmoor Rifles)	1/2 G. R.
1st Battalion 3rd Queen Alexandra's Own Gurkha Rifles	1/3 G. R.
2nd Battalion 4th Prince of Wales's Own Gurkha Rifles	2/4 G. R.
2nd Battalion 5th Royal Gurkha Rifles (Frontier Force)	2/5 R. G. R.
1st Battalion 6th Gurkha Rifles	1/6 G. R.
2nd Battalion 6th Gurkha Rifles	2/6 G. R.
1st Battalion 9th Gurkha Rifles	1/9 G. R.
ROYAL INDIAN ARMY SERVICE CORPS UNITS—	
Headquarters Wazirforce Royal Indian Army Service Corps	....
Headquarters Waziristan Division Royal Indian Army Service Corps	....
Headquarters 1st Indian Division Royal Indian Army Service Corps	....
Rear Headquarters Wazirforce Royal Indian Army Service Corps	....
Headquarters No. 14 District Supply Company	....
No. 1 Temporary Royal Indian Army Service Corps Personnel Depot	....
Headquarters No. 3 Supply Personnel Company	....
Station Transport Officers, Manzai, Dera Ismail Khan, Mir Ali, Wana, Dosalli	....
Advance Base Supply Depots, Bannu and Manzai	....
Field Supply Depots	.....
SUPPLY UNITS—	
No. 1 Supply Issue Section	1 S. I. S.
No. 2 Supply Issue Section	2 S. I. S.
No. 3 Supply Issue Section	3 S. I. S.
No. 4 Supply Issue Section	4 S. I. S.
No. 10 Supply Issue Section	10 S. I. S.
No. 12 Supply Issue Section	12 S. I. S.
No. 21 Supply Issue Section	21 S. I. S.

	Abbreviations used in text.
SUPPLY UNITS—*contd.*	
No. 27 Supply Issue Section	27 S. I. S.
No. 28 Supply Issue Section	28 S. I. S.
No. 29 Supply Issue Section	29 S. I. S.
No. 30 Supply Issue Section	30 S. I. S.
Detachment No. 1 Field Bakery	....
No. 105 Independent Bakery Sub-Section	....
No. 106 Independent Bakery Sub-Section	....
No. 107 Independent Bakery Sub-Section	....
Detachment No. 1 Field Butchery	....
No. 105 Independent Butchery Sub-Section	....
No. 106 Independent Butchery Sub-Section	....
No. 107 Independent Butchery Sub-Section	....
No. 1 Railhead Supply Detachment	....
No. 2 Railhead Supply Detachment	....
No. 15 Supply Depot Section	....
No. 16 Supply Depot Section	....
No. 17 Supply Depot Section	....
No. 18 Supply Depot Section	....
No. 19 Supply Depot Section	....
No. 20 Supply Depot Section	....
No. 21 Supply Depot Section	....
No. 22 Supply Depot Section	....
No. 23 Supply Depot Section	....
No. 24 Supply Depot Section	....
No. 35 Supply Depot Section	....
No. 36 Supply Depot Section	....
No. 37 Supply Depot Section	....
No. 38 Supply Depot Section	....
No. 58 Supply Depot Section	....
No. 59 Supply Depot Section	....
No. 8 Petrol Oil Lubricants Section	....
No. 9 Petrol Oil Lubricants Section	....
No. 10 Petrol Oil Lubricants Section	....
No. 11 Petrol Oil Lubricants Section	....
No. 12 Petrol Oil Lubricants Section	....
No. 13 Petrol Oil Lubricants Section	....
No. 19 Petrol Oil Lubricants Section	....
No. 7 Cattle Supply Section Class II	....
No. 8 Cattle Supply Section Class II	....
Improvised Cattle Section	....
ANIMAL TRANSPORT UNITS—	
No. 1 Animal Transport Company (Mule)	1 A. T. Coy.
No. 2 Animal Transport Company (Mule)	2 A. T. Coy.
No. 7 Animal Transport Company (Mule)	7 A. T. Coy.
No. 10 Animal Transport Company (Mule)	10 A. T. Coy.
No. 15 Animal Transport Company (Mule)	15 A. T. Coy.

Abbreviations used in text.

ANIMAL TRANSPORT UNITS—*contd.*

No. 18 Animal Transport Company (Mule)	18 A. T. Coy.
No. 19 Animal Transport Company (Mule)	19 A. T. Coy.
No. 22 Animal Transport Company (Mule)	22 A. T. Coy.
No. 25 Animal Transport Company (Mule)	25 A. T. Coy.
No. 30 Animal Transport Company (Mule)	30 A. T. Coy.
No. 32 Animal Transport Company (Mule)	32 A. T. Coy.
No. 33 Animal Transport Company (Mule) (less one pack troop)	33 A. T. Coy.
No. 35 Animal Transport Company (Mule)	35 A. T. Coy.
No. 36 Animal Transport Company (Mule) (less one pack troop)	36 A. T. Coy.
No. 39 Animal Transport Company (Mule) (less one pack troop)	39 A. T. Coy.
Detachment No. 6 Animal Transport Company (Mule)	....
No. 37 Animal Transport Company (Camel) (Silladar) (4 troops only)	....
Detachment No. 38 Animal Transport Company (Camel) (Silladar)	....
No. 40 Animal Transport Company (Camel) (Silladar)	....

MECHANICAL TRANSPORT UNITS—

No. 5 Motor Ambulance Unit	....
No. 13 Independent Mechanical Transport Section (30 cwt.)	13 Ind. M. T. Sec.
No. 14 Independent Mechanical Transport Section (30 cwt.)	14 Ind. M. T. Sec.
No. 15 Independent Mechanical Transport Section (3 ton)	15 Ind. M. T. Sec.
No. 29 Independent Mechanical Transport Section (3 ton)	29 Ind. M. T. Sec.
No. 30 Independent Mechanical Transport Section (3 ton)	30 Ind. M. T. Sec.
No. 33 Independent Mechanical Transport Section (3 ton)	33 Ind. M. T. Sec.
No. 35 Independent Mechanical Transport Section (3 ton)	35 Ind. M. T. Sec.
No. 39 Independent Mechanical Transport Section (3 ton)	39 Ind. M. T. Sec.
No. 14 Mechanical Transport Company (30 cwt.)	14 M. T. Coy.
No. 27 Mechanical Transport Company (less two Sections)	27 M. T. Coy.
Detachment No. 28 Mechanical Transport Company	Det. 28 M. T. Coy.
Detachment No. 51 Section No. 27 Mechanical Transport Company attached to 63rd Field Battery (Howitzer) Royal Artillery	....
Detachment No. 18 Independent Mechanical Transport Company attached to 81st Field Battery (Howitzer) Royal Artillery	....
Technical Inspector Mechanical Transport Waziristan Circle	....
Heavy Repair Shops Mechanical Transport, Class III	....
1st Indian Division Mechanical Transport Workshops	....
Field Mechanical Transport Workshops	....
No. 1 Line of Communication Workshop Section	....
No. 2 Line of Communication Workshop Section	....

MEDICAL—

Indian Military Hospital, with British Wing, Bannu	....
Indian Military Hospital, with British Wing, Dera Ismail Khan	....

Abbreviations used
in text.

MEDICAL—*contd.*

Indian Military Hospital, with British Wing, Wana	....
Indian Military Hospital with British Wing, Mir Ali	....
Indian Military Hospital, with British Wing, Manzai	....
Indian Military Hospital, with British Wing, Mari Indus	....
Indian Military Hospital, with British Wing, Razmak	....
Convalescent Depot, Razmak	....
No. 4 Field Ambulance	4 Fd. Amb.
No. 7 Field Ambulance	7 Fd. Amb.
No. 8 Field Ambulance	8 Fd. Amb.
No. 10 Field Ambulance	10 Fd. Amb.
No. 11 Field Ambulance	11 Fd. Amb.
No. 16 Field Ambulance	16 Fd. Amb.
No. 18 Field Ambulance	18 Fd. Amb.
Depot No. 8 Field Ambulance, Bannu	....
No. 3 Sanitary Section	....
No. 14 Sanitary Section	....
No. 2 Depot Medical Stores	....
Military Dispensary, Miranshah	....
Brigade Laboratory, Bannu	....
District Laboratory, Razmak	....
Army Dental Centre, Razmak	....
No. 1 Motor Ambulance Section (Motor Ambulance cars only)	....
No. 5 Motor Ambulance Section	....

VETERINARY—

Deputy Assistant Director of Veterinary Services	....
Military Veterinary Hospital, Class I, Razmak	....
Military Veterinary Hospital, Class II, Bannu	....
Military Veterinary Hospital, Class II, Wana	....
Branch Military Veterinary Hospital, Mir Ali	....
Branch Military Veterinary Hospital, Manzai	....
No. 3 Mobile Veterinary Section	3 Mob. Vet. Sec.
No. 4 Mobile Veterinary Section	4 Mob. Vet. Sec.
Veterinary Aid Posts	....
Advance Remount Section	....
Nucleus Field Remount Section	....
Railhead Remount Detachment	....

ORDNANCE—

No. 2 Ordnance Field Company	....
Ordnance Field Depot, Bannu	....
Ordnance Field Depot, Razmak	....
Ordnance Field Depot, Dosalli	....
Tent Repair Unit	....
Ordnance Mobile Workshop, Bannu	....

	Abbreviations used in text.
POSTAL—	
No. 5 Field Post Office	....
No. 8 Field Post Office	....
No. 9 Field Post Office	....
No. 10 Field Post Office	....
No. 11 Field Post Office	....
No. 13 Field Post Office	....
No. 25 Field Post Office	....
REST CAMPS—	
No. 3 Rest Camp	....
Rest Camp, Bannu	....
Rest Camp, Manzai	....
Rest Camp, Mari Indus	....
Rest Camp, Mir Ali	....
PROVOST—	
Waziristan Divisional Provost Company	....
1st Divisional Provost Company	....
MILITARY ACCOUNTS—	
Field Cashier	....
WORKS—	
No. 9 Labour Company	....
No. 10 Labour Company	....
No. 26 Labour Company	....
CANTEENS—	
Canteen Depot, Bannu	....
TRANSPORTATION—	
Military Forwarding Officers, Bannu, Mir Ali, Manzai, Dosalli	....
MILITARY GRASS FARMS—	
Headquarters, Grass Farm, Bannu	....
Grass Farm, Dera Ismail Khan	....
Grass Farm, Manzai	....
Grass Farm, Razmak	....
Branch Grass Farm, Wana	....
MILITARY DAIRIES—	
Headquarters, Dairy Farm, Bannu	....
Dairy Farm, Dera Ismail Khan	....
Dairy Farm, Manzai	....
Dairy Farm, Razmak	....
Dairy Farm, Wana	....
Dairy Farm, Dosalli	....
CIVIL ARMED FORCES—	
Tochi Scouts	....
South Waziristan Scouts	S. W. S.
Frontier Constabulary	F. C.

Abbreviations used
in text.

ROYAL AIR FORCE UNITS—
Headquarters No. 1 (Indian) Group (Peshawar) . . . .
Headquarters No. 1 (Indian) Wing (Kohat) . . . .
    No. 27 (Bomber) Squadron . . . .
    No. 60 (Bomber) Squadron . . . .
    Bomber Transport Flight (India) . . . .
Headquarters No. 2 (Indian) Wing (Risalpur) . . . .
    No. 11 (Bomber) Squadron . . . .
    No. 39 (Bomber) Squadron . . . .
    Flight No. 70 (Bomber Transport) Squadron . . ....
Headquarters No. 3 (Indian) Wing (Miranshah) . . ....
    No. 5 (Army Co-operation) Squadron . . . .
    No. 20 (Army Co-operation) Squadron . . . .
    No. 28 (Army Co-operation) Squadron (Manzai) . . ....
    A Flight No. 1 Squadron, Indian Air Force . . ....
    No. 31 (Army Co-operation) Squadron (Fort Sandeman) ....

LIST OF MAPS AND SKETCHES.

		Page
A.	General Map of Waziristan. (In pocket)	..
B 37.	Khaisora river from Damdil to River Camp. Jaler Algad. Shaktu river from Mandawam eastward. (At end of Chap. XXVI.)	224-A
C 37.	From Mir Ali south to Ghunda Tizha Algad. (At end of Chapter X)	82-A
D 37.	Ghariom-Madamir Kalai-Shaktu to Mandawam. (At end of Chapter XV)	139-A
E 37.	Area of operations of 1st Infantry Brigade West of Asad Khel 29th March 1937. (At end of Chapter VII)	52-A
F 37.	Shahur Tangi. (At end of Chapter VIII)	65-A
G 37.	Road from Chalweshti to Tiarza Narai and country on either side. (At end of Chapter XXI)	185-A
H 37.	Dosalli-Ghariom-Shawali Algad-Babrakra Algad. (At end of Chapter XVIII)	161-A
I 37.	Pezu Pass. (At end of Chapter XII)	106-A
J 37.	Khaisora R, Dakaikalai to Bichhe Kashkai Camp-Mazai Raghza-Kam Sham. (At end of Chapter XIII)	116-B
K 37.	Sirdar Algad. (At end of Chapter XXIII)	199-A
L 37.	Madamir Kalai to Ahmadwam. (At end of Chapter XIV)	125-A
M 37.	Sharawangi Narai. (At end of Chapter XVI)	152-A
N 37.	Panorama Sketch. (At end of Chapter XVI)	152-B
O 37.	Ladha-Kaniguram-Baddar Algad. (At end of Chapter XXI)	185-B
P 37.	Spinwam. (At end of Chapter XXIV)	208-A
Q 37.	Chaudhwan. (At end of Chapter XXI)	185-C
R 37.	Santala. (At end of Chapter XXII)	190-A
S 37.	Bhitanni country to Kot. (At end of Chapter XXV)	214-A
T 37.	Roads. (In pocket)	..
U 37.	Tribal areas. (In pocket)	..
V 37.	To illustrate system of protection in Razani sector L. of C. (with Appendix I).	243-A

Note.

Where co-ordinates are cited in the text, which are not traceable in the relevant maps provided with this volume, such co-ordinates refer to the gridded Survey of India Maps.

All places and features however, that are essential to a proper understanding of the operations described in this Volume are clearly shown on the accompanying maps; and reference to other maps should not be required unless it is to deal with unforeseen controversial points.

LIST OF ILLUSTRATIONS.

	PAGE
General Sir John F. S. D. Coleridge, G.C.B., C.M.G., D.S.O.	Frontispiece.
Damdil Camp, 1937	43-A
1st Inf. Brigade Camp, Dosalli, May, 1937	84-A
Village Camp, May, 1937, Mtn. Artillery in action against snipers	86-A
Coronation Camp, Sham Plain, 1937	94-A
Kach Camp, May, 1937	95-A
Light Tanks on road protection duty	96-A
Ghariom Camp, 1937	99-A
Sappers and Miners constructing a bridge for the road near Ghariom Camp	99-B
Ghariom Camp and 'Carnarvon Castle.	101-A
View down Sham Algad, and Bahadur Camp	101-B
Spate at Ghariom Camp	} 108-A
Light tanks crossing the Sham Algad in spate at Ghariom Camp	
Transport moving down a nala towards Pasal	109-A
Shaktu River near Gulzamir Kot	116-A
Razmak Column Camp, Torwam, 1937	144-A
The first M. T. through the Nunghar Tangi into Bhitanni country, October, 1937	211-A
Spalvi Camp, 1st Inf. Brigade, 1937	212-A
Spalvi Tangi	213-A
Typical country near Spalvi	213-B
Qalandar Camp	213-C
Lower Shaktu Tangi	220-A
The new road to the Sham Plain	244-A
The Monster at work	} 244-B
Men of the 1st Bn. The South Wales Borderers, Road-making near Ghariom	
The 1st Bn. The South Wales Borderers, marching down the Sham Plain road	244-C

INDEX TO CHAPTERS.

	PAGE.
Chapter I.—Geographical—inhabitants—The General Situation in Waziristan in 1936 and Government's agreement with the Tori Khel in 1935—the "Islam Bibi" case and its immediate results—the Faqir of Ipi	1
Chapter II.—Attitude of Tori Khel Maliks—Factors tending to favour the activities of the Faqir of Ipi—political view of the situation—decision that troops should enter the Khaisora valley	6
Chapter III.—General plan of the operation—routes—advance of Razcol—advance of Tocol—operations of both columns on November 26th and 27th—casualties—R. A. F. co-operation—strength and composition of hostile lashkars—composition of Razcol and Tocol	8
Chapter IV.—Tori Khel to be punished—G. O. C.-in-C.'s appreciation of the situation—delegation of control to and instructions to Commander, Waziristan District—instructions regarding airaction—road to Khaisora river commenced—air warning issued—restrictions on air action—fresh agitation by the Faqir—attitude of tribes—advance to Khaisora river—inactivity of tribesmen—operations of 2nd Infantry Brigade and of Razmak Brigade—R. A. F. co-operation—troops of Waziristan Area—troops comprising Wazirforce	17
Chapter V.—General plan for completion of operations—work commenced on road along Khaisora river—movements and activities of Faqir—Arsalkot bombed—plan for further operations—Razmak Brigade from Damdil and Bannu Brigade from Jaler camp operate in Khaisora valley from 8th January—end of operations—troops withdraw—political control handed back—the Faqir—administration and maintenance of forces—protection on L. of C.	29
Chapter VI.—General situation in February, March and April—murders of Capt. Keogh and Lieut. Beatty—attack on Wana Brigade on 17th February—Tori Khel maliks go to Shaktu to see Faqir—reinforcements sent to Waziristan—Faqir states he will do nothing for one month, openly declares hostility and gets more support—more reinforcements sent to Waziristan—location of troops and re-organisation of areas—Tori Khel ordered to expel Faqir—air blockade round Arsal Kot—attack on Damdil camp piquet.	38
Chapter VII.—Utmanzai jirga visits Faqir—other political measures—attack on 1st Infantry Brigade near Asad Khel on March 29th	47
Chapter VIII.—Utmanzai maliks again approach Faqir—terms announced to Utmanzai maliks—supplies for Faqir—air action taken—events before the ambush in the Shahur Tangi—ambush in the Shahur Tangi April 9th.	53
Chapter IX.—2nd Infantry Brigade arrives in Waziristan—disturbances continue—tribesmen within two miles of attacked troops made liable to air action—Spinwam Post invested—political action against the Jalal Khel and Abdur Rahman Khel—attack on Tiarza Post—attack on piquet at Alexandra Ridge Post—attack on police station Tajori—general situation unsatisfactory—G. O. C.-in-C., Northern Command again invested with political control	66
Chapter X.—Political control assumed by G. O. C.-in-C., Northern Command—decision to operate in the Khaisora vallery area—plan of 1st Division—area of air blockade extended—R. A. F. plan—continuance of Faqir's propaganda—1st Division advances to Bichhe Kashkai—action fought by 2nd Infantry Brigade west of Bichhe Kashkai 29th April—operations of 1st Infantry Brigade, Bannu Brigade and Tochi Scouts 27th April to 3rd May—decision to advance from Dosalli—R.A.F. co-operation—situation continues to deteriorate—raid on Paharpur—attack on Frontier Constabulary patrol near Surkamar—political action against Madda Khel and Bhitannis—troops engaged in Khaisora operations	70

PAGE.

Chapter XI.—Decision to advance from Dosalli—general outline of future plans—conduct of operations delegated to Commander, Waziristan District—9th Infantry Brigade arrives in Waziristan—re-organisation of forces in Waziristan—objects of operations—preparatory moves—allotment of R. A. F. and extension of proscribed area—further activities of Faqir—1st Infantry Brigade advances to village camp 8th May—decision to make converging advance to Sham Plain—efforts to secure secrecy—plan of Commander, Waziristan District—plan and arrangements of Commander. Bannu Brigade—3rd Brigade moves to Dosalli—advance of Bannu Brigade by the Iblanke spur, night of 11th/12th May—advance of 1st Infantry Brigade 12th May—enemy withdraw 83

Chapter XII.—Immediate result of advance to Sham Plain—Faqir's efforts to get support—piqueting of Sre Mela Algad—permanent piqueting on L. of C.—organisation of convoys—responsibility for L. of C.—extension of area proscribed from the air—moves of formations—progress of motor track—supplies dropped from the air—troop movements—reconnaissances by Razmak Brigade—reconnaissance to Ghariom—attack on piquet, Kach Camp—advance to Ghariom Camp 18th May—further preparations at Ghariom Camp—enemy activity—Faqir moves—help to Faqir—attempts to bomb Datta Khel Post and to destroy bridges—raid on Umar Tatta Khel—raid on train in Pezu Pass, 24th May—raid on Tajori 21/22nd May—arrangements to deal with raiders—movements of Wana Brigade. . 96

Chapter XIII.—Plan for advance to Arsal Kot—objects to be attained—routes to Arsal Kot—advance from Ghariom Camp to Pasal, 27th May—arrangements of 2nd Brigade to preserve secrecy—2nd Brigade march to Khaisora river 27th May—route of 2nd Brigade for 28th May—Arsal Kot destroyed, 28th May—March of 2nd Brigade, 28th May—Commander, 2nd Brigade decides to camp—further destruction carried out 29th May, 2nd Brigade marches through rest of Force to Pasal—troops return to Sham Plain, 30th May—column goes to Razani, 27th May—Tori Khel overtures for peace—R. A. F. co-operation 107

Chapter XIV.—Proposals of Commander, Wazirforce for dealing with Mahsuds and for road construction—construction of roads sanctioned—re-organisation of Divisions and their tasks—instructions issued to Commanders, 1st Division and Waziristan Division—allotment of R.A.F.—troop movements—re-adjustment of responsibility for L. of C.—operations of Razmak Brigade and attack on road piquet at Gaj—air action against Bhitannis—arrangements for march of Bannu Brigade to Sororogha—Bannu Brigade marches to Sororogha—peace conditions for Tori Khel—R.A.F. co-operation 117

Chapter XV.—Intimation of further operations in the near future to deal with Mahsuds, their object and method—Razmak Brigade moves to Ladha—Resident interviews Mashud jirgas—activities of Razmak Brigade during period of jirgas—Mohmit Khel refuse road contracts—activities of Faqir and hostile gangs—attack on road piquet of 2/8 Punjab R., 6th June—location of Faqir and of hostile bands—instructions in preparation for early operations from Sham Plain—plan for operations in Shawali area—1st Brigade moves to Waladin—attacks on camp piquet of 2/5 R. G. R.—1st Brigade advances to Lakan 16th June, Bannu Brigade from Razmak advances to 96 grid line—operation repeated 17th June—troops withdraw to Ghariom Camp and Razmak—R.A.F. co-operation—preparations for operation to capture Faqir—plan for the operation—operation carried out on 20th and 21st June 126

Chapter XVI.—Instruction issued by Wazirforce Headquarters for further operations—moves of Brigades during these operations—Bannu Brigade moves to Chalweshti Camp, 20th June—Divisional Headquarters and Razmak Brigade move to Torwam, 23rd June, march opposed—R. A. F. co-operation—Bannu Brigade marches to Torwam, 24th June—arrangements for maintaining the force until the return march to Razmak—sanction given to special punitive air action—Wana Brigade moves to Torwam, 21st to 28th June—attack on Sher Ali's lashkar, 29th June—Wana Brigade commences return march to Wana, 30th June—reconnaissance to Turabaz 30th June—Division less Wana Brigade marches to Chalweshti Camp, 1st July—Paind's house in Pat Khel destroyed, 4th July—Razmak Brigade moves to Asman Manza and Bannu Brigade to Ladha, 5th July 140

	PAGE.
Chapter XVII.—Sanction given for punitive air action against any village known to be harbouring the Faqir or four of his followers, specified by name—measures to quieten the Spinwam Area—half-pay sanctioned for Tori Khel tribal police—air and artillery bombardment of Shawali Algad area—2nd Infantry Brigade visits Dinor villages—other minor offences—Dredonai section of Wuzi Khel fined—air action against Razin—progress of road construction—R.A.F. co-operation	153
Chapter XVIII.—Factors governing the selection of the alignment of the new roads—their alignment—General Sir John Coleridge's intentions regarding the roads—interferences with construction—location of troops protecting road-construction—relief of certain Scouts' garrisons by regular troops .	158
Chapter XIX.—Operations in the Spinwam area—Mahsud maliks visit hostile leaders—activities of Sher Ali—attack on camp piquet at Asman Manza—action taken against neighbouring villages—Faqir moves to Prekari Sar, and attempts to rouse opposition—offences by hostile gangs—the Din Faqir—attempts to enlist the help of Mullah Fazal Din and of the Faqir of Shewa—raid by 9th Infantry Brigade on Karkanwam air action against Faqir's headquarters—Faqir goes to Mandech to attend a conference—initiative for calling conference—meeting transferred to Shawal—conference held, 16th August—expansion of area of 9th Infantry Brigade on L. of C.—distribution of troops of 9th Brigade	162
Chapter XX.—Rumours and their effect on the tribesmen—consideration of disarmament—terms announced to Tori Khel jirga	173
Chapter XXI.—Tribesmen at meeting near Mana disperse—actions of hostile gangs during August—moves of formations in connection with road protection—attempt to capture Khonia Khel—increased raiding into administered territory—punishment for raids announced to Bhitanni jirga—demonstration flight by R.A.F.—warning notice dropped on inhabitants of Shawal—Faqir continues propaganda efforts to get support—Faqir decides to launch offensive with small parties—raid on Chaudhwan—Sher Ali attacks Khassadar Posts—steps taken by Commander, Waziristan Division—air action against special areas—preliminary moves—operations by Razmak and Bannu Brigades from Ladha and Asman Manza Camps, 7th to 14th September, and by Bannu Brigade in Khaisora valley, 18th to 24th September	176
Chapter XXII.—Air action against Khonia Khel's abode—Faqir's meeting at Musa Nika—Musa Khan arranges meeting between Mullah of Karbogha and Faqir of Ipi—Faqir continues propaganda—air action against Faqir's residence at Gumbakai—Utmanzai Wazirs warned—orders issued to Daur jirga—raid on Santala Defile area—dispersal of Pirmullah Khan's gang.	186
Chapter XXIII.—Activities of hostile gang in Spinkamar area—attack on lashkar in Sirdar Algad area, 27th September—Ambush near Razani by 1/2 G. R.—action decided on against Mami Rogha village—second attack on lashkar in Sirdar Algad area, 5th October	191
Chapter XXIV.—Hostile ambush at Sarwekai, 27th September—air action against tribes responsible—march of Razmak Brigade through country from Asman Manza southeast to Kotkai—Sher Ali active in Inzar Narai area—attack on patrol of South Waziristan Scouts—Wana Brigade moves to Inzar Narai—move of Fakir to Barman Sar—offences in Spinwam area instructions issued to Commander, 9th Infantry Brigade to undertake punitive operations—steps to induce hostile lashkar to stay in the area—concentration of column at Mir Ali—destruction of houses at Kot Matagai—advance to Spinwam, 20th October—demolitions carried out, 21st and 22nd October—column returns to Mir Ali, 23rd October . . .	200
Chapter XXV.—Bhitannis have been giving trouble for some time—the Din Faqir—Bhitanni jirga, 12th October—arrangements for advance into Bhitanni country—operations to be carried out by 2nd Infantry Brigade and attached troops country, entered 16th October—operations in Bhitanni country up to 26th October.	209
Chapter XXVI.—Columns located at Miranshah and Mir Ali—further adjustments to administrative areas—political summing up of the situation—orders issued for further movements of 1st and 9th Infantry Brigades—	

	PAGE.
9th Brigade marches to Bichhe Kashkai—1st Brigade marches to Masti Khel—operations in Lower Shaktu area, 17th and 18th November—sanction given for road from Rocha to Karkanwam—work on Kot road continues—orders of Government to Bhitannis—Din Faqir still hostile—road to Kot completed—2nd Brigade leaves Waziristan—Din Faqir goes to interview Political Authorities	215
Chapter XXVII.—Further punishments—Faqir at Kaurai—Madda Khel ordered to expel Faqir—Faqir moves to Afghanistan—existing dispositions suitable to capture Faqir should he return—continued efforts of Faqir and his brother—Faqir returns to Madda Khel country—Bakka Khel and Jani Khel Jirga.	225
Chapter XXVIII.—Conclusion	229
Chapter XXIX.—Points for consideration	231
Appendix I.—System of protection used in the Razani sector of the L. of C. 1937	.. 240
Appendix II.—The employment of the Engineer Units	.. 244
Appendix III.—The Ordnance Service in Waziristan, 1937	.. 249
Appendix IV.—The organization of the L. of C. and the protection of Convoys	.. 252
Appendix V.—The Supply Service and the Transport Service in Waziristan in 1937	.. 254

GENERAL SIR JOHN F. S. D. COLERIDGE, G.C.B., C.M.G., D.S.O.

CHAPTER I.

Introductory.

SEE SKETCH MAP A IN POCKET.

Geographical.

The operations now to be described took place in two distinct parts, the first part comprising those which led to the pacification of the Tori Khel Area, the occupation of the Sham Plain, and the construction of roads in the Tori Khel and Sham Plain Areas, and the second including the steps taken to restore normal conditions west of the Razmak—Jandola road and to drive the Faqir of Ipi from the country.

The area of the first part of the operations lies between Bannu, Spinwam, Mir Ali, Datta Khel, Razmak, the Razmak—Jandola road as far as Ahmadwam, and the Shaktu river to Jani Khel Post.

Flowing through this area are the Tochi, Khaisora, and Shaktu rivers. The Tochi river rises in Afghanistan and flows in an easterly direction by Datta Khel and Miranshah through the Shinki Defile to the Administrative Border where it alters to a south-easterly course, joining the Kurram river near Sarai Gambila. The Khaisora river, rising in the hills north of Razmak, follows an easterly course. It is crossed by the Bannu-Razmak road near Razani, follows that road as far as Asad Khel, and then continues in an easterly direction until it joins the Tochi river a few miles north of Jani Khel Post. The Shaktu rises south of the Sham Plain, skirts the southern edge of that plain, and flows slightly north of east, joining the Tochi by several small channels east of Jani Khel Post.

The country in between these rivers consists of hills of varying degrees of steepness, intersected by numerous valleys. The nature of the hillsides varies considerably. Generally speaking, east of the line Isha-Bichhe Kashkai they are bare, west of that they are covered with low trees and scrub. The valleys vary greatly in width. In places, as for example the Tochi valley between the Shinki Defile and Idak, they open out and cultivation takes the place of rocks and stones. Watercourses are thickly strewn with rocks and boulders. In dry weather in the larger watercourses there is usually a trickle of water which has to be crossed and recrossed frequently. After rain they fill very rapidly and become dangerous torrents.

West of the Razmak-Jandola road, where the greater part of the second portion of the operations took place, there are two main rivers, the Tank Zam, flowing beside the Central Waziristan Road, and south and southeast of Wana the Gumal river. Both these rivers are fed by large tributaries into which numerous lesser streams flow. The country is a mass of hills cut by valleys of varying sizes. The hills are high and in many places covered with trees and thick scrub. The general slope of the country in this area is to the east and southeast, until the road from Razmak to Wana crosses the Tiarza Narai, when the direction of the fall of the country is mainly east and west.

The main portion of the area is inhabited by Mahsuds, the Wana Wazirs occupying the territory west of the watershed running from west of the upper waters of the Baddar Algad to east of the Wana Toi.

Before these operations started there were very few roads in Waziristan, the only ones in existence being from Bannu to Razmak *via* Mir Ali and Isha Post; and on from Razmak to Tank and to Wana *via* Jandola and *via* Kariguram; from Mir Ali to Tal-in-Kurram *via* Spinwam; from Isha Post to Datta Khel *via* Miranshah; and from Old Razani Camp to Datta Khel.

Inhabitants [*ref. sketch map U 37 in pocket*].

The chief inhabitants of this area are the Daurs, the Bhitannis, the Wazirs, and the Mahsuds.

The Daurs dwell on the banks of the Tochi river from Ghazlamai village, north of Datta Khel, to the western end of the Shinki Defile. They are hardworking cultivators and unwarlike by nature, though they have shown brave resistance to attempts to filch their rich lands from them.

The Bhitannis inhabit the borders of the Bannu and Dera Ismail Khan districts and dwell partly in tribal territory. Although in the past they had given little trouble, in the period now under consideration they showed themselves recalcitrant to an extent that required special measures.

The Wazirs consist of two main classes, the Utmanzai and the Ahmadzai or Wana. The great majority are nomadic and migrate with their families every year to their summer grazing grounds. The Ahmadzai pass the summer in the country round Wana and move for the winter to grazing lands on the western borders of the Bannu district. The Utmanzai occupy the Tochi valley and the areas adjoining it, moving to the higher hills in the summer. The main sub-tribe of the Utmanzai Wazirs concerned in these operations is the Tori Khel. They reside chiefly in the area from Spinwam on the Kaitu river across the Tochi and Khaisora valleys to the Shaktu river.

The three main branches of the Mahsuds are the Alizai, Shaman Khel, and Bahlolzai, each of which consists of numerous sections and sub-sections. All these branches are so intermixed that localities occupied by the main branches cannot be defined. Roughly speaking, the area occupied by the tribe as a whole lies between Razmak, Wana and Jandola, with an extension south of the Shaktu river south of the Tori Khel Area.

The Mahsud and the Wazir are independent and democratic. Any man can by his own courage and wisdom achieve the position of Malik. Owing to the hard conditions in which they live, they were accustomed to eking out their existence by plundering their more peaceful neighbours. Their method of life has produced a race of men of fine physique with a remarkable capacity for rapid movement on their hills. They are bold fighters, exceedingly patient in their preparations.

Owing to the hilly nature of the country, the activity of the tribesmen, and the lack of many roads or good tracks, the progress of a column must necessarily be slow. It is difficult to bring the tribesmen to battle. Their role is, rather, to make an advance difficult, to harass the column in every way, and to attack small bodies so situated that a victory would be easy. Their mobility is such that they can break away from an action with ease, and if a tribesman cannot get right away he will hide his rifle and appear as a peaceful villager. (A more comprehensive note on the tribes of Waziristan and their characteristics is to be found in Chap. I of the Official History of Opns. in Waziristan 1919-1920.)

The General Situation in Waziristan in 1936 and the Government's agreement with the tori khel in 1935.

In order to obtain a clear mental picture of the military outlook as it presented itself to the Commanders of the Forces in Waziristan on the unexpected outbreak of hostilities in 1936, it is necessary to understand the situation as it then existed *vis-a-vis* the tribes.

It would hardly be correct to say that Waziristan was at peace, since "peace" as understood in settled or administered Districts has never been applicable to Waziristan. Nevertheless the countryside was in a more settled and peaceful state than had been the case at any time since the end of the Great War 1914—1918. Mobile training columns from the garrisons of Razmak, Bannu, Wana and Mir Ali moved about the country continuously under their own protection, as did "gashts" of the Tochi and South Waziristan Scouts. Opposition to any of these bodies had not been encountered for years, their camps were seldom even sniped at night, and both troops and Militia were generally treated with a considerable degree of respect by the tribesmen. With regard to the Regular troops quartered in Waziristan, these did a tour of duty of two years (the rule for all Frontier Stations) so that in any one year half the garrison of Waziristan was under replacement by fresh troops from India.

Regular troops either in or arriving in Waziristan were never allowed to gain the impression that they were in a "peace station". Although the phrase "Semi active service conditions" was being used in official parlance in regard to Waziristan at this time, the troops were trained always to be ready for hostilities at any moment.

One of the ways by which Government exercises control over the tribes is by means of tribal allowances. In March, 1935 Government had announced to the Tori Khel representatives its readiness to increase their allowances in return for access to and full rights in the Lower Khaisora valley and in the remainder of their territory in the North Waziristan Agency. The Tori Khel had been petitioning for these increased allowances for some years, but some of their sub-sections had refused to accept the conditions. These sub-sections were, however, eventually persuaded, and the agreement was signed by the representatives of the tribe. In February, 1936 the Razmak and Bannu Brigades visited the Khaisora valley and spent two days together at Bichhe Kashkai. No untoward incident occurred.

The "Islam Bibi" case and its immediate results.

As the "Islam Bibi" case first brought the Faqir of Ipi into prominence, a brief account of the case and its immediate results may be given at this stage.

A Hindu girl, a minor, eloped with a young Muslim student. The girl's relations brought a charge of abduction against the student and the girl was recovered. In the meantime, she was alleged to have been converted to Islam, taking the name of Islam Bibi. This raised the question, which community should have the custody of her. The case aroused considerable excitement of a communal nature in Bannu, and on the 7th of April, 1936, the day fixed for the trial of the student, a crowd of two thousand Muslims assembled near the Court to try to overawe the magistrate, and although no disorder occurred, it was not possible to proceed with the case. In the meantime, the Daurs, a tribe living along the Tochi valley west of Bannu and much under the influence of their priests, had been stirred up by agitators from Bannu. The abduction case came up again for trial on the 16th of April at Bannu. The Daurs were now threatening to march on Bannu, the Faqir of Ipi being the most active leader among them. Action was taken against the tribe and by the end of the month their lashkar had been dispersed, the ringleaders had been arrested except for the Faqir who had left for Sham in the Shaktu area, and the tribe tendered abject submission. The decision of the Court at the trial which commenced on the 16th of April was that the girl should be given to the Muslim community. On appeal, later, this decision was reversed and the Hindu community were made her custodians.

Prior to this case, Mirza Ali Khan, the Faqir of Ipi, had not been a
The Faqir of Ipi. man of any notable importance. A member of the Bangal Khel clan of the Maddi Khel section of the Tori Khel Wazirs, he had been born about 1897 in a village near Khajuri Post at the western end of the Shinki Defile, his father owning some property in this neighbourhood. In 1922, he and his brothers sold their property in the Khajuri Post area and purchased some land near Spalga and also in the Sham Plain area, building a house and a mosque on their property in the former place. They lived for a while near Spalga and during this time Mirza Ali Khan frequently visited the village of Ipi to get further religious training under the Mullah of that place. In 1926, he took up his permanent residence at Ipi. In 1928, he performed the Haj, and on his return continued to live a purely religious life, visiting shrines and religious leaders far afield. He thus acquired a reputation for saintliness, and gained considerable influence on this account among the Daurs and Tori Khel Wazirs.

When he left the Daur lashkar which had collected as a result of the "Islam Bibi" case, he laid his curse on the Daurs for their defection and on the Tori Khel for not supporting him. He then departed with his personal following to his property on the Sham Plain area. He did not stay here long, and on the 11th of May 1936, at the invitation of the Zarinai Tori Khel, he moved to Bichhe Kashkai on the lower Khaisora river, here he built himself a house and a mosque, and set himself actively to foment trouble. He persuaded his brother, Sher Zaman, to give up government service, and Sher Zaman now became his right hand man.

In his subversive activities, the Faqir received strong support from certain of the Tori Khel who had supposed grievances about the distribution of the ordinary allowances and of the fresh allowances arising from the 1935 agreement. He also gained further influence by bringing about a semblance of agreement between the different tribes bordering on the Khaisora and Shaktu valleys, the Tori Khel Wazirs, the Mahsuds, and the Bhitannis, who normally were in a constant state of feud with each other. In this, he received the support and help of three well-known men, Khonia Khel, a malik of the Jalal Khel Mahsuds, Din Faqir, a Bhittani mullah, and Mullah Fazal Din, a Shabi Khel Mahsud of Lataka, son of the late Mullah Powindah and spiritual leader of the Mahsuds.

Although this semblance lasted only a short time, to be able to produce even the appearance of unity enhanced his prestige and spiritual authority.

In the early autumn of 1936, he openly adopted the role of Champion of Islam. In this he was assisted by a renewal of public interest in the "Islam Bibi" case. The Faqir did not confine himself to the demand that the girl should be returned to the Muslims, but made wholesale allegations of Government interferences not only in matters of the Islamic religion but also in connection with other supposed local grievances. In this way he was able to acquire supporters in addition to those who rallied to the cry "Islam in danger". Assisted by sympathisers in Kaniguram, he intensified his propaganda among the Mahsuds, urging the leading mullahs of Makin to action and striving to rally the Mahsuds of the Shaktu valley to his support. He claimed miraculous powers and promised his followers many things, among others, that gas and bombs would be made ineffective, and that a few loaves would become enough to feed a multitude. He threatened everlasting disgrace to informers, and promised rewards to the martyrs in his cause. The credulity and superstition of the tribesmen is such that all his promises received wide credence in tribal areas.

CHAPTER II.

The decision that troops should visit the Tori Khel country.

1936.
Nov.

Attitude of Tori Khel Maliks. The Political Authorities were bringing pressure to bear on the Tori Khel either to control the activities of the Faqir for any consequences of which they would be held responsible, or, as it was considered impossible to insist on their surrendering the Faqir, to expel him from their country.

The Maliks admitted their responsibilities, but professed themselves unable to control the activities of the Faqir and his supporters unless Government gave some indication of their ability and intention to avail themselves of their rights under the 1935 agreement. They could not, however, guarantee that the entry of a column into the Lower Khaisora valley would be unopposed. They explained that while they and the majority of their tribe would do their best to help the troops to get into the valley, they could not guarantee their safety. They said that the Faqir's adherents, a collection of malcontents from various sections, would offer opposition.

Factors which tended to favour the activities of the Faqir. Certain factors existed which, later in the campaign, were assessed by Government as being the underlying causes of this unrest among the tribesmen. These made it certain that the Faqir's subversive activities, unless they were quickly checked, would bear fruit to a greater or lesser extent. They may be briefly summarized as follows:—

The latent fanaticism and impatience of control which always actuates the more youthful and turbulent elements in the tribes.

The feeling among the tribesmen that the constitutional changes in India indicated the progressive weakness of the Government.

The boredom, due to the prolonged period of peace in Waziristan, of the irresponsible elements of the tribes. Such men welcomed the chance of trying conclusions with the forces of Government, both for the excitement and for the chances of securing rifles and other loot.

Dissatisfaction, particularly among the Tori Khel, on account of the existing distribution of allowances.

Political view of the situation. Early in November 1936, the Resident in Waziristan recommended that troops should visit the Lower Khaisora valley towards the end of that month. It was thought that such action would very probably result in the expulsion of the Faqir from Tori Khel limits. If he was expelled he would probably go to Mahsud country, and there would be a risk of his getting wider support from the Mahsuds, on whom his propaganda had so far produced no serious result. It was argued, however, that this risk should be accepted, as, otherwise, it was certain that the Government policy of peaceful penetration into the Khaisora valley would lose the ground recently gained, and, further, there was no guarantee that the Faqir's propaganda, if he were not expelled, would not still cause trouble among the Mahsuds, to whom he was paying special attention. In these circumstances, the later and colder the season in which the Faqir was compelled to change his quarters, the less chance would there be of trouble in the really dangerous areas of Makin and Kaniguram.

Government decides that troops shall enter the Khaisora valley. The Government of India decided that on the 25th of November troops should visit that portion of the Tori Khel country which lies south and to east of the Central Waziristan Road between Asad Khel and Khajuri Post, entering the Lower Khaisora area from the North and West.

1936.
Nov.

It was hoped that this move would strengthen the hands of the loyal maliks and check the Faqir's propaganda. The attitude of the Tori Khel as a whole seemed satisfactory, and serious opposition was not anticipated. The most expected was some long-range sniping from the Tori Khel sub-sections who supported the Faqir. (Ali Khel Spin and Pila Khel of the Shoga Khel and Zarinai Haibati), and from other irresponsibles who had joined him. No serious repercussions amongst the Mahsuds were expected. The troops, therefore, were to carry out what was purely a peaceful demonstration on a timed programme, and were to take no offensive action unless forced to retaliate in their own defence.

CHAPTER III.

Operations of the Razmak and Bannu Brigades in the Khaisora valley from the 25th to the 27th of November 1936.

1936.
Nov.

[*Note.—Throughout this History map references have been given of some places not shown on the sketch maps, to enable readers, if they wish to do so, to trace these places on the survey maps.*]

General Plan [*ref. maps A, B 37 (Chap. XXVI) and C 37 Chap. X)*].

In accordance with the orders of the Government of India, it was decided that on the 25th, the Razmak column (entitled Razcol) should start from Damdil, and the Bannu column (called Tocol) from Mir Ali, meeting at Bichhe Kashkai that night, and both returning to their starting points by the same route. Razcol was to move along the Khaisora river, Tocol marching via Hassu Khel, Inarki Qila, the Katira river and the Jaler Algad. The columns concentrated at Damdil and Mir Ali respectively on the 24th . (*See at end of Chapter for composition of Razcol and Tocol.*)

The G. O. C. and G. S. O. I, with the Resident Waziristan and P. A. North Waziristan would accompany Razcol, whilst the G. S. O. II, D. A. Q. M. G., and Assistant Political Agent accompanied Tocol.

Description of routes.

The route to be followed by Razcol was very rough going along the boulder-strewn river bed, the stream having to be crossed frequently. From Asad Khel to Dakai Khula the river flows between high scrub-covered hills, which, between the big south-eastward bend about a mile east of Zerpezai and Shaikh Muhammad Ziarat, form a tangi through which the river bed has an average width of only about fifty yards. The exits from this tangi are dominated by commanding features. Below Dakai Kalai the valley opens out, and the hills become lower and further from the river bed.

Tocol's line was through fairly easy country for the most part, but between the Katira river and the Ghunda Tizha Algad, the track passed through hilly country.

Outline of the arrangements of Razcol for the advance to Bichhe Kashkai.

One section of armoured cars (1st Light Tank Coy.) was detailed to protect the west flank of the advance as far as the pumping station west of Asad Khel, where the column would leave the road and enter the Khaisora valley. This section was to withdraw to Razmak as soon as the column had cleared Musaki.

Eight platoons Tochi Scouts were to provide the more distant protection on both flanks up to a general north and south line just east of Zerpezai, returning to Dosalli as soon as the rearguard was clear of the area occupied by them.

Six platoons Tochi Scouts, which were to go to Bichhe Kashkai, were to precede the advancedguard along the river bed until they approached Zerpezai, returning to Dosalli as soon as the rearguard was clear of the distant protection on the south flank up to about Zikhe, keeping level with the advancedguard. When the column had passed, they were to conform to the movements of the rear guard.

The regular troops were to "close piquet" the route.

The line of the advance up to about Dakai Kalai was divided into two battery sectors each battery being responsible for all artillery support in its own sector. When the rearguard was clear of the first sector, that battery came under command of the Battery Commander of the second sector to support the rearguard if required. The third battery was kept in reserve for the protection of the camp at Bichhe Kashkai.

Work of the Razcol advanced guard. 25th November, 08-30 hours.

At 08-30 hours on the 25th, the 6/13 F. F. Rif. acting as advanced guard and piqueting troops, passed Musaki, preceded by six platoons of Tochi Scouts. No opposition was met with as far as Zerpezai. Here, the Scouts were informed by a Khassadar Subadar that the tangi in front was occupied by considerable numbers of the Tori Khel, and it could be seen that the ridges (sqs. 1640-1740) running north to Zerpezai were strongly held. The advanced platoons came under fire almost immediately.

After a very short interval, more enemy opened fire from a high feature on the north bank (sq. 1841) east of the village. The Scouts, supported by artillery developed a quick attack and the ridges just east and south east of Zerpezai were secured by about 10-15 hours at the cost of a few casualties.

Half an hour later, the advanced guard battalion being now expended, the 5/12 F. F. R. took over advanced guard and piqueting duties. The six platoons of Scouts were now due to leave the river bed and advance along the curved ridge running south east from Zerpezai. In view of the opposition one rifle coy. with a machine gun section of the 5/12 F. F. R. joined the Scouts for the attack on this ridge, the infantry being supported by the 7th Mountain Battery. At the same time another coy. of the 5/12 F. F. R. supported by the 3rd Light Battery was ordered to secure the high feature east of Zerpezai and to establish piquets on it. The troops attacking the curved ridge speedily gained their first objective at the northern end of the ridge. The Scouts leaving the company 5/12 F. F. R. in position to cover the advance, progressed along the ridge meeting with continuous fire. They reached a knoll on the ridge overlooking Sheikh Muhammad Ziarat from the west (182388) and were held up here at about 14-40 hours. The company operating east of Zerpezai accomplished its task at small cost.

In the meantime the eight platoons of the Tochi Scouts had taken up their positions north and south of the Khaisora west of the tangi. No opposition was met with in the process, but owing to the pace of the advance they found some difficulty in reaching their objectives in time to afford the necessary security to the column. They became engaged with the enemy to the east when the advanced guard began to meet with resistance.

Shortly after noon the 1/North'n R. took over the duties of advanced guard. When they reached a point about half a mile west of Sheikh Muhammad Ziarat considerable numbers of enemy were seen on the ridge (1838) immediately overlooking the river bed.

These fired at any movement in the river bed and any further advance was impossible until they had been driven off.

15-00 hours.

At 15-00 hours one company of the 1/North'n R. supported by the Battalion machine guns and a battery, attacked the hill (1838) overlooking Dakai Kalai from the west at the end of the long ridge from Zerpezai on which the Scouts were held up. This attack was rapidly successful, and the company rejoined its Battalion, leaving the Scouts to hold the hill.

1936.
Nov.

16-00 hours. At 16-00 hours the column reached the junction of the Khaisora and the Dakai Algad. The 6/13 F. F. Rif. who had been collected from piquets by the rearguard once more became advanced guard. The van guard and piquets crossing the river bed here were heavily fired on, but piquets were posted, and the advance continued. The advanced guard was not again held up and reached Bichhe Kashkai at 18-00 hours.

Razcol rearguard. Firing at the rearguard and retiring piquets was fairly continuous throughout the day, and piquets were closely followed up on their withdrawal.

The rearguard reached Sheikh Muhammad Ziarat at 17-30 hours and was at Dakai Kalai, three miles from camp, at 18-30 hours. It was now quite dark and clouds hid the moon. Great difficulty was experienced in withdrawing piquets still in position, but by means of lamp, voice, or whistle, all piquets were eventually brought in, though each flash of a lamp drew close enemy fire.

20-15 hours. The rear guard reached camp at 20-15 hours. Meanwhile camp piquets were posted by the advanced guard in the dark without opposition and were established by 21-30 hours.

Tochi Scouts. The eight platoons of Scouts in the area west of the Tangi, as soon as the rearguard was seen to be beyond their help, began to withdraw towards Asad Khel. The party south of the river was engaged by the enemy before its retirement commenced and sustained one or two casualties. The enemy followed them up, but aided by the fire of the platoons on the north bank, they crossed the river without further casualties. The eight platoons then returned to Asad Khel without further interference, avoiding the river and following a north westerly route.

The six platoons accompanying the column followed the rear party when the rearguard withdrew past the junction of the Khaisora and Dakai Algad, and reached camp without any hostile action.

Action of Tocol 25th November. On the evening of the 24th November Tocol Headquarters at Mir Ali received a report that there were small parties of the enemy on the hills south of the Tochi river, that the advance would be opposed, and that the Faqir had ordered his followers not to commence hostilities until the column had crossed the Jaler Algad.

07-00 hours. Tocol started from Mir Ali at 07-00 hours on the 25th. The line it was intended to follow was Musaki, Hassu Khel, Imarki Qila, point 2188 (3053), point 2392 (3050); thence, along the track passing just east of point 2627 (2846) and of point 2336 (2943) and in to Bichhe Kashkai from a north easterly direction.

The advanced guard consisted of the squadron and M. G. troop Probyn's Horse and the 1/17 Dogra R. less a detachment doing rearguard. One coy. less two platoons 1/17 Dogra R. were rearguard, leaving the 3/7 Rajput R. complete in the main body. The flanks were protected by the detachment Tochi Scouts with four infantry platoons on the right and two mounted infantry troops on the left of the column.

08-30 hours. By 08-30 hours, the advanced guard had reached the Katira river. Here a halt was made to allow of the closing up of the transport which had been strung out owing to the numerous water channels. The advanced guard took up a covering position in the low hills south of the Katira, and the Scouts occupied the lower slopes of Zer (2754) on the right and Point 2508 (3152) on the left.

No opposition had been encountered but a number of Tori Khel maliks who had joined the column at Tochi river reported that about 100 hostile tribesmen had spent the night in the hills south of the Katira river and that they intended to attack the main body after the advanced guard had passed.

1936.
Nov.

At 10-00 hours a party of tribesmen was seen on the hills (2950) west of the track south of the Katira river. A troop Probyn's Horse which was sent to investigate was fired on at a range of about forty yards and sustained casualties in men and horses. Heavy and acurate firing then broke out from the hills (2950-3050) on both sides of the line of advance, and it was found that the enemy were in front and on both flanks of the advanced guard at ranges of six hundred yards or less. By 10-30 hours, the advanced guard was held up astride the track at point 2392 (3050) with one platoon progressing slowly along the ridge (2950) forming the south bank of the Katira river. One platoon 1/17 Dogra R. was still in reserve, and this was ordered by the Column Commander to attack through the platoon on the ridge (2950) on the right. By 12-00 hours the advanced guard had progressed about another half-mile. The enemy were now on the low hills (288486) commanding the track from the west, and extended across the front to point 2548 (3048), threatening the left flank of the Column from this point and the south east side of the nullah immediately below it. The R. A. F. who had been called on for support at 11-20 hours, came into action against the enemy in the area of point 2548. Their bombs flushed tribesmen, who became targets for rifle fire.

10-00 hours.

At 12-05 hours the 3/7 Rajput R. were ordered to attack the tribesmen who, from the hills to the right front (2848) were stopping the column's advance. In carrying out the reconnaissance for this attack, Major Tindall and Captain Boyd, 3/7 Rajput R., were wounded the former fatally, and several I. O. Rs. were hit. The forward coy. of the 3/7 Rajput R. was held up by 13-15 hours just short of its objective (288-486) and another coy. was then put in on its right. This attack made ground but was eventually brought to a standstill by fire from concealed positions.

12-05 hours.

As the track forward was still commanded by the enemy orders were given to the squadron Probyn's Horse to carry out a mounted attack on the enemy holding up the Rajputs on the right, to hold on until the Rajputs arrived, and then to push forward to the south bank of the Jaler Algad. The cavalry galloped the hills in about four or five minutes with only two casualties. By 14-35 hours the hills were cleared and the 3/7 Rajput R. were enabled to continue their advance to their objective, the Jaler Algad. Enemy resistance had been determined and casualties were heavy. Another officer of the Rajputs had been wounded, and all companies of the Battalion were now commanded by Viceroy's Commissioned Officers.

14-35 hours.

Whilst the Cavalry and 3/7 Rajput R. were advancing on the right, the Tochi Scouts' infantry detachment, in close touch with the rearguard, had prevented any attack on the right flank. After crossing the Katira river it came under continuous fire, and became engaged with tribesmen who had to be driven out of a sangared position. It was then ordered to push on to point 3025 (2746). The two troops of Scouts mounted infantry on the left flank had been ordered to advance on the left to

1986.
Nov.

point 2548 (3048), but opposition was too strong, and they were unable to get further than the east bank of the nala about five hundred yards from their objective. Here, in touch with a piquet of the 1/17 Dogra R. and with the left flank troop of Probyn's Horse, they held their ground.

At 13-30 hours, the remaining available troops of the 1/17 Dogra R.
13-30 hours. one and a half coys. supported by the machine guns of the Rajputs, were ordered to secure point 2548. The enemy fired two volleys at the Dogras and bolted. The Dogras then steadily worked south along the ridge, and enabled the advance to continue.

No recent news had been received of the position of Razcol. The only reports that had come in had been a wireless message at 11-00 hours when Razcol was halted at Zerpezai and a message, dropped from the air at 12-00 hours, reporting that Razcol was at 180410, about two miles north west of Sheikh Muhammad Ziarat, in the northern portion of the tangi. When the Dogras captured point 2548, a decision had to be made whether the advance was to be continued or not. From the information available at Tocol Headquarters it appeared that Razcol was held up; it was important to get some troops to Bichhe Kashkai that day; moreover there was moonlight. The Tocol Commander therefore decided to continue the advance by night.

The situation at 1745 hours, when the column halted just north of the
17-45 hours. Jaler Algad was that the Cavalry held the ridge overlooking the Algad from the north, (2745-2845), whilst the 3/7 Rajput R. were just in rear of them with the Tochi Scouts infantry on their right, the 1/17 Dogra R. being on the hills which had formed their second objective to the south of point 2548.

The Tochi Scouts mounted infantry, which had been protecting the left flank, had been ordered at 17-00 hours to return to Khajuri Post.

Enemy resistance had now slackened, and the column was ordered to assemble on the north bank of the Jaler Algad preparatory to a night advance.

The advance commenced at 19-30 hours. the sky at this time being
19-30 hours. clear, with a moon, which was, in fact, thought to be rather too bright for the contemplated operation.

Four platoons of the Tochi Scouts formed the advanced guard, and one coy. less two platoons of the Dogras, the rearguard.

As the column crossed the Jaler Algad, it was fired on from the left flank and at the same time fire was directed from close range at the rear of the column. Casualties were caused in the transport, cavalry horses and transport mules stampeded, and touch with the head of the column was lost.

By 20-30 hours order had been restored, and the column was closed
20-30 hours. up again.

At this point a malik arrived with a message from Razcol saying that Bichhe Kashkai had been reached. Tocol Commander, determined to reach his objective if it was possible, decided to continue the advance, and movement was resumed at 20-30 hours. Almost immediately the advanced guard was fired into at point blank range and the Scouts fell back to a flank, some men at the head of the main body were hit, and several animals broke away and stampeded back down the column. There was much confusion, and realizing that it was hopeless to continue the march, Tocol Commander decided to halt for the night and camp about half a mile (2744) south of the Jaler Algad.

23-59 hours. By midnight, a perimeter camp had been laid out and occupied.

1936.
Nov.

The Tochi Scouts held two camp piquets, and the rear guard occupied a ridge three hundred yards north of the camp.

November 26th. There was desultory fire at the camp and piquets during the hours of darkness, and at 04-00 hours an attempt was made by the enemy to attack a rearguard piquet. This was driven off by fire. At 06-30 hours fresh camp piquet positions were occupied without serious opposition. A party was then sent back to the Jaler Algad to recover any transport loads that might be found. Shortly, after daylight the R. A. F. dropped twelve boxes of ammunition on Tocol.

09-50 hours. By 09-50 hours a Razcol detachment which had been despatched from Bichhe Kashkai was in position on the Ghunda Tizha Algad (2642), but owing to the necessity of sorting transport and adjusting loads, Tocol did not move until 11-00 hours. Tocol and the Razcol detachment then moved to Bichhe Kashkai without serious opposition, and with no casualties. Bichhe Kashkai camp was reached at 12-30 hours.

Razcol. 08-00 hours. At 08-00 hours, a Razcol detachment consisting of the 7th Mountain Battery, the 5/12 F. F. R., and the 1/9 G. R. left Bichhe Kashkai to assist Tocol in the latter's march to that camp if necessary. They returned at 12-30 hours.

As it had not been possible to water animals on the evening of the 25th, two water piquets were established at 07-00 hours on the 26th. These were sniped during the day.

During the morning tribesmen estimated at about four hundred strong were found to be collecting in the hills west of the camp. Two extra piquets were established on this flank by the Tochi Scouts. There was firing on both sides, but the Scouts had no casualties. Two battalions and a battery then moved out west of the camp and shelled the village of Dakai Kalai and then withdrew back to camp. In the meantime, camp piquets were strengthened.

Operations November 27th. As the columns were rationed up to the 27th only, and ammunition was running short, and as the early evacuation of the wounded to hospital was an urgent necessity, it was decided that both columns should return to Mir Ali.

Except for a threatened attack on a camp piquet, which was dispersed by fire, the night of the 26th passed quietly.

Tocol moved first from Bichhe Kashkai, their advance being covered by the ten platoons of Tochi Scouts with the 7th Mountain Battery attached.

The Scouts, moving in three groups, right, centre, and left, and covering a front of about fifteen hundred yards, reached their first bound, the Jaler Algad, without opposition. Here, the left group surprised and dispersed a band of some sixty tribesmen, rounding up a number of them in a neighbouring village. With the Scouts clearing the way under continuous fire, Tocol carried on steadily to the Katira river, where it halted and took up a position on the north bank to cover the withdrawal of the rearguard.

1936.
Nov.

Razcol, following Tocol, had the 6/13 F. F. Rif. as rear guard, whilst the 1/North'n R. and the 5/12 F. F. R., in that order from front to rear, on the west and the 1/9 G. R. on the east provided flank protection for the transport of both columns marching in the centre. The rest of Razcol formed the mainguard.

At 09-00 hours camp piquets were **withdrawn without casualties.** Sniping however started again at this hour and continued throughout the day until the Force had crossed the Tochi river.

The withdrawal was carried out at good speed until about 10-30 hours when the firing became heavier as the rear guard approached the Jaler Algad. The enemy attempted to work round the 1/9 G. R. with the object of attacking the transport. The flanks of the 6/13 F. F. Rif. were also harassed, and a machine gun section of this Battalion was followed up at high speed and attacked from the front and flank, suffering some casualties. A company and a machine gun section of the 5/12 F. F. R. were sent to reinforce the 6/13 F. F. Rif., and the withdrawal continued. Shortly after this, the 5/12 F. F. R. relieved the 6/13 F. F. Rif. as rear guard, and remained as such until Razcol passed through Tocol on the line of the Katira river. At about 13-00 hours there was a gap of about quarter of a mile between the front and rear of Razcol, and 1 North'n R. was ordered to take up a position astride the route just south of the Katira river to prevent the enemy getting round the east flank. This battalion withdrew on the approach of the rear guard.

Razcol now passed through Tocol, which in turn was covered into Mir Ali by the 1/9 G. R. on the south bank of the Tochi river.

On reaching the Katira river, the Tochi Scouts infantry were given the task of escorting the transport into Mir Ali. It reached Mir Ali at 17-30 hours, after halting at the Tochi river to water. Two troops of the Tochi Scouts Mounted Infantry had been in readiness since the morning in the Kot Tiwana area (3454) to co-operate if possible, but had not been called on.

The enemy pursuit slackened when the rear of the Force reached the Tochi valley, and though firing continued for the rest of the day, artillery and machine gun fire prevented the tribesmen from again following up closely. The last part of the march into Mir Ali was not interfered with, and the Columns reached that place at 18-30 hours.

Casualties.   During the three days of operations the casualties were as follows:—

Killed		
British officers	2	Major J. B. P. Seccombe 6/13 F. F. Rif. Major J. W. B. Tindall 3/7 Rajput R.
B. O. Rs.	1	
Indian other Ranks	13	
Followers	1	
Wounded		
B. Os.	4	Capt. F. L. Boyd 3/7 Rajput R. Capt. R. R. Phillips 3/7 Rajput R. Lt. W. J. Fletcher 3rd Light Battery Capt. J. R. H. Peacock 6/13 F. F. Rif.
B. O. Rs.	13	
Viceroy's Commissioned Officers	3	
Indian other Ranks	71	
Tochi Scouts	killed 7	wounded 16.

Enemy casualties were estimated at 41 killed and 32 severely wounded.

R. A. F. co-operation.
During the 25th of November, air reconnaissance requirements were met by one flight of No. 5 (Army Co-operation) Squadron. One aircraft was allotted for close reconnaissance on the front of each column for the first two hours. After that, one aircraft had to meet the needs of both. In view of the distance between the columns, the extent of the reconnaissance area, and the difficult nature of the country, it was found that one aircraft for both columns was inadequate. The difficulties were further increased because radio-telephonic communication between Razcol and the aircraft failed when the pack set with the former became damaged during the march. Communication of air reports to both columns, therefore, had to be done by message dropping.

Close support duties were undertaken by a flight of No. 27 (Bomber) Squadron. In order to ensure the safety of the troops it was previously arranged that offensive action in support of them was only to be undertaken if called for by column commander. Such support was given to Tocol on two occasions.

On the 26th of November close reconnaissance and close support sorties were provided during the day, and ammunition, food, and medical requirements were dropped on the columns.

In order to ensure adequate support for the troops during the withdrawal from Bichhe Kashkai on the 27th of November, an additional Flight of No. 27 (Bomber) Squadron was made available. The restriction imposed on the 25th on calling for supporting offensive action had been found to have the result that several opportunities of taking effective action against large numbers of tribesmen opposing the troops had been missed. On the 27th, the Officer Commanding No. 1 (Indian) Wing, who was in charge of R. A. F. operations on this day, on his own initiative removed this restriction, and effective close support was provided on several occasions. In all, five close reconnaissance and six close support sorties were furnished during the day.

Strength and composition of enemy lashkars.
The extent of the opposition offered to the columns was a surprise which exceeded all estimates. In view of the amenability which the Tori Khel had shown previous to the operations the only explanation seems to be that the Faqir's propaganda had succeeded to an extent which had not been considered possible.

The number of tribesmen engaged with the two columns on the 25th does not seem to have been more than five hundred, but exaggerated rumours of the success of the Tori Khel that day spread rapidly, and the lashkars increased considerably during that night and the early morning of the 26th. When the columns united on the morning of the 26th, the situation was deemed to have become more stable, and although considerable excitement prevailed, the tribes as a whole preferred to wait and see what the future might bring forth.

About six hundred enemy actually opposed the Force on the 27th, although the total strength of tribesmen present in the area of operations that day was about two thousand. The majority of this total were Tori Khel, with them were some Madda Khel and other Wazirs, and a mixed

1936.
Nov.

collection of about two hundred Mahsuds including Shabi Khel from the Shaktu valley. No representative parties other than the Tori Khel had, in fact, joined up, and it appears that it was the resistance initially shown by seventy or eighty Mahsuds, who joined the Faqir on 23rd of November, that induced the Tori Khel to join in the fighting.

COMPOSITION OF RAZCOL AND TOCOL.

Detachment Waziristan District Headquarters.

Razcol.	Tocol.
Razmak Bde. Hq.	Bannu Bde. H. Q.
Bde. Sig. Sec.	Bde. Sig. Sec.
22 Mtn. Arty. Bde. H. Q.	One sqn. and M. G. Tp.
3 L. Bty.	Probyn's Horse.
4 Mtn. Bty.	One sec. 15 Fd. Coy.
7 Mtn. Bty.	3/7 Rajput R.
15 Fd. Coy. S. & M. (less one Sec.).	1/17 Dogra R.
1/North'n R.	1 A. T. Coy. (less det.).
5/12 F. F. R.	10 A. T. Coy.
1/9 G. R.	8 Fd. Amb. (Tocol).
6/13 F. F. Rif.	
7 Fd. Amb.	
Det. 1 A. T. Coy.	
15 A. T. Coy.	
25 A. T. Coy.	
35 A. T. Coy.	
Det. Razcol S. I. S.	
Det. Mob. Vet. Sec.	

Two Flights 27 (B) Sqn. R. A. F.
Two Flights 5 (A. C.) Sqn. R. A. F.
Two Platoons M. I. and eighteen Platoons Infantry—Tochi Scouts.

CHAPTER IV.

Operations to punish the Tori Khel. Events from the 28th of November 1936 to the 24th of December 1937.

1936
Nov.—Dec.

The decision of Government to punish the Tori Khel.
During and immediately after the fighting on the 25th of November, the reports current as to the extent to which tribes other than the Tori Khel, in particular Mahsuds of the Shaktu area and Madda Khel Wazirs, were taking part in the hostilities were widely conflicting. It was not possible to gauge what the developments were likely to be. It seemed inevitable, however, that in any case heavy punishment would have to be inflicted on the Tori Khel immediately. Consequently, on the 27th of November the Government of India decided that land and air operations should be undertaken with this object as quickly as possible.

General Sir John F. S. D. Coleridge, K.C.B., C.M.G., D.S.O., A.D.C., General Officer Commanding-in-Chief, Northern Command, was placed in charge of military operations to punish and obtain the submission of the tribal sections which had opposed the march of the two columns on and after the 25th of November. During the course of these operations, a road was to be constructed from Mir Ali to the Khaisora valley, and measures were to be taken to guard against the extension of the disturbances to other areas in Waziristan.

Sir John Coleridge was also invested with, and from the evening of the 29th of November assumed, full political control in the North and South Waziristan Agencies, the Resident in Waziristan being nominated as his Chief Political Officer.

In addition, he was given authority to initiate independent air operations against hostile tribesmen, subject to the proviso that offensive air action was not to be taken against villages in the Khaisora area. All arrangements for the employment of the Royal Air Force were to be made between him and Group Captain N. H. Bottomley, A. F. C., Commanding No. 1 (Indian) Group R. A. F.

Sir John Coleridge's appreciation of the situation.
So far, the unrest appeared to be confined to the Tori Khel of the Lower Khaisora, a few disaffected Wazirs of other sections, and some Mahsuds. It was not possible to predict how far the disaffection would spread. It was not an unlikely contingency that the Faqir of Ipi, wielding considerable influence among the Tori Khel, would be able to spread disaffection through the whole of that section, amongst other Wazirs of the North Waziristan Agency, and also among the Mahsuds. To be ready for such an eventuality, the troops already available in North Waziristan should be increased by two mountain artillery batteries, one infantry brigade, and two light tank companies. Two extra Sapper and Miner companies would be wanted for work on the proposed road, and it would be necessary to supplement Waziristan District transport.

After these reinforcements had arrived, a Striking Force, consisting of the Razmak Brigade with two additional battalions, should move by bounds conforming to the progress of the road which was to start at the twenty third milestone on the Bannu-Mir Ali road. The Bannu Brigade strengthened by extra troops, should go to the south bank of the Tochi river for use as protection to the lines of communication and as a reserve

1936
Dec.

The 2nd (Rawalpindi) Infantry Brigade with two batteries, after concentration at Mir Ali, should be located so as to be able to strike towards the Khaisora or Upper Tochi as circumstances might dictate. After arrival in the Khaisora valley, the Striking Force would undertake punitive action in the Lower Khaisora, an imperative measure if the spreading of unrest were to be prevented. The Tochi Scouts, throughout, were to keep the main road open and be prepared to assist the Bannu Brigade with a detachment.

On the 3rd of December, Northern Command Advanced Headquarters was opened at Bannu. The control of operations and local political control were delegated to the Commander, Waziristan District (Major General Robertson, C.B., D.S.O.) whose headquarters had been established at Mir Ali on the 1st December.

Delegation of control to, and instructions to the Commander, Waziristan District.

To facilitate control, the forces in Waziristan District were re-organized into Wazirforce and Waziristan Area. Wazirforce, commanded by Major General Robertson, comprised all formations and units located within the area of operations. This area included the tribal portions of the Tochi, Khaisora, and Shaktu valleys, the country lying between them, and strips, several miles wide, to the north of the Tochi valley and to the south of the Shaktu river. Waziristan Area, of whose functions some details are given later, consisted of the remainder of Waziristan District.

Instructions were given to Major General Robertson that the disposition of the forces under his command prior to, during, and subsequent to the advance would be at his discretion, that during the advance to the Khaisora river the fact that the rate of advance would be regulated by the speed of the road construction in no way restricted him from taking any offensive action should a favourable opportunity present itself, and that he was to be ready subsequently to operate against guilty tribal sections and to inflict punishment, which might include the destruction of towers and villages, within his radius of action.

Wing Commander J. Slessor, M.C., Commanding No. 3 (Indian) Wing R. A. F., was placed under the operational control of the Commander Wazirforce, to be employed either as air adviser or to accompany columns, as required. His headquarters were established at Mir Ali, with Wazirforce Headquarters. The R. A. F. units at his disposal were the detached flight of No. 5 (Army Co-operation) Squadron, reinforced by another flight of the same squadron, and two flights of No. 20 (Army Co-operation) Squadron, at Miranshah, and Nos. 27 and 60 (Bomber) Squadron No. 1 (Indian) Wing, at Kohat.

R. A. F. units, locations.

During the advance of the Force, air action was to be limited to actual co-operation with the troops and attacks on collections of tribesmen in the proscribed area. Within this zone no bombing of villages was permitted unless the inhabitants showed hostility by firing on troops or aircraft and then only after sanction had been obtained and the usual evacuation warning given. No villages outside the proscribed area were to be bombed unless prior sanction were obtained. The proscribed area, stretching roughly five miles to each flank of the line of advance from the Tochi to the Khaisora river included the latter from Bobali to Sein. All boundaries were defined by outstanding landmarks, the northern

Instructions regarding air action. The proscribed area.

boundary was about two miles to the south of the Tochi rive, the eastern followed the southern extension of the Kharaghora Range, the southern lay along the watershed between the Khaisora and Shaktu rivers, and the western about two miles east of the Central Waziristan Road.

Work commenced on the new road from Mir Ali to the Khaisora river.
In order that no time should be wasted, the Razmak Brigade commenced work on the new road on the 30th of November, the Bannu Brigade joining in a day or two later. The road was to be a fair-weather mechanised transport one, and by the evening of the 4th of December it was fit for use as far as the north bank of the Katira river.

Troop movements.
As soon as the events of the 25th of November had become known, the 12th Mountain Battery R. A. and the 2/13 F. F. Rif. had been moved from Kohat to Bannu, and the move of the 1/10 Baluch R., which was under orders to leave Bannu, was suspended. The 6th and 11th Light Tank Companies (armoured cars) arrived on the 2nd of December at Bannu and Mir Ali respectively. The concentration of the 2nd (Rawalpindi) Infantry Brigade and of other troops required for the operations proceeded rapidly.

Warning from the air.
It was decided that the advance should begin on the 5th of December. On the 3rd of December, aircraft dropped leaflets on the inhabitants of the proscribed area warning them that they must leave that area, special emphasis being laid on the necessity of removing their women and children and on the fact that after the 5th of December any parties of ten or more tribesmen found in the area would be attacked by land and air. Later, it was decided that instead of being liable to attack anywhere in the prescribed area, the area should be a progressive one, extending four or five miles ahead of and to the flanks of the troops. The exact boundaries were specified by Advanced Headquarters Northern Command.

A further restriction in the earlier stages of the advance was imposed by the Force Commander. The available information indicated that the column was likely to be opposed in strength. The G. O. C. was anxious that the tribesmen should be encouraged to stand and not be prematurely dispersed by offensive air action. For this reason he issued orders that aircraft were not to attack parties of the enemy within three thousand yards on either side of or in front of the column. Early in the operations it became apparent that there was little prospect of the tribesmen concentrating with a view to opposing the advance, and that, in consequence, opportunities of inflicting losses on them by aircraft were being missed. The Force Commander, therefore, removed this restriction on the 7th of December.

Fresh agitation by the Faqir.
The lashkars which had opposed the columns in the recent fighting had started to disperse on the 28th of November, and the Tori Khel of the Lower Khaisora began to discuss how they should act in view of the punishment they expected to receive. The Political authorities used their best endeavours to prevent the influence of the Faqir being extended to the Mahsuds. The Faqir at once renewed the efforts to organize opposition. He approached Mullah Fazal Din and other prominent Mahsud leaders and appealed to the Mahsud sections in general. In addition he extended his propaganda to Afghan subjects in the neighbouring province of Khost, and demanded financial assistance from sympathisers in Bannu.

In spite of the heavy casualties suffered by the tribesmen, his prestige had been enhanced by the events of the 25th to the 27th of November. Sympathy with his cause was widespread in North Waziristan and in the adjoining Mahsud country in South Waziristan. Across the frontier in Afghanistan, the withdrawal of the troops to Mir Ali was believed to be a manifestation of the Faqir's piety and miraculous powers, and the fact that apart from close support of the troops in actual contact with the tribesmen, there had been no air offensive was attributed to the same cause.

Attitude of tribes. While the Mahsuds, as a whole, watched developments, those of the Shaktu valley, fearful of punishment for the share taken by individuals in the recent fighting, showed their desire to keep on good terms with Government, the Bahlolzai asking to be given contracts on the new road.

Certain Tori Khel sections in the area north of the Tochi river, and also the Hasan Khel, spontaneously dissociated themselves from any opposition to Government. A jirga of the Lower Khaisora Tori Khel, which was fully representative except for the Zarinai section in whose villages the Faqir had spent the summer months, held on the 2nd of December, showed a satisfactory attitude. At this jirga, the maliks were informed that it was the intention of Government to construct a road or roads in their country, to impose penalties for their misbehaviour, and to inflict severe punishment should the troops be opposed in any way when they now entered the country.

On the other hand, a mullah of the Jalal Khel Mahsuds, with the object of embroiling as many people as possible in the hostilities, endeavoured to instigate that section to commit offences on the Bannu-Mir Ali road. With this same object, the Mahsuds of the Shaktu area and the Tori Khel of the Lower Khaisora who had been actively concerned in the hostilities, were spreading abroad the wildest rumours about the loot obtained on the 25th of November, and efforts were being made to obtain help from the Ahmadzai Wazirs living to the north and north-west of Wana in Waziristan and Afghanistan.

In the meanwhile, the tribesmen engaged in no enterprises. The only incident which occurred was when on the 1st of December a section of armoured cars reconnoitring on the Bannu-Razmak road was fired on by a party of about sixty men near Asad Khel. These, believed to be Madda Khel, dispersed after suffering several casualties.

Composition of Faqir's lashkars. As a result of all this propaganda, when the Faqir, determined to oppose the advance of the troops, went to the Jaler Algad on the 5th of December, a quarter of the fighting strength of the Madda Khel Wazirs was with his lashkars. The rest of his lashkars was composed of some Afghans, Tori Khel and other Wazirs, and some Mahsuds. Their strength was estimated, on the 6th of December, as about seven hundred in the Jaler Algad, with smaller bodies in other places. Although supplies were collected from Bannu, and the hostile tribesmen were distributed amongst the Tori Khel for food and shelter, the problems of accommodation and supply of these parties were acute.

At midnight on the 4th/5th of December, **Wazirforce** and **Waziristan Area** came into being.

The moves of the formations* concerned in these operations were as follows:—

[Ref. Sketch Map B. 37 (Chap. XXVI) and C. 37 (Chap. X)].

1936 Dec.

	Khaicol (see below.)	Tocol.	2nd Brigade.
4th Dec.	At Mir Ali.	At Mir Ali.	At Mir Ali.
5th ,,	to Tochi Camp.	....	....
6th ,,	....	to Tochi Camp.	....
9th ,,	to Jaler Camp.	....	to Tochi Camp.
18th ,,	to Khaisora Camp.	....	....
21st ,,	....	....	to Khaisora Camp.
22nd ,,	to Damdil.	to Jaler Camp.	to Bichhe Kashkai Camp.
24th ,,	....	....	to Khaisora Camp.

The advance to the Khaisora river.

On the 5th of December, the Striking Force, which was now named Khaicol, moved from Mir Ali to Tochi Camp on the south bank of the Katira river. By the evening of this day the 2nd Infantry Brigade was concentrated at Mir Ali. Until required to operate against the enemy this Brigade was to assist in road construction.

The next day, Tocol joined Khaicol at Tochi Camp whilst two battalions of the 2nd Infantry Brigade reconnoitred the slopes of Zer. Tochi Camp was sniped on the night of the 7th/8th of December.

From the 5th to the 9th of December road construction was pushed forward, the work being protected by Khaicol. Despite reports of enemy said to be sangared in and along the Jaler Algad, advances up to and beyond this nullah failed to meet opposition, nor were the enemy induced to follow up the daily withdrawal to Tochi Camp.

On the 9th of December, Khaicol moved forward to Jaler Camp on the Jaler Algad, and the 2nd Infantry Brigade moved to Tochi Camp.

On the 9th, 10th, 11th and 12th, rain fell, making the new road from Mir Ali to Jaler Camp difficult and at times impassable. The R. A. F. came to the assistance of the troops and dropped over a ton of supplies on the 12th at Jaler Camp.

From the 13th to the 15th, all three formations carried out a programme of destruction of certain selected fortified buildings of tribesmen

*For the detailed composition of Khaicol, Tcool, and 2nd Bde. in these operations p. 27 and 28.

known to have taken an active part in the hostilities of the 25th to the 27th of November. During these proceedings Korans found in the buildings were collected and returned to the tribesmen through the Political authorities, an act of grace evidencing the absence of vindictiveness in the reprisals and respect for their religion.

On the 18th of December, Khaicol advanced to Khaisora Camp, three miles east of Bichhe Kashkai, where it was joined by the 2nd Infantry Brigade on the 21st. By this date, in spite of the heavy rain of the previous week, roadhead had reached the Khaisora river, and the portion of the road from Mir Ali to Tochi Camp had been made passable for mechanised transport in all weathers. A number of reconnaissances, meanwhile, had been made by Khaicol in the Khaisora.

During this period, the enemy had not been enterprising. One or two attempts were made to damage bridges on the road between Thal and Spinwam, and some telegraph wires were cut. In spite of the Faqir of Ipi's efforts to persuade the tribesmen to fight, sangars which had been built on the hills in the neighbourhood of the Jaler Algad were not defended, and no opposition was offered except for some sniping.

Inactivity of enemy.

The Faqir's fortunes during this advance appeared to be somewhat on the wane. His followers one third of whom had come unarmed in expectation of loot, had been disappointed of their easy gains, and belief in his powers to work miracles had weakened. The Tori Khel maliks, apprehensive of increased punishment had besought the Madda Khel to leave, and by the 8th of December only about a hundred of them were still in the area. The lashkars now consisted of Ahmedzai Wazirs, some Afghans, and a mixed collection of Tori Khel and other Wazirs and Mahsuds.

In an effort to prevent the tribesmen dispersing, their leaders were driven to spreading lies about the arrival of Mahsud reinforcements. Harassed from the air, and lacking food and shelter, the discomfiture of the tribesmen reached its climax during the rain of the 9th to the 12th. The number of tribesmen from areas outside the Khaisora which, on the 3rd of December, had been estimated at twelve hundred, now dwindled to to about two hundred. Failing to get assistance from Wazir sections of the Lower Khaisora other than the Tori Khel, the main portion of the lashkars dispersed on the 14th of December, after appealing to the Faqir to get Mahsud support.

About this time, the general tribal atmosphere in North Waziristan showed definite signs of returning to the normal. The Faqir, however, remained obdurate and indefatigable. He renewed his appeals to the Mahsuds, especially to those of the Shaktu area, to rally to him after the Id on the 16th of December at the close of Ramzan. He also again solicited the aid of Afghan subjects. As a result of his efforts, there was, somewhat surprisingly, some renewal of interest in his cause, although his continual appeals to Mullah Fazal Din were unsuccessful and a number of influential mullahs on the occasion of the Id urged the tribes to keep aloof. Still, there was no doubt that he had won considerable esteem by the tenacity with which he held to his aims.

Meanwhile, tribal discussions were proceeding among the Lower Khaisora Tori Khel concerning the advisability of coming to a settlement with Government. The Zarinai kept aloof from these discussions. The Faqir informed the other maliks that they were free to enter into negotiations with Government, but that he himself would not do so until Government had signed a guarantee not to interfere in religious matters.

Punitive action in the Khaisora area. By the 21st of December information had come in that although no lashkars were in the field in the Lower Khaisora gangs were watching the movements of the troops, small parties of tribesmen were moving from the Shaktu area towards Dakai Kalai, and that about Dakai Kalai and in the Dakai Algad there were from two to four hundred enemy.

Operations were now planned with the object of destroying fortified towers in the Khaisora valley between Bichhe Kashkai and Bobali. Khaicol, having transferred one mountain battery and two battalions to the other formations, ceased to exist as such and the Razmak Brigade again came into being.

General plan. It was decided that on the 22nd of December, the 2nd Infantry Brigade* should destroy selected buildings in Dakai Kalai and Shaikh Muhammad Ziarat, returning thereafter to Khaisora Camp. The Razmak Brigade, passing through the 2nd Infantry Brigade, was to continue the work of destruction in villages further up the valley and go into camp at Damdil. If the resistance at Dakai Kalai proved substantial, the Force Commander intended to retain the Razmak Brigade and to deliver a combined attack with both Brigades. Tocol was to move from Tochi Camp to Jaler Camp, where it would be more suitably placed to protect the line of communications.

Operations of the 2nd Infantry Brigade *on the 22nd of December. The 2nd Infantry Brigade left Khaisora Camp at 06-15 hours, whilst it was still dark. Piqueting began at about 07-15 hours at the eastern end of Bichhe Kashkai. There was little resistance, and by 09-45 hours, all the protective troops had reached their appointed positions, the 2/4 Bombay Grs. being forward troops, the 2/8 Punjab R. and a portion of the 2/13 F. F. Rif. providing the piquets on the north bank and the Hampshire R. those on the south bank. Protection on the south bank extended up to a col (183387) a few hundred yards along the Dakai Kalai ridge.

R. A. F. Co-operation. Arrangements had been made with the R. A. F. for one reconnaissance aircraft on the front of the 2nd Infantry Brigade throughout the day, one close support sortie from 08-30 hours to 11-00 hours during the approach march, and another from 12-30 hours to 15-00 hours to cover the withdrawal. Complete arrangements were also made for aircraft to be in readiness on the ground from 09-00 hours.

Demolitions accomplished. At 09-45 hours the Sappers and Miners with two companies of the 2/11 Sikh R. went forward to the work of demolition. The buildings marked for demolition were finally blown up at 12-30 hours, the Hampshire R. having been ordered twenty

---

*For composition of 2 Inf. Bde. at this time, see page 27.

1936

Dec. 22nd

minutes earlier to withdraw from the Dakai Kalai ridge. This was somewhat earlier than had been anticipated by the Officer Commanding that Regiment, as it had been intimated the previous day that withdrawal would probably begin at 13-00 hours. The reason for the change was that about 11-00 hours the Force commander had told the Brigade Commander to speed up the preparation of the demolitions, to enable the retirement to begin at 12-30 hours, if possible, so as to allow plenty of daylight in which to conduct the withdrawal. It so happened, however, that when the order to withdraw was received by the 1/Hampshire R. the preparations of this unit were not quite complete.

Withdrawal 22nd December.

Owing to the necessity of covering some dead ground inaccessible to fire from the top of the hill, the most forward piquet of 1 Hampshire R. was in an exposed position (186384) on the forward slope of the ridge. On withdrawing, it came under increasingly heavy fire from enemy to the south of the Dakai Algad, which slowed up the retirement. Further delay was imposed by the difficult nature of the ground. For these various reasons, the withdrawal of the Battalion was much slower than was expected, and it was 13-40 hours before they had cleared the defensive position held by the 2/11 Sikh R. in the valley on a north and south line through Dakai Kalai.

Meanwhile, the forward elements of the 2/2 Punjab R. had been engaged with parties of tribesmen from the time they had reached their positions at about 09-30 hours, and it became evident that they were in contact with appreciable numbers of the enemy. The ground hereabouts was very broken, covered with scrub, and intersected by steep watercourses. The Brigade Commander had anticipated that if there were trouble during the withdrawal it would come from this quarter, and all necessary information to this effect was passed by telephone to the Air Liaison Officer. Eventually, reports from the 2/2 Punjab R. showed that parties of tribesmen, estimated as from twenty five to a hundred strong, were closing in on and above their most forward piquet (205373), which could not be withdrawn until the 1/Hampshire R. was clear of the Dakai Kalai ridge.

At about 14-00 hours it became apparent that the forward company of the 2/2 Punjab R. was in difficulties. The foremost piquet found itself being surrounded, its commander was killed, and ammunition was running short, and it was forced back. This exposed the flank of the company position on which heavy and accurate fire was brought to bear at a range of about one hundred yards. Major Williams, the company commander, and two men were killed. The company fell back taking the dead bodies with it, but being hard-pressed, was compelled to leave them.

At this moment, the Battery supporting the 2/2 Punjab R. had been ordered to move to a rearward position, but the fire of the 2/2nd machine guns was effective in preventing the enemy who were following up closely, from coming too close.

At about 14-30 hours, as a result of a report by wireless from the Battalion Commander, the Brigade Commander asked for air support, saying that he considered that it was a case for low-flying action. Unfortunately, the situation was very obscure, and the location of the forward troops of the 2/2nd was not definitely known. For these and other technical reasons, there was some delay in giving the pilots clear orders, and it was impossible to give more than an indication of the range. At about 14-45 hours two aircraft, a close reconnaissance and a close support machine, attacked the area south of the village of Dakai Kalai, but the enemy could not be seen and action was taken in the area where shells were seen to be bursting.

Meanwhile, the Officer Commanding the 2/2nd, having committed the small reserve at his disposal without success, called on the 2/11 Sikh R., in position in the valley below on his right, for assistance, and one company of this unit was sent immediately. Its original task was to counter attack with a view to recovering the bodies, but it was actually used for the more urgent task of protecting the left flank of the company of the 2/2nd, which was now in a position about halfway (213372) between the top of the ridge and the valley below.

Decision to spend the night of 22nd December at Bichhe Kashkai.

The Brigade Commander, now, at about 15-00 hours in view of the situation of the 2/2nd, and considering the few hours of daylight left, decided at once to camp at Bichhe Kashkai that night instead of returning to Khaisora Camp. Having issued brief orders for piqueting Bichhe Kashkai Camp and for administrative arrangements for the night, he went forward to the headquarters of the 2/2nd, picking up the Officer Commanding 2/11 Sikh R. on the way. After a reconnaissance, he decided that the 2/11 Sikh R. less one company, supported by two batteries ordered forward for the purpose, should counter attack to bring away the bodies of the killed.

A counter attack.

This attack was directed against the spur south of Dakai Khula from which the foremost piquet of the 2/2 Punjab R. had been forced back. With the left flank covered by the company of the 2/11 Sikh R. originally sent to the support of the 2/2nd, and supported by accurate artillery fire and by close support action from the air, it was completely successful by 16-40 hours. No casualties were incurred. Meanwhile, the 2/2 Punjab R. moved up to the top of the ridge (213362) to the left rear of the 2/11th, to cover the retirement of that battalion.

The withdrawal of the 2nd Infantry Brigade was now resumed, the enemy offering very slight opposition. This was attributed to the speed and dash of the 2/11 Sikh R. in their counter-attack, and to the effectiveness of the artillery fire.

From 14-45 to 17-35 hours six aircraft in succession had replaced each other over the critical area, there being two up at the same time between 15-10 and 15-50 hours, and again between 16-45 and 17-35 hours. Very few enemy were seen, but attacks were made at 16-40 hours on a party of about thirty tribesmen and again at 17-15 hours on fifteen men. These men must have been close to the forward troops of the 2/11 Sikh R. during and after their counter-attack.

Operations of the Razmak Brigade.

The Razmak Brigade followed immediately in rear of the 2nd Infantry Bde. from Khaisora Camp on the morning of the 22nd of December, and as only slight opposition had been met by the time the limits of the 2nd Brigade protection were reached, the Razmak Brigade proceeded on its way to Damdil.

1936
———
Dec. 22nd.

Opposition was encountered in the hills (1741,1742) east of Zerpezai, when the high ridge north of the river (1842,1942) and the end of the spur (172409) on the south bank were being secured. The enemy were at once engaged by air attack and by artillery and machine gun fire, piquets pushed on as rapidly as possible, and the enemy withdrew leaving several casualties. After Zerpezai was reached at about 13-40 hours, opposition practically ceased. During the last stages of the march armoured cars and the Tochi Scouts assisted in the protection of the Brigade, the latter securing the ridge north and north east of Musaki from point 4174 to point 4240 (1142,1241).

In order to get clear of the steep sided valley east of Asad Khel and to complete the march as quickly as possible, the Brigade Commander wished to avoid piqueting the highest features on either flank. He asked the R. A. F. to supplement the infantry protection by providing one close support aircraft over the area on each flank from the time the Brigade passed through the 2nd Infantry Brigade until its tail was clear on to the main road at Asad Khel. Two small bodies of enemy were seen and attacked by aircraft during the afternoon.

During the day the Brigade destroyed selected buildings in Zerpezai, Dinor, and Bobali.

The rearguard reached Damdil at 17-45 hours.

Our casualties during this day's fighting were killed, 1 British Officer, Major Williams 2/2 Punjab R., and 4 I. O. Rs., wounded 1 British Officer, 3 British Other Ranks and 9 Indian Other Ranks.

Casualties on the 22nd of December.

The enemy casualties were 20 killed and 21 severely wounded.

During the night of the 22nd/23rd of December the Bichhe Kashkai Camp was sniped from Zairinai villages nearby. On the 23rd, selected houses and towers in these villages were destroyed, and on the 24th, the 2nd Infantry Brigade returned to Khaisora Camp.

Further activities of the 2nd Infantry Brigade.

On two days, flying was interfered with by rain. Otherwise, continuous close reconnaissance was provided daily from dawn until the columns returned to camp in the evening, and frequently, two reconnaissance aircraft were in the air throughout the hours of daylight. Up to the 15th of December reconnaissance was carried out every morning and afternoon to report any unusual actively in neighbouring tribal areas, particularly the Mahsud and Madda Khel country, and to supplement other intelligence sources in obtaining early indication of the movement of lashkars and of the spread of unrest to adjacent tribes. After this date, these reconnaissances were carried out once a day only. The Scouts posts at Madda, Sorarogha, Dosalli, and Datta Khel were visited daily.

R. A. F. Co-operation.

Other activities of the Royal Air Force were the dropping of supplies, photographic reconnaissance, and travel sorties.

A daily air service, also, was instituted for the picking up of orders at Wazirforce Headquarters, and the dropping of these orders on the different camps. Generally, this proved to be the only way of circulating written orders in time, as the road was closed by about 16-00 hours.

1936 Dec.

During this period aircraft were employed for a total of ninety eight hours and forty minutes on close support duties in addition to a number of occasions on which support action was taken by aircraft on reconnaissance duty. From the 5th to the 24th of December air action was taken fortyfive times. A further total of one hundred and thirty-seven hours and ten minutes was expended on various other duties of war flying, including just under thirtynine hours on photography. About four tons of supplies were dropped by parachute during the few days on which the new road proved impassable owing to rain.

Troops of Waziristan Area.

Bannu	2/5th R. G. R.
	Post Group R. A.
	Det. Wazirdist Sigs.
Mir Áli	6 Lt. Tank Coy. (Armoured Cars).
Razmak	Det. Wazirdist Sigs.
	Sec. 20/21 Med. Bty. R. A.
	1 Lt. Tank Coy. (Armoured Cars).
	1/3 G. R. (less one pl. at Dera Ismail Khan).
	4/8 Punjab R.
Wana	Wana Brigade H. Q. & Sig. Sec.
	Det. Probyn's Horse.
	1 Sec. 8 Lt. Tank Coy.
	2 Mtn. Bty.
	3/6 Raj. Rif.
	3/12 F. F. R.
	3/16 Punjab R.
	Post group R. A.
Manzai	4/16 Punjab R.
	3/5 Mahratta L. I.
Dera Ismail Khan	one pl. 1/3 G. R.
	Det. Wazirdist Sigs.
Miranshah and Posts	Tochi Scouts.
Jandola and Posts	South Waziristan Scouts.

Troops comprising Wazirforce.

Wazirforce H. Q.	
Wazirdist Sigs.	(less dets).
Khaicol	Razmak Brigade H. Q. & Sig. Sec.
	22 Mtn. Bde. (less one Bty.)
	1 North'n R.
	2/11 Sikh R.
	5/12 F. F. R.
	2/13 F. F. Rif.
	6/13 F. F. Rif.
	1/9 G. R.

Tocol	Bannu Brigade H. Q. & Sig. Sec.
	12 Mtn. Bty.
	3/7 Rajput R. (less one Coy).
	1/10 Baluch Rt.
	1/17 Dogra R.
2 Inf. Bde.	2 Inf. Bde. H. Q. & Sig. Sec.
	25 Mtn. Bde. (less two Btys.).
	1 Hampshire R.
	2/2 Punjab R.
	2/4 Bombay Grs.
	2/8 Punjab R.
Div. Troops	Probyn's Horse (less one sqn.).
	11 Lt. Tank Coy.
	4 Fd. Coy. S. & M.
	15 Fd. Coy. S. & M.
	18 Fd. Coy. S. & M. (less one sec.).
R. A. F.	20 (A. C.) Sqn.—(less one flight).
	Two flights, 5 (A. C.) Sqn.
Mir Ali	Wazirforce Sigs. (less dets.).
	Det. A Corps Sigs. (one det. Mech. Cable Sec.).
	Det. I Div. Sigs. (one Sig. Office. Group—det. (M. T.) W/T. det. Pack W/T—one pack cable sec.).

CHAPTER V.

Operations to ensure the ejection of trans-frontier tribesmen from the Lower Khaisora valley.

1936.
Dec.

General Sir John Coleridge outlined his plans for these operations in the middle of December. He proposed that, after the Tori Khel had submitted, the Razmak Brigade should return to Razmak and that the Bannu Brigade should remain in the Mir Ali-Jaler Camp area, as considered suitable by the Commander Wazirforce. This was in order to protect the line of communications from Mir Ali to Khaisora Camp in conjunction with the 2nd Infantry Brigade, and to be available as a central reserve.

General plan.

He also proposed that a new road should be constructed eastwards along the Khaisora river via the Sein gorge, and Narmi Khel Khassadar post, to link up with the Central Waziristan Road at Dreghundai near the 8th milestone from Bannu. This extension would have several advantages. It would provide a practically direct route from Bannu to the Bichhe Kashkai area, so being a deterrent in the future to hostile action by the tribesmen in the Sein Area. It would facilitate rapid lateral movement by the Frontier Constabulary when dealing with raiding gangs in that area. It would provide an economic egress for the inhabitants of the Shaktu and Khaisora valleys. It would serve as an alternative to the main road through the Shinki defile, enabling that area to be outflanked if necessary.

[*Ref. sketch map T 37 in pocket*].

With the object of impressing on the Tori Khel that Government was insisting on its rights under the 1935 agreement, it was also recommended that on the withdrawal of the regular troops from the Bichhe Kashkai area when the road was near completion, a detachment of six or seven platoons of the Tochi Scouts should be located temporarily near Bichhe Kashkai until the Tori Khel moved to their summer quarters.

When the whole work was completed, Wazirforce and Waziristan Area would revert to Waziristan District, and, if the situation continued to improve after the submission of the Tori Khel, the R. A. F. detachment at Miranshah would be reduced as found practicable.

The Government of India approved these plans on the 19th of December, and the construction of the road eastward to the Sein gorge was begun without loss of time, work being commenced simultaneously from the Dreghundai end.

Plans approved Work commences.

On the 23rd of December, as it appeared likely that the complete submission of the Tori Khel would follow shortly, the two Flights of No. 20 (Army Co-operation) Squadron R. A. F. were permitted to return to their peace station.

On the following day, the R. A. F. dropped leaflets on the Tori Khel informing them that if they wished to make peace their representatives should present themselves in jirga at Mir Ali on the 29th of December to make known their attitude and to receive the further orders of Government. A jirga was held on that date, being followed by another on the 5th of January, 1937. From the 24th of December to dawn on the 7th of January offensive action in the proscribed area was stopped to facilitate legitimate movement in connection with the jirga and the accomplishment of the preliminary orders of Government.

1936-57
Dec.-Jan.

During this period the improvement of the Mir Ali-Khaisora road and the construction of the new road was continued. The 2nd Infantry Brigade, in order to be more conveniently placed for work on the road, moved on the 31st of December to a new camp, River Camp, further down stream on the Khaisora river (4446).

Successful ambushes.

As the enemy were making considerable use of the well-beaten tracks and even of the roads, when moving to and from the Khaisora between the 31st of December and the 15th of January, the Tochi Scouts and the Razmak Brigade laid ambushes to intercept them. On two occasions these ambushes met with success, 3 enemy being killed and 3 being captured.

Movements and activities of the Faqir of Ipi. [*Ref. sketch map D 37* (*Chap. XV*)].

On the 10th of December the Faqir had taken refuge with the Mahsuds of the Shaktu, and after some changes of residence, finally found an asylum on the 23rd of December at Arsal Kot (on the Shaktu river about nine miles south of Zerpezei). Here he and his small permanent following of Tori Khel irreconcilables remained, the nucleus of opposition. When the Tori Khel maliks were summoned in jirga on the 28th December to hear the preliminary orders of Government, the Faqir tried to dissuade them from attending. He declared that it was foolish for the Tori Khel to make peace as the troops must leave the Khaisora area eventually. He said that Afghans of all tribes were flocking to his standard and that a Mahsud lashkar was collecting. He intimated that an attack would shortly be made on the troops and that, if necessary he himself would lead an attack in the hours of darkness.

In these statements he was partially accurate. A force of some three hundred men, led by one of the Faqir's staunchest supporters, Azal Mir, Haibatai Tori Khel of Sham, did actually arrive close to Jaler Camp during the night of the 5th/6th of January, 1937, intending to make a surprise attack. This enterprise was abandoned at the last moment as the various parties of tribesmen in the force did not agree about the prospects of success. The deciding vote against an attack was cast by Utmanzai Wazirs of Birmal some of whom declared that they had had bitter experience of this form of operation in the past.

There were some grounds too for his declaration that tribesmen were collecting to support him. Although his continued appeals to Mullah Fazal Din for assistance in raising lashkars were still apparently fruitless, and although the Mahsuds as a whole kept aloof, from the 22nd of December onwards Afghans in increasing numbers were attracted to the scene of hostilities. Wild rumours of possible loot were still current across the Frontier, and extravagant stories, such as the fall of Miranshah, were being bruited about. A Gian Khel Zadran, Swalikh Dad, of Birmal gave active assistance in inciting Afghans to help, and the Faqir's former teacher, the Naqib of Chaharbagh, lent his moral support.

Zadrans, Tanis, and Gurbans of Khost as well as Ahmedzai and Kabul Khel Utmanzai Wazirs of Birmal came to the Khaisora Area in some numbers, reaching at one time to a total of about five hundred.

Supplies for the enemy were provided from buried grain dug up in Tori Khel villages and from occasional camel-loads of rice and flour brought from Bannu via the Shaktu valley at the instigation of the Faqir himself or of Janat Mir, Halbatai Tori Khel of Sham, who, like Azal Mir, was one of the staunchest supporters of the Faqir. The problem of supplies, however, was acute, and had its usual effect on the hostile strength.

Many Afghan tribesmen too, disappointed in their hopes of easy and abundant loot, left the Faqir's followers. The Afghan Government, also, discouraged their inhabitants from joining in the hostilities. All these causes contributed to the prevention of any greater incursion of supporters than actually took place.

1937
Jan.

The tribesmen who remained with the Faqir stayed in the Lower Khaisora valley, sheltering by night mainly in deserted Tori Khel villages between Musaki and Dakai Kalai, and by day avoiding observation from the air in broken ground and scrub. Anticipating another advance by the troops from Damdil down the Khaisora, the main body of the enemy prepared to oppose it on ground favourable to itself between Musaki and Bichhe Kashkai, at the same time watching our columns in the hope that some favourable opportunity would occur for an attack.

Below Bichhe Kashkai the enemy showed no activity, and reconnaissances carried out on the 2nd of January by the 2nd Infantry Brigade to a point some three miles below River Camp, and on the 3rd and 6th towards Kaskani Mela and Khoron respectively met with no opposition. These reconnaissances were all kept to the north bank of the river. In order to offer the Mahsuds no excuse for hostilities, reconnaissances south of the river were not permitted.

Instructions were being issued to his tribesmen by the Faqir at Arsal Kot by means of frequent messengers. He was also visited daily by parties of enemy.

Bombing of Arsal Kot.

To put a stop to this, and also to impress the Mahsuds, whose maliks were becoming fearful of the effect which the continuance of operations so close to their people might have on them, it was decided to destroy Arsal Kot by bombing.

On the 31st of December and the 1st of January, after the usual warning had been given, No. 60 (Bomber) Squadron operating from Kohat, attacked Arsal Kot with 230 lb. and incendiary bombs, causing very extensive damage. This had a considerable effect on the inhabitants of the Shaktu valley, particularly on the Mahsuds, many of whom were able to observe the bombing from the high ground south of the Shaktu, the south bank here being Mahsud territory.

Attacks with 112 lb. anti-personnel bombs and surprise visits by aircraft on other missions were continued until the 4th of January, after which they ceased for the time being.

The Faqir took advantage of the cessation of the attacks to re-occupy the place, and in order to maintain the steadying effect on the tribesmen produced by the damage done and to deny its use to the Faqir and his followers, the attacks with anti-personnel bombs were renewed on the 12th of January and continued until the 18th.

The Tori Khel maliks, when interviewed in jirga, had declared that unless Government aided them they would be unable to expel the hostile tribesmen who had come into their territory from other areas. It was decided therefore to take further action against these intruders in the Bobali-Dakai Khula area. The Tori Khel were informed that they could not return to their villages until the intruders had been evicted, and were warned to prevent their tribesmen from entering that area.

Preparations for further operations in the Lower Khaisora area.

1937
Jan.

In preparation for the operations now planned, Headquarters and two Flights of No. 20 (A. C.) Squadron R. A. F. returned to Miranshah on the 7th of January, and Wing Commander Slessor was again placed in control of the R. A. F. units in that place. A section of the 20/21st Medium Battery (6 inch howitzers) was also brought to Damdil from Razmak on the 6th of January.

Plan of Further Operations [*ref. sketch map B 37 (Chap. XXVI)*].

It was decided that on the 8th of January, the Razmak and Bannu Brigades should advance from Damdil and Jaler Camp, respectively, along the high ground north of the valley to positions from which known harbourages of the enemy could be overlooked and engaged. These movements were to be combined with offensive action by the Royal Air Force against all tribesmen in the open or in habitations in a defined "offensive area" which included the Khaisora river from Bobali to Dakai Khula. On the 9th, both Brigades were to advance to camps in the Khaisora valley, remaining there as long as necessary.

The moves of these two formations were as follows :—

	Razmak Brigade.	Bannu Brigade.
7th Jan.	at Damdil.	at Jaler Camp.
8th Jan.	to ground N. W. of Zerpezai Narai and back to Damdil.	to hill above Warmandekai and back to camp.
9th Jan.	to Zerpezai camp.	to Dakai Khula camp.
11th „	....	to Jaler Camp.
13th „	....	to Khaisora Camp.
14th „	to Damdil.	....

Operations on the 8th of January.

On the 8th, the Razmak Brigade first secured point 4285 (1242) and the high ground north of this between Damdil Camp and Sarobi (1545) with one battalion and moved about midway between the Damdil Narai and Shinki Narai to the vicinity of Sarobi. They then advanced to the high ground (1542) just north west of Zerpezai Narai. The Bannu Brigade advanced from the Jaler Camp to the Khaisora river west of Bichhe Kashkai, and from there moved forward to a position in the hills above Warmandekai (2238) with its right about a mile and a half to the north of that place (219407). The two Brigades returned to their camps the same evening, few enemy having been seen. Aircraft of the R. A. F. engaged three small parties during their offensive.

The enemy were expecting an advance down the Khaisora valley itself, and it is probable that unwillingness to leave the more advantageous ground on the south bank, particularly in the neighbourhood of Dakai Khula, and to expose themselves to air action by crossing the open bed of the Khaisora deterred them from collecting to oppose the Brigades.

1937
Jan.

Whilst these operations were in progress, the section of Medium Artillery at Damdil, under cover of a mountain artillery bombardment of villages in the Khaisora valley, registered, with air observation, villages from Bobali to Shaikh Muhammad Ziarat.

During the night of the 8th/9th January harassing fire was carried out **Medium artillery** by the section with the object of surprising tribes- **harassing fire.** men sheltering in the villages. Nine enemy were killed and six were wounded, and the immediate effect of the fire, which was both novel and terrifying, was to create a panic, tribesmen fleeing to the hills in all directions. About 250 Afghans and others left this area immediately.

On the 9th, the Razmak Brigade moved down the Khaisora to camp **Operations on the** (1584413) near Zerpezai. They met with a little **9th of January.** opposition whilst going into camp and were sniped during the early hours of the night. The Bannu Brigade when camping near Dakai Kalai experienced some difficulty in establishing a camp piquet on the north bank (192404). At 14-00 hours, A Coy. (less one platoon) 2/13 F. F. Rif. was ordered to occupy this position and establish a platoon piquet there. On arrival, it was found that the position was commanded by a ridge about four hundred yards away and that there was broken and dead ground right up to the piquet position. All three platoons of the company would be required to hold the extended position necessary to cover the dead ground. A fourth platoon arrived at about 15-30 hours from the battalion reserve, and this platoon was all that was available to construct the piquet defences. Soon after 15-00 hours heavy and accurate fire was opened from the north and north east, causing some casualties, and a party of tribesmen, under cover of this fire, were seen moving into broken ground about three hundred yards from the position. About an hour later a platoon of machine guns arrived, and with them an artillery observation officer from the 12th Mountain Battery. The machine guns came into action, and the artillery engaged the enemy until they came so close that fire could no longer be continued without danger to the troops. A close support aircraft was also in action.

At 16-00 hours the company Commander decided that the whole company would have to remain in the position during the night, and the necessary administrative arrangements were, made.

The enemy's fire made work on the piquet walls almost impossible.

At about 18-00 hours, when it was quite dark the company was ordered to close in and occupy the posts decided on for the night. The enemy followed up this movement, shouting and firing wildly, and attempted to rush the position and seize the piquet stores. They remained close to the position, continuing a heavy fire and at 20-30 hours again tried to rush it. This attempt was beaten off, largely by means of hand grenades, and the enemy withdrew about an hour later.

1937
Jan.

The company was under heavy fire for over six hours, and had beaten off three separate attacks. Its losses were 4 killed and 8 wounded.

It was reported later, that a party of some sixty Kabul Khel Wazirs of Birmal had been responsible for this action.

During the day, the R. A. F. attacked villages where it was thought
R. A. F. Co-operation. snipers might be concealed and also took action against small parties of enemy in the open, besides giving close support, called for by the Air Liaison Officer at Bannu Brigade Headquarters, to the piquet of the 2/13 F. F. Rif.

After dark, the section of Medium Artillery again carried out harassing
Artillery harassing fire. fire against villages in the big bend of the river east of Zerpezai. This night firing combined with the operations of the troops was having a marked effect on the enemy. They depended on deserted villages in the area where the columns were now encamped for shelter from the cold, and they were now reduced to great straits.

On the following day both columns remained in the same area. The
Operations of 10th of January. medium artillery section carried out a dawn shoot with air observation on a village about four miles south of Dakai Khula, where the remnant of the lashkar was reported to have gone. During the day the Razmak and Bannu Brigades carried out reconnaissances in the neighbourhood of their camps, making contact with each other on the hills south of the river. No enemy were met.

The Bannu Brigade withdrew to Jaler Camp on the 11th of January,
Withdrawal of Brigades. and moved thence to Khaisora Camp on the 13th, the Razmak Brigade remaining in camp near Zerpezai until the 14th, when it returned to Damdil. During these movements there was no serious opposition, the enemy confining themselves to occasional sniping.

On the 11th of January, the medium artillery carried out a shoot with
Further artillery harassing fire. air observation at a target in the vicinity of some grass shelters in the Dakai Algad where enemy were reported to be sheltering. On this occasion no enemy movement was seen. On the 14th of January, however, when the medium artillery shelled a small hamlet in the same area, a party of about thirty tribesmen broke out from cover. These were successfully engaged by an aircraft which flew over the spot two minutes later.

The operations from the 8th to the 14th, supplemented by special mea-
End of operations. sures taken to control tribesmen accompanying transborder caravans, had the desired effect. By the 12th of January no Afghans were left in the Lower Khaisora area, and the majority of tribesmen belonging to other areas had departed. The Faqir's following, split up into small wandering gangs, and numbering only about two hundred in all, now consisted of recalcitrant members of the Tori Khel and of wild characters from the different tribes.

In spite of the Faqir's continued strenuous efforts to dissuade them, an almost fully representative jirga of the maliks of the Lower Khaisora Tori Khel assembled on the 15th of January to hear the terms of the Government. These included fines totalling Rs. 50,000 and dismissal for an indefinite period of about 120 Khassadars who had failed in their duties, as well as other penalties, such as the return of loot. The attitude of the jirga was submissive although they expressed doubt as to their capability of returning any loot, most of which was already in Afghanistan.

1937
Jan.-Feb.

As the situation had now become almost normal, the ban on movement in the proscribed area was lifted from the 16th of January, except for an area of two miles round Arsal Kot, against which place air action continued until the 18th.

The Tori Khel began to re-occupy their villages, subject to the restrictions that the tribe guaranteed that no persons hostile to Government would be allowed shelter in the villages from Bobali to Bichhe Kashkai, and that until the tribe could control all its members, villages near Jaler and Khaisora Camps were not to be occupied.

Mahsud and Madda Khel jirgas were held at which these tribes were taken to task for their participation in the disturbances. The Mahsuds protested that they took no interest in the activities of the Faqir of Ipi, a Wazir. Having handed in some rifles as a token of the submission of Malik Khonia Khel, they were treated with some leniency, in recognition of the fact that they had as a whole remained aloof. The Madda Khel, who had previously brazenly denied any share in the hostilities, were punished by the forfeiture of a number of rifles already held in hostage for past misdemeanours, and were warned to expect no clemency if they gave further trouble.

On the 18th of January H. E. the Commander-in-Chief visited Bannu, Mir Ali, Khaisora Camp, and River Camp by car, travelling along the new road from Mir Ali to Dreghundai.

Withdrawal of troops. From the 16th of January Waziristan District replaced Wazirforce and Waziristan Area Headquarters, and returned to Dera Ismail Khan. The Razmak Brigade left Damdil for Razmak on that date and the withdrawal of the additional air and land forces (including the 2nd Brigade) which had been drafted into Waziristan for the operations continued steadily from then to the 5th of February. On the 17th of January seven platoons of the Tochi Scouts occupied a newly constructed camp with an emergency landing ground nearby. This detachment was to stay in this camp until the middle or end of March according to the situation. The Bannu Brigade moved from Khaisora Camp to River Camp on the 31st of January, being expected to return to Bannu about the 20th of Febraury.

Political control handed back. At midnight of the 1st/2nd February General Sir John Coleridge handed back political control to the Governor of the North-West Frontier. He retained control of independent air operations temporarily.

The Faqir of Ipi. The maliks of the Maddi Khel Haibatai Tori Khel, in whose country Arsal Kot, the Faqir's refuge, was situated, were told that they must either expel the Faqir, or assume responsibility for his actions. Air attacks on Arsal Kot were discontinued on the 19th of January to allow them safe approach to him. Some delay was caused in their negotiations with the Faqir, as he fell seriously ill towards the end of January. However, they had an apparently successful interview with him at the beginning of February. The Faqir was said to have stated at this interview that he would abide by the terms of any undertaking Government might require from the Maddi Khel for his future

1937
Dec.

good behaviour, a promise that would hold good wherever he went in the North Waziristan Agency. If Government would not accept their assurance, he would rather leave this country than involve them in further trouble. At the same time, he ordered those tribesmen who were still hostile to keep the peace.

It will be remembered that on the 27th of November, the columns had to return to Mir Ali to refill and the forces had been re-organized into Wazirforce and Waziristan area from midnight on the 4/5th of December. For the operations from the 5th of December onwards, maintenance of the forces was placed on a different footing. Headquarters Wazirforce was responsible for the administration of the troops in the area of operations, which excluded Bannu and Razmak. The Commander of Waziristan Area, whose Headquarters was at Bannu with a rear Headquarters at Dera Ismail Khan, was responsible for the maintenance of Wazirforce as well as for the command and administration of all units and establishments in his own area, and for the protection of all main roads both in the theatre of operations and in his area.

Administration and Maintenance of the forces.

Headquarters, Northern Command controlled administrative matters in both Wazirforce and Waziristan Area by the periodical issue of instructions defining the responsibilities of the two headquarters. It controlled the general administration of the 2nd Echelon which was formed at Bannu, and placed all supplies for advanced base installations at Mari Indus. Base Depots for the supply of ordnance stores were at Ferozepore and Rawalpindi Arsenals and at Lahore Depot. Waziristan Area controlled movement on the narrow gauge railway from Mari Indus to Bannu and Manzai, the latter place serving troops on the Wana line.

The main line-of-communications railhead and advanced base for troops engaged in the operations was at Bannu, although, to avoid congestion, some use was made of Kohat. By the 10th of December a subsidiary advanced base was established at Mir Ali. Maintenance requirements were taken as far forward as possible by mechanical transport, supplies being transferred either to field supply depots located in forward camps as necessary, or direct to the animal transport with columns, giving a three day circuit of action.

The line-of-communications transport moving through Wazirforce area was controlled tactically by Wazirforce Headquarters. That Headquarters was also responsible for road control.

During the period of heavy rain which began to fall on the 9th of December, considerable difficulty was experienced in forwarding supplies along the new road from Mir Ali towards the Khaisora river. On two days, the 12th and 13th of December, it was completely impassable. The R. A. F. came to the assistance of the troops, and between the 10th and 15th of December, furnished thirty-two supply-dropping sorties, during which nine to ten thousand lbs. of supplies were dropped on the camps. Supply-dropping sorties were also provided on other occasions, notably on the 9th and 10th of January, when a total of 5,700 lbs. of supplies were dropped on the Razmak and Bannu Brigades.

By the 18th of December, the administrative system was fully organised and working smoothly.

The maximum amount of mechanical transport required for all maintenance purposes in North Waziristan was three sections of 30 cwt. lorries and two sections of 3-ton lorries with some hired mechanical transport. The 2nd line animal transport was provided by seven mule transport companies with a detachment from an eighth company, and one camel company.

1937
———
Dec.

The carrying capacity of the various transport units was as follows:—

3-ton M. T. Section 25 working vehicles 75 tons.

30-cwt. M. T. Section 25 working vehicles $37\frac{1}{2}$ tons.

Of the seven mule transport companies, six consisted of 4 troops each (1 pack and 3 draught), and one (No. 19) of 3 troops (1 pack and 2 draught).

Pack troop 88 working mules 176 maunds.

Draught troop 48 carts. 480 maunds.

No. 40 Silladar Camel Company consisted of 7 troops.

Troop 88 working camels 440 maunds.

Protection of the lines of communication. For the protection of the main roads, Waziristan Area Headquarters had at its disposal the Tochi Scouts and South Waziristan Scouts and Nos. 1 and 6 Light Tank companies (armoured cars) as well as the troops in the Area. By arrangement with the civil authorities, the Frontier Constabulary located at Dreghundai Post were available to co-operate with the Scouts in protecting the road from Bannu to Mir Ali.

The system of protection was the partrolling of the road by Scouts and armoured cars to support and supplement the protection given by the Khassadar posts.

During the construction of the new road, a proportion of the troops was employed as labour, and brigades furnished protection for the working parties, a section of light tanks usually being allotted to each brigade.

During the hours when the road was thus protected, maintenance convoys were allowed to use the road. On days when the brigades did not open the road for work, an escort of light tanks was provided for small convoys of lorries carrying fresh supplies. From the 22nd of December, when the Bannu Brigade, the rear-most formation, moved from Tochi Camp to Jaler Camp, protection between Mir Ali and Jaler Camp was provided by the troops stationed in Mir Ali. A few permanent piquets were established, mainly in the area of the Sein gorge.

CHAPTER VI.

Events from the 6th of February 1937 to the 21st of April 1937 when the G. O. C. in-C., Northern Command was again invested with Political Control.

1937
Feb.

General.

After the conclusion of the operations in the Lower Khaisora area just described, conditions in Waziristan appeared to be returning to normal and excitement was dying down. This, however, did not last for long.

During February, the situation as a whole deteriorated, largely as the result of intensive anti-Government propaganda spread by the Faqir of Ipi. This propaganda consistently incited all and sundry to kidnap Government officials, commit outrages on communications, and attack Government posts. It was cloaked under the guise of religious agitation, but it is probable that the support given to the Faqir was based on the fear of the Waziristan tribes that the construction of the Khaisora road was only the preliminary to Government action to construct further roads and to destroy tribal independence by opening up the country. The Faqir's appeal was wide and was extended to bad characters and irreconcilables from all tribes in Waziristan as well as Afghan tribesmen from the Afghan Southern Province.

Early in February, two British Officers were murdered, one in Mahsud and one in Wazir territory. These outrages inflamed tribal feeling and frustrated the efforts of the political authorities to force the Tori Khel Wazirs either to control the Faqir of Ipi or to expel him. Further minor hostile acts were committed as a result of which the situation in Waziristan became so uneasy that at the end of February and early in March military reinforcements were sent there as a precautionary measure.

The main lines of action taken included attempts by the Resident of Waziristan to restore the situation by political pressure, limited air action of a purely punitive nature, or limited support of political pressure by proscriptive air action, against certain specified areas at the request of the political authorities. Action by land forces, except for protection of communications, was avoided until political means to restore the situation had proved fruitless.

During March and early April the situation deteriorated further. The Faqir increased his propaganda, other religious leaders began to emulate him, the influx of Afghan tribesmen continued, enemy gangs increased in strength and became more daring, the Tori Khel Wazirs as a whole became more definitely hostile, the Mahsuds were affected, raids in Bannu district became more common, and there were several attacks on road protection troops and on convoys. Particular examples of the last were the attack on a camp piquet at Damdil on the 21st of March, the attack on the 1st Infantry Brigade on the 29th of March between Damdil and Dosalli, when carrying out road protection duties, and the ambush of a convoy in the defile known as the Shahur Tangi on the 9th of April, on its journey from Manzai to Wana. All these incidents were magnified by tribal rumour and made the task of the political authorities increasingly difficult. In spite of the move of further military reinforcements to Waziristan the situation did not improve.

On the 22nd of April, the Government of India again placed the G. O. C.-in-C., Northern Command in full military and political control in Waziristan and in certain tribal areas under the control of the Deputy Commissioners of the Bannu and Dera Ismail Khan Districts, with instructions to pacify the area.

Murders of Capt. Keogh and Lieut. Beatty. The extra troops brought in for the operations described in the previous chapters had hardly left Waziristan, when two incidents occurred which showed that although the Faqir may not have been directly responsible for these incidents, his past propaganda had taken considerable effect.

On the 6th of February, Capt. J. C. Keogh, 1/12th F. F. Regiment, attached to the South Waziristan Scouts, while motoring from Ladha to Jandola with his Scouts orderly, was shot at by a single man on the roadside about eight miles south of Razmak. His orderly was killed and Capt. Keogh died next day from the wound he had received.

The next day, Lieut. R. N. Beatty, Hodson's Horse, attached to the Tochi Scouts and acting as Assistant Political Agent, North Waziristan, was travelling by car from Miranshah via Datta Khel to Razmak with the object of paying the Khassadars in that area. With him in his car were the Khassadar pay clerk and three Khassadar orderlies, a Madda Khel, a Tori Khel, and a Daur. Following him as escort was a lorry in which were two Madda Khel Khassadars and the driver. Lieut. Beatty's car was ambushed by several men at a sharp corner near Boya bridge. Fire was opened from point blank range. Lieut. Beatty was mortally wounded, the Daur and Madda Khel Khassadars in his car were killed and the other two occupants seriously wounded. The murderers then rushed the car and took from it the cash box containing about Rs. 32,000. Fire was opened by the Khassadars in the escorting lorry, who wounded one man, the rest fleeing with the money. The pursuit was taken up by all available Scouts, by about sixty Khassadars who were awaiting their pay at Boya, by Khassadars on duty, and by the village pursuit party, but although they recovered some of the money, which was dropped, they were unable to secure the men.

Territorial responsibility for the safety of the road where Capt. Keogh was shot rested with the Umar Khel Bahlolzai Mahsuds of Makin. The Khassadars of this section, about 120 men, were arrested, and enquiries started. No clue to the identity of the murderer was forthcoming, although this could scarcely be unknown to the Mahsuds. On the 22nd of February, the Mahsuds held a large tribal gathering at Makin at which the outrage was condemned and a reward was offered for any trace of the criminal. This too had no result as the murderer was not produced, and as all sections of the Mahsuds must have known about the affair, it was decided to treat the matter as a Mahsud responsibility and not as a matter for one section only. On the 8th of March the Resident in Waziristan interviewed a jirga at Sorarogha at which the Dre Mahsud tribes were fully represented. He announced a fine of Rs. 75,000 for the murder, and explained that Government considered that responsibility rested on the whole tribe and not on one particular section and was not prepared to tolerate the situation which had been brought about by the unrest and apparent hostility of some sections of the tribe. The Shaman Khel protested their innocence and the

1937
Feb.

1937

Feb.

Alizai stated that should the Faqir move into their country it would be difficult to deal with him. Otherwise no protest was made and the jirga broke up peacefully.

It was established that the murderers of Lieut. Beatty belonged to sub-sections of the Madda Khel inhabiting the Kazha valley* (7659) but to impress their local responsibility on the Hamzoni Daurs, in the area of whose villages the murder took place, those villages were fined Rs. 5,000. The Political Agent, North Waziristan, interviewed a full Madda Khel jirga at Datta Khel on the 14th of February. The maliks agreed that the fullest retribution must be exacted, and promised that tribal machinery would be set in motion at once. Ten days later, they wrote to the Political Agent that they were willing to produce the murderers for trial, but suggested that surrender be conditional on the form of trial and on safe conduct during the proceedings. A reply was given that the surrender must be unconditional. They then refused to give up the men. In the meantime, for reasons in no way connected with the Madda Khel question, a column of troops had been set to Miranshah. This was interpreted by the Madda Khel as evidence of Government's intention to take action against them, and reports came in that they were determined to offer resistance to any force advancing towards Datta Khel. Notwithstanding this, the maliks, after receiving the orders of Government on the 5th of March, left for the Kazha valley in a final effort to induce the surrender of the murderers. The result of this was a letter to the Political Agent openly defying Government, and stating their intention to oppose by force any action taken by Government. They also wrote a letter to Musa Khan Abdullai asking for assistance, which produced no result. On the 10th and 11th of March, the R. A. F. took action against two villages in the Kazha valley which had been harbouring the murderers. The destruction of the villages was undertaken by two Flights of No. 27 (Bomber) Squadron, two Flights of No. 60 (Bomber) Squadron and two aircraft of the Bomber Transport Flight, and involved one hundred and fifty-three hours flying. As a result, three men alleged to have been with the gang when the murder was committed, surrendered on the 12th. These were not the actual murderers, who had moved to the village of Raghzai Kalai (6762). On the 23rd and 24th of March, air action was taken against that place. In April, it was reported that the Madda Khel had expelled the murderers and on the 10th of May a Madda Khel jirga accepted the terms of Government, which were the payment of a fine, the refund of the money looted and the surrender of a certain number of rifles.

Attack on the Wana Brigade 17th of February.

Another incident showing the general unrest in Waziristan though not itself directly connected with the disturbances in the North Waziristan Agency or with the activities of the Faqir of Ipi, was an attack on the Wana Brigade on the 17th of February. This attack was delivered by a party of Kharoti and Suleiman Khel Ghilzais from Birmal* led by a well known bad character, Gul Jan, the son of a Kharoti malik who had been killed some years before by the Zhob Militia.

During the 17th of February, Wana Brigade which had been out on column, was sniped near Obosar (3467) about twenty-two miles west of Wana, near the Afghan border. As the main body was leaving camp at

---

* [Ref. Sketch map A in pocket].

Obosar, the camp site was sniped at a range of about 1,500 yards. Owing to the rising sun, the firers were invisible to men on the camp site and on the perimeter, who were unable to bring effective fire to bear against them. The hostile fire produced some casualties, and some of the animals cast their loads and broke loose, delaying the departure of the column for three hours.

During the remainder of the day, the hostile gang moved through high hills to the east side of the column, and on two more occasions brought fire to bear on the column, causing a few more casualties. The column camped in the open after marching about ten miles. There was no hostile activity during the night and the march was resumed on the 18th of February, and Wana was reached without further incident. Aircraft of the R. A. F. co-operated with the column throughout, and on two occasions took offensive action against the enemy when called on to do so by the ground troops. The total casualties in the column were 2 killed, 2 died of wounds, and 5 wounded. The tribesmen suffered an approximately equivalent numbers of casualties.

Tori Khel maliks go to the Shaktu area to see the Faqir of Ipi. Although when the Maddi Khel maliks visited the Faqir in the Shaktu area at the beginning of February, it appeared that the situation was about to clear, subsequent events showed that this definitely was not so.

On the 12th of February three maliks, when asked by the Political Agent to explain the delay in furnishing sectional security for the Faqir, attributed it to factional and individual jealousies. They were told that they must either effect a settlement or make an open declaration that they had failed and take immediate steps to expel the Faqir from their limits. They were informed of the prevalence of rumours, particularly among the Mahsuds, that the Faqir was still spreading propaganda and plotting mischief after the Id, and were warned that full responsibility for any mischief emanating from the Faqir would fall on the Tori Khel.

After this meeting, the maliks went once again to the Shaktu to see the Faqir. On the 17th of February they returned to Miranshah and at a jirga attended by Tori Khel maliks representing all sections reported results. They had failed to obtain an interview with the Faqir who was said to be too ill to see anyone, but had met his father-in-law Sherzar and his brother Sher Zaman. Asked what the Faqir's attitude was, Sherzar replied that it was the same as when he saw the maliks at the beginning of February, that he was doing no mischief and intended none, and that with regard to rumours he could not be held responsible for what other people were saying. If the Maddi Khel unanimously asked him to leave their country he would do so.

The Tori Khel maliks confessed their failure to achieve unity either to expel the Faqir or to give security for him. All speakers stressed the religious basis of the Faqir's activities and all agreed that it was extremely improbable that anyone would be persuaded to take direct action against him. At the same time they said that the tribe had suffered enough material and monetary punishment and would not support any form of hostilities within their limits.

Tori Khel maliks send a letter to the Faqir of Ipi. Eventually, a petition, signed by all present, was sent to the Faqir by special messenger, informing him that the Tori Khel had made peace with Government and that it was their unanimous desire that he should either come in and abide by the terms of security they were prepared to give or leave their country and save them further suffering.

A few days earlier, the Kikarai Mahsuds in accordance with the orders of the political authorities, had expelled the Faqir's relatives and followers from their area.

Rumours of re-commencement of hostilities.
Many reports were coming in from all over the Mahsud territory and from Bannu of the probability of the recommencement of hostilities after the Id (22nd of February) and of much stronger support for the Faqir being forthcoming than before, particularly from the Mahsuds. It was rumoured that the Din Faqir Bhitanni was collecting followers. In Khost, Gian Mullah and Biba Khel, Zadran maliks, were carrying out extensive propaganda. The Faqir's brother, Sher Zaman, had been touring among the Shaktu Mahsuds.

Despatch of reinforcements to Waziristan.
In view of the disturbed state, the G. O. C.-in-C., Northern Command moved reinforcements into Waziristan consisting of the 1st Abbottabad Infantry Brigade, the H. Q. 25th Mountain Brigade and the 13th and 15th Mountain Batteries, 9th Light Tank Coy. (Light Tanks) and one section 8th Light Tank Coy. (Armoured Cars) No. 10 Field Ambulance, and Nos. 19 and 30 A. T. Coys. These troops had all arrived in Bannu by the 24th of February. On the 19th of February, the Government of the N. W. Frontier Province proposed to the Government of India that the G. O. C.-in-C., Northern Command be granted discretionary powers to authorize air action without delay in areas being used as bases for hostilities. It was pointed out that such action would offer the best hope of preventing a serious conflagration involving the use of troops on a large scale. These powers were not granted and it was decided that the procedure should continue to be in accordance with the rules laid down for the control of operations on the Frontier.

Faqir of Ipi states that he will do nothing for a month.
Contrary to expectation the Id passed off peacefully. Id gatherings throughout the North Waziristan Agency expressed no hostile intentions. The Faqir emerged from his seclusion in the caves at Arsal Kot and presided at the prayers there. Probably on account of the inclement weather very few people were present. After the prayers he granted an interview to some Wazirs and told them that nothing had been decided by him at present and that people should wait for another month until the weather was warmer when he would review the situation.

Faqir of Ipi openly declares hostility.
Within a week of this, the Faqir showed his real intention. On the 26th of February, after Friday prayers, he addressed a mixed gathering of Wazirs and Mahsuds, saying that he had received the assurance of many religious leaders of help in his fight for Islam, and that in the circumstances he proposed to ignore the letter he had received from the Tori Khel in which the maliks had informed him that it was the unanimous wish of the tribe that he should cease from giving trouble or leave their territory, and that he hoped people would now come openly to his help. He proposed to place the letter from the Tori Khel before a council of Mullahs. If the council decided that he was justified in conducting a jehad, he proposed to issue a proclamation to all tribes calling on them to choose between Islam and Kafir.

DAMDIL CAMP, 1937.

Increasing support for the Faqir of Ipi. Support for him continued to increase. A mixed force of about four hundred, mostly armed tribesmen including Birmal Kabul Khel and some Ghilzais, collected in the neighbourhood of Arsal Kot. Some armed parties of the Dreplari Tori Khel, a section which had held aloof during the earlier Khaisora operations, and some parties of Daurs from the Lower Tochi area, started off to Arsal Kot. The Din Faqir of Bhittani openly promised aid to the Faqir and instigated outrages on roads.

1937
Mar.

The Faqir continued to receive a constant stream of visitors from various tribes and he exhorted them to form lashkars and to commit offences on roads. Shots were fired into the perimeter at Bannu. Signs of disaffection appeared among the Mahsuds of the Shaktu area and among the Bora Khel and the Wuzi Khel of the Mohmit Khel Wazirs. Propaganda appeared to be having some effect among the tribesmen of the Southern Province of Afghanistan, a few of whom, consisting principally of Zadrans and Tannis, had moved to the Khaisora area. Food was being sent to the Faqir by his supporters in the Bannu district.

On the 4th of March, the Faqir issued a decree calling on tribal Khassadars and maliks to desert Government service and stating that any who failed to do so would be denied Muslim funeral ceremonies. The pronouncement was not without effect, and numerous desertions that took place must be attributed to it.

Owing to the threat of hostile gangs, traffic on the roads was considerably restricted, and at the beginning of March the only roads left open to normal traffic were those from Isha to Miranshah, from Bannu and Manzai via Tank to Dera Ismail Khan and from Tank via Bain to Ghazni Khel. On the roads from Manzai to Wana via Jandola and from Bannu to Razmak, traffic was run in convoys with armoured car and infantry escorts three times a week.

More reinforcements sent to Waziristan. Further reinforcements were ordered to Waziristan, and on the 8th of March the following Headquarters and troops commenced to arrive, H. Q. 1st Indian Division, one battery (how.) 4th Field Brigade, 2nd Light Battery, No. 4 Field Company Sappers and Miners, 6th Light Tank Company (Armoured Cars), 3rd Indian Infantry Brigade, No. 7 A. T. Company, No. 8 A. T. Company, No. 1 and No. 4, Supply Issue Section, No. 4 Field Ambulance, and one sub-section of No. 3 Sanitary Section.

Location of troops and reorganization of areas. From the 6th of March the Tochi Scouts and South Waziristan Scouts were placed under the Command of the G. O. C.-in-C. Northern Command.

The location of troops in Waziristan on the 15th of March was as under:—

Mir Ali . . .	H. Q. 1st Indian Division .	3rd Infantry Brigade.
Miranshah . . .	Bannu Brigade . .	No. 5 (A. C.) Squadron R. A. F.
Damdil Camp . .	1st Infantry Brigade.	
Razmak . . .	Razmak Brigade.	
Wana . . .	Wana Brigade.	

1937
Mar.

The troops were employed in the protection of communications, a duty that became necessary owing to the desertion of the Khassadars who normally performed this duty and to the presence of numerous gangs seeking opportunities to commit offences.

On the 12th of March troops in Waziristan were re-organized. The 1st Indian Division (Commander, Major General E. de Burgh, C.B., D.S.O., O.B.E.), to which was attached the 66th Field Battery (hows.) and the 9th Light Tank Company was allotted an operational area the boundaries of which were to the north Thal-in-Kurram, to the east, Dreghundai, to the south Madamir Kalai, and to the west, Isha and Dosalli. All formation units, and administrative establishments except the 1st Indian Division and the 2nd Echelon, were placed in the Waziristan District, commanded by Major General D. E. Robertson, C.B., D.S.O. To him was delegated the command of the Tochi Scouts and the South Waziristan Scouts, less those detachments located in the 1st Division operational area. He was made responsible, in consultation with the Commander 1st Division and the Political Authorities, for the timings of all M.T. convoys and other traffic in Waziristan, and for the provision of the necessary protection. He could call on the 1st Division to assist in this protection within the limits of its operational area.

For the time being, operations were to be limited to aggressive action by the R. A. F. and defensive action by the Army, the latter consisting of such measures as were necessary to safeguard the interests of Government. Discretion was given to take offensive action locally if the situation demanded it.

From the 15th of March, sectors for the protection of the line of communications were allotted as follows:—

3rd Infantry Brigade, from inclusive the Shinki defile to milestone 32 (east of Isha post).

Tochi Scouts, at Idak, from milestone 32 to exclusive Isha corner (Isha post).

Bannu Brigade, which had moved from the Khaisora area to Mir Ali on the 27th and to Miranshah on the 28th of February, from Miranshah to inclusive Isha Corner and inclusive point 3461, south of Tal-in-Tochi (about milestone 38).

1st Infantry Brigade, from inclusive the Nariwela Narai (about milestone 39) to inclusive milestone 52 (about six miles west of Damdil).

It was arranged that convoys should run three days a week, the days and timings being liable to variation. The Officers Commanding at Bannu and Mir Ali detailed armoured car, infantry, and engineer escorts. The route was not to be wholly piqueted, but was to be protected by infantry who were to occupy one or more piquets on the route during the passing of each convoy on the outward journey, patrol until the convoy was due to return, and occupy fresh piquets during the passing of the convoy on the return journey, the position of the piquets being varied daily.

The necessity for action to be taken against the Faqir of Ipi, the focus of the whole trouble, was apparent. It was considered that if the Tori Khel had really wished to expel him they could have done so, but, hitherto, they had failed to exert themselves. As the Maddi Khel had failed to deal with him, the political authorities now decided that the whole Tori Khel section should be given the option of expelling him or of submitting to further and more drastic penalties.

1937
Mar.

On the 9th of March a Tori Khel jirga was held at Mir Ali. This was fully representative, except for the Maddi Khel section in whose area the Faqir was still residing. The jirga was informed that unless the Faqir was expelled within a week, severe measures would be adopted. These would include stoppage of Khassadari and of the special compensation granted to the Tori Khel for Razmak which lies in their territory, while members of the tribe would be excluded from administered territory and from the Razmak area.

Tori Khel to expel the Faqir of Ipi or take the consequences.

On the same day a proclamation by the Governor of the N. W. F. Province was broadcast over Waziristan in which the origins of the present unrest were traced and the tribes invited to co-operate in the restoration of normal conditions.

In order to stop the movements into and from Arsal Kot, it was decided to place an area within a three-mile radius of that village under air blockade. The usual warnings were dropped, and the blockade commenced at midday on the 17th of March. On the 24th the area of the blockade was reduced to a radius of one mile from Arsal Kot, and from the 26th it was suspended to allow an Utmarzai jirga to visit the Faqir.

Air blockade round Arsal Kot.

In the meantime, hostile activities continued. Telegraph wires were cut; a bridge in the Shinki defile was damaged; the camps at Razmak, Miranshah, Tal-in-Tochi and Damdil were sniped; men were kidnapped from civilian lorries. On the 19th of March, troops withdrawing from road protection duty were followed up from the direction of Asad Khel by enemy who had been seen in the neighbourhood all day. On the evening of the 19th shots were fired at a relieving camp piquet from the direction of Musaki. Attempts were made to block the road with boulders and to blow up the bridge near Tal-in-Tochi. Culverts on the new Khaisora road were damaged near Sein. Piquets in the Shinki defile and at Idak were sniped. Supplies continued to reach the Faqir from Bannu by night.

Hostile activities continue.

On the night of the 20th/21st of March an attack was made on a camp piquet at Damdil held by the 2/5 R. G. R. This piquet consisted of one N. C. O., 6 riflemen and one signaller, and was placed about two hundred and fifty yards from the camp, inside the main piquet line overlooking a nala which ran towards the perimeter. Owing to the requirements of the more exposed positions, it had not been possible to put up a barbed wire apron. At about 0330 hours the enemy opened fire from close quarters. One of the sentries was killed instantly, and immediately afterwards a tribesman jumped over the wall and killed the signaller. The remainder of the enemy, about thirty to forty in number, followed up immediately, leaping into the post from all sides. In the hand to hand fight which ensued, rifles, kukris, daggers, and stones were used, all the remaining men of the piquet being wounded, some of them seriously. The enemy eventually withdrew leaving three men killed. Only four of the defenders were now able to carry on. The N. C. O. in command was unable to stand. The post was in complete

Attack on a Damdil Camp piquet.

1937
Mar.

confusion, the Verey pistol and lights were not to be found, and the signaller having been killed, none of the remaining men knew how to communicate with camp. The enemy remained in the vicinity of the post until 0600 hours, keeping it under constant fire. The defenders, using bombs and firing from different positions in the post, induced the enemy to believe that it was still strongly held, and no further assault was made. Except for the occasional firing, the action was fought in complete silence, and there was nothing to indicate to the camp that the piquet had been seriously attacked. Apart from the three dead left behind, four rifles, two mills-grenades (1916 pattern), three daggers, and eighty six rounds of ammunition were captured. The piquet lost two rifles and one bayonet.

CHAPTER VII.

Events from the 6th of February, 1937 to the 21st of April, 1937—*contd*.
Action by 1st Infantry Brigade at Asad Khel, March 29th, 1937.

Utmanzai jirga visits the Faqir of Ipi.
As action by the Tori Khel alone to secure the expulsion of the Faqir had proved ineffective, in a further effort to bring this about by political pressure a representative jirga of all the Utmanzai Wazirs was ordered to assemble at Miranshah on the 24th of March, where it was interviewed by the Assistant Resident.

The jirga fully accepted the statement that Government was not interfering in religious matters, and determined to combine to end the present situation. They took power of attorney from the Tori Khel to deal with the situation on their behalf, and agreed to select representatives to go in a body to persuade the Haibati Tori Khel to deal with the Faqir. After the jirga, representatives were selected. These departed for the Shaktu area on the 24th of March and in order to give them freedom of action in that area the air blockade of Arsal Kot was suspended.

On the 27th, the Faqir, arriving at Dakai Khula with a large escort of mixed tribesmen, met the representatives there, being received by them with great cordiality. He interviewed four maliks of each section for about two hours, and then made his announcement to the main jirga. In this he said that he had had no intention of seeking a settlement with Government, but as the jirga of the Utmanzai tribes had come to him he would consider whether it was possible to arrive at one agreeable to everybody. He would consult his followers, and in the course of the next few days would send a letter to Government stating his requests. He also announced that his followers would commit no acts of hostility whilst negotiations were in progress.

The maliks returned to Miranshah in a hopeful mood.

Other political measures.
Another political measure which was taken was the issue of a notification to the disaffected tribes that from sunset on the 26th of March, if it became known that a raiding gang or party which had attacked troops or had committed any heinous offence belonged to or had been assisted by a village in the North Waziristan Agency or in tribal territory of Bannu District, that village would be punished by air action or in any other way deemed most suitable.

Other measures were brought into effect about the same time. Owing to the number of offences which were being committed at night and to the difficulty of distinguishing between honest persons and malefactors any person found outside his village between sunset and sunrise would be treated as an enemy. As Damdil Camp had been attacked on several recent occasions, and as it was difficult for the troops to distinguish friend from enemy, any party of ten or more armed men seen within a radius of three miles from Damdil Camp would be treated as hostile to Government and would be liable to attack without warning. This did not apply to persons using the Government roads. With certain exceptions, and with special regulations in the case of Khassadars in Government employ and Government maliks and their escorts, tribesmen were not to carry rifles on the Bannu-Razmak road or within an area of one mile on each side of it. From the 18th March the use of the Bannu-Kohat road was confined to the hours of daylight, the road being patrolled by armoured cars. Traffic was allowed on the Bannu-Dera Ismail Khan road by daylight only. In Bannu District the strength of the Frontier Constabulary was increased, levies were enrolled, and village defence was re-organized.

1937 March	**Attack on the 1st Infantry Brigade near Asad Khel, March 29th, 1937.***

It soon became apparent that the assurances of the Faqir were of no value, as on the 29th of March, tribesmen made a very heavy attack on the troops of the 1st (Abbottabad) Infantry Brigade† whilst carrying out road-protection duties.

On the 29th, convoys were due to run from Mir Ali to Damdil and back and from Mir Ali to Manzai *via* Razmak. The 1st Infantry Brigade was required to protect the six miles of road from Damdil northwards to the Nariwela Narai and about six miles south and west from Damdil to milestone 52.

The normal arrangements in the Brigade, which were followed on the 29th, were for one battalion, supported by one section of Mountain Artillery, to open the road to the Nariwela Narai. Another battalion, less one company, supported by one section Mountain Artillery, secured the high ground north of the road from the hill west of Asad Khel (096423) known as Ring Contour, to point 4641 (0842). A third battalion, also supported by one section mountain Artillery, varying the route and method on each occasion, secured the road from point 4641 to the 52nd milestone. On this particular day no troops were to move south of the Khaisora river. The fourth battalion of the Brigade normally remained in camp for garrison duties, including the rapid unloading of stores and supplies which came up on each convoy. A large number of men were required for this duty in order to effect a quick turn round. One section of mountain artillery also remained in camp ready to afford support in any direction as required. On the 29th, the units in camp were the 2/5th R. G. R. and one section of the 13th Mtn. Bty.

The 1 S. Wales Bord. with one section of the 13th Mtn. Bty. opened the road to the Nariwela Narai without incident.

0605 hours. The 2/6 G. R., less one company in brigade reserve, left camp at 0600 hours, and by 0725 hours had occupied the Ring Contour and point 4641 without opposition, and had established a forward locality on a lower feature (083418 "W" on the sketch map) about half a mile to the south of point 4641. The 15th Mtn. Bty., less one section, was in position on the col between point 4641 and the Ring Contour.

The 1/6 G. R., less A company and one machine gun section which were to follow later in lorries, with one section of the 15th Mtn. Bty., left camp at 0630 hours moving south of the Ring Contour and passing through the positions held by the 2/6 G. R. The battalion advanced to its first objective, a ridge to the north of the road in the vicinity of milestone 50½.

The country in which the 1/6 and 2/6 G. R. were operating was extremely difficult. Although the Ring Contour, point 4641, and point 4792 (0642) are higher than any ground to their immediate south, the advantages of their commanding position were largely negatived as the country between them and the main road consisted of a series of low ridges covered with a heavy scrub and was intersected by numerous small nalas with steep scrub-covered sides, all affording abundant cover.

---

* [Ref. Sketch map E. at end of Chapter].
† The units of the 1st Inf. Bde. are given on p. 82. In addition 13 and 15 Mtn. Btys. were with it at Damdil.

At 0805 hours, the advanced guard of the 1/6 G. R., consisting of B company less two platoons and one machine-gun section was moving along the low hills (064412-"X" on the sketch map) just north of the road near milestone 51½. Meanwhile, a piquet, supported by one section of machine-guns, had been posted near milestone 49 to watch the south bank, and at 0805 hours, another piquet from C company also supported by one machine-gun section had just moved off from the vicinity of milestone 49 to occupy a spur (0742) running south-east from point 4792. Battalion Headquarters, with one machine-gun section and the equivalent of one weak rifle company in reserve, was now moving on towards milestone 50, working through and searching the broken, difficult ground immediately north of the road, and unable to see the advanced guard. At this moment, fire was opened from the south of the Khaisora on the main body. A few moments later, the advanced guard which was moving along the ridge north of the road also came under fire from the south of the Khaisora. One of the machine-guns of the section with the advanced guard came into action and engaged this enemy from behind the north wall of the road. The detachment of the other gun was shot down before the gun could be mounted. The attention of the troops having been attracted to the south, the enemy now opened a heavy fire on the advanced guard from low ground north of the ridge along which they were advancing. The remaining machine gunners and the men on the slopes north of the road were shot down, and tribesmen who had been lying concealed in a deep wooded nala (0641) north of the road and in other small nalas and even in a road-drainage cut, rushed in with knives. They attacked with fanatical fury and closed with the troops in hand-to-hand fighting. The advanced guard suffered heavy casualties including the British Officer in command and two Gurkha Officers, and the remnants of the party, with their wounded, rallied in a small water course from which they held off the enemy.

No. 1 section of the 6th Light Tank Company was stationed with the Tochi Scouts at Dosalli Post. Just as the Officer Commanding was receiving a report that enemy had crossed to the north of the Khaisora river near Asad Khel, sounds of heavy firing were heard, and he immediately took his cars at top speed down the main road. Enemy were encountered suddenly, some moving up the road, others stripping the rounds from a machine-gun belt, and others, off the road, leading away some mules. Surprised and engaged at short range, the tribesmen sustained at least ten casualties in a short space of time. One sub-section of armoured cars then went towards Asad Khel to see if troops further down the road required support, leaving the other sub-section with the advanced guard. More tribesmen, apparently thinking that all the armoured cars had left, now came into view, and several were shot. In addition to supporting the advanced guard, these armoured cars, later joined by No. 3 section of the same company, which had come with the convoy from Mir Ali to Damdil, patrolled the road and assisted in keeping down hostile fire by engaging the enemy south of the river at long range.

Almost concurrently with the attack on the advanced guard, the piquet of the 1/6 G. R., which had been ordered to occupy the spur running south-east from point 4792, came under heavy fire from the north of the road. Although reinforced by another platoon, it was unable to advance, and it became clear that large numbers of tribesmen were concealed in the nalas north of the road.

1937
Mar.

By about 0820 hours, Battalion Headquarters of the 1/6 G. R., with about thirty men from B and C Companies were in position to the north of the road near milestone 50 ("Z" on the sketch map). Attempts to gain touch with the advanced guard were unsuccessful, partly because all signallers with the advanced guard were casualties, but mainly because of the heavy fire in the forward area which prevented any movement. The remainder of the Battalion, spread over a wide area on the ground to the north of the road and covering the junction of nalas in which enemy were known to be concealed, were unable to do more than maintain their positions, the slightest movement drawing heavy fire from both sides of the road.

0820 hours, 29th March.

It would appear that the advanced guard had got too far ahead and lost touch with the main body. In doing so the advanced guard commander committed his Commanding Officer to an action which the latter was in no way in a position to undertake. There was some excuse for this in that there was very little time for road protection troops to cover the long distance they had to go in order to be in position before the head of the convoy arrived.

At 0835 hours, A company of the 1/6 G. R. arrived at milestone 49. It was ordered to drive the enemy from the nalas north of the road and to establish a piquet on the spur of point 4792, the position which the original piquet had been unable to reach. Although covered by the fire of two machine-gun sections and of the 2/6 G. R., the company was unable to progress very far owing to the close fire of the tribesmen in their concealed positions. After the company commander and several men had become casualties, it was finally held up not far from the forward locality of the 2/6 G. R., to the west of which it had passed in its advance.

0835 hours.

At about this time the enemy began to present good targets to the 2/6 G. R. and to the 15th Mtn. Bty., and the fire of these units effectively secured the main body of the 1/6 G. R. from further attack; but any movement continued to draw instant fire from tribesmen at close range who could not be seen, and the battalion was virtually pinned to its ground.

At about 0900 hours, about three hundred enemy were reported to be working round the west and north of point 4641. These attempted to capture the hill, but were driven off to the north and then were effectively engaged by the section of the 13th Mtn. Bty. in camp. Another party of tribesmen tried to penetrate between point 4641 and Damdil Camp. These were stopped by the company of the 2/6 G. R. which had been in brigade reserve. The company took up a position (090431) to the north-east of point 4641 just in time, and with the assistance of the guns in the Camp, repulsed several minor but determined attacks.

0900 hours.

Earlier in the morning the Brigade Commander Brig. R. D. Inskip, D.S.O., M.C., with his Brigade Major had gone out with the 1 South Wales Borderers and one section 13 Mtn. Bty., who had been given the task of opening the road to the Nariwela Narai. He had reason to expect an attack in his area sooner or later, and decided to be with this Battalion which had not been on the frontier in recent years. He also wished to take the opportunity, if all was quiet, to carry out a reconnaissance of the high ground east of the Nariwela Narai, which had been ordered with

1100 hours.

a view to further operations. As he was completing his reconnaissance he heard continuous gun-fire in his southern sector and hurried back to camp, arriving there at 1100 hours. He found the situation very confused, as it was not possible to discover exactly what had happened to the 1/6 G. R. It was known that there were very large numbers of enemy in the nalas north of the road, south and south-east of point 4792 and between points 4792 and 4641, and there appeared to be little doubt that to extricate the 1/6th was going to be difficult.

The Brigade Commander ordered out the 2/5 R. G. R., placed the escort which had come with the convoy for Razmak in charge of the defence of the Camp, and went off to the Headquarters of the 2/6 G. R. to ascertain the situation.

1200 hours, 29th March. Brigade Headquarters was established on the col between point 4641 and the Ring Contour by 1200 hours. By this hour the convoy for Mir Ali had left Damdil Camp and the S. Wales Bord. had commenced their six-mile withdrawal.

To relieve the pressure on the 1/6 G. R., the 2/5 R. G. R. were ordered to make an attack from the north on point 4792 and on the spur on which the 1/6 G. R. had been unable to establish a piquet. After attaining this objective, the battalion was to work southwards, cut off all the enemy lying in this area, and drive them out of the nalas.

1300 hours. The attack started at 1300 hours, and in spite of strong opposition on the southern slopes of point 4792, was successful. A large number of the enemy were practically surrounded; many were driven out of the nalas by shell fire and were engaged by all three battalions. It was estimated that a high proportion of the casualties sustained by the enemy was incurred during this phase of the fighting.

1630 hours. "A" company of the 1/6 G. R. was now withdrawn, covered by the fire of the 2/6 G. R. and the 15th Mtn. Bty., and the Officer Commanding the battalion, under heavy and persistent fire from tribesmen in the scrub and nala area, took about thirty men forward to the advanced guard position. Motor Ambulances and lorries were sent forward to the vicinity of milestone 50, and, covered by the Armoured cars, without whose assistance it is doubtful whether it could have been done successfully, the advanced guard casualties were evacuated to camp, except for some dead whose bodies were brought in by the Tochi Scouts the next day. The survivors of the advanced guard were then brought away, and at about 1630 hours, the 1/6 G. R. withdrew through the 2/6th, and took up a position to cover the retirement of that battalion.

1700 hours. It was now getting dark and it was obvious that the withdrawal of the 2/5 R. G. R., who had had some casualties on the southern slopes of point 4792, and whose route thence crossed very difficult rising ground exposed to enemy fire, would present difficulties.

The 2/5th had asked for assistance, and the 1. S. Wales Bord., who had arrived at the camp at about 1600 hours, were ordered to occupy a position north-east of point 4792. Covered by the latter, the 2/5th, having collected and evacuated all their casualties except three dead men, under great difficulties, commenced their withdrawal. A strong concentration of Artillery fire was put down on the eastern and western slopes of point

4792 and in the nalas in that area, and the enemy did not follow up the withdrawal. This allowed the 2/5th to work their way back up the slopes without suffering further casualties.

At about 1845 hours, the 2/5 R. G. R. were clear of the 2/6 G. R., who then withdrew, followed by the 1 S. Wales Bord., the last of the troops reaching camp at 1945 hours.

Owing to the nature of the country, which enabled the tribesmen to conceal themselves very effectively, an early morning reconnaissance had failed to discover their presence. There had been no previous intimation of an attack, and the earliest information received at Brigade Headquarters had been a report by the Political-Naib-Tahsildar at about 0800 hours, that a Khassadar piquet had informed him earlier in the morning that there were tribesmen on both sides of the road in readiness to attack the troops. This report had hardly been received when sounds of firing were heard.

The enemy, whose strength was estimated to be about 700 at the commencement of the attack, increasing to 1000 during the course of the day, sustained casualties amounting to 94 killed and 64 severely wounded. There is little doubt that if the action could have continued they would have lost many more, as a large number had been trapped in the area north of the road.

The casualties in the 1st Infantry Brigade were:—

Killed: Captain O R. Bethune, 2/5 R. G. R. F.F.
Lieut. R. A. L. Marks, 1/6 G. R.
Gurkha Officers.—2.
Gurkha Other Ranks.—30.

Wounded: Lieut. P. F. C. Nicholson, 1/6 G. R.
British Other Ranks—1.
Gurkha Officer—1.
Indian and Gurkha Other Ranks—41.

By the morning of the 30th, the tribesmen had evacuated their position in the battle area and had withdrawn out of reach of the troops, only one party being seen at a distance during the day.

Aircraft of No. 5 (A. C.) Squadron R. A. F. were active over the area throughout the day on reconnaissance and close support duties, and gave much assistance to the ground troops.

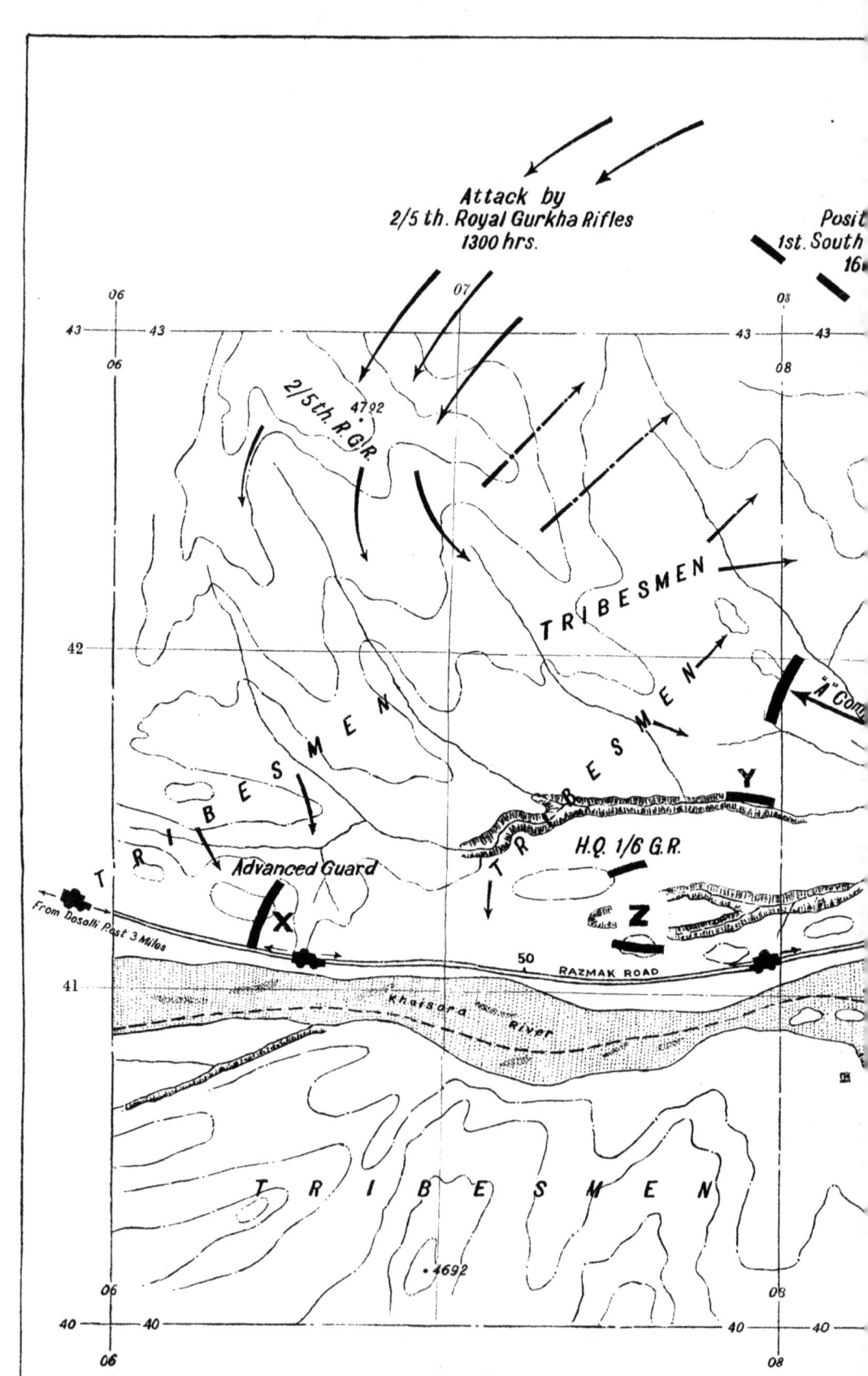

Map E. 37.

Sketch Map to Illustrate the
ACTION OF THE 1st (ABBOTTABAD) INFANTRY BRIGADE
South West of DAMDIL, 29th March 1937.
(Part of Map Sheet 38 L/I)

CHAPTER VIII.

Events from the 6th of February 1937 to the 21st of April 1937—*contd.*
Ambush in the Shahur Tangi, April 9th.

1937
April

The lashkar responsible for the attack on the 1st Infantry Brigade on the 29th of March had been led by the more prominent among the Tori Khel hostile strong adherents of the Faqir, who had in the past acted closely under his orders. It was considered that if he did not actually order this breach of his own undertaking given to the Utmanzai jirga that his followers would not commit any act of hostility for the time being, he had connived at it, and had it in his power to stop it.

Utmanzai maliks again approach the Faqir of Ipi. The Utmanzai maliks expressed their annoyance at the attack near Asad Khel and sent a deputation to seek an explanation from the Faqir and to ask him once again to make peace. A messenger, despatched by the full jirga, before the departure of the deputation, on his return stated that the Faqir had told him that he had written to representative mullahs and maliks of Wazirs, Mahsuds, and Bhitannis, whose views he must obtain before opening negotiations for peace. If these agreed that peace was desirable, he would have no hesitation in urging negotiations. He himself desired peace. In the meantime, Government should not try to force a settlement prematurely.

The deputation itself produced no result, as on arrival at Arsal Kot it spent the night there without meeting the Faqir. Later, the Faqir sent a letter saying that he had not been able to consult all the representatives of other tribes, and suggested that the Government should help him to collect them.

There was no doubt that the Faqir's prestige had been considerably enhanced by the importance given to him as a result of the negotiations with the Utmanzai jirga, and although the heavy casualties received on the 29th of March had a sobering effect on his followers, this was very temporary and there was no reason to suppose that the Faqir and his supporters had any intention of abandoning their plans.

Terms announced to the Utmanzai maliks. As no settlement with the Faqir had been achieved, on the 5th of April, the Resident interviewed the Utmanzai jirga at Miranshah. He pointed out the deterioration which had taken place in the situation in spite of the forbearance shown by the Government. The Tori Khel were held responsible. The Resident announced that the following terms were imposed on the Tori Khel. These terms would not be relaxed until they made submission, cleared their country of hostiles, and expelled the Faqir.

(a) From 1200 hours on the 6th of April the following areas would be closed by air blockade to all persons and cattle.

Arsal Kot and an area within a radius of three miles; two miles on either side of the Khaisora valley from (exclusive) Musaki (1141) to (inclusive) Sein (3844); one mile on either side of the Shaktu valley between Tabai Algad (3743) to one mile short of Arap Kot (3131).

(b) The Khaisora allowances were withdrawn, the Tori Khel not having fulfilled conditions on their part.

(c) All Tori Khel maliks' allowances and Khassadari were suspended from the 5th of April and any contracts held by the Tori Khel were cancelled.

1937

April

(d) Bannu District and Razmak area were closed to Tori Khel until further orders.

(e) All Tori Khel villages within three miles of the Bannu-Razmak road must be evacuated by Tori Khel by 1200 hours on the 7th of April and kept empty until further orders.

(f) After 1200 hours on the 7th of April any Tori Khel seen by Government forces would be liable to arrest except in the case of Jirgas coming to the political authorities.

Supplies for Faqir of Ipi.

Sympathisers of the Faqir's cause in Bannu had been making a regular practice of sending camel loads of supplies to him. The object of the proscription of the Shaktu valley area was to put a stop to this. Other measures to this end were also taken in Bannu. It had been found that the sale of food supplies to tribesmen at Miranshah had increased considerably, and a limit was placed on the number of civilian lorries leaving Bannu for North Waziristan. All the passes, too, from Bannu to North Waziristan between Kui in the south to the point where the Khaisora river crosses the boundary in the north were closed.

Air action taken.

On the day of this jirga, a formation of three squadrons R. A. F. demonstrated over Waziristan, in particular over the Shaktu valley.

Offensive air action in the prescribed areas began on the 6th of April, the operations being carried out by No. 1 (Indian) Wing R. A. F. The procedure was similar to that adopted in the previous operations against the Arsal Kot area. Orders were issued that the object was to be attained with the minimum destruction of life and property. During the first two days bombs were dropped on a large number of villages within the areas, to make the inhabitants realize that it was unsafe for them to remain there. Subsequent action was directed chiefly against any movement of men or animals seen in the areas. A few bombs were dropped in various villages, and delay action bombs, timed to explode during the night, were used in different localities. There was so much cover in the areas that it was impossible to prevent a certain amount of movement. To cope with this, instantaneous and delay action bombs were dropped in nalas and among trees near cultivation, small-arm fire also being largely used to search out probable places of concealment. There was a shortage of reconnaissance flares, and night sorties were restricted to occasions when there was sufficient moonlight to enable pilots to pick up positions accurately.

All these measures excited the hostility of the younger members of the tribe. Propaganda by the Faqir had greatly increased, but there was still some hope that the action taken would enable the tribal elders of the other Wazir sections to regain control over their irresponsible elements. Military action, therefore, was still confined to the protection of communications, whilst air action was only taken at the request of the political authorities.

At their request, steps were taken to deal with the Dreplari Tori Khel. This section, which lives in the Spinwam area, was giving considerable trouble by looting the mail and passenger lorries and damaging the road between Mir Ali and Spinwam. It was decided to punish this particular section by bombing some of its villages. The Datta Khel villages were selected for this purpose, and notices were dropped on the 9th of April that destruction would commence on the 10th. The bombing was carried out by two Flights of No. 11 (B) Squadron and two Flights of No. 39 (B) Squadron of No. 2 (Indian) Wing Risalpur. The first attacks were delivered from Risalpur and the subsequent ones from Arawali. Each flight made two attacks on the 10th April and three on the two following days. Incendiary bombs were also discharged on the villages. High explosive bombing ceased on the 12th, but incendiary bombing continued until the 16th. The next day, notices were dropped informing the inhabitants of the area that the bombing had ceased.

1937
——
April

Early in April, the Faqir made further attempts to gain the support of the Mahsuds, who were further inflamed by exaggerated rumours which reached them of the action of the 29th of March. In addition to Mahsuds who had already joined the Faqir, several gangs were formed which sought opportunities for outrages in the Sorarogha area. The attitude of the tribal elders was, however, outwardly satisfactory, and information, generally, pointed to North Waziristan as being the probable scene of any outrage contemplated by the Faqir or his adherents.

On the 3rd of April, an officer travelling with the Wana Convoy reported that he had seen small parties of men in the broken ground above the road in the dangerous defile known as the Shahur Tangi, in places having a good command of certain sections of the road. He said that these men were certainly not Khassadars, and they gave the impression of "being engaged in a tactical exercise". On the same day, a report was received from political sources that the local villagers were saying that the Wana convoy would be attacked.

Report of movement in the Shahur Tangi.

These reports were referred to the political authorities, and, in the meantime orders were issued that convoys would not travel on this route. Later this prohibition was removed.

Convoys to Wana stopped and then resumed.

Regular troops not being available for the protection of the routes from Manzai to Razmak and Wana, this duty was carried out by the Scouts under military control and by Khassadars under political control.

On the 8th of April an M. T. convoy ran between Razmak and Manzai without incident.

On the 9th of April a convoy left Manzai for Wana at 0600 hours. A very early start was unavoidable as paucity of transport and other considerations made it necessary for convoys to return to Manzai the same day, and unless a start was made at dawn it was not possible to complete the round trip of about a hundred miles before dark. The hour of start could not, therefore, be varied, and the tribesmen had possibly observed the regular routine of days and timings to which convoys adhered.

Ambush in the Shahur Tangi*.

Crossing the bed of the river at Chagmalai, the road winds along the hillside north of it, on a rising gradient as far as about milestone 8½, near which point the defile is at its narrowest. From there it descends to cross the Splitoi tributary of the Shahur. The slopes to the north are steep, and in many places precipitous. The main ridge at point 3940 (0882), fourteen hundred feet above the level of the road, rises another fourteen hundred feet some distance to the north. The lower slopes, defiladed by the shape of the ground from the higher points, are very broken and are

---

* [Ref. Sketch map F 37 at end of Chapter].

1937
April

strewn with boulders, big overhanging rocks in places offering shelter to as many as six men at a time. Coming round a prominent bend at milestone 7, the road winds round some sharp turns until it passes through a cutting near milestone 7½. The deep narrow gullies in this area provide excellent positions for tribesmen intent on ambush. Unnoticeable until the last moment, from here men can command the road at point-blank range at places where lorries must be slowed down by the windings of the road and by the ascending gradient. From the low wall bordering the south edge of the road there is a precipitous fall to the river bed. About three hundred feet up from the river bed on the far side is a false crest affording good cover within easy range of the road, and beyond this rise hills as high and forbidding as those to the north. The road itself, though wide enough for two-way traffic, gives insufficient space for turning a large vehicle. particularly an armoured car, except with some difficulty.

The posts at Splitoi and Chagmalai, at either end of the defile, and the two-storied masonry piquets above the defile had been vacated for some time. The latter, gutted of their wooden flooring and staircases, were almost useless for defence in their existing state. The nearest garrisons of the South Waziristan Scouts were at Jandola and Sarwekai, and on the morning of the 9th of April, patrols were working from these places towards Kotkai and Suragarh respectively. The actual protection of the Shahur Tangi on this day devolved on the Khassadars of the Abdur Rahman Khel and Jalal Khel Mahsuds, in whose territory it lay.

Composition and organization of convoy.
On the 9th of April, the convoy consisted of fortynine military and hired civilian lorries and two private cars. As escort it had four armoured cars, and a party of fifty one Indian other ranks and two light machine-guns of the 4/16th Punjab Regiment from Manzai under a Viceroy's Commissioned Officer and one sub-section 19 Field Company with demolition equipment, the two parties being carried in some of the lorries. In addition to the escort there was a party of seventytwo other ranks returning from leave, most of whom were armed. The two senior officers awaiting transport to Wana at the time were detailed to command the convoy and the infantry with it, the vehicles being under the command of Major T. Z. Waters, M.C., R.I.A.S.C., an officer who had travelled with many convoys recently, and who had made the report about tribesmen in the defile on the 3rd of April.

The organization of the convoy for the march was the usual one for that particular road, and was the result of experience. Vehicles were arranged in blocks of five, each block being under the command of a N. C. O. One armoured car, "Chitral", preceded the vehicles the second one, "Crecy", was in rear of the fourth block about one third of the way down the convoy, the third, "Corunna", behind the ninth block, two thirds of the way, with the fourth, "Candahar", bringing up the rear of the column. This distribution of the armoured cars had been evolved after much practice on the Wana road. It increased the length of the convoy by about eight hundred yards, but provided protection in the middle as well as at the front and rear—in certain areas where the windings of the road and the nature of the country bordering it strongly favoured hostile action. The infantry escort was divided into three parties, one party consisting of the V. C. O. ten I. O. Rs. and one L. M. G., travelling in the fourth lorry, being followed immediately by a sub-section of a Field Company. The second party of thirty I. O. Rs. and one L. M. G. was carried in the nineteenth and twentieth vehicles, just in front of the second armoured car, the O. C. escort being just behind them. The third party of a N. C. O. and ten I. O. Rs. was in the forty third vehicle near the tail of the column. The seventy two leave details followed immediately behind the second party. The infantry were purposely concentrated near an armoured car to afford them as much protection as possible.

Subsequent reports show that prior to the 9th of April a gang of Mahsuds arrived by night from the Shaktu area *via* Sorarogha and occupied the Shahur Tangi. Their presence in the neighbourhood was not reported by either maliks or Khassadars, who were supposed to be loyal and protecting the defile. Actually, the bulk of the Khassadars were not carrying out their duties and were not in position on the 9th of April. Patrols of South Waziristan Scouts were working respectively from Jandola towards Kotkai and from Sarwekai eastwards towards Sura Ghar. Information available at the time showed that these areas were more potentially dangerous than the Shahur Tangi area. On the morning of the 9th April, the Shahur Tangi itself was not patrolled by the South Waziristan Scouts.

The convoy marched from Manzai at 0600 hours, leaving Jandola an hour later. Early morning reconnaissance by the R. A. F. revealed no indication of tribesmen in position in the Tangi and everything appeared quiet as the leading armoured car, "Chitral", entered the defile at about 0735 hours. Major Waters, when passing Chagmalai Post, noticed a moulvi and some Khassadars on the roadside watching the convoy, an unusual circumstance, and later, when in the defile, observed that there were no Khassadars in position along the road, and that no one was visible on the hillsides.

0745 hours 9th April. Attack commences. At 0745 hours, when the head of the convoy was near milestone 3½ and the tail well inside the defile about milestone 7, intense and accurate fire was opened simultaneously along its whole length, being most intense against the leading half.

The tribesmen were in skilfully chosen positions on both sides of the road, but mainly to the north of it, from which they could bring enfilade fire to bear on its various windings. Concealed behind rocks and in catchment drains on the spurs and in the re-entrants, on the north side of the road they were in some places not more than fifteen to twenty yards from it, and in many cases were completely protected from air attack under big overhanging slabs of rocks in front of which they had built walls.

Intense fire was kept up by the tribesmen for fifteen minutes without relaxation. There were many casualties at once before anyone could leave the lorries. The survivors, with a few exceptions, dismounted, many being hit whilst doing so, and took what little shelter there was in the shallow drain on the north side of the road. The infantry, shot down if they attempted to scale the precipitous slopes to the north, as many gallantly attempted to do, took what cover could be found behind boulders and on the sides of the nalas and engaged such enemy as were visible. Several drivers were hit at once, and their lorries slewed across the roads. Other vehicles were abandoned in the middle of the road. The armoured cars immediately opened fire, but had difficulty in firing uphill at the slopes to the north. Unable to move along the convoy on account of the blocks created by the

1937
April 9th

abandoned vehicles, or to turn except with great difficulty owing to the narrowness of the road, the protection they were able to afford was necessarily restricted, particularly as the numerous re-entrants made it impossible for them to cover the whole area. Although the enemy's fire was less fierce after the first fifteen minutes, during which time most of the casualties of the day were incurred, any individual who exposed himself momentarily came at once under fire, and a period of stalemate ensued in which, while the armoured cars and infantry could not extricate themselves, the tribesmen were prevented from over-running the convoy. Attempts were made during the day to get some of the leading and rear lorries away, always under heavy fire. Relieving troops arrived from Sarwekai, Wana, and Jandola in the afternoon. They succeeded in establishing themselves on the high ground some distance north of the road, but the tribesmen remained in their positions near the road, and the condition of stalemate continued throughout the day.

After the firing commenced, Lieut. Hopkinson, commanding the leading armoured car, "Chitral", escorted the three leading lorries, the driver of one of which was wounded, clear of the defile. He ordered the three lorries, to go on to Sarwekai, and took his armoured car back into the Tangi to the vicinity of the fourth lorry, whose driver was a casualty, and opened fire on the occasional tribesmen who disclosed themselves and on areas on which hostile fire appeared to be coming.

Three leading lorries leave the Tangi.

The second armoured car "Crecy" was moving about a hundred yards behind cars carrying officers and servants, lorries containing part of the infantry escort and some men of the Royal Corps of Signals going to join their unit at Wana. The opening volley of the tribesmen killed or wounded practically every man of the infantry escort before they could dismount and all but two of the signallers. The officers and servants succeeded in getting out into the ditch beside the road. "Crecy" immediately opened fire and succeeded in dislodging some of the enemy on the south side of the road, but the steepness of the slope on the north side made effective action in that direction very difficult. "Crecy" tried to move west up the road, but found that the rear lorry, driverless, formed an impassable obstacle. Movement east, also, was blocked by the leading lorry of the next batch of vehicles, which was in the centre of the road. The armoured car was then placed so as to give protection from the south to the party which had dismounted. It remained in this position throughout the morning, effectively covering the party, which was augmented by one or two individuals who managed to make their way to it by crawling along the north edge of the road. Attempts to move from the shelter of Crecy to extricate the blocking lorries proved abortive on account of the accurate sniping of the enemy, and until late afternoon action was of necessity confined to co-operating by fire with the remaining armoured cars of the section.

Second armoured car, Crecy, blocked.

"Corunna" was separated from Crecy by about twelve lorries, but could only move a very short distance in either direction owing to blocks in front and behind, caused by the adjacent lorries whose drivers had become casualties. "Corunna" like "Crecy" immediately opened fire, successfully neutralizing enemy fire from the south, and also engaging the enemy on the slopes above "Crecy".

Third armoured car, Corunna, blocked.

Rear armoured car, Candahar, also blocked. "Candahar" at the rear of the convoy, was also unable to move up the convoy. It came into action, and on one occasion forced the enemy to go to ground, though throughout the day the firing in this area was less intense than it was in the front and centre.

0915 hours. No. 3 section 8th L. Tank Company arrived from Sarwekai. Attempts to extricate lorries at head of columns— 1015 hours—Arrival of Khassadars from Sarwekai. News of the ambush had reached Lt. Wetherell who, with No. 3 section of the 8th Light Tank Company was at Sarwekai. He immediately moved his section to the Tangi. As his advanced guard sub-section reached the ninth milestone just inside the Tangi, it encountered a small party of tribesmen trying to block the road. Fire was opened on these at once, and they quickly dispersed at least two enemy having been killed.

No. 3 section reached the head of the convoy at 0915 hours, an hour and a half after the initial opening of fire by the enemy. Lt. Wetherell ordered his cars to turn so that they faced the western exit from the Tangi, and placing his own car "Busaco" alongside "Chitral", learnt the details of the situation, and formed a plan to extricate the lorries at the head of the column. The leading lorry, standing diagonally across the road, formed an effective block, and it was obvious that its removal was an essential preliminary to any attempt to get the remaining vehicles out of the Tangi. Arrangements were made for covering fire from the armoured cars and the infantry on the spot and instructions given that the drivers of the adjacent vehicles should in turn attempt to mount and drive out of the Tangi when the leading vehicle had moved. At about 1015 hours heavy fire was opened on spots likely to be occupied by the enemy, who remained invisible, and Lieut. Wetherell, dashing to the lorry, succeeded in starting it, under a hail of bullets. There was a slight delay whilst the civilian driver, who was lying wounded under the lorry was dragged clear and then Lieut. Wetherell drove the lorry clear of the Tangi escorted by an armoured car. The remaining adjacent lorries were unable to follow as the driver of the next lorry, a 3-ton Thorneycroft was shot while attempting to start it, and the road remained blocked. When clear of the Tangi the lorry was sent on to Sarwekai. Soon after, Lieut. Wetherell met Capt. Lowis, the Assistant Political Agent, who was coming from Wana to the Tangi. Informing him of the situation, Lieut. Wetherell then forced his way into the deserted fort at Splitoi, and reported by telephone, to the Commander of the Wana Brigade. At the request of Capt. Lowis he sent a telephone message to Sarwekai to send up as many Khassadars as possible in lorries to Splitoi. This party arrived very quickly and occupied with little or no opposition the piquets on each side of the road commanding the western entrance to the Tangi.

Advanced party of South Waziristan Scouts arrives 1200 hours. About 1200 hours, the advanced party of the South Waziristan Scouts arrived at Splitoi from Sarwekai, and took over the piquets at the western end of the defile from the Khassadars, the operation being supported by fire from Lieut. Wetherell's armoured car and by another armoured car under Lieut. J. P. Stoker which had been escorting the South Waziristan Scouts. As soon as the piquets were taken over the two armoured cars returned to the head of the convoy whilst the Khassadars joined Capt. Lowis at Splitoi.

1937
April 9th

1937

April

Whilst Lieut. Wetherell was at Splitoi, Lieut. Hopkinson organised a successful attempt to tow out the Thorneycroft now at the head of the column. The lorry's engine had been pierced and it could not be driven under its own power. A tow rope was attached to the armoured car "Badajos" and a volunteer R. I. A. S. C. driver steering the vehicle, it was towed away under heavy fire to Splitoi. The remaining vehicles of the group had been started and were moving slowly in rear of the towed Thorneycroft, when the leading lorry was hit and set on fire by a bullet which struck its petrol tank. The short advance made enabled the lorries to halt off the crown of the road, but the fierceness of the flames made it impossible to pass the burning lorry for some hours, and once again the efforts at extrication to the west had to be suspended.

Removal of more lorries from head of column made impossible for some time.

For several hours the situation in this area became static. The enemy continued to maintain a heavy fire at the least sign of movement, and the armoured cars engaged any targets that presented themselves. No attempt could be made to drive or to tow out any of the remaining vehicles until the blaze of the burning lorry had subsided, and offensive action by the Scouts and the party of Khassadars was delayed in view of the expected arrival of Scout reinforcements from Wana.

Attempts were being made, also, at the tail of the column to extricate lorries to the east. At about 0815 hours, a report of the occurrences had reached Manzai, and Capt. L. M. Jones, took No. 2 section 8th Light Tank Company to the Tangi, reaching the rear of the convoy at milestone 7¼ at 0950 hours. Here it was possible to move some lorries into the side of the road, and a sub-section was ordered to make its way up the convoy. Unfortunately, the leading armoured car "Assaye" in endeavouring to pass two civilian lorries which had been deserted in the middle of the road with their gears in neutral and their brakes off, became jammed and formed an impassable obstacle. Soon after the arrival of No. 2 section enemy fire in this area increased, and any attempt at movement drew accurate fire.

0815 hours—0950 hours—Arrival of No. 2 section 8th L. Tank Company from Manzai—Impassable block at tail of column.

At about 1030 hours, a force escorted by the armoured car "Cambrai", arrived at Chagmalai from Jandola consisting of one rifle company and one machine gun platoon of the 4/16th Punjab Regiment with three platoons of the South Waziristan Scouts. The three platoons of the Scouts immediately advanced on to the Tera Shah ridge, establishing themselves there without opposition. The detachment of the 4/16th Punjab Regiment remained in the area of Chagmalai to counter any threat of attack from the south.

1030 hours—Arrival of troops at Chagmalai—Scouts advance to Tera Shah ridge.

Shortly after this, a bus carrying maliks arrived in the Tangi. These maliks had come with the intention of trying to persuade the enemy to withdraw. One of them was, however, immediately shot dead by an enemy sniper, and the rest withdrew, abandoning their bus in a position where it half-blocked the only practicable turning point in the vicinity.

In the centre portion of the convoy enemy fire had been fiercer than anywhere else. The larger portion of the infantry escort and of the leave details had been travelling in this section, and the first burst of hostile fire had killed and wounded a larger number of them. Major T. Z. Waters, M.C.,

Movement impossible in centre portion of column.

R.I.A.S.C., with a small party of survivors succeeded in finding a temporary refuge where they dismounted. There was very little cover and the party, pinned to the ground by enemy fire, was unable to move for a considerable time.

1937
April 9th

Situation at 1200 hours.

At about 1200 hours on the 9th of April, the situation was as follows:—

Five lorries had cleared the west end of the Tangi and had arrived at Splitoi or Sarwekai, the remainder being still in the defile, which was blocked by broken down vehicles at each end. All three sections of the 8th Light Tank Company were in or adjacent to the defile. Five armoured cars under Lieut. Wetherell were at the western end of the convoy, "Crecy" and "Corunna" were in the centre of the column, separated from each other by about ten lorries, and the remainder, under Capt. L. M. Jones, were in the rear. Sniping was directed on to the road almost continuously, any attempt at movement being greeted with heavy fire. Troops, arrived from Jandola and Sarwekai, were attempting to operate against the enemy on the heights north of the road. On the west, the two piquets covering the exit from the Tangi had been occupied by the South Waziristan Scouts, while Capt. Lowis, the Assistant Political Agent, was at Splitoi with a number of Khassadars, awaiting the arrival of further reinforcements from Wana. To the east, the detachment of the 4/16 Punjab R. and of the South Waziristan Scouts was commencing an advance with the heights north of the roads as their objective.

Movement of troops from Chagmalai north of the road—1345 hours.

Shortly after 1200 hours four more platoons of the South Waziristan Scouts and two platoons of the 4/16 Punjab R. reached Chagmalai. There was now sufficient strength at this end of the Tangi to attempt to seize the high ground to the north, and the Commander gave orders for the capture of the ridge in square 1083, the intention being to push on from there and to effect contact with the platoons at the west end of the defile. Three platoons of the South Waziristan Scouts with one platoon of the 4/16 Punjab R. reached the ridge without opposition, one platoon of the 4/16th being dropped to protect the eastern end of the ridge, the remaining three platoons of that Regiment taking up positions from the Tera Shah piquet to the north-west.

1515 hours—1630 hours.

The three platoons of the South Waziristan Scouts were then ordered to work forward from the ridge, their first objective being a small knoll about six hundred yards west. Heavy fire broke out at once and continued for about half an hour, some casualties being incurred. It was obvious that there was not time to take their objectives and also to withdraw to Chagmalai before dark, and orders were given for the withdrawal to commence. The enemy followed up closely with fanatical bravery, being at times not more than fifty yards from the rearmost platoon, and repeatedly tried to envelop both flanks. Considerable delay, too, was caused by having to re-occupy vacated positions to remove casualties. Leaving Tera Shah piquet occupied for the night, the troops reached Chagmalai at about 1900 hours.

1937

April 9th

Movement of troops and Khassadars and further extrication of lorries at the western end.

To return to events at the head of the column. The extrication of any more lorries was impracticable, owing to the intense rifle fire, until the enemy had been forced by ground action to evacuate their positions commanding the road. Information had been received by telephone that three platoons of South Waziristan Scouts had left Wana—some forty miles away—in lorries, and their arrival was anxiously awaited.

1600 hours.

About 1600 hours, as there were no signs of the arrival of Scouts reinforcements, Capt. Lowis decided to take his Khassadars into the Tangi in an attempt to clear the enemy from the immediate north of the road in the neighbourhood of the leading lorries, and he led his party of about sixty down the road escorted by two armoured cars. The enemy's fire which up to this time had been considerable, now ceased abruptly, and the Khassadars scrambled up the slopes, occupying the cliffs on the northern edge of the road without a shot being fired.

1830 hours—extricated lorries leave for Sarwekai.

Surviving drivers were collected, dead and wounded loaded into lorries, and one by one eleven vehicles were driven or towed clear of the Tangi. Subsequently, about 1830 hours, they were escorted to Sarwekai by a sub-section of armoured cars.

1700 hours—Three platoons South Waziristan Scouts arrive and capture point 3940—1800 hours.

While these lorries were being moved from the defile, at 1700 hours three platoons of the South Waziristan Scouts arrived from Wana. The commander of this force was given orders that with the help of the platoons already holding the western exit he was to occupy the high ground north of the Tangi and eject the enemy from that side; if the convoy was not released by nightfall, he was to close piquet it. He decided first to seize a knoll just north of milestone 8 (079816) and then to capture point 3940. The advance commenced at 1800 hours. There was considerable close fighting, but the Scouts pushed on and captured point 3940 as it was getting dark. Having left some men at the knoll, realizing that close-piqueting of the convoy would involve the evacuation of point 3940, a dominant feature, the commander decided to hold the point for the night.

2100 hours.

Two of the original platoons of the South Waziristan Scouts from Sarwekai withdrew to Splitoi at 2100 hours leaving one platoon in position where it was.

More vehicles extricated to the west— 2100 hours.

Whilst the leading portion of the convoy was being cleared from the Tangi, Lieut. Stoker in his armoured car had reached the two lorries which had blocked "Crecy's" movement westward. An attempt was now made to get these clear. The drivers who had been sheltering in the road ditch, mounted. Immediately they did so, the sniping which had died down recommenced. There was some confusion before the lorries started off. Whilst controlling this situation, Major H. W. D. Palmer 3/16 Punjab R., who had been in command of the escort, was killed. The leading lorry then drove off to Splitoi. The driver of the second, hired lorry, left his vehicle and again took refuge in the ditch. However, the lorry was now in such a position that it was possible to pass it. It was removed a little later and the next lorry behind it was towed away, this being completed about dusk. The next batch of lorries were 3-ton Thorneycrofts. These vehicles were on a rising gradient in a narrow cutting and it was clearly impossible to remove them without considerable organization. No survivors remained in this part of the road, and Lieut. Wetherell decided to take his section back to Splitoi, where they arrived at 2100 hours.

1937
April 9th

As a result of the efforts at extriction to the west, some twenty vehicles had been cleared from the Tangi during daylight, and all survivors and dead had been sent to Sarwekai.

2100 hours.

At 2230 hours two platoons of South Waziristan Scouts which had been in the piquets at the western end of the Tangi arrived at Splitoi. It was decided to make a further attempt to get vehicles clear of the defile under cover of darkness.

2230 hours.

The Scouts, preceded by one sub-section of armoured cars and covered by the other, entered the Tangi. On arrival at the leading lorry piquets were sent out. These were unable to scale the face of the cliffs which rose practically sheer from the road. The enemy opened fire as efforts were made to start the engine of the leading Thorneycroft. Its mechanism had been damaged and an attempt was then made to tow it away. This was found impossible as the lorry, standing on an upward gradient was too heavy to be moved by an armoured car. It was considered that further efforts during the night were useless, and the party returned to Splitoi, arriving there at 0430 hours on the 10th.

2355 hours.

In the centre portion of the convoy during the afternoon, Major Waters and his small party of survivors succeeded in moving a little further to the east and eventually reached the armoured car Corunna. At about 1400 hours they moved from the place where they had originally dismounted from the cars and lorries, and creeping round a spur immediately to the east of them, found a temporary shelter in a catchment drain. Any movement continued to draw fire, but a little later they managed, all the time under fire, to get round another spur. There they found the armoured car Corunna. Major Waters succeeded in getting to the car, being wounded in doing so. To enable the car to turn it was necessary to fill in a part of the ditch, and this was done by Major Waters and his party. Before the car began to turn, Major Waters, already twice hit, was again wounded and was taken into the car. The car moved slowly off, but after passing three vehicles it came to a block and had to halt. Here it remained for the rest of the afternoon and night, firing on any enemy it could see. Major Waters' party remained with it, taking what cover they could under and round the car.

Events in the centre portion of the column.

During the night a party of tribesmen came down to the road to strip the dead and to loot the lorries. These were easily driven off by the fire of infantry and armoured cars. In spite of considerable sniping which continued throughout the night until about 0600 hours, when it ceased, endeavours were made during the hours of darkness, but only with partial success, to clear various road obstacles.

During the night, information was received at Chagmalai that the 2/11 Sikh R. would arrive at about 0900 hours on the 10th from Bannu. As it appeared that the force then available would be sufficient to secure the hills commanding the defile, it was decided that the infantry already present should advance on to the Tera

Troops advance on 10th of April.

1937
April 9th

Shah ridge and the adjacent heights shortly before dawn on the 10th of April whilst in the Tangi itself a simultaneous attempt should be made to clear the vehicles eastward under cover of fire from the armoured cars.

The 4/16 Punjab R. and the South Waziristan Scouts reached the Tera Shah ridge just before dawn, and continuing their advance in the general direction taken on the preceding day, occupied the whole of the dominating feature without difficulty, the enemy on this side having apparently dispersed during the early hours of the morning. Some of the enemy, however, still remained on the south side of the river at dawn, and continued to fire at the road until the arrival of the 2/11 Sikh R., when they withdrew.

The armoured cars took up their positions in the Tangi, and as dawn broke, parties went in to remove the obstacles and extricate the lorries. Major Waters, in spite of his wounds, actively arranged for the clearing of the rest of the convoy. Extra vehicles and spare drivers were sent out from Manzai, and by about 1400 hours the road had been cleared. Many vehicles could not be moved under their own power owing to damaged engines, petrol tanks, or radiators, and to punctured tyres. It was found that the lorries in the vicinity of the cutting, in ground dead to the fire of any armoured cars or infantry, had been systematically looted. Major Paton R. A. commanding the convoy, who had been wounded in the first burst of enemy fire on the 9th and had been rescued and taken to Sarwekai late that evening, reformed the portion of the convoy that reached that place, and took it on to Wana.

Remaining vehicles extricated.

Except for the burnt-out lorry, the Tangi was cleared of vehicles by about 1200 hours. The troops were then withdrawn and returned to their normal stations, the South Waziristan Scouts leaving small garrisons at Chagmalai and Splitoi.

At the commencement of the action on the 9th one aircraft of No. 5 (A. C.) Squadron R. A. F. was co-operating with the convoy. Later, the same unit provided continuous close support until 1900 hours when it became dark, bombing and machine-gunning such enemy as could be seen and by their action being of great value in keeping down the enemy fire. At 1430 hours on the 9th, an aircraft made a forced landing in the neighbourhood of Chagmalai Post having been shot through its petrol tank. Covered by two armoured cars which arrived on the scene almost at once, and with the help of some Sappers and Miners, the aircraft was dismantled, and except for the main planes, was loaded on to a lorry sent from Manzai and removed to safety. During the latter part of this operation the party came under increasingly accurate fire from tribesmen coming from the direction of the Tangi.

R. A. F. co-operation.

The gang which had carried out this attack had come from the Shaktu at the instigation of the Faqir of Ipi, one of the two chief leaders being Khonia Khel, a Jalal Khel Mahsud, a murderer and notorious bad character. Their presence in the neighbourhood had been reported neither by maliks nor by Khassadars, and afterwards, local villagers professed ignorance of the intention to attack the convoy. At the beginning of the action, the gang numbered from sixty to eighty men, but during the day, as parties from neighbouring villages including Abdur Rahman Khel joined up, their strength increased to about three hundred. Their casualties, confirmed later, were sixteen killed and twenty six seriously wounded.

Composition and casualties of enemy.

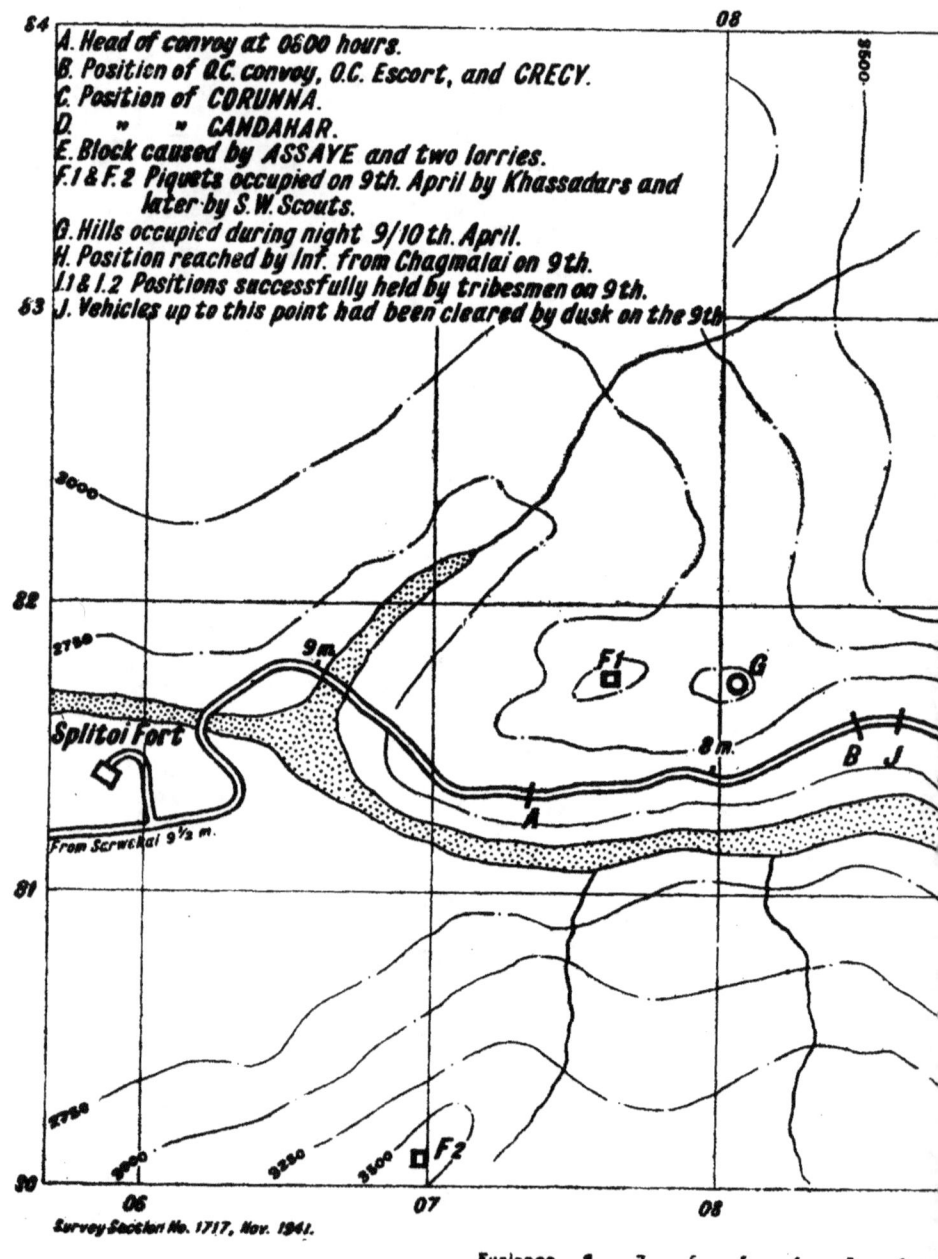

F. 37.
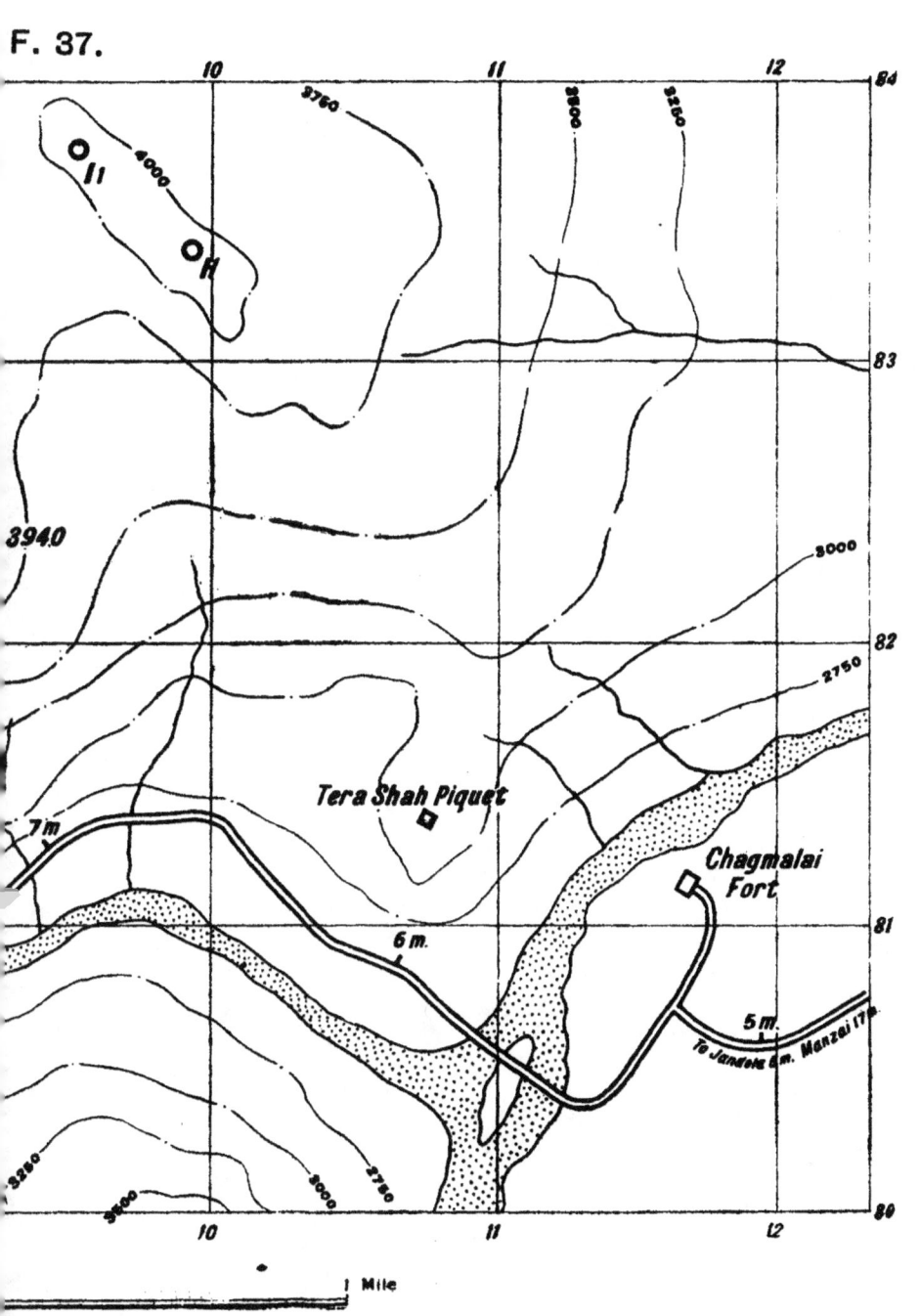

Casualties. The casualties in the convoy were as follows:—

1937
April 9th

Killed—British officers 7
    Lieut. M. Earle, 2 Mtn. Bty.—Lieut. E. G. L. Hinde, 19 Fd. Coy.—Lieut. F. I. R. France, 3/7 Rajput R.—2-Lieut. G. L. Scott, 3/12 F. F. R.—Major H. W. D. Palmer, 3/16, Punjab R.—Capt. M. B. Courtnay, 3/16 Punjab R.—Capt. N. M. Durrani, I. M. S.

    British other ranks 2
    Indian other ranks 27
    South Waziristan Scouts 7
    Followers 1
    Civilian drivers 3

Wounded—British officers 5
    Major A. Paton D.S.O., M.C., 2 Mtn. Bty.—2 Lieut. L. H. M. Parsons, Probyn's Horse Capt. S. D. Wilcock, S. W. S.—Lieut. F. D. Robertson, S. W. S. Major T. Z. Waters, R. I. A. S. C.

    British other ranks 1
    Viceroy's Commissioned Officers 2
    Indian other ranks 32
    South Waziristan Scouts 4
    Followers 3
    Civilian drivers 3

CHAPTER IX.

1937
April

Events from the 6th of February to the 21st of April — (Continued).

Arrival of 2nd Brigade. — The remaining brigade of the 1st Indian Division, the 2nd (Rawalpindi) Infantry Brigade, was ordered to Waziristan, and by the 15th of April was concentrated at Mir Ali.

Disturbances continue. — Disturbances continued, and the increasing state of disorder was indicated by several minor episodes. Hostile parties fired on lorries and attempts were made to interfere with the Razmak and Manzai water supplies. Gangs moved about the country looking for further opportunities for mischief. The Tori Khel Khassadars in the Razmak area who had been dismissed were replaced after a little difficulty by Mohmit Khel, and the ex-Khassadars sniped their successors heavily for several nights after the change had been made.

Tribesmen within two miles of attacked troops liable to air action. — According to the standard instructions regulating the offensive action of aircraft in support of troops, it was impossible for aircraft crews to take offensive action against any enemy unless the tribesmen were firing on aircraft, engaged with our troops, or in a declared proscribed zone. Representations were made to the Government of India, and sanction was accorded that in the event of any attack on troops or posts in Waziristan, all tribesmen within a radius of two miles of the troops or post would be liable to attack. In order to give every opportunity to tribesmen with peaceful intentions to avoid attack from the air, it was arranged that offensive air action against tribesmen within this radius and not directly opposing our forces, should be withheld until a period of half an hour had elapsed from the beginning of any engagement.

On the 12th of April, owing to attacks on the posts in the Shinki defile, an area of three miles on each side of the main road from Kajuri Post to Saidgi Post was proscribed to all movement.

*Investment of Spinwam Post. — A more serious incident was the surrounding of the Spinwam Scouts Post by about three hundred of the Dreplari Tori Khel. They kept it under fire for three days, making movement from the post impossible. At the same time, the road Mir Ali—Thal-in-Kurram was blocked in several places, and a reconnaissance by tanks and armoured cars on the 15th of April was held up in the Tabai Narai (4277). It was decided to take action against the offending villages, but on the 15th of April the Dreplari sent a message to the Post to say that they wished to come to terms with the Government. Punitive action was therefore suspended, to test the sincerity of their advances. Their further attitude was peaceful and there were no more incidents in their area. In consequence of this, Government later opened their area to those of the Tori Khel who were not disposed to enmity.

Political action against the Jalal Khel and Abdur Rahman Khel. — The chief consequence of the Shahur Tangi action was to promote great unrest and excitement amongst the Mahsuds. The Jalal Khel Jirga was summoned to Jandola on the 13th of April but failed to arrive. They came to Sorarogha on the 14th and were sent on to Jandola where they were interviewed by the Political Agent on the 15th. They

---

* [Ref. Sketch map P. 37 (Chap. XXIV)].

were interviewed again on the 17th by the Resident, and ordered to hand over Khonia Khel and Dilbogh, another leader of the Shahur Tangi ambush, within seven days. Failing this, they were to hand over thirty other hostages, and return to their winter encampments within seven days. If this was not done, the whole tribe would be treated as hostile and their allowances and Khassadari would cease. They tried to comply with these terms, but were unable to deal with Khonia Khel. The jirga of the Abdur Rahman Khel were seen on the 13th and 22nd of April. Their attitude at the latter interview was satisfactory and they handed over twelve hostages as ordered.

1937
April

*Attack on Tiarza Post.

Unrest was not confined to these two sections only. The Mahsuds in the Khaisara valley, in South Waziristan, mainly Urmar Khel, Nekzan Khel and Kikarai also became troublesome. An Urmar Khel mullah, Sher Ali Khan, reported to be receiving money from the Faqir of Ipi, arrived in Urmar Khel Kile village on the 13th April. A considerable number of followers joined him immediately, and it was reported at Tiarza Post, which was held by a detachment of the South Waziristan Scouts, that this party was likely to fire on a Scouts patrol or to attack the Post. At daylight on the 16th of April fire was opened on the Post from all round it. The fire continued until the early part of the afternoon. Small parties of enemy were seen moving about, and were engaged with machine-gun fire. The night was a peaceful one. On the 17th, at about midday, a few shots were fired at the Post. The R. A. F. bombed Urmar Khel Kile during the day, the tribesmen retaliating by shooting at the aircraft. Bombing continued on the 18th and 19th. There was no hostile action against the Post, though shots were fired at the bombers. The village suffered extensive damage, but the mullah's cave was not touched. On the 20th of April, the area being reported quiet, normal routine was again adopted by the garrison of the Post. The Khaisara jirga, interviewed at Sariwekai on the 22nd of April, said they desired peace. The Urmar Khel handed over seven hostages and the Nekzan and Kikarai two each, as an earnest of good faith.

For the time being, hostile activity appeared to have been largely transferred to the Razmak area, and large numbers of the enemy were reported to have moved there from the Khaisora and Shinki valleys. The road was damaged in several places, and a bridge near Razani was made unserviceable.

Lashkars comprising Tori Khel and Mahsuds at the Engemal and Naidal Narais, Afghans in the Sirdar Algad, and Mahsuds and Madda Khel in prepared concealed positions about Spin Kamar, were reported to be planning attacks on the Razmak water supply, which had already been damaged on the 14th of April. This water supply, normally guarded by Khassadars, came from springs in the Sirdar Algad, some five miles west of Razmak, and was brought to Razmak by a pipe-line. Other hostile bands were located in the Shinki defile area, about Zer in the Katira and Jaler Algad areas, and in the Shaktu.

On the 19th of April an attack was made on a piquet from Alexandra Ridge post (five miles North of Razmak) held by a detachment of the 4/8 Punjab R., which was protecting the watering party from that post.

* [Ref. Sketch map G 37 (Chap. XXI)].

1919
April

Attack on piquet at Alexandra Ridge Post*.

The post is situated on the broadest part of the ridge. North of the post the ridge divides into two parallel spurs, each crowned at its north end by a slight eminence, the eastern one being known as White Rock Spur and the western as Sangar Hill. Between the post and Sangar Hill is a Knoll, and west of Sangar Hill, separated from it by a col, is another hill-top known as Left Spur. East, south east, and South west of the post are other slight eminences. The distance between the Knoll and Sangar Hill is about sixty yards, and the other points mentioned are all within short range of the post and of each other. The watering point for the post lay below and to the north of Left Spur, and the main path to it, after passing along the western face of the main ridge crossed the col between Sangar Hill and Left Spur and wound down their northern slopes. The whole area is thickly covered with dense scrub. Movement from the post could always be safely observed by concealed tribesmen. To protect the watering party, a small piquet usually established itself on Sangar Hill, the only feature commanding most of the track.

On the 19th of April two sections (fourteen men), under the command of a Naik, were detailed to protect the party. At 1115 hours the naik occupied the Knoll, six men taking up a position there to cover the advance of the remaining eight to Sangar Hill. The remainder of the post garrison, with the exception of a small working party on the parade ground between the Knoll and the post, stood to in the post. When the advancing eight men were in the dip between the Knoll and Sangar Hill, tribesmen, until then silent and concealed suddenly opened fire from White Rock Spur and the area east of the post on the covering party on the Knoll. These men changed position at once to engage this enemy. Immediately after this, heavy fire was directed from the Sangar Hill area on the men in the dip, whilst some ten or fifteen tribesmen rushed across from Left Spur. When the fire opened from Sangar Hill, some of the men on the Knoll changed front again and engaged that portion of the enemy with fire. The charging tribesmen were dispersed by fire from the post. The eight men in the dip at once advanced to assault Sangar Hill. Seven of them were killed immediately. Six of these fell in ground directly in front of Sangar Hill, invisible from the Knoll. The enemy dragged their bodies behind the hill and looted their rifles and equipment. The Naik commanding the covering party dashed forward and brought back the rifle and equipment of the nearest casualty, while the Naik in charge of the working party with two men carried the eighth man back to the post under heavy fire.

The action had so far taken about five minutes, during which time the post itself was heavily fired at by tribesmen in position to the north, east and south east. The enemy's fire then began to slacken. The post Commander took out a platoon from the post, and, under fire from three sides, the dead bodies were collected. No further casualties were sustained, and the operation was concluded by about 1300 hours. The tribesmen were estimated to be about fifty to eighty strong, and they left definite evidence of having sustained some casualties.

In the Bhitanni area also, unrest was taking a more active form. The police station at Tajori (61) was attacked on two nights in succession, the 17th/18th and 18th/19th of April, by a gang of about one hundred Bhitannis.

*Bhitannis attack police station at Tajori.

---
* [Ref. Sketch map A in pocket].

There were no casualties among the Police, but at least one of the enemy was killed.

General situation unsatisfactory. The general situation was very unsatisfactory. The measures adopted in the case of the Tori Khel, the chief object of which was to compel that tribe to force the Faqir of Ipi to give up his anti-Government activities, had not succeeded. The focus of the trouble had moved towards South Waziristan, the majority of the gangs now operating being Mahsud, with a smaller proportion of Wazirs, and Bhitannis. Throughout the present troubles one object of Government policy had been to avoid, if possible, involving the Mahsuds as a tribe in hostilities. Although a great majority of the Mahsud maliks were still friendly and most of their Khassadars were still working, a number of their youths and bad characters were involved in hostilities against the Government, and the suppression of this trouble was an urgent necessity. Action of the kind already taken, such as the air action against Arsal Kot and Sher Ali's village and political measures against the Jalal Khel and Abdur Rahman Khel, was not likely in existing circumstances to have any speedy effect even if extended to other sections. The only kind of action which appeared to be likely to bring things to an issue speedily, and speed was now most necessary, was action by troops. It was essential to concentrate those tribesmen, still hostile, in one area, opposing the advance of troops, in order to make it feasible to punish them, and at the same time it was necessary to confine the trouble to as small an area as possible.

G. O. C.-in-C., Northern Command invested with political control. On the 22nd of April, the G. O. C.-in-C., Northern Command was again invested by the Government of India with political control in Waziristan and in the adjacent tribal tracts which were under the jurisdiction of the Deputy Commissioners of Bannu and Dera Ismail Khan districts, and with control of air operations, and was instructed to bring about the pacification of the area.

CHAPTER X.

Operations of the 1st (Indian) Division, the 23rd of April to the 3rd of May 1937.

1937
April

Political control assumed by the G. O. C.-in-C., Northern Command.
On the 21st of April, the Government of India gave General Sir John Coleridge his formal instructions. His task was to restore peaceful conditions in Waziristan and in the tribal areas on the Waziristan border which were under the control of the Deputy Commissioners of the Bannu and Dera Ismail Khan Districts. He was vested with full political control in these areas from midday on the 22nd of April, the Resident in Waziristan acting as his Chief Political Officer. He was also vested with the command and control of air operations, the authority already given by the Government of India to undertake air operations under certain conditions and in certain specified areas remaining effective.

Decision to operate in the Khaisora valley area.
During March, the question of the military action to be taken if the Tori Khel did not comply with the demands of Government announced to the Utmanzai jirga on the 5th of April, began to receive consideration. At a combined political and military conference on the 22nd of March General Coleridge outlined a proposal for striking from the direction of Dosalli at the Faqir of Ipi in his headquarters at Arsal Kot. This proposal, however, remained dormant for the time being. Another proposal was discussed at a conference on the 12th of April. This was to try to induce the enemy by an advance from Mir Ali to collect again and to fight on ground favourable to troops.

Three possible areas were considered for such action, the Khaisora valley (approached by the new road from Mir Ali), Spinwam, and Spalga near Tal-in-Tochi.

General Coleridge decided on the first of these as the route would not require the establishment of permanent piquets for its security, the ground was favourable for the employment of tanks, and the operation could be combined with the re-provisioning of Khaisora Scouts Post.

*On the 19th of April instructions were issued by Headquarters Northern Command to the Commanders Waziristan District and 1st Indian Division which stated that in order to afford an opportunity of bringing large numbers of enemy to battle, which had not been possible since the action of the 29th of March, it was the intention of the G. O. C.-in-C., Northern Command to stage an operation towards the Khaisora Valley from Mir Ali. It was politically desirable that, prior to the operation, all those Tori Khel who did not wish to be hostile, should be enabled to move away from this area, and for this reason the area of the existing air blockade would be extended. The operation was to be considered in three phases, first, the extension of the air blockade, the preliminary arrangements for concentrating the force for the operation, and the closing of the greater portion of the lines of communications to convoys; second, an advance with air co-operation into the Khaisora valley; third, the re-organization and re-opening of the lines of communication on the conclusion of the operations. The advance was to be made under the direction of the Commander, 1st Division along the Mir Ali—Khaisora Scouts Post road, with the dual object of visiting the Khaisora Scouts Post for the purpose of re-victualling

---

*[Ref. Sketch maps B 37 (Chap. XXVI), J 37 (Chap. XIII) and C 37 (Chap. X)].

it and restoring its water supply and of inflicting the greatest possible loss on any tribesmen who might oppose the force. If the Commander, 1st Division, saw a favourable opportunity of employing the 1st Infantry Brigade at Damdil in co-operation eastwards with his striking force, he was empowered to do so with the proviso that it must be able to return to its camp the same day. The advance was to begin on the 23rd of April, and as the Commander of the 2nd Infantry Brigade, and most of his troops were already familiar with the proposed area of operations, that formation should be used as the striking force.

Plan of 1st Division*.

As the force would have to be north of the Tochi river again by about the 1st of May because of the uncertain attitude of the Mahsuds and of the necessity of re-opening the main line of communications, the Commander, 1st Indian Division, calculated that he could count on a period of nine days only in which to conclude the operation. Information that the enemy were present in some strength near the Tochi River and in the Jaler Algad indicated the advisability of supporting the *Striking Force with as much artillery and as many light tanks as possible.

The force was to make a deliberate advance in three stages in order to induce as many tribesmen as possible to oppose the advance. In the first stage, the 2nd and 3rd Infantry Brigades were to move forward to Tochi Camp, in the second, the advance was to continue to Jaler Camp and in the third the striking force was to operate in the vicinity of Khaisora Scouts Post. In the last stage the distribution of the 3rd Infantry Brigade would be one battalion at Mir Ali, two at Tochi Camp, and one at Jaler Camp. This would be weak road protection as far as the infantry was concerned, but it was considered that the weakness in infantry would be compensated for by the use of armoured cars and tanks for which the terrain was very suitable. In the third stage, the 1st Infantry Brigade at Damdil was to advance as far as point 4332 (1442) north of the Khaisora river, to distract attention from other operations and to bring fire to bear on the valley as far as Zerpezai.

The line of communications of the striking force was divided into sectors. From the 22nd of April, Headquarters Waziristan District would be responsible for the security of the road from Bannu to (exclusive) Mir Ali, an extra battalion being sent from Kohat to Bannu to assist in this task and to protect Bannu itself. The 3rd Infantry Brigade was responsible from Mir Ali southwards. The road from Mir Ali to Razmak was to be closed to convoys from the 21st of April until the conclusion of the operations. The maintenance of the troops on the Khaisora road was to be done by daily M. T. convoys to road-heads. (In actual practice this system did not turn out to be satisfactory, and the line of communications had to be closed from time to time while operations were in progress, a reserve of two or three days supplies being built up previously at Jaler Camp, the road head).

Area of air-blockade extended.

It had been decided to extend the area of the air blockade, and on the 18th of April the proscription of all Tori Khel country between the Tochi and Khaisora rivers was announced. This new area was bounded on the east by the Karaghora Range, on the south by the Khaisora proscribed area,

---

*For details of Troops including Striking Force employed in Opns. of 1st Ind. Division from 23rd April to 3rd May 1937, See p. 82 (end of Chapter).

1937

April

on the west by the Central Waziristan Road from Tal-in-Tochi to Asad Khel, and on the north by a line one mile south of the Tochi river. The tribesmen were warned that proscription would become effective from first light on the 22nd, and that areas already proscribed would remain so, (*i.e.*, the Shinki defile area, the lower Khaisora valley from Musaki to Sein, and the short stretch of the Shaktu east of Arap Kot). At the same time the Tori Khel were told that as the Dreplari had assured Government that they would commit no further offences, air operations against that section would be suspended, and if they kept their promise, the Spinwam area would be safe for all peaceable Tori Khel.

R. A. F. plan.

In preparation for the operations, the advanced Headquarters of No. 3 (Indian) Wing R. A. F. were established with the Headquarters 1st (Indian) Division at Mir Ali on the 19th of April. Two (A. C.) squadrons, R. A. F., Nos. 20 and 28, arrived in Waziristan. The former relieved No. 5 squadron at Mir Ali on the 20th of April, and the latter arrived at Manzai on the 24th. No. 20 squadron was placed under the operational control of the Headquarters 1st Division and No. 28 under that of Headquarters Waziristan District from the 24th of April. Two more squadrons, Nos. 27 and 60 (Bomber) Squadrons of No. 1 (Indian) Wing at Kohat, were also available for the operations. Offensive action in the proscribed areas was to be carried out from the 23rd of April by No. 1 Wing, but in order that aircraft crews co-operating with the force should have the latest information, it was arranged that air operations in the immediate vicinity of the line of advance should be the responsibility of the Officer Commanding No. 3 Wing under the direction of the Commander 1st Indian Division, a portion of the proscribed area being withdrawn from No. 1 Wing and taken over by No. 3. As previously, the orders for offensive air action in the proscribed areas directed that the least possible destruction of life and property was to be caused.

Continuance of Faqir of Ipi's Propaganda.

Meanwhile, the Faqir continued his intensive propaganda amongst the tribes, appealing especially to the Madda Khel and to Mullah Fazal Din, telling them that operations by the tribesmen would begin on the 25th of April. He had summoned a large part of the Razmak lashkars to the Khaisora area, and reports showed that the lashkars there, and about Zer in the Katira and Jaler Algads, were being reinforced. Accurate figures of the enemy's strength were not available, but on the 23rd of April it was estimated that there were about one thousand in the Shaktu valley, and it was known that only about one hundred and fifty remained round Razmak. Movements of Mahsuds and Afghan subjects to join the Faqir had been reported, and it was probable that there were at least another thousand hostile tribesmen in the Tochi—Khaisora area.

Establishment of Tochi Camp, 23rd April.

Before the commencement of the operations the Commander 2nd Infantry Brigade had been informed that though the ostensible reason was to re-provision the Khaisora Scouts Post, the main object was to bring the enemy to battle and to inflict the maximum losses on him whenever opportunity occurred.

On the 23rd of April, the 1st (Indian) Division (less the 1st Infantry Brigade at Damdil) moved out from Mir Ali. The intention for the day was that the 3rd Infantry Brigade should open the road to the south bank of the Tochi river where they would establish a bridge head to enable the 2nd Infantry Brigade to pass through and seize the Tochi camp site where both brigades would encamp for the night.

The bridge head was secured by 0810 hours, and at 0830 hours the leading battalion of the 2nd Brigade the 2 Bombay Grs. (supported by all four batteries of the 23rd Mountain Brigade) advanced to capture the spur from Zer into the plain (295545 to 300545). There was some opposition and a few casualties were incurred, but the spur was secured by 0935 hours.

The original plan of the Brigade Commander had been, as soon as this spur was captured, to relieve the 2 Bombay Grs. there by one company and one machine-gun platoon of the 2 A. and S. H., the 2 Bombay Grs. then going on to take the second objective, the low foothills beyond and south of that spur from approximately Waligai (2953) to the Katira nullah (302517).

Realizing that it would take some time for the 2 Bombay Grs. to re-organize for the attack on its second objective, he decided to send the 1/11 Sikh R. forward for its capture, bringing the Bombay Grenadiers into reserve as soon as they were relieved on the captured spur.

The 9th Light Tank Company, which had been kept concealed in the hope that more enemy would be attracted to the fight and so provide more targets for their fire, now advanced to the low ground due south near the Katira river.

The 1/11 Sikh R. captured this objective without opposition by 1007 hours.

The 2/8 Punjab R., supported by three of the four mountain batteries, the fourth remaining in support of the two battalions already on the objectives, then advanced to capture the final objective, the Tochi camp site area. With the exception of some sniping from the left flank, they met with no opposition, and were in position by 1107 hours.

As the large number of lorries had to be unloaded in a confined space and to return to Mir Ali the same day, it was necessary to keep the road open for a considerable time, and the withdrawal to Tochi camp was not completed until 1900 hours.

Jaler Camp occupied, 24th April. On the 24th of April the advance continued to Jaler Camp. There was no opposition, and all troops were in the Camp by 1715 hours.

Scouts' Post re-provisioned 25th April. The next day, the 25th, was spent in re-provisioning the Khaisora Scouts' Post. This was done with no opposition, though a few parties of the enemy were seen and engaged by the 9th Light Tank Company.

Further plans to bring enemy to battle. Although the first object of the force, the re-provisioning of the Scouts' Post, had been achieved, there had been no opportunity as yet of bringing the enemy to battle, and the Commander, 1st (Indian) Division decided that a further advance to Bichhe Kashkai was necessary. During the morning of the 26th, the Brigade Commander, accompanied by the Commander 1st (Indian) Division made a reconnaissance towards Bichhe Kashkai. The reconnaissance was escorted by the 1/11th Sikh Regiment, and no opposition was met.

1937

April

As a result of this reconnaissance the Brigade Commander came to the conclusion that an advance up the Khaisora river to Dakai Kalai, while probably bringing on a battle, would do so on ground particularly favourable to the tribesmen. He decided, therefore, to make his attack on the hills to the south of the river towards Mazai Raghza (1934). By doing this he would force the enemy to leave the cover of the innumerable rocks and scrub which exist on the hills up the Khaisora valley, and to come out into the more open country at the tops of the hills where they would present more favourable targets for the aircraft, artillery, and machine gunners. It was essential for this plan that the enemy should be made to think that the advance would be made up the Khaisora, and the first step towards deceiving the enemy was made at this time. The Political Agent, North Waziristan, was asked to have enquiries made, (not too discreetly), with regard to the amount of water available at Zerpezai.

*Striking force advances to Bichhe Kashkai, 27th April.

On the 27th of April, the 2nd Infantry Brigade with the 9th Light Tank Company advanced to Bichhe Kashkai at 0830 hours, the camp site and piquets being secured by 1040 hours. In order to enable the 2nd Infantry Brigade to operate as a complete brigade, the 1/17 Dogra R. was attached and held all camp piquets. As there were persistent rumours of an intended attack on all unwired camps and camp piquets, it was decided to put down a single apron round all camp piquets. Two which were more isolated were given a double apron. The troops covering the occupation of the piquets, the 2/4 Bombay Grs. and the 1/11 Sikh R., were subjected to some opposition, but with the aid of the 9th Light Tank Company on the south bank of the river and of the artillery, had no difficulty in taking up their positions.

At 1430 hours the Brigade Commander, who had gone across the river to the Water Piquet (244390) earlier in the day to make his plan for the next day's operations, issued his orders from that spot for the attack on the hills in squares 2236, 2237, 2136 and the ring contour at 207360.

During this time, the Brigade Commander's pennant was being prominently displayed by the 2 Bombay Grs. from their Headquarters north of the river.

Throughout the day large numbers of the enemy had been seen at a distance on both banks of the Khaisora valley, and it became increasingly obvious that the object of bringing the enemy to battle would be attained.

Attack on camp piquets and camp, Bichhe Kashkai, night 27th/28th April.

At about 1715 hours, very shortly after the withdrawal of the covering troops to camp, the camp piquets situated to the west of the camp, Nos. 1, 2, 3, and 3A, began to come under heavy fire from the ridge running north-west about 226391. Several bodies of the enemy were seen on this ridge and were engaged by artillery from camp until darkness intervened.

The enemy attacked these piquets with varying degrees of intensity throughout the night. Many heavy attacks were made on No. 1 piquet by large parties, using bombs, but all were beaten off. Of the fourteen men in the garrison nine were wounded. No. 2 piquet also was fiercely attacked. On three occasions the enemy, using bombs, succeeded in reaching

---

*For Composition of Striking Force See p. 82.

the barbed wire, but each time the garrison drove them off. The casualties in the piquet were one man killed and five wounded. One enemy party which approached No. 3 piquet called out to the piquet commander to hand the piquet over, saying that if the garrison was Mussulman and surrendered their rifles they would be permitted to go unmolested. This invitation was replied to by a burst of fire.

1937
April

At about 2200 hours sniping of the camp increased considerably and shouting was also heard from the south west. The moon was now rising, and at 2230 hours tribesmen were seen on the top of the river bank to the south west about fifty yards from the perimeter. A few minutes later they were also seen on the western face. On this face a small nullah and a large graveyard gave access and cover for tribesmen approaching the perimeter. A party in the graveyard opened covering fire, and the enemy made an attempt to rush the perimeter gate. They got to within twenty yards before being driven off. They now moved round to the north of the camp and attempted to creep up to the perimeter posts on the ridge overlooking the camp, but were again driven off by fire. Later, about 2330 hours, they were again seen in small numbers round the camp.

About this time all communication with Nos. 2 and 3 piquets was lost, and no sound of firing from them could be heard.

Decision to postpone for one day the advance planned for 28th April.
The attack which had been planned for the 28th was to commence at 0530 hours, and the Brigade Commander had to make up his mind whether it should take place or not. Unwilling as he was to be diverted from his purpose, the following reasons influenced him in asking permission to postpone his attack for twenty four hours. The battle was not yet over; the security of the camp was not assured, all touch with two of the camp piquets having been lost the troops had been up all night and would by no means be fresh for the arduous work which would be expected of them in the contemplated attack; some twenty five mules had been either killed or wounded, entailing a redistribution of animals; ammunition would have to be replaced and machine-gun belts refilled when the night action was over; the ground required to be cleared.

The Commander 1st Division agreed to the postponement of the attack, and arrangements were made for covering parties to go out beyond the camp piquet line as soon as it was light for the relief of the Dogra Regiments camp piquets by other units and for the clearance of the battlefield.

During the night the casualties were one Indian other rank killed, one British officer wounded, twenty six Indian other ranks wounded, and twenty five mules and two horses killed and wounded. The enemy succeeded in getting away all their dead and wounded before daylight, but there were many evidences of casualties all over the area of the fighting.

At about 0900 hours on the 28th the Commander 1st Division visited the camp and discussed the situation with the Brigade Commander. There seemed no doubt at this time that the enemy were collecting in increasing numbers, that the prospect of bringing them to battle was good, and that the objective was of little importance provided that severe punishment could be inflicted. It was decided therefore, that the objective for the next day should be a large rounded feature (230370) near Zikhe, and that if it were possible, a further advance should be made up the ridge running west and south west towards Mazai Raghza (1934).

1937

April

Plan for advance on 29th April.

At about 1430 hours the Brigade Commander issued his verbal orders for the attack on the 29th from a point on the ridge immediately north of camp.

The plan of operations was as follows. As soon as it was light, the whole of the 1/17 Dogra R. with the 2nd Light Battery were to advance westward near the river bed as ostentatiously as possible, with the object of giving the impression that the force was advancing up the Khaisora. On arrival at the ridge at about 226391, the 1/17 Dogra R. was to establish a rifle company and a machine-gun platoon on it while the 2nd Light Battery took up a position to the east on the spur near No. 1 piquet. The object of this was to bring fire to bear across the river on targets moving up towards the main attack. As soon as the rifle company and battery were established, the remainder of the battalion was to return to camp. The capture of the rounded feature (230370) was to be accomplished as follows. The 2/8 Punjab R. on the right and the 2/2 Punjab R. on the left, leaving camp at 0530 hours, were to cross the river, and go straight for the feature as far as some rocky outcrops about three quarters of the way up, dropping piquets as flank protection on the spurs up which they advanced. The 2 Bombay Grs. were then to advance up the left spur through the 2/2 Punjab R. and seize the top of the hill. The 1/11 Sikh R. was to advance up the centre to about half way up and to take up a defensive position there pending further orders. Both the two leading battalions were to be supported by batteries as far as their objectives, the fourth battery being kept in Brigade Reserve on the foothills to take on any targets not engaged by other batteries. The 9th Light Tank Company was to protect the left flank of the attack, watching particularly the approaches and tracks leading down from Mazai Raghza. After the capture of the feature, the Brigade would exploit towards Mazai Raghza.

Operations by Striking Force, 29th April

The night of the 28th/29th was a peaceful one, only slight sniping taking place, and on the morning of the 29th, troops left Bichhe Kashkai as arranged, the 1/17 Dogra R. preceding the remainder of the force by fifteen minutes. The 2/2 and 2/8 Punjab R. captured their objectives with the greatest speed, both battalions being on them by 0605 hours. The 2 Bombay Grs. were in possession of the top of the rounded feature by 0630 hours with a large part of the battalion in hand.

The Brigade Commander, who was also on top of the rounded feature by this time, now ordered the 2 Bombay Grs. to swing to their right and push on up the spur towards the height at 220366. Up to this time no enemy had been seen, but when the 2 Bombay Grs. approached the summit some opposition was met which was driven off with loss to the enemy. As the battalion moved up successive ridges of the spur parties were left behind to hold these ridges and the flanks for the protection of the withdrawal. Seeing that the 2 Bombay Grs. were about to be used up, the Brigade Commander at 0750 hours ordered the 1/11 Sikh R. to pass through the Bombay Grenadiers and to advance along the narrow ridge along which a track runs in square 2136. Dropping parties on each successive position along the spur, the 1/11th Sikhs at 0930 hours reached a small Knoll at 206360, when the battalion had no troops left for a further advance. From this point excellent observation was obtained and Dakai Kalai was shelled.

While the advance was in progress many reports were received of large parties of the enemy climbing the hills beneath. One party of a hundred and fifty and another of six hundred were reported, and air action and artillery fire brought to bear on them. Other parties were engaged by the 2nd Light Battery and by the machine-gun platoon of the 1/17 Dogra R. on the north bank of the river. Good targets were also obtained by the flanking piquets and by the aircraft as the troops advanced and flushed the enemy.

1937
April-May.

The problem now before the Brigade Commander was to decide how long to remain on the position gained. It was obvious that the withdrawal would be energetically followed up and if he stayed too long it would be very difficult to get casualties away by hand over such a long carry in steep rocky country back to camp. On the other hand, to withdraw at once would mean that the movement up the hill by the tribesmen would not be sufficiently punished. The Brigade Commander decided to wait for one and a half hours on his position, during which time as much loss as possible was to be inflicted on the enemy as they climbed up the slopes towards the position.

The withdrawal was ordered to commence at 1100 hours. It was carried out with great speed, the 1/11 Sikh R. passing through the 2/4 Bombay Grs., and the latter through the 2/2 and 2/8 Punjab R. The enemy followed up closely and succeeded in inflicting some casualties, but the pace of the withdrawal combined with the very effective protection afforded by the flanking parties, close support aircraft and artillery, prevented a larger casualty list.

It had been anticipated that the 2/8 Punjab R. might have difficulty in getting away owing to the ease with which the enemy could approach over the foothills on their right flank. In order to help them off, one section 9th Light Tank Company was posted along the low ground south of Zikhe to shoot up the reverse sides of the foothills. In spite of this the rear party suffered some casualties, and the Battalion was compelled to halt and put in a local counter attack to recover two wounded. This was successfully accomplished with the support of the 8th Mountain Battery and some machine guns of the 2/2 Punjab R. on the left flank.

By 1330 hours all the troops except the company and machine-gun platoon of the 1/17 Dogra R. north of the river had returned to camp. This company was in some difficulty as a party of the enemy reported to be about three hundred had reached some dead ground immediately under the ridge. It was expected that they would rush the ridge from this cover as soon as the withdrawal commenced. The close support aircraft and the artillery were directed on to the target and another company of the 1/17 Dogra R. was sent out to assist in the withdrawal. As a protection for the camp the withdrawal was not allowed to commence until 1715 hours, when it was successfully accomplished with only one casualty.

The casualties in the force during the day's operations amounted to twenty one. Heavy casualties had been inflicted on the enemy, pilots, gunners, and machine-gunners all reporting excellent targets successfully engaged. After this action the enemy were rarely seen and then only in small numbers, and sniping practically ceased.

On the 27th of April and again on the 28th, the 1st Infantry Brigade at Damdil carried out an advance to point 4332, north of the Khaisora, meeting with no opposition.

1937
May.

Operations by 1st Infantry Brigade, Bannu Brigade, and Tochi Scouts, 27th April to 3rd of May.

On these two days piquets of the 1st Infantry Brigade saw considerable movement of tribesmen northwards from the Khaisora area, apparently by the Kam Sarobi nala which crosses the Bannu-Razmak road about half way between Tal-in-Tochi and Damdil. On the night of the 29th/30th of April attempts were made to intercept these parties.

At 0200 hours on the 30th, Headquarters Bannu Brigade with the 2/4 G. R. and the 7 Mtn. Bty., left Miranshah with the object of taking up a position before daylight in the Pawana Ghundai area, south of milestone 46 on the Miranshah—Datta Khel road, where three of the main routes used by the tribesmen could be watched. This force was unable to reach the position originally intended as the deep irrigation ditches running through the crops on the north bank of the Tochi river were found to be impassable for mules. A suitable position was found, however, about a re-entrant near Raghzai Kalai (0859) and this was occupied by 0540 hours. Three platoons of Tochi Scouts had also left Miranshah some time before this, at 2345 hours on the 29th, for the Panakzai Nala areas (0859) where it was possible to command two other routes. Moving over difficult country this party was in position before daylight. A third ambush was provided by a section of the 6th Light Tank Company (armoured cars) in the vicinity of Boya. About one hundred tribesmen, in small parties, approached the Bannu Brigade troops and the Tochi Scouts as dawn broke on the 30th, and were successfully engaged, losing some thirty casualties including eleven men captured.

On the 1st and 3rd of May Tochi Scouts from Datta Khel Post also operated successfully against some small parties of tribesmen, inflicting some casualties.

Decision to advance from Dosalli.

General Sir John Coleridge had for some time been considering a plan to strike at the Faqir in his headquarters at Arsal Kot from the direction of Dosalli. He determined that as the operations in the Khaisora area appeared to have fulfilled their object, they should now cease and be followed at once by further operations from Dosalli. Orders were issued for the return of the force to the Tochi Valley. It was decided to evacuate Khaisora Scouts Post at the same time as it was thought that the retention of a garrison there might prove a source of embarrassment during subsequent operations.

On the 30th of April, with the object again of deceiving the enemy about future intentions, the 2nd Infantry Brigade carried out a reconnaissance north east of Dakai Kalai and north of the river. At the same time the Brigade Commander made a personal reconnaissance in a tank southwards to the Zarinai ridge overlooking the Pasta Algad, with a view to an advance down the Algad on the following day for the purpose of executing an R. E. road reconnaissance.

Orders had been received that the 2nd Infantry Brigade was to return from Bichhe Kashkai to Jaler Camp via the Pasta Algad, on the 1st of May the Khaisora Scouts Post also being evacuated on that day. This operation was carried out with very little opposition, only a few long-range snipers being encountered, and all the troops including the party of Tochi Scouts from the Post were in Jaler Camp by about 1330 hours.

On the 2nd of May two battalions of the 3rd Infantry Brigade withdrew to Tochi Camp, and on the 3rd, Headquarters 1st Indian Division and the 2nd Infantry Brigade returned to Mir Ali, and the 3rd Infantry Brigade to Idak, Jaler and Tochi Camps being evacuated.

1937.
———
April-May.

The total casualties among the troops taking part in these operations from the 23rd of April to the 3rd of May were five killed and fifty four wounded. From reports received later it was estimated that in the operations from Mir Ali and Damdil and the ambushes from Miranshah the enemy lost two hundred and fifty seven severely wounded.

During the operations of the 1st Indian Division, air co-operation was provided by No. 20 (A. C.) Squadron. Close support and reconnaissance duties were carried out continuously. Close support action was taken on several occasions, and particularly good targets were obtained by close support aircraft on the 29th of April. The squadron also provided photographic, supply-dropping, and travel sorties.

R. A. F. co-operation.

The Khaisora column was accompanied throughout its march by the O. C. No. 3 (Indian) Wing, who acted as liaison officer with the Column Commander, and at the same time attempted to control and co-ordinate the operations of Nos. 20 and 28 (A. C.), Squadrons. He was also accompanied by an Intelligence Liaison Section. He found that though his work with the column proved most valuable he was unduly isolated from his squadrons. As a result of these experiences, in future columns an experienced officer from the (A. C.) Squadrons replaced him with the column.

It was found that the current orders in "Instructions regarding the control of operations, including the employment of air forces, on the North-West Frontier of India", which limited air action to within two miles of the force engaged, resulted in the missing of several chances of inflicting damage on hostile tribesmen. On the urgent representation of the Political Authorities, after this operation had been completed, the regulations were modified to the extent that aircraft were permitted to continue to operate against such tribesmen, except in villages, without strict adherence to the two-mile limit, provided that the crews were able to keep the offending tribesmen in sight throughout the engagement. Pursuit by aircraft beyond the "Three mile limit" of the Durand line was not, however, permissible in any circumstances.

In spite of the success of the operations in the Khaisora Valley, the general situation in Waziristan continued to deteriorate, and there seemed to be dangerous possibilities in South Waziristan where the Mahsuds were watching events with increasing interest. Although the Faqir of Ipi remained with the Tori Khel and was technically harboured by them, at the same time he continued to enjoy the sympathy and support of all the Mahsud sections of the Shaktu area who also virtually sheltered him. The Kikarai Mahsuds, the Abdur Rahman Khel, and the Mahsuds of the Khaisora valley appeared ready to comply with the orders of Government, and produced the hostages demanded as security for their good behaviour, but the Jalal Khel Mahsuds, against whose summer grazing grounds air action was begun on the 28th of April, remained recalcitrant, stated that they were unable to control Malik Khonia Khel, and failed to comply with any of the terms imposed on them. It was known, too,

General situation continues to deteriorate.

1937.
May.

that the Faqir, whose propaganda was now being intensively directed at the Mahsuds, especially at the Bahlolzai of Makin, was in constant communication with Mullah Fazal Din, and it was suspected that the latter was inciting the Mahsuds to action. Parties of Bahlolzai were leaving Makin openly to join the Faqir. Mullah Sher Ali, in spite of the security given by the Nano Khel for his good behaviour, was plotting mischief. The migration of Afghan nomads, including the Ghilzai and Zadrans from the Frontier districts, was complete and they would now find themselves free to participate in Waziristan lashkars. In fact, the numbers of Afghans moving to join the Faqir was now on the increase. The nomad Ahmadzai Wazirs of the Wana and Birmal areas had reached their summer locations and were taking a renewed interest in the Faqir's cause and were already showing signs of restlessness, the Faqir being in correspondence with their leading men and asking them to join him. Although as a result of the operations in the Khaisora valley, the lashkars there had decreased in size, there was a considerable number of hostile tribesmen in the areas of Razmak, the Sham, and the Shaktu valley, ready to give what trouble they could whilst the operations had been in progress. Telegraph wires had been cut, attempts made to damage bridges, and civilian lorries looted, and the main Bannu-Razmak road made temporarily unfit for traffic at several points. An unsuccessful attempt had been made to ambush a wood cutting party from Alexandra Ridge Post, and opposition, though slight only, had been offered to the Razmak Brigade on the several occasions when it moved out to reconnoitre the Sardar Algad area to relieve the Alexandra Ridge piquet, or to cover repairs to the road.

Raid on Paharpur in settled district. Bold raids in the settled districts also had been carried out, instigated by the Faqir of Ipi. A gang of about seventy men, mostly Mahsuds, made a raid on the village of Paharpur south east of Pezu in the Dera Ismail Khan District on the night of the 1st/2nd of May. When news of this raid was received on the morning of the 2nd at Waziristan District Headquarters, a detachment of one and a half sabre squadrons and two machine gun sections of the Scinde Horse, stationed at Tank, was warned to be ready to move at short notice. Headquarters Waziristan District decided to try to intercept the raiders when making their way back to tribal territory by watching the line of the road between Pezu and Dera Ismail Khan with police and armoured cars and that of the Bain-Tank road with the Scinde Horse detachment and the Frontier Constabulary. The Scinde Horse detachment, with a W/T lorry, leaving one sabre troop in Tank, marched out at 14-30 hours, and by 18-30 hours was established in a number of positions from the Rud Soheli Nala to Tajori on the general line of the road, the Frontier Constabulary extending the line on either flank. The raiders did not appear that night, and fresh arrangements were made for the next night. Keeping as concealed as possible, the Scinde Horse by 18-30 hours occupied fresh positions covering the Rud Soheli near Pai, the Takwara Nala near Tajori, and likely routes in between them. At 23-20 hours a party of raiders, led by two men with torches, approached by the Takwara Nala, where one sabre troop and the two machine gun sections were posted. Fire was opened by the ambush party at short range, and the raiders, taken by surprise, scattered and opened fire. They then attempted to close in on the troop from all sides, while making partially successful attempts to remove their casualties from the Nala. At the first burst of fire, several horses took fright, dragged their pegs out of the ground, and stampeded. Portions of the gang approached the positions held by two other troops during the next hour, and fire was opened on them bloodstains seen after daylight showing that casualties had been inflicted. Intermittent firing continued until about 05-00 hours, though it was thought that the main body of the raiders left at about 03-30 hours. In the action the Scinde Horse lost one man killed. One seriously wounded tribesman and four dead bodies were found after daylight. The raiders were forced to leave behind three rifles and a considerable portion of their loot. The majority of the horses which had stampeded were found close to the position, the remainder being brought back later by local inhabitants.

The day after this, another raid was made on Surkamar, fifteen miles south of Manzai. A gang of about a hundred and twenty tribesmen attacked a detachment of Frontier Constabulary less than half its strength which had been sent out to intercept the gang. In the fight the police were pinned to their positions and were unable to move. Another party of Constabulary from Drazinda Post, patrolling routes along which, it was thought the Paharpur raiding gang might be travelling, came to their assistance, followed by more Constabulary reinforcements from Tank. Aircraft from Manzai also came into action, and the raiders were eventually driven off with loss.

Attack on Frontier Constabulary patrol near Surkamar.

The Political authorities were impressing on the maliks the advisability of keeping their sections in control, but, though most of them were willing enough, their power to do so was waning. Political action had been taken against the Madda Khel on account of the murder of Lieut. Beatty, and the tribe had accepted the terms of Government. Action had also been taken against the Bhitannis, whose maliks had failed completely to carry out their undertaking to control the Din Faqir who had been actively supporting the Faqir of Ipi, and whose efforts on behalf of the latter had been causing the increasing restlessness of the tribe in the area round Jandola. Maliks' allowances were stopped, it was announced that any Khassadars who failed to appear for duty would be suspended, and hostages had been demanded. As the hostages were not produced on the appointed date, air action was threatened. This threat proved effective and the hostages were produced. The Din Faqir, however, remained at large and continued to assist the Faqir of Ipi.

Political action against Madda Khel and Bhittanis.

1937.
April-May.

TROOPS ENGAGED IN THE KHAISORA OPERATIONS 23RD OF APRIL TO 3RD OF MAY.

Headquarters 1st Indian Division.
1st Divisional Signals.
Detachment Tochi Scouts.

Striking Force.

2nd (Rawalpindi) Infantry Brigade.
    2/2 Punjab R.
    2/4 Bombay Grs.
    2/8 Punjab R.
    1/11 Sikh R.
66 Fd. Bty. (H).
23 Mtn. Bde. Headquarters.
3 Mtn. Bty.
8 Mtn. Bty.
15 Mtn. Bty.
No. 2 Fd. Coy. S. and M.
9th Light Tank Company (less 1 section).
4th Field Ambulance.
Detchment No. 3 Sanitary Section.

Line of Communications.

3rd (Jhelum) Infantry Brigade.
    2 A. and S. H.
    3/9 Jat. R.
    1/14 Punjab R.
    1/17 Dogra R.
81 Fd. Bty. (H).
2 Light Bty.
Post guns, Mir Ali
No. 4 Fd. Coy. (less 2 sections).
One section 9th Light Tank Company.
7th Light Tank Company (Armoured cars) less one section.
Detachment 11th Field Ambulance.
Detachment No. 5 Sanitary Section.

Damdil.

1st (Abbottabad) Infantry Brigade.
    1 S. Wales Bord.
    2/5 R. G. R.
1/6 G. R.
2/6 G. R.

Map C 37

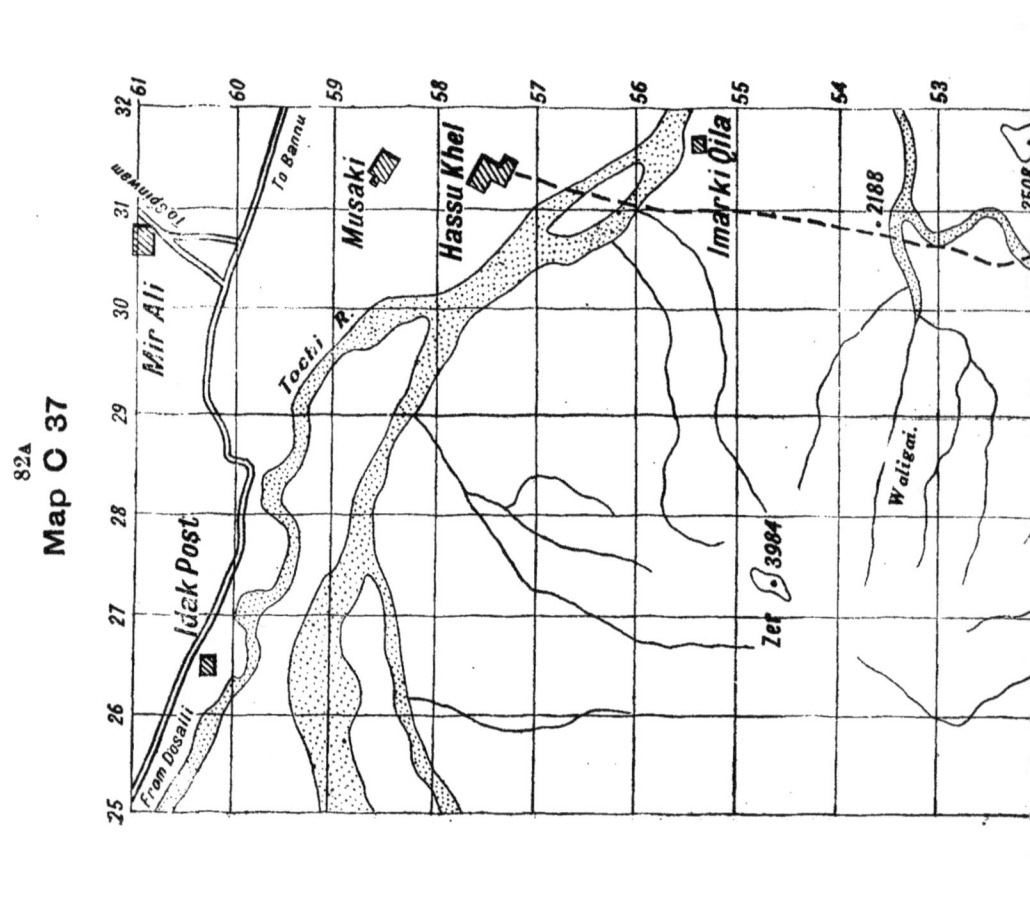

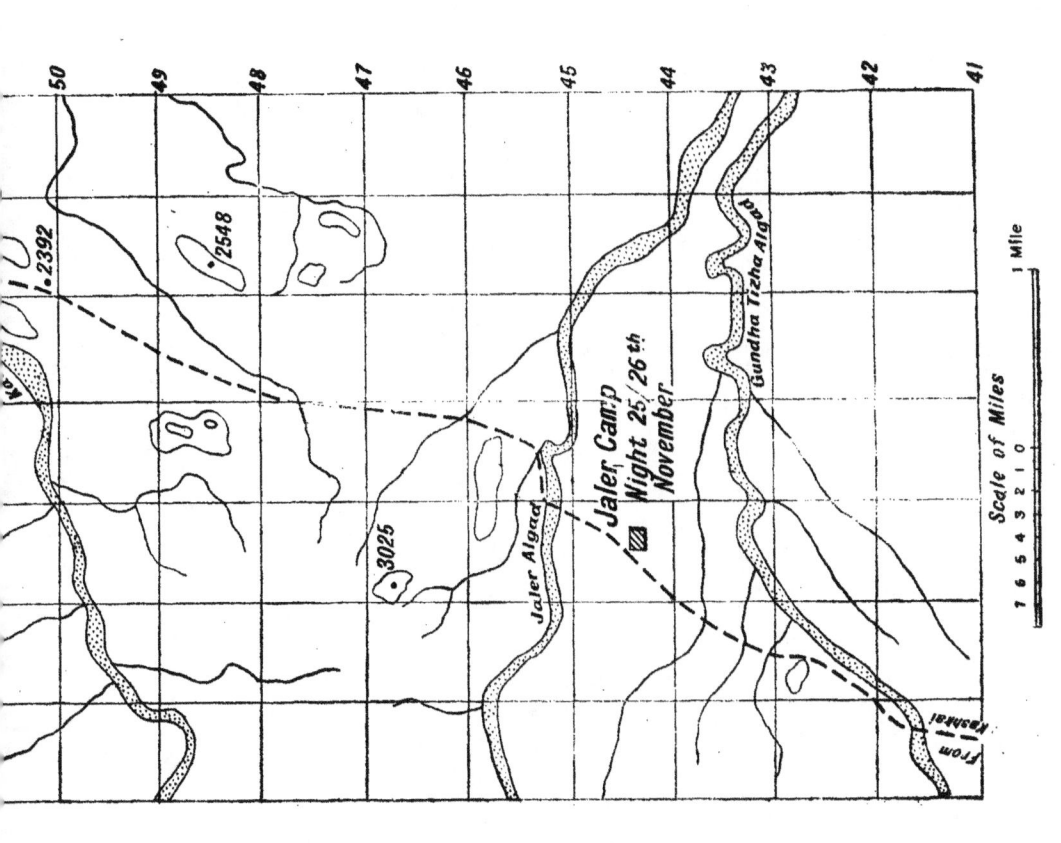

CHAPTER XI.

Concentration of troops and advance to the Sham plain, May 1937.

Decision to advance from Dosalli.

It was plainly evident that the Faqir of Ipi was the focus of all the trouble in Waziristan, and before the task of pacifying the country as a whole could be satisfactorily achieved, it was necessary that he should be forced either to vacate his present headquarters so that his activities might be brought under control, or to leave Waziristan altogether. It was this conviction that influenced General Sir John Coleridge in making his decision to advance on Arsal Kot. The Faqir had frequently declared that his sanctuary at Arsal Kot was inviolate. If it were destroyed, therefore, it was hoped that his influence and prestige might be shattered. Tribesmen were likely to collect in considerable strength to oppose any advance on this place, and if they did so, decisive results might be gained which would greatly facilitate the restoration of general peace.

It would be difficult to capture the Faqir by a surprise raid owing to the distance from Arsal Kot to the nearest suitable starting point. A deliberate advance would be unlikely to result in his capture as he would almost certainly take alarm as soon as troops came within striking distance of him. The best solution of the problem, therefore, in the circumstances appeared to be to construct a motor road to the vicinity of Arsal Kot. Such a road would enable this hitherto inaccessible area to be more easily reached by troops, and would ensure its future domination. At the same time, with so many troops in Waziristan, the present circumstances presented a very suitable opportunity for a comprehensive scheme of road-making which would open up the area from several directions.

From a military point of view it was important that there should be as little delay as possible between the withdrawal from the Khaisora valley area and the advance on Arsal Kot. Three routes of advance had been considered, the first, from Dosalli via the Sham Plain, the second, from the Khaisora valley near Bichhe Kashkai via Mazai Raghza, and the third, from Ahmedwam via Madamir Kalai. Any one of these routes would fit in with a future scheme of motorable roads. The third route traversed Mahsud country throughout its length, and as the attitude of the Mahsuds was most uncertain, an advance by this line might well result in a war with that tribe, a complication to be avoided for many reasons. The other two routes passed through Tori Khel country. The Tori Khel, it was considered, were not likely to offer serious resistance as a tribe in view of the measures which had already been taken against them. Malcontents from both tribes were likely to oppose the construction of a road whatever route was selected, but if the road was made in Tori Khel country, there was less likelihood of the Mahsuds entering the field as a tribe than if it was started from Ahmedwam. Satisfied therefore that the choice must rest between the first two lines of approach, General Sir John Coleridge decided in favour of a road from Dosalli. This route had the particular advantage that it followed, generally, a higher level than the other. With the approach of the hot weather, the question of the effect of the climate in its effect on the health of the troops became an important factor.

1937.
May

1687.

May.

General outline of future plans.

To ensure the rapid construction of a motorable road, and to be ready to meet the most serious situation that might arise, resistance from the combined Mahsud and Tori Khel tribes, General Sir John Coleridge decided that the initial advance from Dosalli should be made by two infantry brigades with a strong proportion of artillery, while adequate forces were kept in reserve to assist the striking force if required and to subdue possible risings elsewhere. The first objective was to be the Sham Plain, and when the line of communications from Dosalli to the Plain were established the advance was to be continued to Arsal Kot. After that village had been destroyed and the Faqir evicted, the Mahsud country would then be visited and a clear demonstration given to that tribe that Government forces would move through their country at will. When these further operations were commenced, the contemplated programme of road making would be commenced.

Conduct of operations delegated to Commander, Waziristan District.

Responsibility for the conduct of the advance from Dosalli to the Sham Plain was delegated to Major General A. F. Hartley, C.B., D.S.O., who had recently succeeded to the command of Waziristan District.

Further reinforcements.

It was decided to bring further reinforcements to Waziristan, and on the 29th of April orders were issued for the move of the 9th (Jhansi) Infantry Brigade and ancillary units.

Re-organization of forces in Waziristan.

In order to relieve Major General Hartley of the considerable administrative responsibilities which had devolved on the Headquarters, Waziristan District since the re-arrival of reinforcements in Waziristan in March, and to leave him free to concentrate on the prosecution of the task now given him, the forces in Waziristan were re-organized from the 28th of April. Wazirforce was formed comprising all formations, units, and administrative establishments, under the command of General Sir John Coleridge. Headquarters, Wazirforce, formed from Northern Command, Headquarters, was divided into two echelons, Headquarters at Bannu, and Rear Headquarters at Dera Ismail Khan. General Sir John Coleridge, in chief command, controlled all operations, the general protection of the line of communications, and the general administration of the force. His Rear Headquarters dealt with the peace routine work normally carried out by Headquarters, Waziristan District. The formations under Wazirforce, Headquarters were the 1st Indian Division with headquarters at Mir Ali, the Waziristan Division with headquarters at Dosalli, the Bannu line-of-communications area, and the Manzai line-of-communications area. The Wana Area was brought into existence on the 5th of May. The Advanced Base, as before, was located at Bannu. Responsibility for the protection of the Central Waziristan Road was laid on the Bannu Area from that place to milestone $14\frac{1}{2}$, thence to milestone 52 on the 1st Division, and from milestone 52 to Dosalli, on the Waziristan Division.

Objects of operations.

In the instructions given to Major General Hartley, the attainment of two objects was specified, firstly, to inflict a decisive defeat on hostile lashkars when and where met, and secondly, to occupy Arsal Kot and its neighbourhood with the minimum of delay in order to destroy the influence and prestige of the Faqir of Ipi. He was also told that a fair-weather motor track was to be constructed as

1ST INF. BRIGADE CAMP BOSALL, MAY 1937.

the troops advanced. The force under his command, known as the Waziristan Division, was to consist of the *Bannu Brigade, the *1st Infantry Brigade, (temporarily detached from the 1st Indian Division) the 9th Light Tank Company and the Artillery and Sappers and Miners attached to the infantry brigades, and a detachment of Tochi Scouts. He was permitted to use the *Razmak Brigade if the Mahsud situation permitted, failing which another Brigade would be placed at his disposal.

Whilst these operations were taking place, the 1st Indian Division was to be prepared to take quick offensive action against any gangs of hostile tribesmen who might interfere with the main line of communications within its area. All possible steps, also, were to be taken to intercept tribesmen moving through its area either joining or leaving lashkars. The Commander, 1st Division was also to be ready to despatch an infantry brigade group from Damdil, if called on to do so, to co-operate with the main advance on Arsal Kot. If the attitude of the Mahsuds deteriorated, he was to be prepared to send an infantry brigade group to Razmak, with a view to operations in the Makin-Kaniguram area. He was, also, to watch carefully the attitude of the Madda Khel and to be ready to anticipate any offensive action by that tribe.

Preparatory moves. Immediately after the return of the troops of the 1st Indian Division from the Khaisora, units and formations began to move to their new destinations in readiness for the proposed operations. The 1st Infantry Brigade group occupied Dosalli Camp, near the Scouts' Post, on the 6th of May, being followed by the Headquarters, Waziristan Division, and by the Bannu Brigade group the next day. The 9th Light Tank Company arrived at Dosalli a few days later. On the line of communications, by the 6th of May the *2nd Infantry Brigade was distributed between Mir Ali, Idak, Miranshah, and Tal-in-Tochi, the *3rd Infantry Brigade was at Damdil, and the 9th Infantry Brigade, which had completed its concentration in Waziristan two days previously and had come under the command of Headquarters 1st Division, was on its way to the latter place. On the 11th of May the 3rd Infantry Brigade moved to Dosalli. On the 10th of May Headquarters No. 3 (Indian) Wing moved from Mir Ali to Miranshah, this being the most convenient centre for communication with Army formations and for control of Army Co-operation units. Senior Royal Air Force officers were attached as liaison officers to Headquarters, 1st Division and Waziristan Division to accompany column Headquarters and to advise on the requirements of air co-operation generally and of close support action in particular.

Allotment of R. A. F. Extension of proscribed area. Royal Air Force co-operation continued to be provided by Nos. 1 and 3 Wings R. A. F. Of the latter, No. 20 (A. C.) Squadron was placed under the operational control of Headquarters, Waziristan Division from the 5th of May, whilst No. 28 Squadron came under the direct operational control of Wazirforce Headquarters.

In anticipation of the possible necessity for extending the area proscribed by air action, sanction had recently been obtained to such extension when considered necessary, to include the catchment area of the Sham Algad, Sre Mela Algad, and the Babrakra Algad. It was now thought desirable to try to drive as many hostile tribesmen as possible into the area in which

---

* For units of Bannu and Razmak Bdgs. see page 15 *ante*. For units of 1st, 2nd and 3rd Inf. Bdgs see page 82.

1937.
May.

the Waziristan Division was about to operate. Orders were issued extending the proscribed zone from the 5th of May, to include a part, only, of the whole area sanctioned. The former southern boundary was extended to its permissible southern limits, thereby joining up with the proscribed Arsal Kot area; on the west the boundary was placed along the western limits of the Dakai, Nargesa, and Wedon Algads up to point 4987 (0739), and from there it was taken *via* point 4580 (1040) to point 4050 (1140) where it joined up with the original western boundary. Control of air operations in this area was allotted to No. 1 (Indian) Wing until the advance of the troops began. The area roughly west of the 06 grid line (*i.e.*, roughly N. & S. through Ghariom) was then taken over by No. 3 (Indian) Wing which was working in close co-operation with the troops.

Further activities of the Faqir of Ipi.

When the 1st Indian Division withdrew from the Khaisora valley and the Khaisora Scouts' Post was evacuated at the beginning of May, rumours, instigated by the Faqir, were spread abroad that the troops had retired in disorder, that the Post had been vacated through fear, and that troops would shortly be going to Razmak to effect a withdrawal from that place. Wana, too, was to be evacuated. The retirements from the Khaisora area were quoted as examples of the current policy of the Government of India to give up Waziristan owing to the inability of Government to control the tribes. These tales were believed to the extent that some tribesmen arrived at Wana bringing camels to remove the loot. Fresh appeals were made to Khassadars to desert their posts. The Mahsud situation was giving signs of becoming worse. It was reported that Mullah Fazal Din was using his influence to encourage the Mahsuds to join the lashkars, and parties of the tribe were still leaving Makin openly for the Shaktu or Razmak areas. The Faqir had instructed his followers to attack troops on the road between Isha and Razmak and to make the road impassable for lorries. He also announced his intention to hold up the Razmak Brigade if it moved towards Razani, and to concentrate the remainder of his followers in the Shawali Algad and Sham Plain areas. On the 6th of May serious harm was done to the Pariat Bridge near Razani and to the road itself between Razani and Razmak Narai, and the water supply at Razani was badly damaged. On this date it was estimated that there were about 2400 hostile tribesmen in the Khaisora—Shaktu area, about half of whom were Afghan subjects.

*Advance of 1st Infantry Brigade to Village Camp, 8th May.

Owing to the arrival of large numbers of troops at Dosalli camp the question of the water supply there was now beginning to produce difficulties. The combined strength of the Waziristan Division and the Scouts' detachment at Dosalli Post totalled some ten thousand six hundred men and four thousand animals. Some water was brought from the Asad Khel pumping station in lorries, but some dispersion of this force was inevitable. A reconnaissance by the 1st Infantry Brigade on the 6th of May ascertained that water for an infantry brigade group was available in Dosalli village about two miles to the south. It was decided to move the 1st Infantry Brigade to that place. It was realized that this would probably leave the enemy in no doubt of the intention to advance to the Sham Plain, but it was considered that in the circumstances this was not a matter of

---
* See Sketch Map H 37. (p161A).

VILLAGE CAMP MAY 1937. MTN. ARTILLERY IN ACTION AGAINST SNIPERS.

great importance. On the 8th of May the 1st Infantry Brigade advanced to establish Village Camp to the immediate west of Dosalli village.

The advance was assisted by the Brigade Headquarters, 2/11 Sikh R. and 2/4 G. R. of the Bannu Brigade, who provided the advanced guard and right flank protection as far as the village, and by eight platoons of the Tochi Scouts who were responsible for the left flank.

It was known that hostile reinforcements had been collecting on the Sham Plain, and considerable bodies of tribesmen were reported in the neighbourhood of the Sham Narai and about Ghariom in the Sham Algad. They were also said to be contructing sangers covering the approaches to the Sham Plain at the upper exits from the Sre Mela Algad. The Faqir's brother and active supporter, Sher Zaman, had come to organize opposition to the anticipated advance, and to exhort them on behalf of the Faqir, to attack the troops between Dosalli and the Sham Plain and to resist them to the utmost. Any tribesmen in the vicinity of Dosalli Camp, however, appeared to be certain that the next move of the troops would be westward along the road to Razani, as, on the morning of the 8th, a party of about two hundred of them were occupying a position covering the main road near Gardai. They had doubtless been led to this conclusion by observing a reconnaissance of the damaged Pariat Bridge and of the water supply at Old Razani Camp, carried out from Dosalli Camp the previous day with the express purpose of misleading them.

Whatever the reason, no enemy were met as far as the site of Village Camp, which was reached at 10-00 hours.

At this time the troops of the Bannu Brigade were disposed as follows. The 2/11 Sikh R. had halted on an east and west line just north of the village. The 2/4 G. R. protecting the right flank, had reached a big feature (000386) about one thousand yards west of the village.

The detachment of the Tochi Scouts, on the left flank, was posted up to the lower slopes (014378) of a spur about half a mile south east of the village.

At 10-00 hours, the 2/5 R. G. R. of the 1st Infantry Brigade passed through the 2/11 Sikh R. to secure the camp site, and occupied a position on a north east and south west line astride the Sre Mela Algad about two thousand yards south of the village. Parties of tribesmen began to arrive about 11-00 hours in the area south and south west of the camp site, and firing commenced. By this time work on the construction of most of the camp piquets had begun. Of these, No. 4 (996379), No. 5 (002378) and No. 6 (001376), south west of the camp were to be established by the 1/6 G. R. This Battalion had been rearguard to the Brigade, and arriving last in camp, were unable to start work on their piquets as soon as other units. As soon as the men were available, a platoon was sent with a British Officer to the site of No. 6 piquet. As this party reached its destination, it came under heavy fire from the south west and sustained several casualties, including the British Officer who was severely wounded.

It was impossible to construct the post until the firing was overcome. By 14-00 hours it was evident that the enemy's strength was increasing and that they were approaching closer from the south west towards the piquet site. With the object of covering the construction, a company of the 2/6 G. R., who were holding piquets north of the 1/6 G. R., supported by a section of machine guns, advanced from the vicinity of No. 4 piquet, but was brought to a halt by a very deep Nala which had not been shown on the map.

1937.
—.
y.

By this time, Nos. 4 and 5 piquets had been established, and it was now decided to concentrate on these and to defer the construction of No. 6 piquet to the following day.

The 2/5 R. G. R. were also engaged with the enemy, and when they withdrew at 17-00 hours, they were closely followed up until they were within two hundred yards of the camp, the tribesmen exposing themselves more freely and offering good targets to the artillery and machine guns.

The hills in the neighbourhood of Village Camp were covered with heavy scrub. Throughout the day it had been most difficult to locate any tribesmen and to find targets to engage. Owing to the dense cover they were able to remain concealed until the troops were almost on them or to creep forward and get close up to the troops without being discovered. A dust storm which arose at about 16-00 hours also made visibility very poor, and increased the difficulties of co-operation by the Royal Air Force.

During the day parties of the enemy were seen in sangars on the hills to the east of the Tochi Scouts. These were successfully engaged by the R. A. F.

The troops of the Bannu Brigade commenced their withdrawal at 18-00 hours. They met with some opposition on the way, but brushed it aside without incurring any loss, and reached Dosalli Camp about an hour and a quarter later.

The casualties in the force, all in the 1st Infantry Brigade, were as follows:—

Wounded—. . British Officers . . .	1	(Captain G. L. S. Vaughan, 1/6 G. R.)
British other ranks . . .	1	
Gurkha other ranks . . .	20	
Tochi Scouts	1	

The enemy remained active during the night, harassing the camp piquets and cutting the channel which, running along the side of the Sre Mela Algad, conveyed the water on which the supply of the camp depended. Fortunately, however, the water from the channel found its way along the bed of the Algad, and no serious inconvenience was caused.

Whilst the operations were in progress on the 8th of May, the Razmak Brigade which had marched out to the Razmak Narai for the day to cover the repair of the road near milestone 66, had a small engagement. The advance in the morning met with no resistance, parties of enemy seen being engaged by artillery and by aircraft. The return to Razmak in the afternoon was closely followed up by about one hundred and fifty tribesmen. The Brigade was hampered by poor visibility, due to a dust storm, of which the enemy took full advantage, following up the troops right to the gates of Razmak. The Brigade lost ten men, one of whom died of wounds, at a cost to the enemy of about twenty killed and wounded.

On the 9th of May an M.T. track was made from Dosalli to Village Camp, and this was taken into use on the 10th, when, a convoy ran to Village Camp.

Hostile tribesmen continued to snipe Village Camp and its piquets day and night. About 00-30 hours on the 10th, they made an attempt to assault the Camp. One party was seen approaching from the north down the Nala, which, some three hundred yards west of Dosalli village, passed along the western side of the camp. Another contingent was observed on the slopes of the spur under No. 5 piquet south west of the Camp. Covered

Attempted attacks on Village Camp, 10th May.

by considerable fire from the east, the tribesmen began to creep in towards the camp from the northwest. Fire was opened on them, and the attack was checked, some of them having got to within thirty yards of the perimeter wire. After about an hour they withdrew. A little later, at about 03-00 hours, another effort was made. This was less determined and was driven off more quickly.

1937.
May.

At about 21-15 hours the same day they again tried to close with the troops, this time under cover of a heavy thunderstorm. They repeated the tactics of their earlier attempts, but gave up after about half an hour.

Information was received that they intended to attack the Camp again on the night of the 11th/12th May. No attack was made, however, and during that night the Waziristan Division resumed its advance to the Sham Plain.

The presence of the 1st Infantry Brigade in Village Camp had enabled arrangements to be made with the inhabitants of Dosalli village for a share of their irrigation water to be made available for the troops in Dosalli Camp. The water was brought from the village in pipes and its security was ensured by the threat that if it was interfered with in any way, the towers of the leading maliks of the village would be destroyed.

Water difficulties solved. Completion of concentration of troops at Dosalli, 10th May.

The problem of the water supply having been satisfactorily settled, the expansion of the advanced base installations at Dosalli Camp was completed on the 10th of May, and by the 11th all was ready for a further advance.

Tribesmen had been concentrating in the Sham Plain area, and had reached a total which, on the 11th of May, was estimated to be about four thousand. In spite of reported dissensions between the Wazirs and Afghan tribesmen, a high proportion of the latter were still with the lashkars. An increasing number of Mahsuds, also, appeared to be joining the enemy.

Decision to make a converging attack, the Bannu Brigade column advancing by the Iblanke spur and the 1st Infantry Brigade by the Sre Mela Algad.

They had been preparing actively to defend the northern approaches to the Sham Plain. Reconnaissance by the Royal Air Force had confirmed the existence of sangars east and west of the Sre Mela Algad. Later, many of these were found to have been very skilfully camouflaged and carefully concealed.

The direct line of advance to the Sham Plain would be by the main Sre Mela Algad. This valley becomes steadily narrower as it nears the Plain, while the hills commanding it are increasingly more densely covered with scrub. The position selected by the tribesmen to oppose the troops would favour their guerilla tactics, enabling them to collect and inflict losses and then slip away undetected. To turn them out of any position where they elected to stand would be a difficult and possibly costly operation. Moreover, little help could be expected from the Royal Air Force in such close country. There was every probability that with these conditions, the enemy would be able to inflict severe losses on troops advancing this way at little cost to themselves, and that the rate of advance would be very slow.

The Commander, Waziristan Division decided, therefore, that the lodgment on the Sham Plain should be effected by out manœuvring and surprising the tribesmen.

1937.
May.

To effect this, the Bannu Brigade would advance on the night of the 11th/12th of May from Dosalli Camp along the Iblanke Spur, the 1st Infantry Brigade advancing in the early morning of the 12th up the main branch of the Sre Mela Algad. This would place the Division very suitably for an attack from the front and flank on the enemy's position.

Before adopting the line of advance by the Iblanke Spur it had been difficult to decide whether this route was practicable. Little could be ascertained by the use of field-glasses, and although a close study was made of air photographs, the information gained from them was limited as the track itself was largely obscured from view by the scrub on the spur. Reconnaissance could not be made because of the vital need for secrecy. However, the Tochi Scouts who had used the Iblanke spur during their patrolling operations, reported that the route, though very difficult, was passable for men and for animals, and reliance was placed on this report.

Efforts to secure secrecy.

Very thorough arrangements were made to ensure the secrecy on which success depended, and to deceive the tribesmen. Written orders and instructions were not issued by Headquarters, Waziristan Division until 12-10 hours on the 11th of May. Brigade Commanders were told of the proposed operation on the 9th. Other officers were given verbal instructions in sufficient time, only, to enable adequate preparations to be made, and the smallest possible number of individuals were informed of the real objective. Thus, in the Bannu Brigade, Commanding officers of units were not taken into the confidence of their Brigade Commander until the afternoon of the 10th of May, and the troops in general were not told their true destination until after night arrangements were in force on the 11th. Meanwhile, reports were spread about that the Division was to move to Razani to put the water supply there in order and to repair the road to Razmak. Colour was lent to this report by a reconnaissance of the Razani water supply on the 10th of May and by the issue of orders to the Razmak Brigade to move there on the 12th, these orders not being cancelled until 23-00 hours on the 11th, when there was no possibility of the truth leaking out before the operation began. Orders to the same effect were issued to the Bannu Brigade.

The Commander of the 1st Infantry Brigade had told the local inhabitants that his Brigade was moving back from Village Camp, from which all surplus baggage was back-loaded to Dosalli on the 10th of May. The success of these efforts was shown when some four hundred tribesmen gathered in the Razani area to oppose any movement in that direction.

Plan of the Commander Waziristan Division, 11th May.

The written orders issued by the Headquarters, Waziristan Division on the 11th of May specified the intention to establish two new camps the next day, Camp "A" about 021333 by the Bannu Brigade on the northern edge of the Sham Plain, and "Kach Camp" by the 1st Infantry Brigade, about 006356, on the lower slopes of the spur directly to the west of the upper portion of the main branch of the Sre Mela Algad. The Bannu Brigade with eight platoons of the Tochi Scouts was to leave Dosalli Camp at 21-30 hours on the 11th of May, and moving southwards over the high ground east of the Sre Mela Algad, was to be established on the northern slopes of the Sham Plain by or as soon as possible after first light the following morning. Camp "A" having been secured, vigorous action was to be taken against the hostile tribesmen as opportunity offered, particularly in the direction of Kach Camp to assist the advance of the 1st Infantry Brigade. Brigadier Maynard, commanding the Bannu Brigade, was instructed that the best means of providing this assistance was to seize the feature (to be known as Kach Hill) immediately south of Kach Camp. The 1st Infantry Brigade, leaving Village Camp at 06-00 hours on the 12th of May, synchronizing its movements as far as possible with those of the Bannu Brigade, was to establish Kach Camp and relieve the Bannu Brigade on Kach Hill. When relieved the latter formation was to return to Camp "A". The Royal Air Force was to provide a close reconnaissance sortie and continuous close support for each formation from first light on the 12th, an additional sortie being kept ready from the same hour for relief purposes or for taking any action which might be necessary.

1937.
May.

Reports which later were proved true indicated that the enemy was concentrating astride the Sre Mela Algad to oppose the advance, that they were probably occupying the woods south of 36 Grid Line and that they had constructed sangars east and west of the Algad.

Plan and arrangements of the Commander, Bannu Brigade, 11th May.
The Commander, Bannu Brigade, decided that it was of the first importance to establish himself on the high ground in square 0336 just north of the Iblanke Narai by first light, so as to be above the enemy when daylight came. He decided to cover his advance with the eight platoons of Tochi Scouts who were ordered to advance independently to the 36 Grid Line, dropping piquets on the features in square 0337. These piquets were to be relieved by the Advanced Guard as it came forward. One battalion, 2/11 Sikh R., was to act as advanced guard, with a second battalion, 2/4 Gurkha R. as piqueting troops. No artillery accompanied the advanced guard as it would have been an encumbrance at night. It was anticipated that both these battalions would be used up by dawn, and the third battalion, 2 A. and S. H., was to move in rear of column headquarters at the head of the main body, accompanied by both Mountain Batteries of the column. The fourth battalion, 1/17 Dogra R., was to provide the rear guard and the escort to the transport.

To ensure the success of this advance over unknown and difficult country it was necessary to work out the arrangements in very careful detail. The column was to march as light as possible, and animals accompanying the column had to be reduced to a minimum, everything which could be dispensed with being left to be brought on later. It was arranged, therefore, that rations for the 12th and 13th May should be carried on the man, two days grain being carried by each animal. No fodder was to be taken. The only baggage permitted was one greatcoat or blanket for every two officers and men. All riding animals, including those normally required for the wounded, were to be left behind in camp. By this means, the total number of animals with the column was reduced to seven hundred and twenty five, of which sixty, only, were 2nd line Transport. Full unit echelons of ammunition and the normal number of water mules were included in this figure. As the season of the year demanded that as ample a supply of drinking water as possible should be available and as the amount of the local supply was unknown, filled chaguls were to be taken in addition to the pakhals on the mules. Every animal in the column was to be led separately, infantry battalions providing the extra leaders themselves, men for the mules sent to other units being supplied by the R. I. A. S. C. The escort for the 7 and 19 Mtn. Btys. was to be provided by one company of

1937.
May.

the 2 A. and S. H., for No. 8 Field Ambulance by one section of No. 12 Field Company, and for the transport by two companies of the 1/17 Dogra R.

Guides, provided by the Tochi Scouts, were to move with the advanced guard, main body, and rear guard.

Intercommunication between the various portions of the column and the headquarters was to be maintained by liaison officers from each unit at column headquarters and by means of W/T sets, one set each being allotted to the advanced guard, column headquarters, No. 12 Fd. Coy. and the rear guard.

Piqueting troops were to protect the column from the spot where the route left the main road. Piquets were to consist of five rifles, at intervals of approximately one hundred yards on alternate sides of the route and at any point where the track might be mistaken, and not more than ten yards from the track. To facilitate the posting of piquets, the normal organization of the battalion was broken up and platoons were organized in parties of five. Platoon headquarters itself was organized as a piquet with the platoon commander as road sentry, and was posted as the last piquet found by the platoon. Piquets were posted personally by the Commanding officer, and to ensure that they were instantly available when required, each piquet commander was instructed to catch hold of the Commanding officer's left hand when he found himself the leading piquet in the battalion.

A camel convoy with supplies for both formations and with the surplus baggage, animals, and followers of the Bannu Brigade column, was to be sent forward on the 13th of May from Dosalli Camp to Kach Camp, the 1st Infantry Brigade sending on the supplies, etc. for the Bannu Brigade column to Camp "A" (later named Coronation Camp). In case of accidents, the Royal Air Force was asked to be prepared to drop by parachute on the Bannu Brigade during the 12th and 13th May sufficient supplies for the 14th.

Move of 3rd Brigade to Dosalli Camp.

In order to relieve the forward troops of responsibility for the security of the line of communications from Dosalli to Kach Camp the 3rd Infantry Brigade was moved to Dosalli Camp from Damdil during the 11th and 12th May where it came under the orders of the Commander, Waziristan Division.

Start of night advance, 11th May.

The pace expected from the Bannu Brigade was one mile an hour. To get on to the hill tops as early as possible, and to allow for possible delays on the way, the starting time was fixed for 21-00 hours, half an hour earlier than was originally intended.

At this hour the Bannu Brigade column was formed up on the main road near Dosalli Camp. The order of march was the Tochi Scouts, who were to advance independently, 2/11 Sikh R. advanced guard, 2/4 G. R. piqueting troops, Column Headquarters, 2 A. and S. H. less one company, 7 Mtn. Bty., 19 Mtn. Bty., No. 12 Fd. Coy. less one section, No. 8 Field Ambulance less detachments, No. 28 Supply Issue Section, 2nd Line Transport, and rear guard, 1/17 Dogra R. less two companies escorting the transport.

The actual time of start had to be put back for a few minutes as the moon had not yet set, and if the Tochi Scouts started before it was quite dark, the success of the operation might have been prejudiced. They left shortly after 21-00 hours, and moving fast, reached their objective, 36 Grid Line, at 00-30 hours, a report to this effect reaching Column Headquarters at 01-00 hours (12th May).

When the column started the night was clear with a starry sky, visibility being limited to a range of fifteen to twenty yards. It quickly became apparent that the progress of the troops was to be slower than had been anticipated. Four hundred yards from the starting point the route left the main road and followed a track into the Khaisora. This necessitated moving in single file, and the head of the main body was unable to move off until 22-00 hours.

Difficulties of route.
The physical difficulties of the route now turned out to be much greater than had been expected, making the rate of march exceptionally slow, and owing to the need for absolute quiet, nothing could be done to improve the path. After climbing the steep, trackless slope, covered with bushes and loose rock, from the Khaisora river on to the Iblanke spur, the route followed the crest of that spur which was frequently "knife-edged" with the sides falling away steeply. Footholds were hard to discover, mule-leaders often finding themselves temporarily unable to move forward or back. Mules fell down the precipitous slopes, some of them rolling a hundred feet down before being checked by a bush or a tree and being pulled or pushed back to the crest.

Halt, 01-10 hours, 12th May.
The orders for the march had laid down half-hourly halts. Owing to the slowness of the pace, the Commander had cancelled this order early in the march. At about 01-10 hours, however, having then heard that the Tochi Scouts had gained their objective, as the reports received from the rear indicated that the column was very much strung out, he decided to halt to allow of its closing up. At this hour, the rear-guard was just clearing the starting point, and it had taken the column four hours to get completely on the move. By then the Advanced Guard had relieved the piquets posted by the Tochi Scouts on the high ground in square 0337, but were not in touch with the Headquarters of the Scouts. The head of the main body was about half a mile south of point 5419 (0238). The Tochi Scouts had reported the presence of some enemy in front of them. Tribesmen had been heard calling to one another, saying that it was only the "Militia" who had arrived. They had also shouted to the Scouts that they would not be allowed to cross the Iblanke Narai.

0200 hours advance resumed.
By 02-00 hours, the column had closed up and the Advance was resumed. The advanced guard was ordered to push on and take over the position of the Tochi Scouts, the latter being ordered to seize the Iblanke Narai (035355).

At about 03-30 hours the advanced guard reported that the route was becoming even more difficult. Brigadier Maynard, who was determined that no difficulties should be allowed to prevent the successful accomplishment of his task, gave orders for the advanced guard to push on and himself started forward to their headquarters to assume control.

Progress was slow, but by 04-30 hours, the advanced guard regained touch with the Tochi Scouts Headquarters and it was possible to pass on to the latter the orders to secure the Iblanke Narai.

04-30 hours. Tochi Scouts advance to seize Iblanke Narai.
The Tochi Scouts moved forward at once, drawing immediate fire from the tribesmen, but pressing on resolutely along the difficult knife-edged feature to their front, they attacked the eastern of the two steep scrub-covered hills (042854 and 035355) commanding the Narai.

1937.
May.

05-00 hours precautions on approach of daylight.

It was now 05-00 hours, Brigadier Maynard had reached advanced guard headquarters about 035357. Daylight was approaching. The advanced guard commander was ordered to occupy certain prominent features to cover the column in daylight, and to occupy the Narai when it was captured. The 7 Mtn. Bty. was ordered to come into action to support the advance to the Narai and the support company 2/4 G. R. was sent to give additional support from a hill (035364) in rear of the advanced guard.

05-30 hours attack on hills commanding Narai.

Half an hour later the head of the main body was about five hundred yards north of the Narai. Enemy fire broke out from the east, south, and west. The Tochi Scouts were advancing from the hills east of the Narai to those on the west, closely followed by the 2/11 Sikh R. and supported by one section of the 7 Mtn. Bty. in action. The other section came into action almost immediately. The fire of the Battery and the support company stopped the hostile fire from the west and south. At the same time, one platoon 2/11 Sikh R. attacked a feature (about five hundred yards east of the position of Column Headquarters) from which accurate fire had been causing casualties in that battalion.

06-30 hours, hills captured.

By 06-30 hours the hills east and west of the Narai and the feature attacked by the platoon were captured and the Iblanke Narai was in our possession. The losses in in this fighting had been three Indian Officers and two Indian other ranks of the Tochi Scouts wounded, one Viceroy's Commissioned Officer and two Indian other ranks 2/11 Sikh R. killed and four Indian other ranks wounded of the same battalion. With the exception of one Sapper who was injured during the night march, these were the only casualties sustained by the Bannu Brigade column in the whole course of the operation.

Advance continues.

The 2/11 Sikh R. now took over the Narai from the Tochi Scouts, and extending east and west of it, they with the Tochi Scouts, continued the advance. Reports from the R. A. F. indicated a general withdrawal of the enemy from the ridge in front, during which the close support aircraft did much damage to retreating parties of the enemy.

By 07-15 hours, the leading troops of the 2/11 Sikh R. were astride the Nala in square 0334 about 35 Grid Line, and the 2 A. and S. H., supported by the 19th Mountain Battery, assumed the duties of advanced guard and continued the picketing. No. 12 Fd. Coy. followed close behind them to improve the track if necessary. The 2/4 G. R., the original piqueting battalion, was ordered to collect and come into reserve.

09-00 hours, 12th May. Tochi Scouts on hills over-looking camp site area.

Once the Iblanke Narai was captured there was little opposition. The Tochi Scouts advanced boldly, and by 09-00 hours were in possession of two hills just north of the proposed camp site. They then pushed on and occupied hills to the north west and west of the site.

09-50 hours. 2/4th G. R. advance to picquet camp area.

At 0950 hours, the 2 A. and S. H. had reached the north eastern edge of the Plain. The 2/4 G. R. were then ordered to advance and secure the camp site, occupying hill 016344, already held by the Tochi Scouts, and the hills to the west of the camp about 012332. Their advance across the Plain was slowed up slightly by fire of some of the

CORONATION CAMP, SHAM PLAIN 1937 (MADE BY TO'OL ON CORONATION DAY OF H. M. KING GEORGE VI).

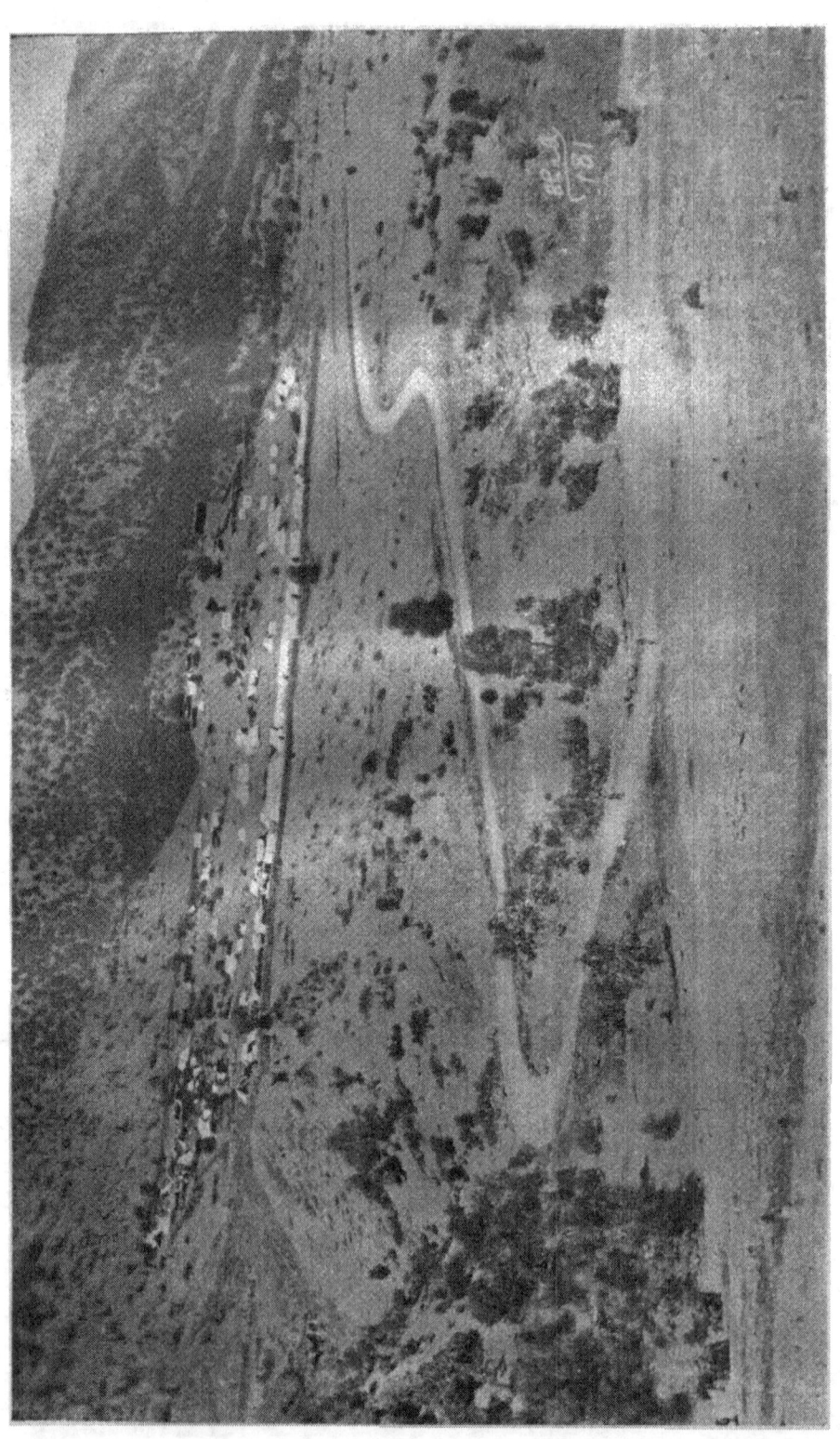

KACH CAMP, MAY 1935.

enemy from the hills west of the Plain who had retreated in front of the Tochi Scouts, but by 1130 hours the Battalion had crossed the Plain and was in occupation of the Camp piquets.

1937.
May.

1130 hours. 2/4 Gurkhas in position. 1320 hours rear guard arrives in camp.

The Brigade Commander then went forward to the camp site which was occupied by the Tochi Scouts at 1205 hours, and decided on the exact position of the camp, the column following him into the camp. The rear guard, which had not been followed up, arrived at 1320 hours.

0615 hours. 12th May. 1st Infantry Brigade advance.

In the meantime the 1st Infantry Brigade, to which one section of the 9th Light Tank Company had been attached for the day's operations, left Village Camp at 0615 hours. The 1/6 G. R. protected the right flank of the Brigade to the exits of the Sre Mela Algad from the hills. The left flank was secured by the 1 Bn. S. Wales Bord. with their forward troops on the highest point (018352) of the ridge overlooking the site of Kach Camp from the east. The 2/6 G. R., moving up between the two battalions to the camp site had obtained a footing on Kach Hill by 1215 hours, the Light Tanks supporting the advance from the nala bed.

The movement throughout was regulated according to the progress made by the Bannu Brigade. Hostile opposition was not serious, only one casualty being sustained by the 1st Infantry Brigade during the day. Camp piquets were established without difficulty although about five hundred tribesmen were estimated to have been present on this part of the front.

1330 hours. Kach Camp established. R. A. F. co-operation.

Kach Camp was established at 1330 hours.

Co-operation by the R. A. F. from dawn was very effective and the aircraft engaged several good targets successfully. At least two sorties used up all their bombs and ammunition, being relieved immediately by sorties "Standing by" in the air above them.

Enemy withdrawal and casualties.

The operations to establish the force on the Sham Plain had been most successful. The enemy were prepared to resist strongly an advance from the north. The brilliant advance by the Bannu Brigade column up the Iblanke spur and the attack on the hostile right flank and rear had surprised and demoralized the enemy to such an extent that serious opposition practically vanished. Although some snipers remained concealed in the dense scrub, there was a general withdrawal by the large majority of tribesmen in a south-westerly direction to escape the converging movement of the columns. In their efforts to get away they presented many targets, and their casualties were estimated as being at least fifty-five.

CHAPTER XII.

Events between the arrival of Waziristan Div. on the Sham Plain and the further advance to Arsal Kot.—May 1937.

1937
May

Immediate result of advance to Sham Plain.

As an immediate result of the successful advance by the Waziristan Division to the Sham Plain, there was a marked decrease in the number of tribesmen in the field. The combined effect of the dissensions going on between the Afghan tribesmen and the Wazirs, of the recent reserves, and of the shortage of food and scarcity of ammunition, showed itself in the departure of many Afghans and of fighting men belonging to the tribes of Waziristan.

Faqir of Ipi's efforts to get support.

In spite of this, the Faqir continued vigorously to try to entice aid to his cause. He himself remained at his cave area at Arsal Kot, guarded by a strong escort of tribesmen, declaring that he would not leave it until troops entered the territory of the Maddi Tori Khel. In defiance of the Afghan authorities, who were still trying to prevent their tribesmen from going to Waziristan, he sent appeals for support once more to Khost. His propaganda among the Mahsuds was intensified. Mullah Fazal Din and the Mahsuds, generally, were sufficiently interested to hold meetings to discuss what they should do. Although the decision was against a tribal rising, there was considerable sympathy for the Faqir's cause and an increasing number of small parties set out to join the lashkars. Mullah Fazal Din, apparently disappointed at the unsatisfactory response made hitherto by the Mahsud tribe to anti-Government propaganda, and afraid of the consequences to himself of his surreptitious support of the Faqir, thought it prudent to ensure his own relations with the Government, and in a somewhat clumsy effort to do so, provided confirmation of his double dealing.

Permanent piqueting on L. of C.

The security of convoys moving from Dosalli Camp to the forward troops up the Sre Mela Algad presented some difficulties owing to the close and difficult nature of the country. To assist the infantry employed on road protection, therefore, the scrub was cleared off the upper slopes of certain dominating hills and permanent piquets, provided with strong barbed-wire defences, were installed on them, whilst Tanks were used to patrol the track and its vicinity.

These arrangements coincided with the introduction of a system of permanent road piquets on the main line of communications from Bannu.

Prior to the 1st of May, as it had been considered wasteful of manpower to render troops immobile by putting them into permanent piquets, the method employed had been to open the road daily with mobile troops from central points. This had involved the employment of escorts of armoured cars and of infantry in lorries with all convoys. It had been found that this method entailed the employment of a large number of troops. Owing to the difficulty of varying the daily procedure, it was now felt that it invited attack, resulting possibly in an unnecessary casualty list. Permanent piquets were found to save the road-protection troops much time and fatigue and to make it easier to adopt different ways of occupying other essential points from day to day. They also put the tribesmen at a disadvantage if they tried to follow up when the troops

LIGHT TANKS ON ROAD PROTECTION DUTY.

withdrew. An unavoidable disadvantage of this system was that the re-provisioning of piquets was often an undertaking of some magnitude, entailing as it did the employment of a large number of men and animals.

Organization of convoys.
With the introduction of permanent piqueting, it was decided to abandon the plan of running all the vehicles which had to be forwarded in one day, a considerable number, as one large convoy. The daily convoys were now organized into sections of twenty five vehicles each at intervals of twenty minutes, control stations being established and sections moving in accordance with a definite time table. If there was an excessive number of vehicles the size of sections, and not the number, was increased. Close infantry escorts were dispensed with. Close escorting by armoured cars was also discarded, the opinion being that these provided better protection by patrolling their allotted sectors before the arrival of the convoy and by securing dangerous localities, constantly varied, during its passing.

Responsibility for L. of C.
By the 16th of May the 1st Division had completed its arrangements for permanent piquets. As the 3rd Infantry Brigade was now in the Dosalli area, the responsibility for the security of the road from the eastern end of the Shinki defile (milestone 14½) to the Rocha Algad (milestone 52) about one mile east of Dosalli Post, lay with the 2nd and 9th Infantry Brigades. These Brigades had their headquarters at Mir Ali and Damdil respectively their sectors meeting at the Nariwela Narai about milestone 40. Towards the end of the month, when the 2nd Infantry Brigade left Mir Ali to take part in operations, their sector was taken over by the 9th Infantry Brigade which came under the direct operational and administrative control of Headquarters Wazirforce. Sometime later, after the road from Dosalli to Razmak which had been closed temporarily during the Sham Plain operations had been re-opened, the 9th Infantry Brigade having been given additional troops was made responsible for the road to the north of Razani.

Extension of proscribed area.
For the security of the troops who had established themselves on the Sham Plain, the Commander Wazirforce decided to extend the area proscribed from the air to the limits for which sanction had been obtained, and with effect from the 13th of May the catchment area of the Sham, Sre Mela, and Babrakra Algads were included in the area.

Moves of formations.*
The next step in the operations was to destroy Arsal Kot and capture the Faqir or drive him away.

The following table shows the moves and their dates, of the three formations concerned in this part of the operations.

Date.	1st Bde.	Bannu Bde.	2nd Bde.
13th May	at Kach Camp	at Coronation Camp	at Mir Ali and L of C.
18th „		to Ghariom	
24th „	to Ghariom		

* [Ref. sketch maps D (chap. XV) and H (chap. XVIII)].

Date	1st Bde.	Bannu Bde.	2nd Bde.
27th May	to Pasal	to Pasal	to Balmoral (near Bichhe Kashkai).
28th „	to Arsal Kot and back to Pasal.	to Arsal Kot and back to Pasal.	towards Arsal Kot.
29th „	to Arsal Kot and back to Pasal.	to Arsal Kot and back to Pasal.	to Pasal.
30th „	to Ghariom.	to Ghariom.	to Coronation.

Progress of motor track. Work on the rough motor track from Dosalli Camp to the Sham Plain commenced immediately and progressed steadily, its head reaching Kach Camp on the 17th of May, and Coronation Camp, (the name given to Camp "A" in memory of the Coronation on the 12th of May of Their Majesties King George VIth and Queen Elizabeth) on the 19th.

Supplies dropped by aircraft. Supplies were forwarded to the camps by a combination of lorry and camel transport. On the 13th of May, as no convoy could reach Coronation Camp, supplies were dropped for the Bannu Brigade by aircraft Approximately 13,000 lbs. in 101 loads were dropped by parachute. Some loads were damaged, but only a few were lost. The surrounding country was so precipitous and air currents so strong that one lightly loaded parachute, instead of dropping on the Plain, was carried three thousand feet above the aircraft before finally coming to the ground.

Troop movements. In preparation for further moves, two battalions of infantry, the 5/12 F. F. R. and the 1/3 G. R., were sent from Razmak to garrison Coronation and Kach Camps respectively. Two more companies of Sappers and Miners were sent to Coronation camp for work on the roads. Troops of the 3rd Infantry Brigade, also came up from Dosalli Camp for line-of-communication duties.

Operations by the Razmak Brigade. In case they might be able to intercept enemy leaving the Sham Plain area, the Razmak Brigade carried out a series of reconnaissances round Razmak visiting Bare Patch, the Engemal Narai, Kabutar Scouts camp, Mir Alam Kot, and Nazhe Narai Algad between the 13th and 20th of May.

Reconnaissance forward for new camp site. On the 14th of May, the Bannu Brigade made a reconnaissance southwards along the Sham Algad in search of a new camp site, more suitably located than Coronation Camp as a starting point for the final stages of the advance. A detachment of Tochi Scouts co-operated, taking up a position to secure the right flank of the earlier part of the advance. An adequate supply of water was found at Ghariom (0527). The withdrawal commenced at 1030 hours. There was no real opposition, enemy activity being confined to long range sniping which caused no casualties.

GHARIOM CAMP 1937.

SAPPERS AND MINERS CONSTRUCTING A BRIDGE FOR THE ROAD NEAR GHARIOM CAMP.

Attempt on a Kach Camp piquet. The camps were subjected to a considerable amount of sniping, but the only attack carried out by the enemy was on the night of the 14th/15th of May, when they made an attempt on one of the Kach Camp piquets. They cut through the barbed wire fence under cover of the scrub and threw a bomb into the post. The bomb was flung back and exploded among the enemy, and they withdrew.

1937
May

More troops arrive at Coronation Camp. On the 17th of May, the 2/1 Punjab R., 1/14 Punjab R., 5/12 F. F. R., and 13 Mtn. Bty. arrived at Coronation Camp for road-protection and garrison duties when the Bannu Brigade column advanced.

Advance to Ghariom Camp 18th May 1937. This advance took place on the 18th of May, when the Bannu Brigade column, reinforced by one section of Light Tanks which had reached Coronation Camp the previous day, left that Camp to establish a new one in the fork of the Sham Algad in square 0527. The name first given to this camp was "Camp B", but it was later changed to "Ghariom".

A camel convoy was to go to Ghariom with the column, and when unloaded return to Coronation Camp.

The first mile and a half of the route was piqueted by the 1/14 Punjab R. supported by the 13 Mtn. Bty., the Bannu Brigade column taking on the protection of the route from there.

This Battalion experienced some difficulty in establishing its final piquets on the right flank on the hills fringing the southern end of the Sham Plain. "A" company was ordered to secure a position in these hills (016314, 024313). As the two forward platoons, Nos. 2 and 4, neared the company objective heavy firing broke out. Meanwhile, the company commander, anticipating that the tribesmen might cause trouble from the direction of two knolls on a spur (028314) to his left front, ordered No. 3 platoon to seize them. As this platoon approached the crest, it was received with heavy fire at ranges from five to twenty yards, and in a determined attempt to assault its objective lost one man killed and four wounded. The company commander, seeing what was happening, took forward his last platoon, No. 1, to the assistance of No. 3, and arrived in time to defeat an enveloping movement by some fifteen or twenty tribesmen against the left flank of the latter. In doing so, the platoon came under fire at point-blank range, and at once lost four men killed, the enemy removing three of their rifles before anything could be done to stop them. A fight now ensued in which another outflanking movement was defeated by fire, and the two knolls were captured. The fire fight continued at close range, and eventually, the tribesmen were compelled to withdraw for a short distance. Later, the company commander organized a further successful advance in which hand grenades were used, and the bodies of the killed were recovered. The ground over which the action was fought was covered with dense scrub and the range of vision seldom exceeded ten yards. It was estimated that about fifty enemy opposed Nos. 1 and 3 platoons, and that these formed part of a much larger body, which, from the tactics employed, seemed to have intended an attack on the left of the company's allotted position.

As soon as the 1/14 Punjab R. had established its piquets, the advanced guard and piqueting troops of the Bannu Brigade column, consisting of the 2 A. and S. H., the 1/17 Dogra R., two rifle companies of the 2/4 G. R., and the 7 Mtn. Bty. passed through them, preceded by eight platoons

1937
May 18th

of the Tochi Scouts, who were given the role of advanced guard mounted troops. As the Tochi Scouts were reaching their second bound, about two miles north of the Ghariom camp site, a detachment on the right, advancing to a thickly wooded feature (037294, afterwards given the name "Conical Hill"), came into contact with tribesmen holding sangars on the edge of the plain. At the same time, enemy opened fire on them from Conical Hill. Two platoons of the Tochi Scouts advanced across the bare open plain to attack this hill. As they were suffering casualties in the advance, a third platoon was sent up to reinforce them. The fire from Conical Hill and from other features east of it intensified, and the Tochi Scouts were finally held up on the north side of a deep open nala running between the plain and their objective.

The two companies of the 2/4 G. R. were furnishing piquets at this time. "A" company had been expended, and it was now the turn of "B" company. Subedar Sahabir had been ordered to take two platoons of this company to piquet Conical Hill. He quickly reached the position where the Tochi Scouts were lying unable to advance. Strong supporting fire was necessary to enable any troops to cross the nala, and the Subedar placed his two light machine guns on a knoll just in rear of the Tochi Scouts for this purpose. Under cover of their fire and of the fire from other piquets already posted, he doubled his command across the nala, where he was joined by the Tochi Scouts. They then rushed the feature and drove off the enemy. In this small action, the Gurkhas lost two men. It was reported later, that the enemy, who were mostly Mahsuds, lost fifteen killed and seventeen wounded. Conical Hill was found to be covered with cleverly built sangars invisible from both ground and air observation.

Whilst this action was taking place on the right flank, strong opposition was being offered by the enemy to the posting of a piquet, from the same company of the 2/4 G. R., on the left. A platoon, supported by artillery and machine-gun fire, had been ordered to hold a hill on this flank, (053314) but was held up about four hundred yards from its objective. Major Weallens, commanding the detachment of the 2/4 G. R., as his companies were now used up, went forward with his headquarters party of six men to this platoon. On reaching the platoon, he found that it had had one man killed and two wounded, and that heavy fire was being brought to bear on it from three directions, one party of about thirty enemy being only a few yards distant just over the crest to the right front, another of twenty about one hundred and fifty yards ahead between the platoon and its objective, and the third on a different feature to the left front. He decided to advance with all available men on the objective in front, supported by artillery and machine-gun fire which was to give moving covering fire along the ridge in front, one rifle section covering the right flank and keeping the thirty enemy engaged, the fire from the left front being kept down by a light automatic weapon. About fifty minutes after Major Weallens reached the platoon the advance began. The enemy to the right front and to the front withdrew, the position of the latter being reached without loss. Just forward of this point there was a clearing in the scrub some fifty yards wide, and beyond it was the piquet's objective. As the platoon entered this clearing, a volley was fired by the enemy at close range from the right flank. Major Weallens heard enemy to the front and saw a party of them working their way through the bushes round his left flank, and realized that his party was heavily outnumbered. He withdrew to the under feature from which he had started and began to

GHARIOM CAMP, AND CARNARVON CASTLE.

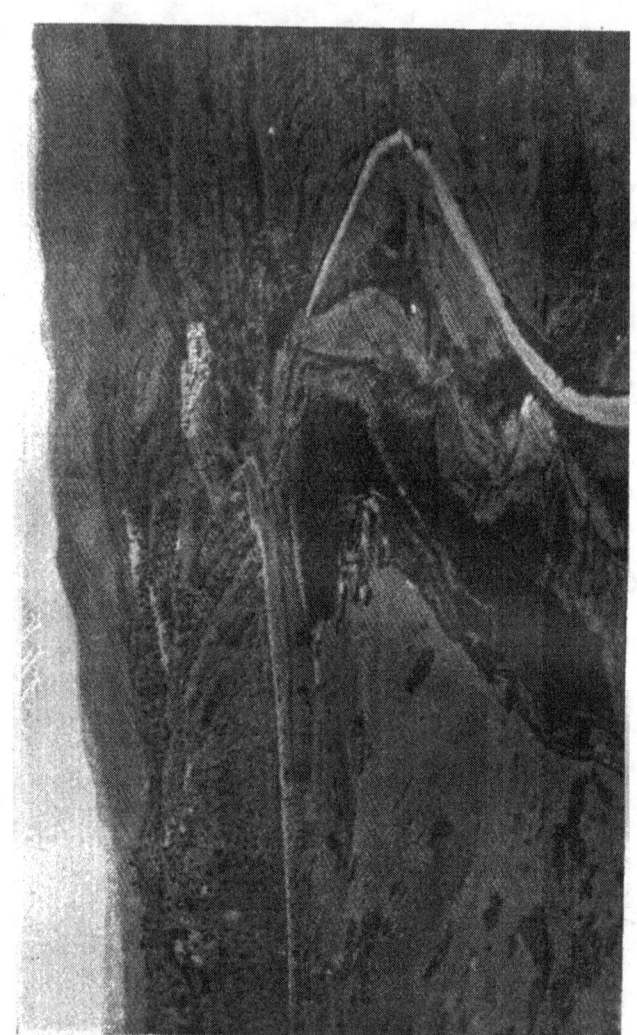

VIEW DOWN SHAM ALGAD, AND BAHADUR CAMP.

organize it for defence. Shortly after this at about 0920 hours a company of the 1/17 Dogra R. supported by the section Light Tanks arrived, and passing through the platoon, occupied the whole position, the enemy retiring as the company advanced. It was found that in this area, also, there was a considerable number of carefully constructed and concealed sangars.

The column now continued its advance, slight opposition being encountered from both flanks and in front. This opposition died away in the afternoon, and camp was reached at 1420 hours, the rear guard which had not been followed up arriving three hours later.

The casualties incurred during the day were, including the Tochi Scouts, seven Indian other ranks killed and twenty three wounded. It was estimated that between three and four hundred tribesmen had been in action against the column, their losses being, approximately, thirty seven killed and thirty seven severely wounded.

Further preparations at Ghariom Camp.
During the next few days troops were assembled in Ghariom camp and final preparations were completed for the advance to Arsal Kot. Stocks of supplies were built up at the camp. Construction of a motor track to the camp was pressed forward so rapidly that on the 23rd of May a motor convoy was able to run from Dosalli Camp and back. The next day, Headquarters Waziristan Division and the 1st Infantry Brigade arrived picking up Nos. 3 and 12, Field Companies Sappers and Miners on the way. The 3rd Infantry Brigade took charge of the protection of the line-of-communication forward to Coronation Camp. The 2/1 Punjab R. of the 3rd Infantry Brigade and the mechanized 4 Fd. Bty. (hows:) were also moved up to Ghariom Camp, to protect the camp with the 1/6 G. R. of the 1st Infantry Brigade during the absence of the Division. Piquets on the main line-of-communication held by units of the 2nd Infantry Brigade were relieved by other troops, and that Brigade was concentrated at Mir Ali, ostensibly for its move to Dosalli Camp. Two additional battalions were brought into Waziristan for employment on the line-of-communication. One battalion, the 3/1 Punjab R., was taken temporarily from line-of-communication duties and attached to the 2nd Infantry Brigade for use in the first stage of the movement of that formation.

Enemy activity.
The enemy who had withdrawn mainly to the east of the Sham Algad when Ghariom Camp was established, continued their activities. Snipers constantly harassed the troops on the Plain and on the line-of-communication, causing a certain number of casualties to men and animals. Parties of tribesmen hovered round, ready to seize any chance of attacking small bodies of troops, watching particularly the relief of piquets. A piquet of the 1/10 Baluch R. was unsuccessfully attacked on the night of the 20th of May at Dosalli Camp, a place where the tribesmen had not hitherto displayed any special activity. On the 21st, the Tochi Scouts were in action against the enemy in the neighbourhood of Ghariom Camp. On the 22nd, the tribesmen made a determined attempt against a small body of the 2nd Battalion The Argyll and Sutherland Highlanders. To reduce the amount of sniping to which the camp was being subjected, some of the piquets to the west were re-sited. One of these re-sited posts was constructed by a party of the 2 A. and S. H., covered by a rifle platoon of the same battalion. When the latter began to withdraw shortly after 1200 hours, one of its forward sections was fiercely attacked by tribesmen, dressed in Khaki clothing similar to that worn by the Tochi

1937
May

Scouts and estimated to be over one hundred in number. Shooting and throwing hand grenades, the enemy killed two and wounded nine of the platoon. The Battalion launched a counter attack from the Camp with a rifle company supported by machine guns and artillery. This party met with long-range sniping, only, and the platoon was brought back to camp. The enemy casualties were estimated to be about the same number as our own.

The following day, tribesmen attacked troops of the 1/17 Dogra R. covering the construction of a piquet (062257) to the south-east of Ghariom Camp. Working up close, the enemy got to within fifty yards of them at one point, but were held off by rifle fire and by grenades, and the withdrawal to camp was carried out without any casualty.

Move of Faqir of Ipi.
From the 20th of May onwards it had been rumoured that the Faqir had at last left his headquarters at Arsal Kot. Eventually, confirmation was received that on the night of the 19th/20th May he had been taken away from Arsal Kot by his personal body guard, a party of some eighty Wazirs and Mahsuds charged with his protection to the point of removing him forcibly if necessary, on the command of Mullah Fazal Din. To prevent his departure becoming generally known no outsiders were allowed to approach the Arsal Kot cave area. The Faqir, however, found an asylum temporarily at Bhawana Manza, some six miles south east of Arap Kot, with Malik Khonia Khel.

Help to Fair of Ipi.
Some of the Faqir's leaders visited the Tori Khel who were showing definite signs of tiring of the hostilities. He himself, despairing of their support, was depending increasingly on the Mahsuds, Bhitannis, and Afghan tribesmen. A number of the Mahsuds had come to join him, and the Bhitannis were responding to his propaganda. Mullah Fazal Din was said to be still helping the Faqir, especially with presents of money, although he had openly declared that he would not oppose the Government unless the Mahsuds definitely declared war. Afghan reinforcements continued to arrive despite the efforts of the Afghan authorities to stop them. The Faqir also spread reports that the Faqir of Shewa, a man with a wide reputation for sanctity, wielding considerable influence particularly among the Kabul Khel Wazirs, would shortly declare himself hostile to Government and was raising lashkars to take the field. The Faqir of Shewa had consistently used his authority on the side of peace and resisted the approaches made to him by the Faqir of Ipi's agents, but this piece of propaganda was well calculated to disturb tribal feelings.

Expecting an attack from both Ghariom Camp and the Khaisora, the majority of the hostile tribesmen, about one thousand in number, remained on the watch in the area to the east of the Sham Algad and in the valleys round about, within easy reach of the force. Altogether, the total number of tribesmen now under arms was much the same as before, between seventeen hundred and two thousand.

Attempts to bomb Datta Khel Post and to destroy bridges.
Those not in the Sham Algad neighbourhood sought opportunities of raiding and of doing what damage they could. An unsuccessful attempt was made during the night of the 18/19th of May to throw a bomb into the Tochi Scouts' Post at Datta Khel. Two nights later, a bridge on the road between Datta Khel and Boya was destroyed. On the night of the 27th of May three

charges of gunpowder were laid in the structure of Idak bridge on the Central Waziristan Road. Two of the charges exploded, but no damage was done.

Tribesmen carried out three serious raids between the 19th of May and the end of the month.

Raid on Umar Tatta Khel.
On the night of the 19th/20th of May a successful raid was carried out by a gang of some seventy Mahsuds on the village of Umar Tatta Khel, in Bannu District, about 9 miles north of Pezu, in which four Hindu girls were kidnapped and a quantity of loot removed. In the course of this enterprise the gang had received, either voluntarily or as the result of pressure applied, promises of help and co-operation in future raids from an inhabitant of Shahbaz Khel, a village about 6 miles north of Pezu. On the 20th of May this raiding gang returned to Bhitanni territory, and having distributed the girls and loot, resolved to organize a fresh raiding gang on a more ambitious scale, fixing as their objective one of the trains travelling from Bannu to Manzai.

*Raid on train in Pezu Pass, May 24th.
On the 24th of May the escort for the train was provided by one rifle company and one machine-gun section, 1/13 F. F. Rif., which was going to Tank to augment the garrison there. The train left Bannu at 0815 hours and at 1045 hours arrived at Lakki.

South-west of Lakki the dangerous section of the line begins. The railway here crosses the Bhitanni hills. This range, bare, stony and almost waterless, rises abruptly from the plains and forms the dividing line between the Bannu and Dera Ismail Khan districts. Scored by deep valleys and precipitous nalas, the range is crossed by two passes. The Pezu Pass lies to the southeast, and through it runs the railway to Tank, in a series of deep cuttings. Further to the north-west is the Bain Pass, over which runs the motor road from Lakki to Tank. The administrative border adjoins the Bain Pass, guarded by a chain of Frontier Constabulary posts at Khairu Khel, Fakir Chauki, and Bain.

On arrival at Lakki the troops were disposed for the protection of the train. The object was two fold, to engage any tribal gangs that might be encountered by fire from the train, and to facilitate rapid detrainment with a view to taking offensive action.

The railway is a single line of 2' 6" gauge, rolling stock is limited, and even with two engines the length of train that can be drawn is governed by the gradients to be negotiated in the pass. It had not at this stage been possible to provide special armoured trucks, though these were improvised later.

The troops were disposed in the following way. One light machine-gun was placed on the leading engine, to fire forward and clear the track. The machine-gun section was mounted on the leading coach, to cover each side of the train. One rifle platoon, ready for action, was disposed in each of the next four carriages. One compartment was reserved as a hospital. The engine-driver was to give a pre-arranged signal by whistle if danger or attack was apprehended.

---

*[Ref. sketch map I 37 (Chap. XII)].

1937
May 24th

The raiding gang, now increased to about three hundred and sixty tribesmen, the large majority being Bhitannis, assembled on the evening of the 23rd of May at a village some seven miles from Bain.

They started off at dusk, and crossed the Bain Pass between the Frontier Constabulary posts at Faqir Chauki and Bain. From the Bain Post onwards the raiders were in the danger area and piquets were therefore dropped at intervals along the hills with a view to securing the unmolested retreat of the gang, hampered, as they hoped to be, with booty. About two-thirds of their total strength was employed on this duty, another forty were left as a reserve and to assist in conveying the loot at a place where water existed, whilst the remainder, sixty men, went on to carry out the actual hold-up.

In the early morning of the 24th they arrived at a rainwater pond near the village of Wazir Khan, west of Shahbaz Khel. Here they were met, by pre-arrangement, by five men from Shahbaz Khel village, who brought food and meat for the party. Discussion then took place as to the most suitable time and place for the raid, the leaders basing their plans on the local knowledge and information given them.

Having settled their plan, the raiding party moved to Pezu Pass, and at about 1415 hours took up positions in the hills by a railway cutting some five hundred yards north of Pezu village. A party was despatched to damage the track with a view to derailing the train, but the first sleeper had not been removed when the train came in sight.

It was climbing the Pezu Pass when there was a signal whistle from the engine, and simultaneously, a burst of fire from the light machine-gun on the engine, which engaged and scattered the party on the line. The leading engine-driver, losing his presence of mind, brought the train to a standstill in a cutting so deep and narrow that it was impossible for the troops to detrain or to open fire. The raiders now opened fire along the whole length of the train. This fire was largely ineffective, particularly on the leading coaches, as the fire of the light machine-gun on the engine and later of the machine-guns in the leading coach prevented the tribesmen from showing their heads over the bank of the cutting. Some casualties, however occurred among the troops crowded in the narrow carriages, the wooden sides of which were not bullet-proof.

After a short period of a little over a minute the engine-driver was prevailed upon to start the engine again. As the train left the cutting, the troops were able to engage the raiders by fire and inflicted three casualties on them. The train now quickened its pace, and the raiders continuing to fire for a few minutes at lengthening range.

Casualties amounted to two men of the escort and one passenger killed and four men of the escort wounded.

Surprised at finding troops on the train, and disappointed of loot, the raiders at once began to withdraw along the line of their previously posted piquets. As they did so they were observed by an aircraft of No. 28 (A.C.) Squadron R. A. F. which attacked with machine-gun fire and wounded at least two raiders.

As soon as information of the raid was received, measures to intercept the raiders were set on foot. One company of infantry supported by one and a half sections of armoured cars, two squadrons of cavalry, and a force of Frontier Constabulary were posted on a general line between Amakhel and Khairu Khel, astride the Bain Pass across the line of withdrawal of the gang. Meanwhile four platoons of Frontier Constabulary moved out from Pezu with the object of driving the raiders against this cordon. The raiders, however, were aided by a heavy dust storm which gave place later to a thunderstorm, natural agencies whose favourable intervention was attributed to the Faqir of Ipi. Although touch was gained with them on three occasions, the raiding gang, which by now had split up into smaller gangs the better to escape observation, succeeded in evading the cordon, and crossing the Bain Pass at about midnight in a heavy thunderstorm, reached Bhitanni tribal territory.

Another raid was carried out on the night of the 21st/22nd of May by a gang of about one hundred and twenty five Mahsuds and Bhitannis on Tajori village, nine miles north-west of Tank. A Hindu woman and a boy who offered some resistance were shot dead, and shops were looted and burnt, the raiders getting away without loss.

Raid on Tajori.

In order to deal more effectively with raiding gangs, the Commander Wazirforce had made certain special arrangements. The more important of these were the following.

Arrangements to deal with raiders.

He was given personal discretion to authorize air action against raiding gangs wherever found, provided that he had no doubt about their identity and that they were not returning with kidnapped victims. Temporary Bhitanni Khassadars, whose pay was to be met by deductions from the allowances of the Dera Ismail Khan Bhitanni Maliks, were sanctioned. In addition to the military forces already stationed in Tank and Manzai, one company of regular infantry and one troop of mounted infantry of the South Waziristan Scouts was to be located at Tank, and one sub-section of armoured cars would go to Bannu for patrolling work in the Pezu Pass area. A striking force of about three hundred and twenty men of the South Waziristan Scouts would be formed at Jandola to deal with raiding into the Tank sub-division. They would be assisted as feasible by the Royal Air Force and by the Civil and Military forces in the Manzai—Tank area.

The civil forces had already been increased in the Bannu-Dera Ismail Khan area. Additional Frontier Constabulary had been brought in, posts had been strengthened, and new ones established. Levies had been raised, and arms had been issued to the inhabitants of certain villages. In May a Civil Defence Officer, with his headquarters at Tank, was appointed, to control the civil operations.

As military forces were now being employed on anti-raiding duties in increasing numbers, General Sir John Coleridge was authorized on the 30th of May to take control of the dispositions of the Frontier Constabulary, the Levies, and the Khassadars in the Bannu and Dera Ismail Khan districts. This control was delegated by him to the commanders of the Bannu and Manzai areas, these officers being instructed that when any operation was contemplated or undertaken, they were to act in the closest co-operation with the Civil Defence Officer, who retained tactical command of the civil forces.

The military commander at Manzai, about the 4th of June, in consultation with the Civil Defence Officer, prepared a co-ordinated scheme for operations against raiding gangs using routes in the Bain Pass area, which was as follows.

The Frontier Constabulary were to form a cordon along the Bain Pass, sangared posts being prepared for use when the occasion arose. Armoured

1937
May

cars supported this party on to their positions. Detachments of regular troops from Khairu Khel and Ghazni Khel and the Bannu Mobile Column, accompanied by Frontier Constabulary, were to extend the cordon north of the Pass to the vicinity of milestone 40, and beyond if necessary. The headquarters of this sector was at Khairu Khel. South of the Pass the cordon was to be taken to about Ama Khel by the South Waziristan Scouts from Mullazai and by the Mobile Columns from Tank and Manzai, their headquarters being at Bain. The detachment of eight platoons of the South Waziristan Scouts at Jandola, if it was not required for other operations, was to go to Pezu, and advancing over the hills between the Pezu and Bain Passes, was to drive any enemy who might be lying up there towards the Bain Pass or out into the plains. An infantry battalion from Mir Ali, which had also been made available if not otherwise employed, was to rendezvous at Ghazni Khel, dropping a detachment at Bannu to replace the troops of the mobile column from there. If the South Waziristan Scouts at Jandola were not available, this battalion was to carry out the "Drive" over the hills. The Commander Manzai Area, with his headquarters probably at Bain, and accompanied by the Civil Defence Officer, was responsible for the conduct of the operations.

To provide an alternative route to the Bain Pass between Lakki Marwat and Tank, the construction of a motorable road between Pezu and the village of Gul Imam was started.

To deal with raids elsewhere beyond the capacity of Area Mobile Columns, reinforcements were to be "stepped up" as the circumstances demanded, either to replace mobile columns which had left their permanent stations or to reinforce them in the area of operations.

In South Waziristan also, there were now some indications of trouble.

Movements of Wana Brigade.* In the early part of May, the Zilli Khel Wana Wazirs showed signs of disaffection, and a lashkar gathered at Chinikwa to the south west of Tanai. This was promptly dispersed by the maliks, who were successful in preventing further large hostile gatherings. Mullah Sher Ali who had led the lashkar which had threatened the Tiarza Scouts' Post in April, tried strenuously to incite the Mahsuds of the Khaisara† valley to embark on hostilities. He received no encouragement, however, from the Mahsud maliks, who were not desirous of hostilities in their own country, and only succeeded in collecting a following of about one hundred individuals from the different sections. He sent small parties to harass the Wana Brigade, and Wana and its piquets were sniped on various occasions. On the 13th of May, the Wana Brigade began an operation with the object of drawing off Khaisara Valley gangs from around Sarwekai and other parties which might be intending raids into the settled districts. A motor track was made northwards towards the Inzar Narai, and the intention was, when the road head had reached a point four miles from the Narai, to establish a camp there and to make a reconnaissance of the Narai on the following day. By the 19th of May Sher Ali had collected his following in the Pakkalita area to oppose any further advance. On that day, however, General Sir John Coleridge decided that in view of projected operations to take place in June the Wana Brigade should not proceed with its plan. Sher Ali and his lashkar remained in the vicinity for a few days in the hope of finding an opportunity of attacking the Brigade, and then dispersed.

*[Ref. sketch map A. in pocket.]
† *N.B.*—The Khaisara Valley in South Waziristan is not to be confused with the Khaisora R. in North Waziristan.

Sketch Map I. 37.

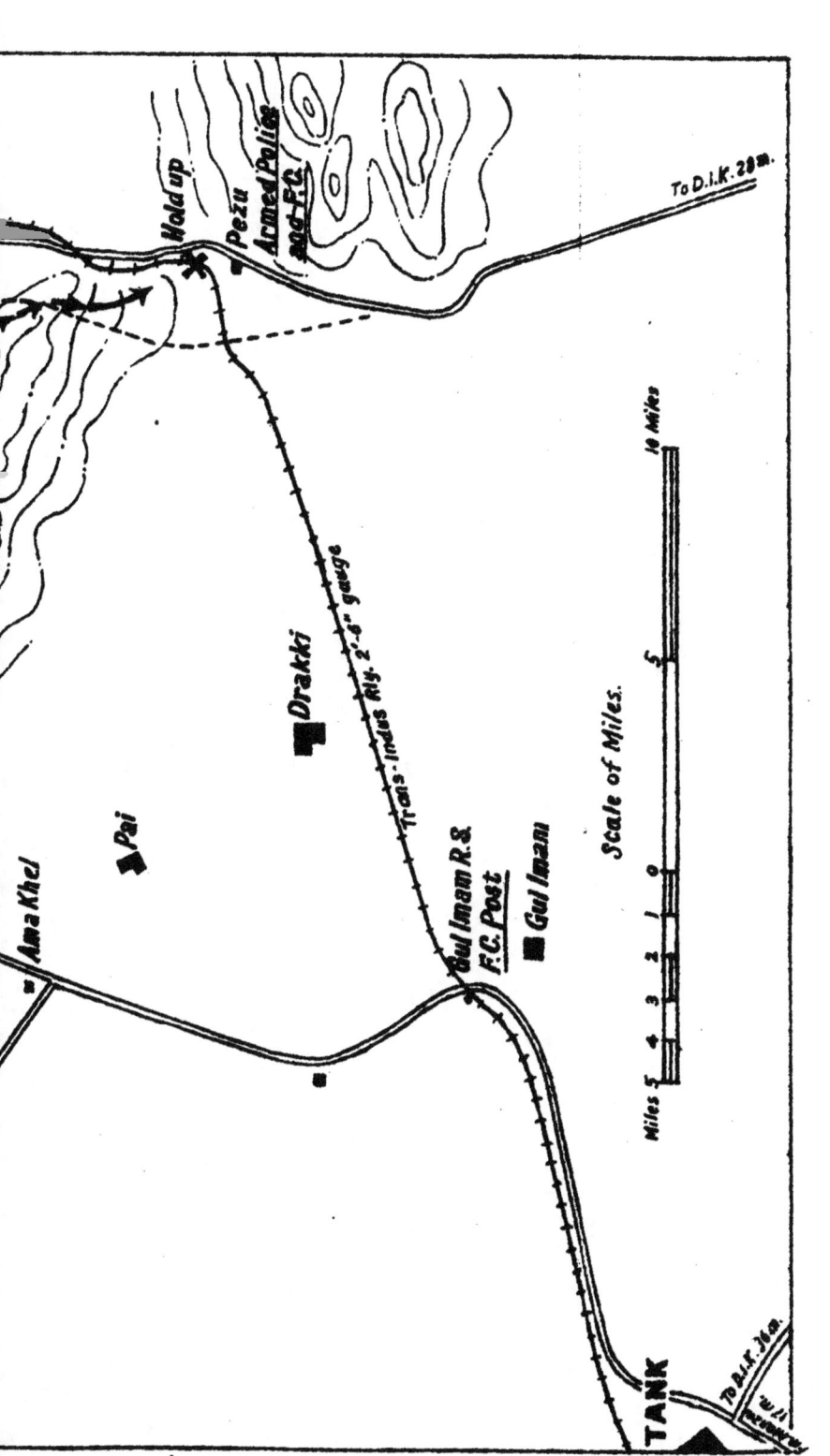

CHAPTER XIII.

Destruction of Arsal Kot and return of the 1st Infantry Brigade and the Bannu Brigade to Ghariom Camp, and of the 2nd Infantry Brigade to Coronation Camp.

<small>* Plan for advance to Arsal Kot.</small>
To carry out his intention of advancing to Arsal Kot the Commander Wazirforce had decided that this advance should be made by a converging movement on two lines. The Bannu and 1st Infantry Brigades were to advance from the Sham Plain, whilst the 2nd Infantry Brigade at Mir Ali would move via Biohhe Kashkai on to Arsal Kot from the northeast. It was considered that the move of the 2nd Infantry Brigade by this route, apart from the advantages of the converging movement itself, would have a good effect in demonstrating to the tribes the ability of the forces to move about their country at will. It would also enable an engineer reconnaissance to be made of the Pasta Algad—Mazai Raghza—Kam Sham route with a view to the possibilities of the construction of a road for mechanical transport. The 2nd Infantry Brigade would have to cover a long distance out of reach of support. The route included a climb from Bichhe Kashkai of over four thousand feet and a march along winding and little known tracks, at a time of the year when the heat is excessive and water supplies at their lowest. It was realized that this march could only be undertaken against slight opposition. It was considered, however, that this condition would be satisfied, as it was likely that the advance from the Sham Plain would draw the majority of the tribesmen in that direction, and, further, the number of enemy in the Lower Khaisora valley did not exceed two hundred and fifty, and there was little doubt that the Tori Khel were weakening in their opposition.

<small>Objects to be attained.</small>
On the 22nd of May Headquarters Wazirforce issued instructions vesting the Commander Waziristan Division with responsibility for the conduct of the advance to Arsal Kot. The objects to be attained were the infliction of a decisive defeat on the hostile lashkars when and where met, the occupation of Arsal Kot and its neighbourhood and the complete destruction of the Kot itself as well as of all property and food materials found therein and adjacent to it. The commander Waziristan Division was made responsible for deciding the hours of start on the same day of the converging columns from Ghariom Camp and Mir Ali and was instructed to effect their junction in the vicinity of Arsal Kot on the following day, thereafter withdrawing both columns to Ghariom Camp.

<small>Routes to Arsal Kot.</small>
One route for the advance from Ghariom Camp was down the Sham Algad to its junction with the Shaktu river at Madamir Kalai and then along the Shaktu to Arsal Kot. This had the considerable disadvantage of bringing the force into early contact with the Mahsuds dwelling just to the south and southwest of Ghariom and might entail conflict from Madamir Kalai onwards with the Mahsuds south of the river.

A more northerly route, therefore, appeared preferable.

There were two possible alternatives, both involving a march for about one and a half miles down the Sham Algad to a point (073265) where a

*[Ref. sketch maps D 37 (chap. XV) and J 37 (Chap. XIII).]

1937
May

track was shown on the map leading off in an easterly direction, and along this track until it met the next tributary of the Shaktu to the east (093266). From this spot, the force could either continue along the track to the next tributary, so avoiding the Shaktu altogether and moving on Arsal Kot from the northwest, or it could follow the tributary from 093266 down its course to its junction with the Shaktu about two miles northeast of Madamir Kalai, and then advance down the Shaktu.

As it was impossible to make any reconnaissance and as the need of secrecy precluded the prosecution of any enquiries about the country to be traversed, when coming to a decision reliance was placed on air photographs. From a careful study of these it appeared that the track across the hills to the second tributary, though marked on the map, was most unlikely to be fit even for camels of the country, and much less so for the several hundred camels from the Punjab which, for lack of pack mules, formed part of the 2nd Line Transport. On the other hand, although no track was shown on the map, the route down the first tributary was better suited for camel transport.

It was decided to use the route from the track-tributary junction (093266) down the first tributary, the march on the first day, the 26th of May, having Pasal Kot (117252) as its objective. On this day, the 2nd Infantry Brigade was to advance from Mir Ali to Bichhe Kashkai, and the next day both columns were to advance to Arsal Kot.

Postponement of advance for 24 hours.

As it was intended to carry out this operation as rapidly as possible and the troops were not to stay in the Arsal Kot area longer than necessary, all arrangements were based on a three-days' absence from Ghariom Camp, and non-essential baggage and supplies were to be left behind at that place. The advance was planned to take place on the 26th of May. On the afternoon of the 25th there was an exceptionally violent storm of rain and hail. Streams came down in spate. The road from Dosalli, particularly between Kach and Coronation Camps, was badly damaged. Ghariom Camp was swamped, rations which were in the process of preparation were spoiled, and the baggage, completely soaked, became heavily overweight. The operation therefore, had to be postponed for twenty four hours. Heavy rain again fell on the 26th rendering the road to Ghariom Camp once more unfit for normal traffic, but the Commander 1st Division decided that unless conditions made it quite impossible to do so, the force must advance without fail on the 27th of May, and orders were issued for a start on the 27th.

Advance from Ghariom Camp to Pasal, 27th May.

Troops left camp before daylight on the 27th protection at the start being ensured by a camp piquet which had been established previously with this object, well forward on the southern flank.

The Tochi Scouts preceded the rest of the force, securing their first objective, a saddle over which the route passed after leaving the Sham Algad, (078265) at 0445 hours without opposition.

The Bannu Brigade, with two battalions of the 1st Infantry Brigade, the S. Wales Bord. and the 2/5 R. G. R. and with the 7, 15, and 19 Mtn. Btys. provided the advanced guard and piqueting troops. In addition, the 4 Fd. Bty. from Ghariom Camp was in support of the initial stages of the advance. The 1/17 Dogra R., starting from the hill on which the southern camp piquet was situated and supported by the 4 Fd. Bty., protected the right flank on the hills about one thousand yards south of

LIGHT TANKS CROSSING THE SHAM ALGAD IN SPATE AT GHARIOM CAMP.

SPATE AT GHARIOM CAMP.

TRANSPORT MOVING DOWN A NALA TOWARDS PASAL.

1937
May 27th

the track as far as the tributary leading to the Shaktu river. The 2/11 Sikh R.. with the 7 Mtn. Bty. in support, assembled in the Sham Algad at 065272. and on the orders of the Brigade Commander, advanced to protect the left flank, moving by the spur running north east from 074273 to point 6031 (0828) and thence along a ridge in a south easterly direction The actual route was secured by the 2/4 G. R. aided by the 19 Mtn. Bty. until the Battalion was used up, when they were succeeded by the 2 A. and S. H. The later stages of protection were carried out by the 1 S. Wales Bord. and by the 2/5 R. G. R.

Troops left camp at 0430 hours, for their assembly positions, and the advance commenced at 0515 hours.

The enemy showed no signs of their presence until the Tochi Scouts, who had been relieved by the advanced guard on their first objective at about 0545 hours, were nearing their second objective, a ridge immediately north of Pasal village. Here there was some slight opposition by a small party of about thirty tribesmen, but the party withdrew south of the Shaktu. The advanced guard reached the river at about 1030 hours. Fifteen minutes later, two companies of the 2/5 R. G. R., with the Tochi Scouts on their left, advanced to secure positions for camp piquets south of the river. Fire was opened on these companies.

Hostile opposition now began to increase steadily, not only south of the river, but also against the rearguard, and piquets on the southern flank of the line of advance.

Although the 2/5. R. G. R. and the Tochi Scouts gained their objectives without loss and a number of casualties were inflicted on the enemy, the tribesmen kept up persistent sniping whilst the camp piquets were being constructed and succeeded in hitting some of the troops. The country on this side of the river favoured the tribesmen as the tops of the hills were too far from the site selected for the camp for it to be practicable to locate piquets on them, and consequently, the sites of the piquets were commanded from higher ground. Hostile fire increased in intensity when the covering troops began to withdraw at 1815 hours. and they were unable to get their casualties away, until three platoons of the Battalion came out from camp to their assistance.

In spite of the difficulties of the route, the transport of the column made good progress, and reached the camp site at about 1245 hours.

The rearguard, the 1st Infantry Brigade less the battalions attached to the Bannu Brigade, met with some opposition during the latter part of the withdrawal. During a rainstorm, early in the afternoon, a piquet of the 2 A. and S. H. on the south flank (0925) was attacked at point-blank range by about fifty enemy when withdrawing from its position on a forward slope, and sustained some losses. In the attempt to bring away their first men hit, more men became casualties, the piquet losing altogether six men killed and seven wounded. A counter attack, made by a company of the 2/6 G. R. was successful in extricating the piquet, although it was not found possible to remove some of the dead.

The enemy continued to follow up the rearguard, which reached camp at 1810 hours.

1937
May 27th

The casualties incurred during the day were six British Other Ranks killed and seven wounded in the A. and S. H., one Gurkha other rank killed and nine wounded, 2/5 R. G. R., and four Indian other ranks wounded, Tochi Scouts.

It was clear that the enemy had intended to offer serious resistance. A large number of unoccupied sangars were found during the march from the saddle onwards, and a position had been prepared round point 6031 (0828). Evidently, the enemy, themselves taking shelter from the inclement weather, had not thought that the force would be ready to start from Ghariom Camp quite so soon. The country in this region would have been very favourable to their tactics, the hills being steep and serrated, and requiring a large number of piquets to ensure the security of the column. They were covered with grass, and had patches of scrub. There were dense masses of scrub in the valleys.

Arrangements of the 2nd Brigade to preserve secrecy.

In order to keep the move of the 2nd Infantry Brigade as secret as possible, no attempt was made to concentrate it before the march. Arrangements were made for the two battalions farthest away to be carried in mechanical transport. In addition, it was given out that the destination of the Brigade was Dosalli Camp, not even Commanding Officers being told the true objective until the 26th of May. No packing up or loading of lorries at Mir Ali was permitted until after the night arrangements had come into force on the day preceding the advance. To reduce transport to its lowest limits no blankets or kits of any sort were allowed, and rations for the 29th were to be drawn from the Waziristan Division. As it was reported that there was no water in the Khaisora river and only a very little at Mazai Raghza, each unit carried a double echelon of water pakhals and every mule carried a chagul.

The orders for the 2nd Infantry Brigade were that they were to camp on the Khaisora river in the neighbourhood of Bichhe Kashkai on the first day of the operations, moving on the second day by Mazai Raghza and Kam Sham to join the Ghariom Camp column at Arsal Kot and continuing with that column to the Sham Plain.

2nd Brigade march to the Khaisora river, 27th May.

For the march to the Khaisora, the Brigade was organized in two columns, a mechanical transport column and a marching column.

The mechanical transport column consisted of the 1/11 Sikh R. from Tal-in-Tochi, the 2/8 Punjab R. from Idak, and one section of No. 2 Fd. Coy. and a supply column from Mir Ali. The two battalions in their lorries met the detachment from Mir Ali at 0530 hours on the 27th of May at the junction of the Bichhe Kashkai track with the Central Waziristan Road. Escorted by one section of the 9th Light Tank Company and by two sections of the 6th Light Tank Company (armoured cars), the column reached the site of the new camp, Balmoral, to the west of the old Bichhe Kashkai camp, at 0820 hours. The construction of the camp was started immediately. The marching column, in which was Brigade Headquarters 2/4 Bombay Grs. (who joined up at the starting point from Khajuri Post at the western end of the Shinki defile), 2/2 Punjab R., 3/1 Punjab R., the 3 and 8 Mtn. Btys. and 1st Line Transport mules of the whole column, left the starting point on the Central Waziristan Road at 0845 hours, and reached Balmoral Camp at 0920 hours. The 3/1 Punjab R., which was not accompanying the Brigade any further in this operation, took over the defences of the camp. With the object of confusing the enemy about operations on the following day, early in the afternoon the 2/8 Punjab R. and the 1/11 Sikh R. made a demonstration a little way up the Khaisora valley. At the same time the Commanding Officers of the two battalions made a reconnaissance south of the river in preparation for the next day's march.

1937
May 28th

No enemy showed themselves during the day.

Route of 2nd Brigade for 28th May.
Brigadier Noyes, commanding the 2nd Infantry Brigade, had been instructed that after concentrating his force at Bichhe Kashkai on the 27th of May, his object was to reach Arsal Kot as quickly as possible so as to allow himself as much daylight as he could for settling in to camp, and that he was, therefore, to make a very early start on the 28th. He decided to leave camp at 0330 hours and to move under cover of darkness up the low Zarinai ridge, south of the Khaisora river, and to be astride the Pasta Algad by first light. From here, the column was to follow tracks to Mazai Raghza via the track junction at 211335. From Mazai Raghza the route was by a south westerly track to Kam Sham via the cross-tracks at 176330, and on via the track junction at 149303, to meet the 1st Infantry Brigade about one mile north of Arsal Kot. As the country, except for the first part of the march, was unknown, a Mahsud had been provided to guide the column.

Destruction of Arsal Kot, 28th May, 1937.
Operations from Pasal on the 28th of May had as their object the destruction of Arsal Kot and the concentration of the 2nd Infantry Brigade with the rest of the force. The Bannu Brigade was to secure the route as far as about three quarters of a mile north and north east of Arsal Kot and carry out the demolition of the village. The 1st Infantry Brigade, passing through the forward line held by the Bannu Brigade, was to advance northwards about one mile and a half and take up a position astride the route by which the 2nd Infantry Brigade would arrive.

The Bannu Brigade left Pasal camp at 0600 hours, moving along the broken plateau above the left bank of the Shaktu river, and thus avoiding the piqueting of the difficult country to the south of the river. It had been reported that the enemy, who had been strengthened by the arrival of Khonia Khel with a party of Mahsuds, were in the hills south of the river about two miles from Arsal Kot. During the night Pasal camp had been sniped, but no enemy were seen during daylight on the 28th.

At about 0730 hours the Bannu Brigade had reached its forward positions, the 1st Infantry Brigade passed through, and preparations for the destruction of the village commenced. As a result of the air bombardment Arsal Kot was almost a complete ruin, only one corner being left standing. A good deal of timber had been salved by the inhabitants and hidden in nalas. This was all burnt before the withdrawal of the troops. There were several buildings and towers in the vicinity however, which had not been damaged by bombs. These were destroyed in the course of the morning. The eight caves, which had been used by the Faqir of Ipi and his following, were grouped on both sides of a deep nala on the hill side about a thousand yards north of Arsal Kot, and by their location afforded immunity from bombing. The largest, presumably that used by the Faqir himself, had four chambers, each about twelve feet in diameter,

1937
May 28th

off a passage about forty feet in length with a height and width of seven feet. The other caves averaged about ten feet in diameter. All the caves were about thirty feet below the level of the ground.

A search of the caves revealed no one in hiding, but a collection of documents found in them was seized.

All demolitions were completed by 1400 hours, the caves requiring 1900 lbs. of gun cotton to destroy them.

The 1st Infantry Brigade established communication with the 2nd Brigade by 1230 hours. As it was unlikely that the latter brigade could reach Arsal Kot in time for the withdrawal to Pasal to be completed in daylight, the commander of that Brigade decided, about an hour later, to halt for the night where he was.

The 1st Infantry Brigade began its withdrawal at 1530 hours, and the rearguard of the Bannu Brigade reached Pasal camp at 1905 hours.

March of 2nd Brigade 28th May.

The 2nd Infantry Brigade left Balmoral camp, as decided, at 0330 hours. Owing to the nature of the country, animals were compelled to move in single file. The protection of the column during the early part of the march was provided by moving flank guards, sixteen platoons Tochi Scouts being employed on each flank. To protect the column as it climbed up the Mazai Raghza spur, the 9th Light Tank company less one section took up a position at first light across the northern end of the Pasta Algad. As soon as the column was out of range of the Tanks, the latter withdrew to Balmoral camp. The 3/1 Punjab R., leaving its protective detachments at the camp, moved out at 0315 hours, quarter of an hour before the start of the Brigade, and advanced up the Khaisora, to create the impression that the Brigade was going to operate in that direction. The Battalion, in accordance with its orders withdrew at 0700 hours, and at 1515 hours, escorted by the Light Tank companies, returned in lorries to Mir Ali. In order to assist in the deception of any enemy, artillery from Damdil Camp fired during the morning on pre-arranged targets in the Lower Khaisora valley as far east as Zerpezai.

The country over which the Brigade was advancing was very broken and difficult, but at 0800 hours, the head of the column reached the vicinity of the track junction, (211335) about one and a half miles south east of Mazai Raghza. Here a halt of one and a quarter hours was made, to allow the column to close up. By 1030 hours the leading troops were at Mazai Raghza, the animals still in single file traversing the long narrow col leading to the village. It was now apparent that the moving flank guards could no longer keep up with the column, and ordinary piqueting commenced. This change necessarily entailed some delay, and the rate of march was unavoidably reduced. By midday the Brigade was passing over an open plain said by the Mahsud guide to be the Kam Sham Plain. Actually, it was not the Kam Sham but another, unidentifiable on the map, running parallel to and east of the Kam Sham, but this was not realized at the time. Half an hour later, at 1230 hours, touch was gained with the 1st Infantry Brigade, and messages were received indicating that Divisional Headquarters required the head of the 2nd Infantry Brigade to be well behind the forward troops of the Division by 1400 hours, that assistance could not be given if the 2nd Infantry Brigade used a route other than that decided on, and that the 1st Infantry Brigade would have to begin its withdrawal at 1530 hours if it was to reach camp before dark.

At 1340 hours, Brigadier Noyes, who had joined the rearguard to give some special instructions in person, saw the head of the column in the distance moving up a steep spur in a southerly instead of a westerly direction. Arriving at the head about twenty minutes later, he ordered a halt to be made. It was now clear to him that the Brigade, misled by the Mahsud guide, was not on the correct route. His troops were considerably exhausted. In addition to the long march of the previous day, they had had some twelve hours of marching and climbing, including some heavy piqueting, in oppressive heat. More severe climbing would be necessary before the position of the 1st Infantry Brigade could be reached. As it was now impossible to comply with the order to be well behind the line of the 1st Infantry Brigade by 1400 hours, Brigadier Noyes decided that the interests of the Division would best be served if he made up his mind at once to halt where he was for the night, so enabling the two brigades in the Arsal Kot area to return to their camp in good time before darkness fell.

1400 hours. 28th May. Commander 2nd Brigade decides to camp where he is.

1937
May

A camping ground (169307), suitable in every way for defence, was found, but water was not available. The animals, which had been watered earlier in the day, had to go without it. The arrangements which had been made for extra water with the column enabled every man to have a small quantity, but this was not sufficient after the hot and trying march.

The tribesmen had taken no action during the day except to fire a few long-distance shots. However, always alert to take advantage of a mistake, a few of them lay in waiting over a rain-water hole, in a nala below the camp. Here, three men, one of whom was killed and two were wounded, paid the penalty for their lack of discipline in creeping out of camp before the perimeter defences were completed to search for more water.

When night fell, the temperature dropped sharply, and there being no blankets, little sleep was obtainable owing to the cold.

The following day, the 29th of May, the 1st Infantry Brigade and the Bannu Brigade moved out to the positions they had held on the 28th. The 2nd Infantry Brigade, assisted by aircraft which showed the line of the track to be followed by firing Verey lights over it, passed through these two brigades and went to Pasal Camp. Meanwhile, further demolitions of Tori Khel property in the Shaktu valley were carried out. All the troops were back in Pasal Camp by 1545 hours.

29th May. Further destruction carried out. Brigades from Pasal advance to meet 2nd Brigade which marches through to Pasal.

On the 30th of May, the Waziristan Division, including the 2nd Infantry Brigade, marched back to the Sham Plain, following the route which had been taken on the 27th. The Bannu Brigade, reinforced by the Tochi Scouts' detachment and the 1st S. Wales Bord. of the 1st Infantry Brigade, formed the advanced guard and piqueting troops. The two remaining battalions of the 1st Infantry Brigade, with one rifle company and a machine gun platoon of the 2/4 G. R. from the Bannu Brigade composed the rear guard. The 2nd Infantry Brigade was in the main body.

30th May. Force withdraws to Ghariom and Coronation Camps.

1937

May 30th

The advanced guard started at 0400 hours and piqueted the route to Ghariom camp without meeting any opposition.

Contrary to expectation, although some sniping began at 0730 hours, the withdrawal of the camp piquets from the south of the Shaktu river was not seriously interfered with until the last of the troops had crossed to the north bank about one and a half hours later. A large number of enemy had been seen crossing the river about a mile to the west and making for the southern flank of the line of withdrawal.

The tribesmen followed up the rearguard which was provided by the 2/5 R. G. R. and the 2/6 G. R. alternatively. They not only engaged the retiring piquets at close quarters but advancing along the bed of the nala itself behind the rear party, showing great skill and boldness in endeavours to close with the troops. On one occasion a party of four tribesmen were shot down at a range of only one hundred yards. The withdrawal of the piquets went on successfully until about 1100 hours, when a piquet of the 2nd Battalion The Argyll and Sutherland Highlanders had difficulty in getting away. This party was on a position (about 098254) in the vicinity of the place where one of their piquets had been attacked on the 27th of May. It came under heavy fire and eight men were wounded. The enemy were pressing hard. The situation was relieved by the advance of two rifle platoons of the 2/6 G. R. from the rearguard. which covered the retirement of the piquet, any further advance by the enemy being then effectively checked by artillery fire directed on to the vacated position.

Later on in the withdrawal, an attempt by the tribesmen, whose pressure increased as the day wore on, to attack a piquet of the 2/4 G. R., was defeated owing to arrangements made in advance for covering fire. It was anticipated by the Commanding Officer that this piquet might have some difficulty in withdrawing, as, having left the ridge on which the piquet was posted, the men would have to move across a steeply sloping plain with no cover and in full view of covered positions from which the enemy could open fire. It was arranged that, as soon as the piquet commenced to retire, the fire of ten 3·7" howitzers should be brought down on the far side of the piquet site, whilst twelve machine-guns fired at the crest line. As the piquet left its position a party of about sixty enemy rushed forward towards it. As soon as they realized the volume of the covering fire they ran back again. The piquet got away without a shot being fired at it.

The portion of the route which followed the tributary of the Shaktu, and against which the enemy concentrated their efforts, presented many obstacles to the movement of animals and at times there was considerable congestion of the transport towards the rear. This prevented troops of the rearguard from moving back to fresh positions, and twice a stand had to be made by the rear party to hold off the tribesmen until the press of animals had been cleared. As soon as the rearguard reached the high ground on the east bank of the Sham Algad, where the Division was in direct touch with the permanent piquets of Ghariom Camp and well within range of the field battery there, the enemy drew off.

The enemy strength during the day was estimated at from two to three hundred, of whom a large proportion were Mahsuds. This was evident from the way in which they employed enveloping tactics and the

1937 May

manner in which individuals on occasions freely exposed themselves. Twenty three of them were believed to have been killed.

The casualties in the Waziristan Division for the day were one British Officer and one British other rank killed, nine British and four Indian and Gurkha other ranks wounded.

Enemy casualties between the 23rd and 30th of May, both dates inclusive, had been fifty nine killed and forty five severely wounded. These figures include twenty four Mahsuds killed and seventeen severely wounded.

These figures bring the total of enemy casualties from the 25th of November 1936 to the 30th of May 1937 to seven hundred and fifteen killed and six hundred and fifty seven wounded. During the same period, the casualties among the forces in Waziristan had been one hundred and sixty four (including fifteen British officers) killed and four hundred and thirty one (including fourteen British officers) wounded.

If slightly wounded be included, the enemy's total casualties may be taken as not less than two thousand.

The 2nd Infantry Brigade and attached troops dropping two battalions at Ghariom Camp, marched through to Coronation Camp, at which place their baggage and animals from Mir Ali had already arrived. The rest of the force occupied Ghariom Camp.

All troops were in camp just after 1700 hours.

The Waziristan Division, which, on the 27th of May had negotiated the same route, then unknown, in fifteen hours, had this day covered the six and a half miles of mountain track in just over thirteen hours, having with it all the additional troops and animals of the 2nd Infantry Brigade.

27th May. Small column goes to Razani to repair the road and to intercept any hostile parties.

Whilst these operations were going on from the Sham Plain, a small column was sent to Razani on the 27th of May to undertake the repair of the Pariat Bridge and of other damage in its vicinity, a thing it had not been practicable to do any earlier, and to intercept any hostile parties leaving the lashkars opposing the Waziristan Division.

The column was commanded by Major A. Felix Williams, M. C., Commandant of the Tochi Scouts, and consisted of thirteen platoons of the Tochi Scouts, one section of the 63rd Field Battery, one section of No. 15 Field Company, one rifle company and a machine gun platoon of the 1/2 G. R., with Signals, Transport, and Medical detachments.

Although ambushes were laid nightly on the 27th, 28th and 29th of May only one small hostile party was met.

A diversion round the Pariat bridge was made, enabling motor traffic to and from Razmak, which had been interrupted for about three weeks, to be resumed, and the bridge itself was repaired by the 1st of June, the running of convoys to Razmak being resumed on the 4th of June.

Tori Khel overtures for peace.

When it was decided at the end of April 1937 to make the Tori Khel country south of the Khaisora river an area proscribed from the air, a sanctuary was established in the Spinwam area for those members of the tribe who did not wish to oppose Government. This region had been used to an increasing extent by hostile tribesmen as a haven of refuge in which to

1937
May

recuperate before returning to the field. Two warnings given by the Political Authorities about this practice had been disregarded. Eventually, the threat of the withdrawal of the concession drove the Dreplarai Tori Khel, who were responsible for its abuse, to mend their ways. At about the same time the Shogi Tori Khel of the Sein area begged that the air proscription of their territory might cease, giving an assurance that they would submit to the terms of Government and refrain from any further hostilities. These defections, the forced departure of the Faqir from Arsal Kot, the effects of the air proscription in their territory which had led to a general deficiency of supplies and much hardship, and the persuasion of some maliks of importance belonging to other tribes, all combined to bring about a general decision of the Tori Khel to ask for peace. Messengers from all sections came in to announce that they were prepared to submit to the orders of Government.

On the 30th of May they were told that if there was in fact a general desire for peace, their jirga should assemble at Spalga, on the 3rd of June to discuss matters among themselves, and that two days later the jirga should assemble at Miranshah.

Meanwhile the air proscription, which had been lifted from the Arap Kot area on the 19th of May, and from the Sein area on the 20th, was stopped over other parts of their territory except in the Shinki area and in the immediate vicinity of the troops on the 30th of May, to enable the maliks to meet in safety.

Throughout this period air co-operation was provided by units of No. 3 (Indian) Wing. The major task of tactical reconnaissance and close support of troops was carried out by No. 20 (A.C.) Squadron, a Flight of No. 28 (A.C.) Squadron, being moved from Manzai to Miranshah to assist them between the 24th and 31st of May. During the four days of the advance to Arsal Kot and the subsequent withdrawal, No. 20 (A.C.) Squadron averaged over forty eight flying hours per day, and during the month of May they flew 919 hours. No. 28 (A.C.) Squadron, with a strength of two flights, during this period flew a total of eight hundred and eight hours.

R. A. F. co-operation.

R. A. F. Officers accompanied the various columns during these operations.

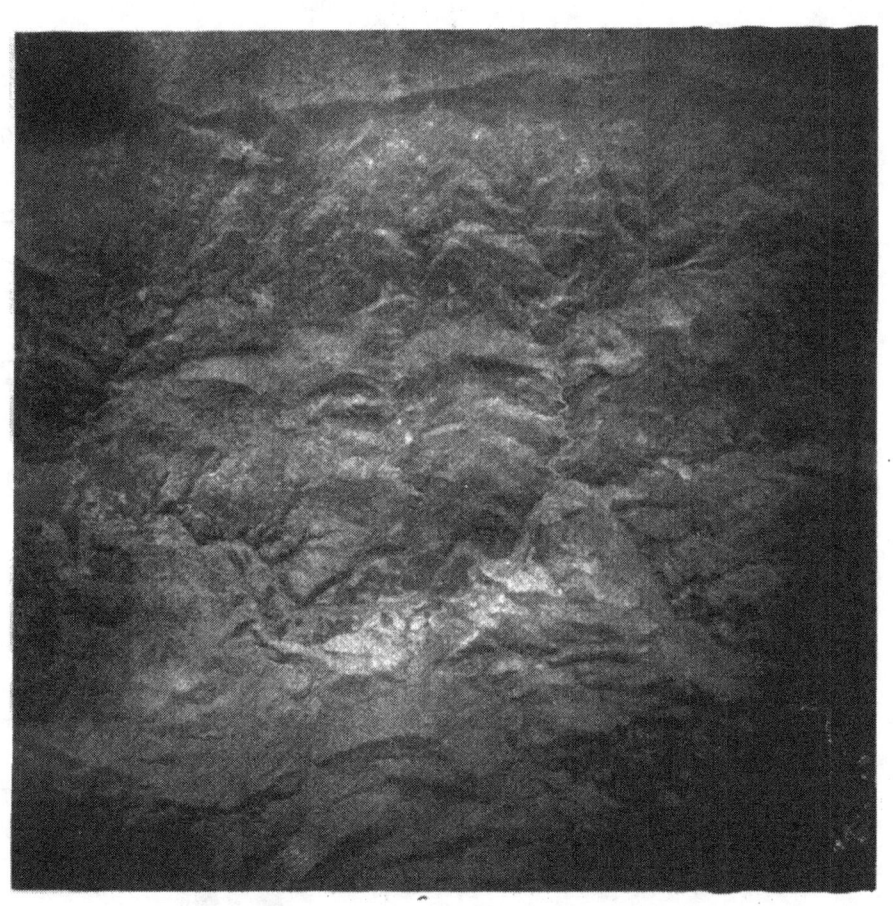

SHAKTU RIVER NEAR GULZAMIR KOT.

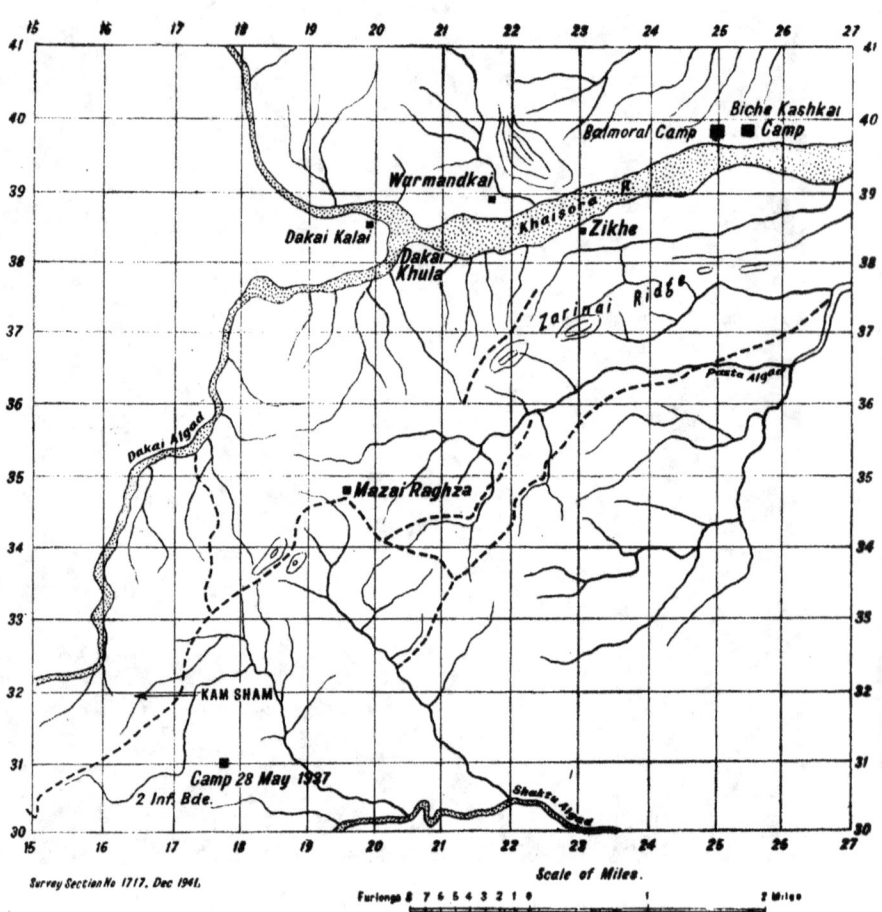

CHAPTER XIV.

Return of Bannu Brigade to Razmak *via* Sora'ogha. June 1937.

1937
May

At a conference held at Dosalli on the 15th of May, General Sir John Coleridge, besides explaining his intentions for the advance to Arsal Kot, had outlined his proposals for dealing with the Mahsuds as soon as the current operations were concluded, and had also announced his views on road-making.

*Proposals of the Commander Wazirforce for dealing with the Mahsuds and for road-construction.

After consultation with the Governor of the North-West Frontier Province, he had forwarded his recommendations regarding the roads to be made to the Government of India on the 16th of May. It was pointed out that the area which it was desired to open out was cut by the Shaktu river. To the north of this river lay Tori Khel Wazir territory, and to the south, that of the Shabi Khel, Kikarai, Galeshai, and Jalal Khel Mahsuds. In this latter area, also, were found small numbers of other Mahsuds tribes as well as the "Hill" Bhitannis. The first essential therefore was considered to be a road from Dosalli to Ahmedwam *via* the Sham Plain and the Barari Narai which would go through the heart of what was termed "the back area". The second essential was thought to be a road running down the Shaktu valley. If financial considerations permitted and it were technically possible, it was recommended that this latter road should start from Razmak and go over the Engemal Narai to the sources of the Shaktu river, as, without this direct communication with Razmak, troops in Razmak would have to go a considerable distance before reaching the road. At the eastern end, it was suggested, the road should either be taken to Jani Khel or be joined up near Sein in the Khaisora valley to the road recently constructed to Dreghundai. To complete the system other roads were recommended as desirable. These were, one to connect the road-head at Bichhe Kashkai with the Shaktu river, another to connect Piaza Raghza with the Razmak-Shaktu river road, and a third leading from the Barari Narai on the Dosalli-Ahmedwam road eastward along the top of the watershed to the Sammal Narai, overlooking the country of the "Hill" Bhitannis. Looking to the future, this third branch might be extended from Sammal Narai into Gabbar and Saraghar, the strongholds of the Bhitannis, with outlets to the plain at Tajori and Jandola. Some of these roads, it was suggested, could probably be made by means of contracts given to the tribesmen provided that the troops were still in occupation of the country. It would not be safe to assume that after evacuating the country it would be possible to enforce construction by tribal means, and it would have to be made plain to the tribes that if they were unwilling to make the roads they would be made by force.

Referring to the Dosalli-Ahmedwam road, General Sir John Coleridge pointed out that work had already started on the section from Dosalli to Madamir Kalai as part of the operations then in progress, and asked for immediate sanction to complete it and to begin construction of the portion from Madamir Kalai to Ahmedwam during the next fortnight. He hoped that the latter could be made by tribal labour under their own contractors, and on authority being received the tribes concerned would be informed of Government's intentions.

---

*[Ref. sketch maps A. T 37; and U 37, in pocket.]

1937
May

Construction of roads sanctioned.

On the 22nd of May the Government of India sanctioned the construction of the complete road from Dosalli to Ahmedwam *via* Madamir Kalai and also agreed to the construction of a road from Razmak to Bichhe Kashkai joining up with the former road. Other roads recommended were thought not to be necessary for the present. No announcement was to be made to the tribes of the intention to build the roads, whether under tribal contract or by force, until the operations aiming at the occupation of Arsal Kot had been successfully concluded.

Re-organization of Divisions and their tasks.

General Sir John Coleridge decided that on the return of the troops from the Arsal Kot operations, the brigades of the Waziristan and 1st Divisions should return to the command of their respective divisional commanders as soon as possible, with a view to further operations. Major General de Burgh, commanding the 1st Division, was to resume command of his three brigades and to assume operational control in the Sham Plain-Shaktu River area. The 1st Division was to remain in that area to deal with any further opposition and to cover the road-making, on which a proportion of the infantry was to be employed. Work on the Dosalli-Ahmedwam road was to be pressed on, its construction and security taking priority over punitive operations, subject to circumstances. The Waziristan Division was to march through Mahsud territory, the first step being a march by the Bannu Brigade from Ghariom Camp to Razmak *via* Janata and Sorarogha, the Brigade returning to the command of Waziristan Division Headquarters on arrival at Sorarogha. After this, the Razmak Brigade was to carry out operations round Ladha. This would necessitate the return to Razmak of the two infantry battalions which had been sent to the Sham Plain in May for work on the motor track. Finally, the Waziristan Division was to concentrate in the Khaisora valley, the Wana Brigade moving to Sarwekai and thence northwards. The 9th Infantry Brigade would be responsible for the main line of communications to Dosalli from the east, and a detachment of the Tochi Scouts was to be established between Razani and Razmak to assist in the protection of the road west of Dosalli. The completion of all these movements would, it was considered, besides restoring the lines of communications between Dosalli and Razmak, result in the re-opening of them between Jandola and Razmak and Jandola and Wana. The latter line had been closed for some weeks, supplies being delivered in Wana by Mahsud lorries.

Instructions issued to Commanders 1st Division and Waziristan Division.

In accordance with these decisions, Headquarters Wazirforce issued instructions to the Commanders of the 1st and Waziristan Divisions on the 29th of May which specified that the following objects were to be attained.

A. To repair and open the road from Dosalli to Razmak. This was to be carried out under the orders of the Commander Waziristan Division.

B. To move a column from the Sham Plain to Sorarogha Scouts' Post, and thence to Razmak, thus traversing territory occupied by the Kikarai, Shabi Khel, and Galeshai Mahsuds, who had contributed a large number of fighting men to assist the Faqir of Ipi. The march was to be undertaken by the Bannu Brigade, which, coming under the orders of the Commander 1st Division on the 31st of May, was to march *via* Janata assisted by the 1st Infantry Brigade as far as Barari Narai. On the day of the advance of the Bannu Brigade to Janata, the 6th of June, Mahsud villagers living between the Barari Narai and Janata were to be ordered to remain in their villages until the Brigade was established in its camp. On arrival at Sorarogha the Bannu Brigade was to revert to the command of the Commander Waziristan Division, who was instructed to arrange for the Razmak Brigade to move to Piazha Raghza by the 8th of June to assist the advance of the Bannu Brigade on the next day. After this, the Razmak Brigade was to go to Ladha, the Bannu Brigade moving to Razmak. Detachments of the South Waziristan Scouts from Sorarogha or Ladha were to co-operate with regular troops in all these movements.

C. To construct a permanent motor road from Dosalli Post to some place on the Shaktu river, to be settled later. Protective arrangements for this were to be made by the Commander 1st Division. Eight platoons of the Tochi Scouts, released from the Waziristan Division, were to come under his command from the 31st of May.

The Commander 1st Division was made responsible for the maintenance of the existing motor track to Ghariom Camp from the same date, and was informed that the work on the permanent motor road, to be carried out by military and contract labour as circumstances permitted, would begin as soon as labour could be made available.

D. The despatch of columns to areas which would be specified in due course. The Commander 1st Division was to be prepared to undertake this, the column or columns being based on a three days' circuit of action.

Allotment of R.A.F. From the 31st of May, No. 20 (A. C.) Squadron Royal Air Force was to be transferred from the Waziristan Division to the 1st Division; and from the 8th of June, No. 28 (A. C.) Squadron, less the daily sorties was to come under the Waziristan Division. Headquarters, No. 3 (Indian) Wing, Royal Air Force, was to be located at Miranshah.

Troop movements in preparation for further operations. During the last three days of May and the first three days of June, movements were carried out to get Headquarters and units into their right places for these forthcoming operations. Headquarters 1st Division opened at Dosalli on the 29th of May, the operation headquarters going to Ghariom Camp the next day to control the arrangements for the march of the Bannu Brigade. Waziristan Division Headquarters moved to Razmak on the 2nd of June, the 5/12 F. F. R. and the 1/3 G. R. left the Sham Plain on the 31st of May, arriving in Razmak on the 3rd of June. The 1st Infantry Brigade, the Bannu Brigade, and two battalions of the 2nd Infantry Brigade remained at Ghariom Camp, the rest of the 2nd Infantry Brigade staying in Coronation Camp. The 3rd Infantry Brigade continued grouped in the Dosalli-Kach Camp area. The 2 A. and S. H. left the Bannu Brigade and went to Dosalli, their place in that Brigade being taken by the 2/1 Punjab R. The 1/2 G. R. also, moved to Dosalli from Miranshah.

Re-adjustment of responsibility for L. of C. From the 1st of June the 1st Division was made responsible for the protection of the line of communications between milestones 52 and 54 on the Central Waziristan Road and from Dosalli Post to the Sham valley. From milestone 54 to Razmak protection was provided by the Waziristan Division. The 3/15 Punjab R., with one section of the 7th Field Battery and one section of the 9th Light Tank Company was sent to Razani for the protection of the Razani sector. On their arrival, the column commanded

1937

June

by Major Felix Williams at Razani broke up, ten platoons of the Tochi Scouts establishing a new camp at Razmak Narai, the remaining three platoons returning to Miranshah. The troops in Razmak provided for the security of the road from Razmak to near Alexandra Ridge Piquet, the gap from there to the Razani sector being filled by the Tochi Scouts at Razmak Narai.

On the 3rd of June, the former 1st Division Area became the 9th Infantry Brigade Area, the Brigade having under its command all the regular troops and Scouts in the area except the 2nd Infantry Brigade and attached troops previously under the 1st Division. It became responsible for the security of the line of communications from milestone 14½ near Saidgi to milestone 52 and to Miranshah.

The Razmak Brigade continued its reconnaissances and operations con-nected with securing the road, meeting with no opposition except on the 4th of June.

*Operations of Razmak Brigade. Attack on road piquet at Gaj.

On this occasion, the Brigade was piqueting the main road to Razmak Narai for the protection of a convoy, and a platoon of the 6/13 F. F. Rif., which was ordered to secure a hill (883279) not far from Gaj Piquet, was attacked.

On arrival at their position, the troops saw a party of armed tribesmen at a tower on a ridge a few hundred yards to their southwest. Suspecting that these men were a potential danger, the piquet commander, an Indian Commissioned Officer, reported their presence. He was given orders that as they were in Mohmit Khel country fire was not to be opened on them unless they fired first or acted in a suspicious manner, but they were to be kept under close observation. Finding that it was not possible to see from the piquet position into a nala to the north of it, the piquet commander took forward two rifle sections (a total of seven men) to a point about one hundred yards from the main piquet position and posted them in three groups. The scrub in this area was so thick that these groups could only see about forty yards of the nala.

When the sections arrived at this forward position three men had been seen ploughing in the fields nearby. By the time the forward sections had been posted one of these men had disappeared, presumably to give information to the armed party. The piquet commander called up one of the remaining two to him, intending to hold him as a hostage. He was returning with this man to the main position when a man purporting to be a Khassadar although he had no badge (actually it was no unusual thing for a Khassadar to have no outward sign of identification), came up from the nala and said that he had orders to take the person whom the piquet commander had with him back to the Assistant Political Officer. Having been warned that a Khassadar was on his way to join him, the man was handed over. The Khassadar then volunteered the information that this man and the other one working in the fields were relatives of his, and asked that the tower should not be fired at as it belonged to his family. He also asked whether any armed men had been seen near the tower, and being told that they had though they were no longer visible said no more and departed with his relative. Neither of these men reached the Assistant Political Officer. Later in the day

---

* [Ref. sketch map K 37 (Chap. XXIII).]

the man still working in the fields was joined by another, and the former taking a water jar, went off to some huts near the tower, reappearing shortly afterwards without it.

When the red flag of the rearguard came in sight on the road to the north, the piquet commander decided to withdraw his forward party in order to be ready to retire when he received the permissive signal. As these men got to their feet a volley was fired at the centre pair from the direction of the tower, killing one man and wounding the other. The party continued to withdraw leaving the dead sepoy on the ground, and the piquet commander ordered an immediate counter attack with his remaining section. Light Machine-gun and rifle fire was opened at the place from which the enemy had fired, considerable movement was seen near the tower, and firing became general. The section which had been ordered to counter-attack, taking the men of the forward sections with it, reached the forward position within four or five minutes of the opening volley, but in that time three of the enemy, as was seen from a neighbouring piquet, had rushed in, apparently from the nala to the north and had seized the dead sepoy's rifle and equipment and had got away.

As soon as the firing started an artillery observation officer was sent to the piquet. The guns opened fire, and after an action lasting for about quarter of an hour, the piquet withdrew without further trouble.

At the beginning of June and again later on in the month offensive air action was taken against the Bhitannis. Their jirga was summoned on the 29th of May. Their representatives admitted complicity in the kidnapping of the Hindu girls from Umar Tatta Khel and also in the raid on the train in the Pezu Pass. They also admitted their responsibility for stopping raiding gangs passing through their country and for safeguarding the passes. They were informed that as a punishment Government had decided to destroy certain of their villages. For this reason an area two miles round Kot (4113) and an area two miles round Allahdad Qahata (3007) seven miles west of Kot were to be completely evacuated by midnight on the 31st May/1st June, since thereafter these areas would be subject to offensive action until further notice. They were informed that these areas were not to be re-occupied until Government had given them notice that it was safe to do so. They were also informed that Government had decided to enlist one hundred and twenty additional Khassadars of their own choice, the pay, Rs. 20 a month, of these men being deducted from the Bhitanni allowances.

*Air action against the Bhitannis.

On the 1st of June the destruction of the three villages of Bara Kile and Raghzai Kile near Kot and Lowazhi near Allahdad Qahata (Map A) was undertaken by one flight of No. 27 (B) Squadron and one flight of map "A" No. 60 (B) Squadron from Kohat. Both explosive and incendiary bombs were used. Bombing was continued on the 2nd of June, when the work of destruction was completed. Ninety per cent. of hutments and surrounding serais were completely burnt out during the operations.

As the Bhitanni maliks still failed to produce the kidnapped girls, air action was taken on the 12th of June against Tali Palosai (4013) and on the watermill and homestead of the Din Faqir near Kot. Bombing of these targets was carried out on the 13th and 14th of June also, with considerable success. On the 21st of June the three girls were

---
*[Ref. sketch map S 37 (Chap. XXV).]

1937

June

brought into Tajori Post by Jani Khel maliks, the Bhitanni maliks themselves paying Rs. 1,200 to the kidnapper to avoid the further punishment expected.

On the 21st, a full jirga was held with the Bhitanni section. The jirga was submissive but stated their inability to accept responsibility for the actions of the Bhitanni sections of Dera Ismail Khan and the adjoining tribal territory. The Waruki section of the Dhanni Bhitannis had not yet handed over their hostages. The situation regarding the Bhitanni, therefore, although improved, was not yet satisfactory.

*Arrangements for the march of the Bannu Brigade to Sorarogha were now complete.

*Arrangements for march of Bannu Brigade to Sorarogha.

On the 2nd of June the 1st Infantry Brigade at Ghariom had carried out a reconnaissance of the route down the Sham Algad towards Madamir Kalai (1022) improving the track as much as possible.

Although it was hoped that the column would be met and assisted by the local maliks, the attitude of the inhabitants of the country to be traversed was still uncertain, and any plan made had to take into consideration the possibility of opposition. An air reconnaissance to Janata had in fact shown that sangars were being constructed in that area. The route from Ghariom Camp to Janata (0514) *via* Madamir Kalai and the Barari Narai (0718) was known to be difficult, requiring work on it in several places before it would be fit for pack transport. Throughout its length, the country on either side of the track was mountainous and in many parts close and difficult, requiring extensive piqueting. In view of these considerations, the Commander 1st Division decided that, although the original intention had been for the Bannu Brigade to march through to Janata eleven miles in one day, a halt would have to be made at Madamir Kalai, supplies for both Brigades being put in at that place.

The plan adopted was that the 1st Infantry Brigade should move on the 4th of June to Madamir Kalai, protected for part of the march by the Bannu Brigade. No 12 Field Company, the 2/11 Sikh R. of the Bannu Brigade, and the 2/8 Punjab R. of the 2nd Infantry Brigade would accompany the 1st Infantry Brigade. The Field Company was to improve the track. The 2/11 Sikh R. were to unload the supply column immediately on its arrival at Madamir Kalai. The supply transport had to return to Ghariom Camp the same day, and as it consisted of more than six hundred camels, carrying two days' supplies for the Bannu Brigade and three days' for the 1st Infantry Brigade, special arrangements for rapid unloading were necessary. The task of the 2/8 Punjab R. was to establish and occupy the camp piquets, in order to release the whole of the 1st Infantry Brigade for covering the advance of the Bannu Brigade to the Barari Narai. On the 5th of June the Bannu Brigade would arrive at Madamir Kalai, moving the next day to Janata *via* the Barari Narai. On the 7th of June the Bannu Brigade would arrive at Sorarogha, the 1st Infantry Brigade returning to Ghariom.

For the purpose of control a small operational Division Headquarters was organized which accompanied the 1st Infantry Brigade. This consisted of the G.O.C. and A.D.C., G.S.O. I, G.S.O. II, S.C.(Q), O.C. 1st Divisional Signals, Cipher Officer, R.A.F., Liaison Officer, A.L.O., Political Officer and one "G" clerk.

---

*[Ref. sketch maps D 37 (Chap. XV) and L 37 (Chap. XIV).]

This organization was found to be barely sufficient, especially in the number of "G" and "Q" officers. It was the bare minimum for this kind of short operation and would require to be augmented in the event of more prolonged ones.

1st Brigade moves to Madamir Kalai, 4th June. The operations were successfully carried out as planned, but it was not clear until the last moment what the reception of the column was going to be. This meant considerable suspense for the troops, as, in order not to start hostilities unnecessarily, the rule that the troops were not to open fire unless fired at was enforced.

The Political Agent, South Waziristan, and a large party of Maliks representing all the local Mahsud sections met the 1st Infantry Brigade at Madamir Kalai on the 4th of June. The maliks showed great friendliness and said that they would try to ensure that the column was not opposed when the advance was continued to Janata. In this they were successful, as they dispersed a lashkar of Afghan and other tribesmen, about one hundred and fifty strong, at the Barari Narai, and, as the advance (of Bannu Bde.) to Janata progressed, prominent features were found to be occupied by tribesmen with white flags.

Although during the march there had been no opposition, the camp was subjected to sniping during the night, three men being wounded and fourteen mules killed and wounded as a result.

5th June, Bannu Brigade moves to Madamir Kalai. The following day, the Bannu Brigade reached Madamir Kalai without incident. The camp was again sniped that night, but no casualties, except two mules, were incurred. Considerable discomfort was caused by the temperature which now rose to about 110 degrees.

6th June, Bannu Brigade to Janata. On the 6th of June, the Bannu Brigade moved on to Janata, the route being secured as far as the Barari Narai by the 1st Infantry Brigade, which withdrew to Madamir Kalai when the Bannu Brigade had passed through. A detachment of South Waziristan Scouts from Sorarogha co-operated in the final part of the march. Not a shot was fired, and throughout the march the column was accompanied by large numbers of Mahsuds who gave the impression that they considered that the force was marching through that country on their invitation and with their consent. Water was scarce at Janata, and the supply was made more difficult by the fact that every landholder had decided to water his fields that day and refused to allow the Sappers to draw off the water unless exorbitant compensation was paid.

That night Janata camp was not molested. There was very little sniping at Madamir Kalai. A party of the 1/6 G. R. laid a successful ambush for the snipers, inflicting at least three casualties on them, and this effectively put a stop to serious sniping.

7th June, Bannu Brigade to Sorarogha, 1st Brigade to Ghariom. On the 7th the 1st Infantry Brigade returned to Ghariom and the Bannu Brigade marched to Sorarogha, in both cases without any serious opposition. The route from Janata to Sorarogha was extremely bad, both in respect of the track and of the "bigness" of the country. Had opposition been encountered, the column would have had difficulty in getting through.

1937

June

The Razmak Brigade meets the Bannu Brigade. The Bannu Brigade marches to Razmak.

To assist the Bannu Brigade during the latter part of its march to Razmak, the Razmak Brigade moved down to Piazha Raghza. On the 7th of June it marched to Tauda China where it camped for the night. During the night it was heavily sniped. The next day, the 8th, whilst the Bannu Brigade was marching to Sorarogha, the Razmak Brigade moved on to Piazha Ragbza. Here, again sniping was heavy during the night. On the 9th of June the Bannu Brigade joined the Razmak Brigade at Piazha Raghza after an uneventful march. That night, Mahsud Khassadars piqueted the camp, at a distance to prevent sniping, and the night was quiet. The next day the two Brigades marched to Tauda China. That night, again, the camp was heavily sniped. It was reported that the leader of the sniping at Tauda China was Bahram Khan, a Band Khel. On the 10th of June the Commander Waziristan Division interviewed a jirga of the Mahsuds of Makin and informed them of his intention to destroy the house and tower of Bahram Khan as a punishment for his hostile activities. The jirga asked to be allowed to take action themselves. On the 11th they handed over Bahram Khan and his brother and destroyed his house. This action, which was probably without precedent, showed the determination of the Mahsuds to avoid hostilities in their country if possible.

That afternoon the Bannu Brigade marched to Razmak, being slightly sniped on the way. The Razmak Brigade remained at Tauda China.

Peace conditions for Tori Khel.

Whilst the march from Ghariom Camp to Sorarogha was being carried out the Tori Khel jirga was being again interviewed at Miranshah by the Resident in Waziristan on the 5th and 6th of June. The Commander Wazirforce, also, was present on the 5th. The attitude of the maliks was entirely submissive, but they were told that before the final orders of Government could be given to them they must give proof of their good intentions. They were taken to task for their misdemeanours and informed that they must give a written guarantee to suppress the recalcitrant members of their tribe, to expel hostile members of other tribes from their territory, and to turn out the Faqir of Ipi if he should attempt to take refuge with them again. They must also ensure the release of all kidnapped persons detained in their territory. If they failed to comply with all these orders, Government would be compelled again to take strong measures against them. When the Government was satisfied that the tribe was fulfilling its responsibilities, its jirga would again be summoned to hear Government's final orders. The maliks pressed strongly for the re-instatement of their Khassadars, without whom, they said, it would be very difficult to carry out their promises. They were told that Government did not require their Khassadars for the present and that if the tribe wanted a police force it should organize one for itself. The maliks agreed to call up their Khassadars and employ these, without pay, as tribal police, and it was arranged that they should meet the Resident on the 13th of June to decide how these should be used. They were told that the air blockade of their country was now removed, that they would no longer be liable to arrest on sight, that the Razmak area would be re-opened to them, that they would be allowed to re-occupy villages within three miles of the Central Waziristan Road, but that they would not be permitted to visit British Territory except with a pass from the Political Agent. The release of their hostages

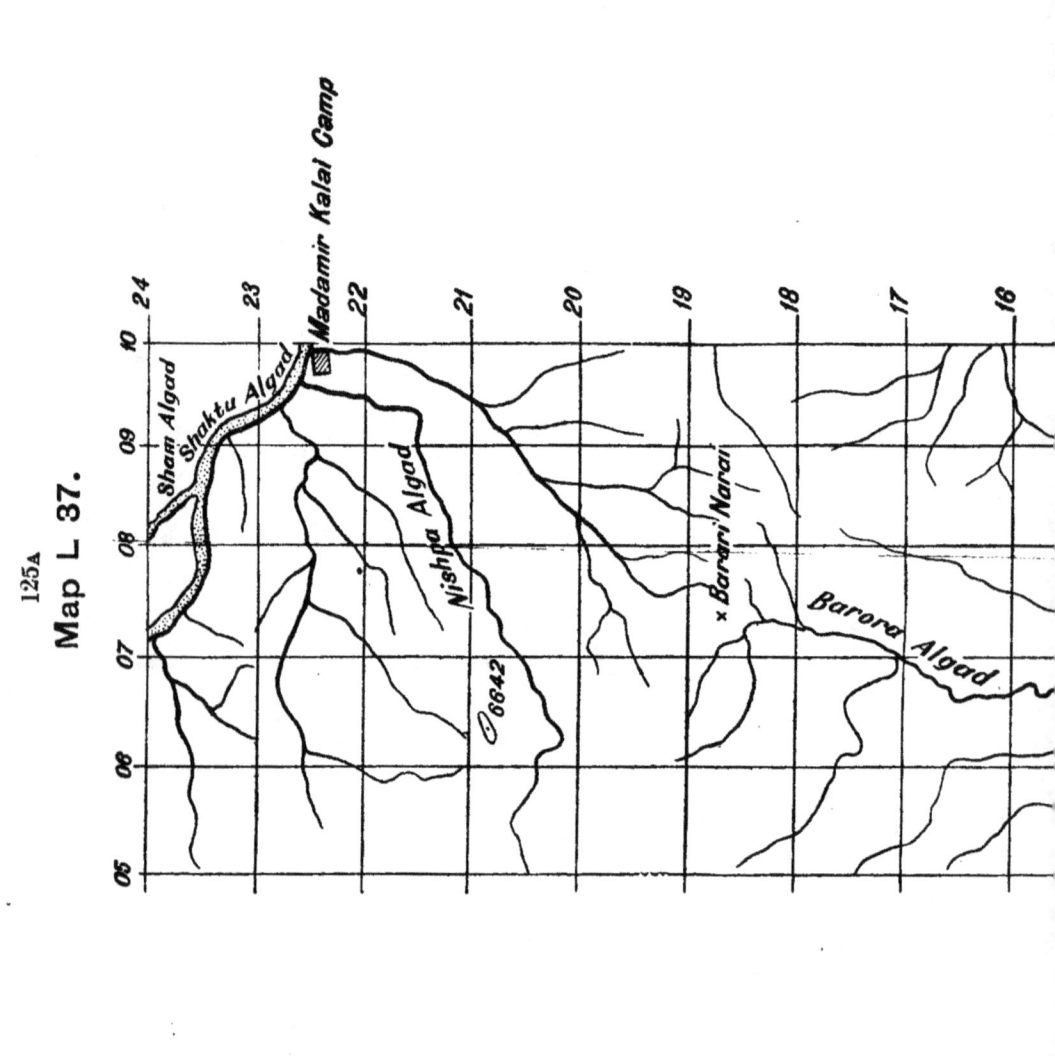

125A
Map L 37.

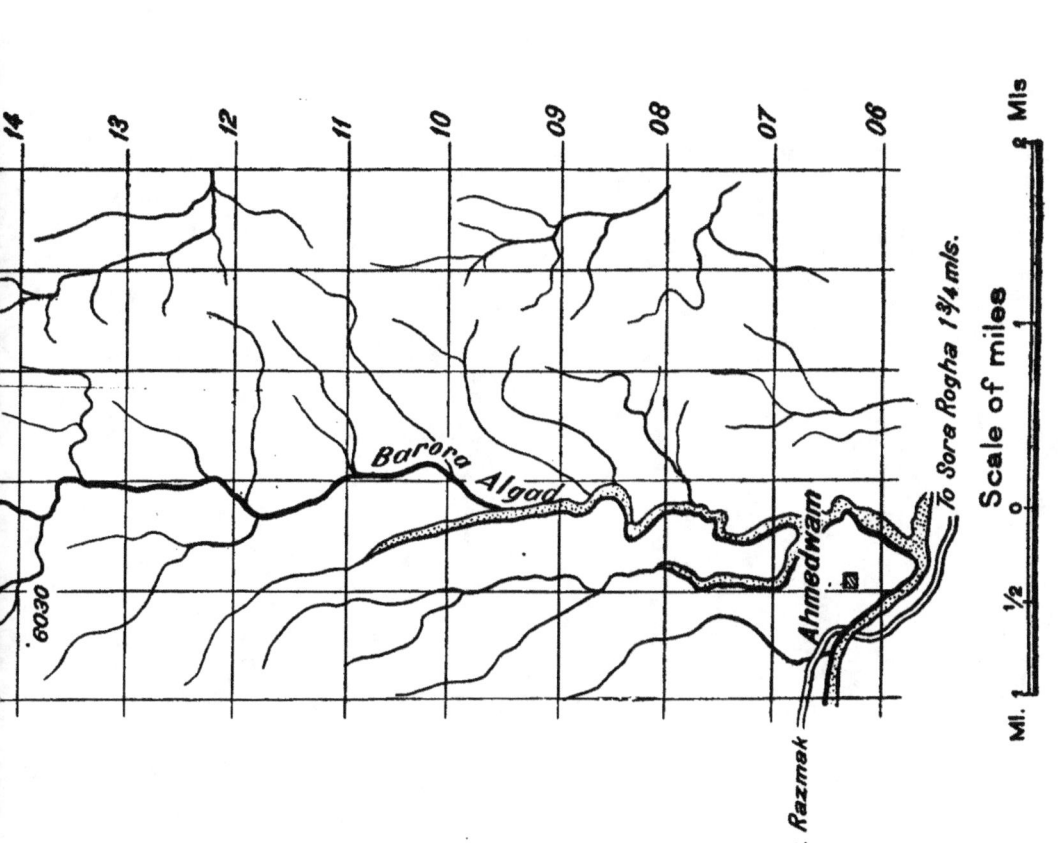

was strongly pressed by the maliks, and after some discussion the jirga was informed that they would be released on the deposit of one hundred rifles. This gesture was appreciated by the jirga, and their spokesman exclaimed "Peace has now been made".

In all the operations of the advance to and withdrawal from Arsal Kot and of the march to Sorarogha, reconnaissance and close support duties were carried out by the R. A. F. not only for the formations concerned in the operations, but also for road protection troops and convoys on the line of communications, and for trains in the area of the Pezu Pass. In addition to this, the supply of the Wana garrison had been carried out by aircraft of the Bomber Transport Flight (India) and by the Flight of No. 70 (Bomber Transport) Squadron which arrived at Risalpur from Iraq on the 31st of May. Although Mahsud lorries had been running to Wana there had been no regular M. T. Convoy for some weeks, and there was an accumulation of personnel and stores at Mauzai which could not be taken by Mahsud transport. These were conveyed by air.

R. A. F. co-operation.

CHAPTER XV.

Operations of Razmak Brigade Based on Ladha. Operations of Bannu Brigade and 1st Brigade in the Upper Shaktu Area.

Intimation of further operations in the near future to deal with the Mahsuds.

On the 7th of June another operation instruction was issued by Wazirforce Headquarters to the Commanders of the Waziristan and 1st Divisions. In this it was explained that although the Mahsud maliks had apparently done their best to restrain the majority of their people from opposing Government and their Khassadars had generally remained on duty, in some cases offering opposition to hostile gangs, and although supplies had been carried regularly to Wana and Razmak in Mahsud lorries, and the Army's communications generally had not been destroyed, yet some of them had been guilty of the attack at the Shahur Tangi and on Tiarzha Scouts' Post, had taken part in raids into the settled districts, and had allowed men of their tribes to join the Faqir's lashkars. They were therefore deserving of punishment. This punishment, if it were to be made as effective as possible, should be imposed on those who had actually committed offences. This would, in addition, be the best way of restoring the authority of the maliks. It would also be necessary to punish the tribe as a whole by means of fines and in other ways, to bring home to them their tribal responsibility.

Objects of these operations.

The objects of the forthcoming operations, therefore, were to mark down those who had offended and to administer punishment to them. The attainment of the first object would be the responsibility of the Political Authorities. The gaining of the second would be entrusted to the Waziristan Division, assisted, if necessary, by the 1st Division.

Method of operations.

Accordingly, the Razmak Brigade was to go to Ladha on the 12th of June, and from there visit certain areas, to be arranged by the Commander Waziristan Division in conjunction with the Political Authorities, while the Resident in Waziristan held jirgas with the various Mahsud tribes. The Bannu Brigade was to start at Razmak, but from the 16th of June was to be prepared to move out as necessary. The Wana Brigade was to be ready to co-operate with the remainder of the Waziristan Division during this period. The 1st Division was to locate two brigade groups in the Ghariom—Madamir Kalai area, ready to operate, if necessary, with a three days' radius of action in Mahsud country.

Razmak Brigade moves to Ladha. Resident interviews Mahsud jirgas.

Backed by the Razmak Brigade, which marched from Tauda China to Ladha on the 12th of June, the Resident in Waziristan held separate interviews with fully representative jirgas of the Manzai Mahsuds, the Shaman Khel, the Aimal Khel and Band Khel Bahlolzai, the Nano Khel and Shinghi Bahlolzai, and the Shabi Khel. These began on the 14th and were completed on the 19th of June. The procedure was the same at each jirga. As a preliminary, some of the leading maliks were interviewed on the question of bringing home individual guilt. They all agreed that some action to this end was advisable both as a deterrent and in order to uphold their authority. A previously prepared list of men who had been prominent in the recent hostilities was discussed and the names of the more prominent were selected with the maliks' advice. At the jirga the misdeeds of the tribes were enumerated. They were told that punishment was inevitable and were asked to explain their conduct. They all protested that as tribes they had remained friendly towards Government and that those individuals who had engaged in hostilities had done so in spite of the restraining efforts of the maliks and of other responsible elements in the tribes. They pointed out that as many of their people were hungry and without a livelihood the prospect of loot was too much for them. They agreed that it was necessary to bring home individual guilt in certain cases and they promised to surrender as hostages in a few days' time certain individuals, named by the Resident, who had been the most prominent in the disturbances. They were told that if these men were not given up action would be taken against any property they possessed. The jirgas were then informed that it was Government's intention to make certain roads in Mahsud country either by military labour or by contract, that the first of them would be from the Shaktu valley to Sorarogha, and that there would not be any question of "rights" as far as contracts were concerned. They were warned against any hostile interference with the troops either during this road-making or later. Finally, they were told that the orders of Government concerning their recent conduct would be announced at a future date.

The attitude of each jirga was very friendly. It was clear that they did not want trouble in their own country and were prepared to go to considerable lengths to avoid it. Several hostages were handed over at once. No objections were raised to the making of roads in their country, and the maliks seemed anxious to obey any orders given to them.

Activities of Razmak Brigade during the period of the interviews. Whilst these interviews were taking place, the Razmak Brigade which was at Ladha with detachments of the South Waziristan Scouts, carried out four one-day reconnaissances in various directions. Except for a few long-range shots on one day, no opposition was encountered.

The tribal situation, generally, was beginning to show signs of improvement, although the Faqir of Ipi still had his following and was still very active in his propaganda. The Tori Khel were returning to their summer locations. The Haibatai section, only, at first appeared to be unwilling to provide their quota of tribal police. This section gave way after a little while, and by the 15th of June details for the employment of some four hundred men as tribal police had been satisfactorily settled. The attitude of the Mahsud maliks was satisfactory. They had succeeded in restraining most of their younger hotheads and had managed to recall most of their fighting men. The Mahsuds of the Shaktu valley, who had evacuated their villages whilst the offensive against the Tori Khel was taking place, now decided to reoccupy them and to deny their territory to potential lashkars. On the 8th of June the Jalal Khel Mahsuds agreed to hand over more hostages, with the result that malik Khonia Khel's personal following would be considerably reduced. Mullah Fazal Din, moreover, had declined to attend a meeting, to which he had been invited, to discuss plans with the Faqir of Ipi and his lieutenants, and was reported to have advised the Mahsuds not to take part in further hostilities for fear of the consequences.

Mohmit Khel refuse road contracts. The Mohmit Khel, who had taken over Khassadar duties on the defection of the Tori Khel, and whose conduct had on the whole been satisfactory, were now not co-operating so activity, particularly the two sections which had been offered four miles of contract work on the Dosalli—Sham road which lay inside their particular territory. At first they were willing

1937 June

to accept the contract, but later changed their minds. They were interviewed in jirga by the Resident on the 11th of June. They ventilated several grievances, to which explanations were given by the Resident, but eventually refused to take the contract, and were told that there was no compulsion to accept it and that their relations with Government was not affected by the refusal.

Activities of Faqir of Ipi.
The Faqir himself quickly showed that he had no intention of submitting. He issued letters to the Afghan tribes soliciting their support and informing them that although the Tori Khel had decided to make their peace with Government his own attitude was unchanged. After the Tori Khel jirgas on the 5th and 6th of June he gave out that the tribes should finish harvesting their crops and that then he would raise another lashkar. He also sent messages to the tribes that they should contribute tithes of their harvest for his use, and it was known that he was receiving supplies from both sides of the border. He kept in close touch with certain well-known supporters of his, notably his brother Sher Zaman, Azal Mir, Malik Khonia Khel, and the Din Faqir Bhitanni. In conference with them it was decided that for the present their tactics should be to harass roads and piquets, particularly between Razmak and Dreghundai, with the special object of murdering British Officers. For this purpose they determined to use gangs of Mahsud and Wazir bad characters and of those Tori Khel who were resolved not to submit to Government.

Small parties of Mahsuds and Ghilzais joined Mullah Sher Ali in the Khaisara valley, and it seemed possible that larger bodies of Kabul Khel Wazirs and other Afghan subjects were also on their way to reinforce the Faqir's following.

It seemed in fact that if there was to be a recrudescence of trouble it was likely to come with an increased influx of tribesmen from Afghanistan. The Faqir had lost no time in renewing his propaganda there, and that interest was still being taken in his cause was shown by the visit to him of some Afghan Mullahs. He appears now to have concentrated on inciting the Ghilzais to action as well as on stirring up the Kabul Khel Wazirs of Birmal to further hostilities. The latter were also said to be urging the Ahmedzai Wazirs of Wana, Shakai (N. of Wana) and Birmal (Map A) to take up arms.

Strong propaganda was put about that large reinforcements of Ghilzais were shortly to be expected in Waziristan, and there were persistent rumours of the arrival of these in Shawal, the area between Razmak and the Durand Line. Much pressure also continued to be exerted on the Faqir of Shewa. Numbers of Mahsud and Afghan tribesmen including Sher Ali, the notorious Mahsud irreconcilable, visiting him for the purpose of paying their usual religious respects, tried to persuade him to declare for hostilities. Every effort was made to compromise him. Letters signed by the Faqir of Ipi were sent to the Ahmedzai Wazirs instructing them to join the Faqir of Shewa. Persistent rumours were spread amongst the Mahsuds that the Faqir of Shewa was actually inciting his people to fight. A notice was even found in the mosque of the Miranshah serai stating that he had risen against Government with the Kabul Khel Wazirs of the Spinwam area and voicing an appeal to all Muslims to renew their courage and fight for freedom. Doubts arose, inevitably, for a time about the loyalty of the Faqir of Shewa, but he held to his policy of peace and gave to no one any encouragement or support.

Activities of hostile gangs. In accordance with the plans of the Faqir of Ipi several parties were reported to be on the prowl awaiting their opportunity for doing mischief. A civilian lorry was held up on the main road near Razmak, some of its passengers were murdered and its contents looted. Telephone and telegraph wires were cut. Cattle were lifted from a village in the Bannu district. A threatened attack on the 8th of June by a gang of about two hundred men on the down Manzai-Mari Indus train at Pezu was only averted by the precautionary measures taken.

Attack on road-piquet of 2/8 Punjab R. Attempts were made, also, on the troops. On the night of the 6th of June a party of about thirty tribesmen made an unsuccessful attack on a piquet on the Tal-in-Tochi bridge provided by the 3/1 Punjab R. On the 9th of June a gang of about forty men tried to surprise a road—protection piquet of the 2nd Infantry Brigade. Two platoons of the 2/8 Punjab R. were attached to the "road-opening" battalion on this day. One of them, No. 4, advanced in two lines to occupy a position on a ridge (033311). As it approached the crest of the hill, the enemy, who were hidden in the scrub and disposed in small parties giving each other mutual support, suddenly opened fire from a range of about forty yards. Some of the leading line of the platoon became casualties at once, and a few tribesmen started forward with the evident intention of seizing the rifle and ammunition of a dead sepoy who was somewhat in advance of the rest of the line The remainder of the leading line at once took up a position. The naik commanding the platoon immediately led up the second line to its support. The dead man and his rifle were brought in before the tribesmen could reach him. The naik sent his platoon light machine gun to one flank and organized the platoon defence. He was then severely wounded, and although unable to move and in great pain, continued to encourage his men. Another naik then took charge and led the platoon forward to the attack, covering fire being given by the light machine-gun, which was fired from the shoulder by a sepoy standing up as the scrub obscured the view from the lying position. The enemy did not wait for the attack, and sustained casualties when the platoon reached the crest and opened fire on them. The other platoon of the 2/8 Punjab R. had now come up. Its arrival, coupled with the advance of a section of Light Tanks, which performed the difficult task of coming into action up the boulder-strewn and scrub-covered hillside, and with the fire of the artillery, confirmed the success gained by the piquet. In this spirited action the 2/8 Punjab R. lost two men killed or died of wounds, whilst the enemy's casualties were at least four killed and six wounded. That same night, a piquet of the 2nd Battalion, The R. Norfolk R. near Asad Khel, was twice attacked, the tribesmen reaching the barbed wire before they were driven off.

Location of Faqir of Ipi and of hostile bands. The gathering of hostile tribesmen in the Shawali Algad area, between the Shaktu river and Razmak, reported on the 3rd of June as between one hundred and fifty and two hundred strong, had been gradually increasing in strength. By the 15th of June it was estimated that there were some four or five hundred fighting men mainly Afghan subjects and Bhitannis, in the upper Shaktu and in the Shawali and Babrakra Algads.

The Faqir of Ipi, with his personal escort of fifteen Tori Khel Wazirs and twenty Jalal Khel Mahsuds, continued to take shelter with the Mahsuds of the lower Shaktu, but although he was known to have left Shawane

1937
June

Manza, reports concerning his actual location were conflicting. His food supplies were reported on the 10th of June to be stored at a shrine in Baramand, an area about one mile east of Arsal Kot, but it was said that he intended to remove them from that place shortly. It was thought that he himself was probably somewhere between Arsal Kot and Mandawam. (2429). It was evident that care was being taken to conceal his place of residence, which probably was made known to his more confidential intimates only, as he was no longer receiving the streams of visitors who had been coming to see him previously. Sheltering by day, he was said to visit his Tori Khel and Mahsud friends by night.

On the 12th of June, formal instructions, confirming verbal ones already given to him, were issued to the Commander 1st Division, informing him that if the Mahsud situation remained quiet, General Sir John Coler.dge considered that two operations should be undertaken in the near future.

Instructions in preparation for other early operations from the Sham Plain to destroy a lashkar in the Shawali Algad* area and to attempt to capture the Faqir.

These were:—

A. To attack and inflict the greatest possible loss on the hostile lashkar in the vicinity of Waladin and the Shawali Algad.

B. To capture the Faqir of Ipi.

A. would be carried out with the forces at his disposal. For B a force of eight platoons each of the Tochi Scouts and of the South Waziristan Scouts was to be placed under his command. These were to be supported by an infantry brigade and attached troops. As soon as reliable information was received of the exact location of the Faqir, he was to be prepared to act forty eight hours after the receipt of orders from Wazirforce Headquarters. This delay was imposed to allow of the concentration of the combined force of Scouts in the Sham area, the arrangements for which would be made by Wazirforce Headquarters.

The Commander 1st Division decided to use the 1st Infantry Brigade for the operations in the Shawali Algad and issued orders for it to advance to Waladin on the 15th of June and to establish a camp there.

It was known that three of the Faqir's lieutenants Sher Zaman, Azal Mir, and Khonia Khel, had joined the lashkar, and further reports indicated that the enemy had been considerably reinforced and had been joined by the Faqir. General Sir John Coleridge decided to use the Bannu Brigade and ten platoons of the Tochi Scouts, operating under the orders of the Commander Waziristan Division, to assist the 1st Division to destroy the hostile gathering and to prevent the escape of its members to the west and north west.

The general plan was as follows. The 1st Infantry Brigade column after establishing its camp at Waladin on the 15th of June, was to occupy a line west of Lakan (9825) on the 16th. At the same time, the Bannu Brigade column leaving Razmak in the early morning, was to reach a position astride the Shawali Algad approximately along the 96 north and south grid line by 1000 hours. The Tochi Scouts column was to be in position about Kach Manza and the Shini Narai by the same hour, blocking the exits westward from the Babrakra Algad. All troops were to withdraw at 1400 hours, the 1st Brigade returning to Waladin Camp, the Bannu Brigade camping for the night in the neighbourhood of Yowa (9326). Six platoons of the Tochi

Plan for operations in the Shawali Algad area*.

---

* [Ref. sketch map H. 37 (Chap XVII)].

Scouts were to return to Razmak Narai, four platoons staying for the night in the Shini Narai area. On the 17th the forces were to return to their bases. Waziristan Division operation headquarters was to be installed at Alexandra Ridge Piquet from 0900 hours to 1600 hours on the 16th of June; otherwise, it was to be at Razmak.

The carrying out of the operations was complicated by the fact that although a hostile lashkar was reported in the area, conditions in the Shawali Algad were considered to be normal, and the usual inhabitants, who were said to have no hostile intention, were occupying their villages and pursuing their normal life. The operations would, therefore, have the dual purpose of engaging the lashkar should it oppose the advance and of "showing the flag". These conditions made it necessary to impose certain restrictions on the activities of the troops. There was to be no indiscriminate firing of any kind; there was to be no reply to long distance sniping unless the safety of the command was endangered; in the absence of hostile action there was to be no registration of piquet positions prior to occupation; villages were not to be subjected to interference unless fire was opened from them, in which case the action to be taken was to be ordered by the Column Commander; damage to crops was to be avoided if possible; offensive action was not to be taken by the Royal Air Force except at the request of column headquarters, and piquets were not to display their call signs for urgent support from the air until permission had been given. Except for the orders relating to villages and crops, and indiscriminate firing, these restrictions were removed, later, for the operations of the 16th.

The Political Authorities were to warn all inhabitants in the Shawali Algad area that they must either confine themselves and their flocks to their villages or remove their families and flocks to such a distance from the line of advance that their security would be ensured should fighting develop.

Before the operations started, the 1st Infantry Brigade was reinforced by the 1/10th Baluch Regiment of the 3rd Infantry Brigade. The role of this Battalion was the defence of the camp at Waladin, to enable the 1st Infantry Brigade to be at its full strength for the advance up the Shawali Algad.

1st Brigade move to Waladin Camp 15th June. Leaving Ghariom Camp at first light on the 15th of June, and assisted by the 3rd Infantry Brigade who protected a short portion of the route, the 1st Infantry Brigade column marched up the Sham Algad to a point (046277) due east of Waladin, and moving thence across country, established itself on the camp-site (018265) by 1100 hours. Up to this time the 1st Infantry Brigade had met with no opposition, the only shots that had been fired being a few at a battalion of the 3rd Infantry Brigade which was putting up piquets to protect the initial stage of the advance.

As the leading troops of the 1st Infantry Brigade advanced to secure the commanding ground to the west of the camp, a party of about forty armed tribesmen were seen in the lower ground near the junction of the Shawali and Babrakra Algads. Artillery were ready for action and could have engaged this party successfully, but in view of the restrictions which had been imposed, immediate action was not taken against them as they withdrew without firing. When this party reached a spur (005265) to the west of the camp, they fired about forty shots at the camp and at a covering party between them and the camp, but caused no casualties. Sniping of the camp from the southeast, south, and southwest continued during the

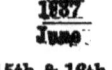
1937
June
15th & 16th

remainder of daylight, one Indian other rank being killed and two being wounded.

During the course of the day information was received that Khonia Khel with a party of about eighty Bhitannis had quitted the lashkar. The bulk of the hostile tribesmen, having expected that the troops would advance to Madamir Kalai, had gone to the Shin Starge Algad the preceding night leaving about one hundred men in the Shawali Algad.

Towards evening more tribesmen arrived in the vicinity and the enemy came closer in to the camp as darkness grew, be-

Attacks on camp piquet of 2/5 R. G. R.

coming more active in their sniping after dark. They made three separate attacks on one piquet, held by men of the 2/5 R. G. R. This post had been subjected to persistent sniping from the thick scrub round it whilst the defences were being constructed and when it was occupied. The fire died down at about 2000 hours, but an hour and a half later shouting and singing were heard on the side of the piquet away from the camp, and some fifty men advanced to the attack. The enemy appeared to have been organized in four parties, two of which gave covering fire at a range of about one hundred yards while the remainder came on in two lines. On a whistle signal the covering parties opened heavy fire, and on a second whistle signal the fire stopped and the assault was delivered. The garrison withheld their fire until the enemy came close in and were approaching the wire obstacle. Brought to a halt by the small arms fire and bombs of the piquet and by artillery fire directed by the Gurkha officer in command, (the piquet had been used during the day as an artillery observation post and the telephone line to the camp had been left in position), the enemy drew off into dead ground, shouting in Urdu to the troops not to fire and to let them in to the post. They delivered another attack at 2150 hours from a slightly different direction and were again driven off. At 2230 hours they made another very determined assault, covered by fire as before, but were once more forced to retire. Ten minutes later they left the scene of the action, leaving one dead man, an Afghan, at the wire in spite of several attempts to get him away. In their determined defence the piquet suffered no casualties. The ground round the piquet was very thickly wooded and the enemy were difficult to see, but it was estimated that several casualties were inflicted on them.

After dark, sniping of the camp became continual but finally died down at about 2310 hours. It met with some success, the casualties being, wounded, one British officer, Major G. L. Tomkins, M.C., 1/10 Baluch R., two British other ranks, and two Indian other ranks.

Reconnaissance showed that the country beyond Waladin camp up the Shawali Algad was very close and difficult, the hills being big and thickly wooded. The Commander 1st Infantry Brigade decided that his advance on the 16th of June must take place by stages, with a pause for further reconnaissance on the completion of each stage, and that all the country up to Lakan should be searched. He also decided to make a long pause on reaching the final objective in order that any enemy caught between the two brigades might be dealt with. The withdrawal to Waladin camp, also, was to be carried out by stages, so that if any enemy tried to follow up, the retirement could be stopped and a counter-attack delivered.

The instructions issued by Wazirforce Headquarters for the operations on the 16th were that the 1st Infantry Brigade was to advance to Lakan and occupy a general line just west of Lakan. The Bannu Brigade was ordered to move to a general line just west of 96 north and south grid line.

Advance of 1st Brigade on 16th June. Leaving camp at 0445 hours, the 1/6 G. R. the leading battalion of the 1st Infantry Brigade, had secured the Brigade's first bound, astride the Algad at 000257, a few hundred yards east of Mir Ali, by 0820 hours. As the right flank troops of this battalion reached their objective, (at 005265) they came into conflict with a band of about thirty tribesmen, inflicting some casualties on them. A little later, another party of about twenty enemy were successfully engaged on the left flank, (about 004253), three vigorous attempts being made by the tribesmen here to rush a forward platoon. Camp piquets of the 3rd Infantry Brigade at Ghariom Camp sent a report to say that at 0630 hours they had seen about one hundred tribesmen taking up a position about a mile south of Waladin Camp. As the country on the left flank of the 1/6 G. R., in which this party was reported to be, was even more difficult than had been supposed, and as fire was coming from that direction, one rifle company of the S. Wales Bord., who were in brigade reserve, was left with the 1/6 G. R., to enable them to deal with anything that might happen on their left.

The second objective, a line roughly north and south just west of Mir Ali astride the Algad, was secured by the 2/6 G. R. by 0925 hours.

Finally, the 2/5 R. G. R. went on to take the village of Lakan (9825) and the spurs west and south of that place. Not having enough troops now in hand to secure the high ground in squares 9826 and 9926, the Commander ordered one company of the 1. S. Wales Bord. to carry the right flank back to about 990259. These final objectives were reached at 1030 hours. During the last two stages the advancing troops met with long-distance sniping and minor opposition only. Parties of tribesmen were seen on the left flank and were engaged by guns, machineguns, and aircraft. Artillery effectively shelled a collection of about a hundred tribesmen seen in a water course (981254) during the advance to the final objectives.

Advance of Bannu Brigade on 16th June. The Bannu Brigade column moving via the Nawal Narai and Yowa reached Anztalai (9526) at 0840 hours, having dropped a party at the Nawal Narai to prepare a camp there. Advancing eastward from Anztalai, by 1000 hours their forward troops were in position approximately on the 96 grid line, the final objective given to the Brigade. They had met with no opposition on the way, although, as they approached Anztalai, a volley was fired at the leading troops. It was ascertained that the object of this volley had only been to slow up the troops who were advancing too fast, so as to allow the village women time to reach shelter. They had not seen more than a few small parties of tribesmen, but were aware that large numbers were in front of them.

The Tochi Scouts' detachment, also, was in position from the Shini Narai to Kaeh Manza with the left flank thrown back by 1000 hours, and had seen no sign of any enemy.

Both Brigades, having used up their troops, were unable to advance any further.

Decision to repeat the operation on the 17th of June. As it appeared to the Commander Waziristan Division that the 1st Infantry Brigade had not reached the objective given them, he sent a message to the Commander Wazirforce proposing that in order to deal effectively with the enemy in the area instead of both Brigades withdrawing to their bases the following day, they should repeat the advances they had just made. The Commander Wazirforce, who was at Ghariom

1927
June 17th.

Camp with the Commander 1st Division, considering that the 1st Infantry Brigade had to all intents and purposes gained their objective, decided that the plan should be carried out as already arranged. The Commander Waziristan Division then suggested that, to bring the enemy to battle, the Bannu Brigade should camp for the night at Anztalai and move towards Waladin the next morning at dawn, the 1st Infantry Brigade moving up the Algad to meet it. On this the Commander Wazirforce decided that the Bannu Brigade column and the Tochi Scouts should remain out one more night. The Bannu Brigade column camping at the Nawal Narai was to advance on the 17th as far as possible towards Waladin in order to cover the withdrawal of the 1st Infantry Brigade. On the suggestion of the Commander 1st Division this plan was altered to the extent that the 1st Division was to advance towards Mir Ali before withdrawing to Ghariom Camp.

The 1st Infantry Brigade commenced its withdrawal from its position west of Lakan at 1400 hours. A few sniping shots were fired but the enemy did not follow up and the column was in its camp at Waladin by about 1625 hours. It was estimated that the enemy engaged had numbered between two and three hundred and that their losses had been at least twenty killed and forty wounded. The casualties in the Brigade during the day were three Indian other ranks killed, one British officer, two British other ranks, and seven Indian other ranks wounded.

The original orders had laid down 1400 hours as the starting time for the withdrawal of both Brigades. Owing to the discussion on the next day's plans, the time of starting the withdrawal of the Bannu Brigade was delayed. It began to move back at 1430 hours and all the troops were in camp at the Nawal Narai by 1800 hours. The latter part of their withdrawal was slightly followed up, and two Indian other ranks were wounded.

As the Bannu Brigade column had not brought enough rations for the extra day now to be spent on the operations, a small supply column left Razmak at 1600 hours for Nawal Narai camp, escorted by the 4/8 Punjab R. and taking with it reinforcements of two rifle companies and one machine-gun platoon of the 1/9 G. R. No enemy were met with and the ration mules were back in Razmak by 1930 hours.

Orders for operations on the 17th of June.

Orders for the next day's operations were issued by Wazirforce Headquarters between 1830 and 1900 hours. These laid down that the 1st Infantry Brigade would advance to grid line 99 and exploit to grid line 98, the Bannu Brigade advancing to grid line 96 and exploiting to grid line 97. The 1st Infantry Brigade was to commence its withdrawal to Ghariom Camp at anytime after 0900 hours, making the fullest possible use of the Royal Air Force to assist its retirement. The Bannu Brigade was not to withdraw before that hour. The Tochi Scouts were to co-operate on the same lines as on the 16th.

Advance on 17th June practically unopposed.

These orders were received by the 1st Infantry Brigade too late to allow fresh plans and orders to be issued, and the operation on the 17th was conducted on the same plan as for the 16th, the starting time being 0445 hours, as before. The troops now knew the ground and pauses for reconnaissance were not necessary, and, consequently, the advance was much quicker, the final objective being reached at 0840 hours. Only a few enemy were seen. The Bannu Brigade met with no opposition and reached its final objective at 0800 hours.

From the lack of opposition it seemed clear that the lashkar had left the Shawali Algad.

Withdrawal, 17th June.
The withdrawal commenced at 0915 hours. A few enemy who fired at the forward troops of the 1st Infantry Brigade when retiring were immediately engaged by artillery and machine-gun fire, and thereafter the movement to Waladin Camp was unmolested. Some slight opposition was offered by tribesmen, believed to be local Mahsuds, when withdrawing from Waladin to Ghariom Camp, and a piquet of the 1/10 Baluch R. on the Waladin feature inflicted casualties on a party of about a dozen men who were seen crawling up to the position just before the piquet retired. The Bannu Brigade, whose retirement was at first unopposed was later followed up and lost one man wounded. The column reached Razmak at 1900 hours. The Tochi Scouts were not engaged with the enemy, and returned unattacked to Razmak Narai Camp. Enemy casualties during the day numbered about fifteen.

R. A. F. Co-operation.
During these three days R. A. F. co-operation was provided by Nos. 20 (A. C.) and 28 (A. C.) Squadrons, which carried out continuous tactical reconnaissance and close support duties.

Tribal situation at the end of Opns. 15th to 17th June 1937— (Ref. Sketch maps 'A' & 'U').
As soon as the fighting had begun in the neighbourhood of Waladin, parties of tribesmen on the spot had, as usual, been reinforced by others from further afield. The majority of the Bhitannis, however, and a large proportion of the Afghan tribesmen left the lashkar during the night of the 16/17th, some of the latter remaining behind to collect their casualties, whom they removed on camels hired from the local Mahsuds. After the conclusion of these operations it was reported that there still remained about two hundred and fifty of the original lashkar in small parties in the hills south of the Shawali Algad

The Din Faqir, who had been responsible for collecting the Bhitanni portion of the lashkars and had quitted the area before the fighting had begun, was now said to be trying to raise a new lashkar, with the object, as he stated, of opposing an advance of the troops into Bhitanni country.

Rumours still persisted that Ghilzais, Kabul Khel Wazirs of Birmal, and other Afghan tribesmen were collecting in large numbers in Shawal* and opinion among the tribes was that when the gathering had gained sufficient strength, it would compel the Faqir of Shewa to declare himself hostile to Government. The Kabul Khel Wazirs of Birmal had decided to allow parties of Ghilzais to traverse their country without interference. Another report indicated that a large lashkar of Ghilzais and Kabul Khel Wazirs of Birmal had arrived at Mandech. and that some had gone on to join the hostile tribesmen in the Upper Shaktu whilst others had left for the Upper Baddar valley. Their intention was said to be to commit offences in Mahsud territory. Their arrival gives an interesting sidelight on the mental processes of the tribesmen. It was learned that the Tori Khel, who realized fully that they had been misled by the Mahsuds and ascribed all their misfortunes to that tribe, had appealed to Afghans of the Southern Province, especially to the Kharotis and other Ghilzais, to send lashkars to the Mahsud country and to try to implicate them in war with Government.

---
*Note.—The Shawal lies between Razmak and the Durand line (see Map 'A') and not to be confused with the Shawali Algad area where opns. had just concluded.

1937
June.

It is possible, that the Faqir of Ipi too, may have been concerned in this as he was said to be displeased at the lack of support on the part of the Mahsuds. Mullah Sher Ali had by now collected a larger following and was located in the area west of the Sharawangi Narai, where he was said to have been joined by a party of one hundred and twenty Bahlolzai Mahsuds. That the more responsible Mahsuds seemed to be trying to co-operate with Government was shown by a report that some Afghan tribesmen returning to their homes from the Shawali Algad had been attacked by Abdullai Mahsud Khassadars.

Information had also been received that tribesmen were collecting in the Baramand area, north east of Arsal Kot. It was in this area that the Faqir of Ipi's food supplies were said to be stored. It was now reported that a communal kitchen had been started which was attracting many undesirable persons. Finally, on the 18th of June a reliable report was received according to which the Faqir of Ipi's residence was in some caves in a nala (about 146268) west of Gul Zamir Kot* (1426).

Preparations for operation to capture the Faqir. Measures to ensure secrecy.* Prior to the formal instructions issued on the 12th of June to the Commander 1st Division informing him that the capture of the Faqir of Ipi should be attempted in the near future and that he was to be prepared to act forty eight hours after the receipt of orders to carry out this operation, he had been personally informed of this intention.

Since some preparations were essential to enable effect to be given to the plan without delay when it was decided to carry it out, it was necessary to send out some preliminary instructions in advance giving details of troops to be employed and preparatory moves. In the interests of secrecy, these instructions, which were issued on the 11th of June, omitted all reference to any attempt to capture the Faqir, but were framed to cover two tasks which it was stated, had been assigned to the 1st Division to be carried out at short notice. These tasks were the provision of protection for a road reconnaissance from Ghariom Camp via Madamir Kalai to Pasal and back to Ghariom Camp, and the provision of a column for operations along the line of the Shaktu river. The 1st Infantry Brigade and attached troops were nominated for these tasks, and warning was given that, in the event of the second task being carried out, the column would be joined at Ghariom Camp by detachments of Scouts on the day before its departure. As in the ordinary course of events when preparations were being made for an operation complete secrecy was unattainable, it was hoped in this way to account reasonably for the sudden appearance of a considerable force of Scouts and to keep the actual object of the operations concealed.

Instructions issued on 18th of June that the operation was to take place between the 21st and 23rd June. As the whereabouts of the Faqir now seemed to have been established, the time appeared to have arrived to make the attempt to capture him. Further instructions were issued to the Commander 1st Infantry Brigade on the 18th of June to the effect that the road reconnaissance would be carried out from the 21st to the 23rd of June, the fiction of the reconnaissance being maintained by the statement that the Commander Royal Engineers, Wazirforce, would join the 1st Infantry Brigade for the purpose on the 20th. The remainder of the instructions, with the one exception of the route to be

*[Ref. Sketch map D 37 (Chap. XV)].

followed which was amended later, were as applicable to the operation intended as to the objects already given out. Accordingly, all preparations made by the 1st Infantry Brigade remained appropriate, although undertaken for an intention which was not actually the real one. It was also arranged that the 3rd Infantry Brigade should be relieved of various routine duties during the period of the operations, as, although this was not mentioned, this formation was to assist the 1st Infantry Brigade.

Up to this time, except for the Commander 1st Division only two officers, the senior representatives of the General and Administrative Staffs at 1st Division Headquarters, had been informed of the real intention. A staff officer of these Headquarters visited the Commander 1st Infantry Brigade on the 19th and delivered to him in person the Divisional operation instruction in manuscript, in which the complete arrangements for the operation were given in detail.

Orders for the concentration of the Scouts at Dosalli Post had already been given by Wazirforce Headquarters at a conference which had been held with the Commandants of the Tochi and South Waziristan Scouts, and at which it had been decided, that eight platoons of each Corps would provide sufficient strength to carry out the searching of the area.

Concentration of detachments of Tochi and South Waziristan Scouts at Ghariom Camp.

The Commandants decided that a start from a common base was preferable to a converging movement from Sorarogha and Dosalli which would have been a complicated movement and difficult to execute with accurate timing. The eight platoons of the South Waziristan Scouts, therefore, leaving Jandola on the 19th of June in motor transport, moved through the Bain Pass and Bannu to Mir Ali for the night. No halt was made in Bannu as it was feared that the sympathizers of the Faqir there would speedily have passed on information about this unusual move. The next day, this party joined up at Dosalli Scouts' Post with the eight platoons of Tochi Scouts who had arrived from Razmak Narai Camp. There they rested for the day while rough plans for their part in the operation were made. At 1800 hours, the combined detachments, in their lorries, moved on to Ghariom Camp, escorted by light tanks. In order to ensure that their arrival at Ghariom Camp was kept secret, night dispositions in that place were adopted at 1745 hours and no person was allowed to leave camp. After arrival, the Commandants had a final conference with the Commander 1st Infantry Brigade.

At 1745 hours, when the Camp was closed for the night, the Commander 1st Infantry Brigade held a conference attended by unit commanders only. The real object of the operations was now revealed and orders in manuscript were given out personally by the Brigade Major.

Plan for this operation.

The combined detachments of Scouts were to leave Ghariom Camp that night and move to the nullah junction 116252 on the Shaktu river following the same route as that taken by the Waziristan Division on the 27th of May. On reaching the Shaktu the detachments were to separate and moving along north and south of the river were to occupy the high ground on either side of the river, putting blocks in the actual river bed. The Tochi Scouts were to be responsible on the north side from just east of Arsal Kot to just west of a knoll at 152273, with a block in the river about 153269 south of the knoll. On the south, the South Waziristan Scouts would hold the high ground just south of Gulzamir Kot and extending east and west of that place (154264 to 148263), with a block in the Shaktu south of Arsal Kot.

1937
June.

These positions were to be occupied by 0445 hours. The South Waziristan Scouts were then to search the nala in square 1426 from the nala-track junction 144263 to the junction of the nala with the Shaktu. When this had been completed, the ground within about half a mile on all sides of their respective positions (in squares 1427, 1527, 1426, and 1526) was to be thoroughly searched by the detachments. The two parties were then to fall back independently to Arsal Kot, and having assembled there, they were to withdraw on to the 1st Infantry Brigade. The 1st Infantry Brigade was to leave Ghariom Camp at 0400 hours on the 21st of June, and following the route of the Scouts, was to advance to a line about one mile east of Pasal astride the river in support of them, acting thereafter as the situation demanded. The Brigade was to camp for the night at Pasal, returning to Ghariom Camp on the 22nd. The detachments of Scouts would either stay with the 1st Infantry Brigade for the night or come straight back to Ghariom Camp, depending on the time by which the operation for the day was finished. To help the 1st Infantry Brigade the 3rd Infantry Brigade was to hold a line by 0500 hours on the 21st about half a mile east of the Sham Algad until the tail of the 1st Infantry Brigade was about a thousand yards east of them, doing the same thing again on the 22nd when the 1st Infantry Brigade returned.

Shortly before the Scouts left Ghariom Camp a report was received that a small party of Mahsuds had posted themselves in that part of the route which followed the tributary to the Shaktu river. This caused some uneasiness, but it was decided that the risk of meeting this party was preferable to the difficulties arising from making a detour through the very difficult hills.

Operations of Scouts 20th June 1937.
The two detachments marched off at 2300 hours on the 20th. Tochi Scouts led the way as they had been over the ground before during earlier operations. Pasal camp site was reached without any opposition at 0210 hours on the 21st. Here, the detachments separated and went off to their respective areas, being in forming up positions at 0400 hours. At 0445 hours, just before it began to get light, they moved forward into their appointed positions. By 0500 hours it was light enough to make a further reconnaissance and at 0515 hours the search of the areas began. By 0630 hours all the allotted tasks had been performed and orders were issued for a co-ordinated withdrawal.

The few people found in the area had been taken completely by surprise and no opposition was offered, except in one case, where a tribesman, when called on to surrender, finding that he could not run away, lay down and prepared to shoot. He was shot dead before he could fire. This man was found to be a mullah of repute, and had been carrying out the duties of quartermaster for the Faqir of Ipi for some time. Eleven prisoners were captured and taken back to Ghariom Camp. The most important of these was a Tori Khel, Arsal Khan, the owner of Arsal Kot, the host of the Faqir for a long time, and a bitter opponent of Government. In a village on the north side of the river the Tochi Scouts found and released two Hindus who had been kidnapped and kept captive in a dark room, with their feet in home-made stocks, for three or four months.

The withdrawal of the Scouts was carried out without any difficulty, and after handing over their prisoners to the 1st Infantry Brigade, they returned to Ghariom Camp, and in due course, to their respective bases.

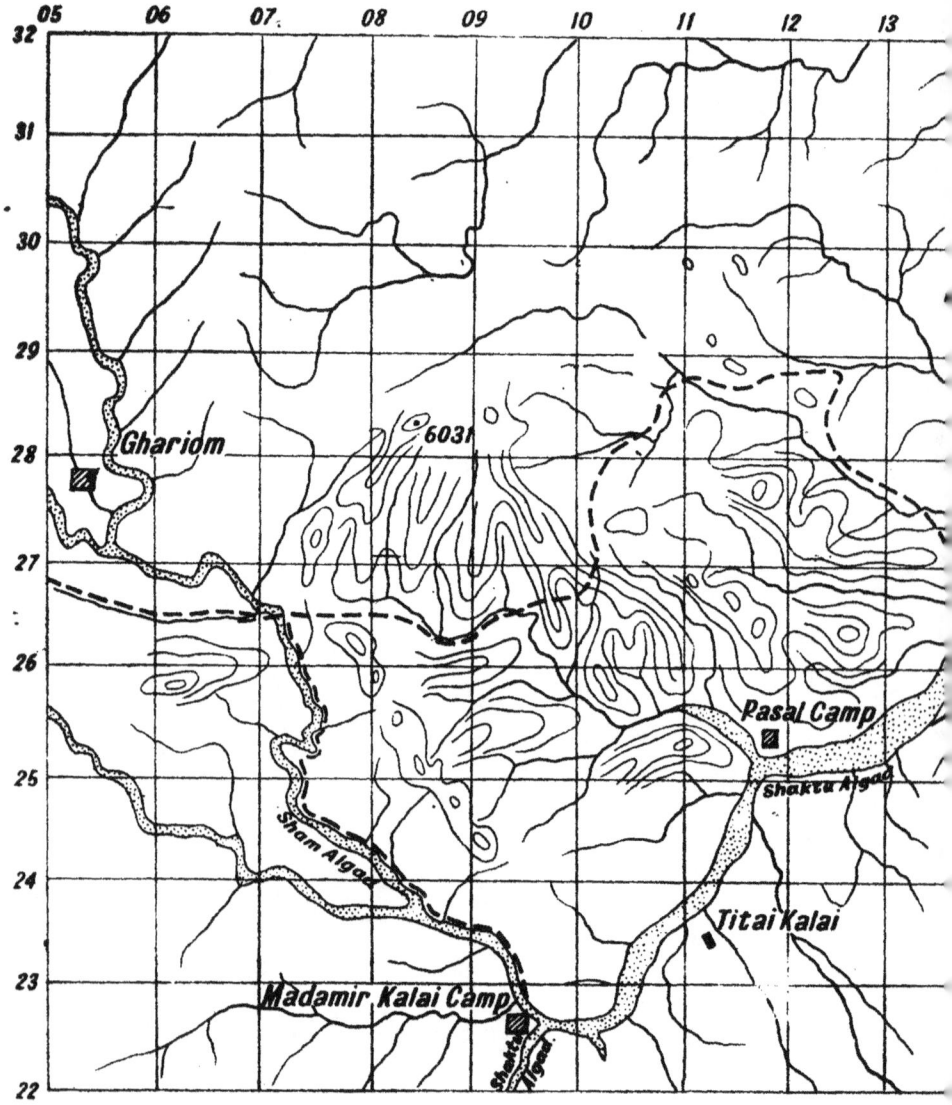

Survey Section No 1717. Nov 1941

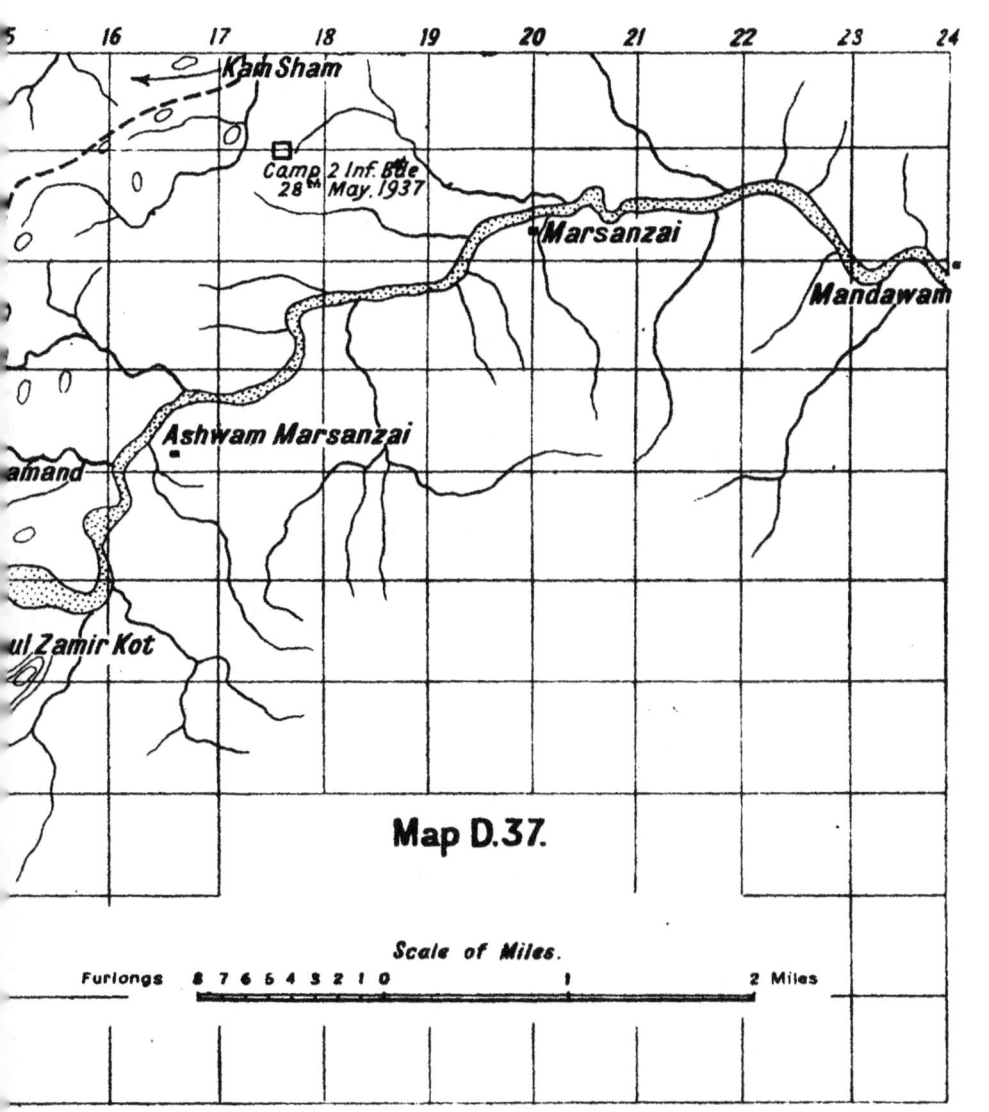

The 1st infantry Brigade left Ghariom at 0400 hours on the 21st, and the advanced guard, consisting of the 1 S. Wales Bord. and the 1/6 G. R., supported by the 25th Mountain Brigade R. A. (less two batteries) passed through the position held by the 3rd Infantry Brigade and secured the route as far as the junction of the nala with the Shaktu river, west of Pasal, and a spur on the south bank of the Shaktu.

The 3/9 Jat. R. then passed through, and moving along the north bank, secured Pasal camp site and features to the north-east, whilst the 2/5 R. G. R. secured features along the south bank. The Brigade reached its final position by 0830 hours as the Scouts were withdrawing.

After the Scouts had passed through, the 1st Infantry Brigade withdrew to Pasal where camp was made. The day passed quietly, but a few shots were fired at a piquet that night and at a party sent out to bring back stores from one of the piquets early on the 22nd. There were no casualties.

The 1st Infantry Brigade returned to Ghariom Camp on the 22nd of June, the few tribesmen in evidence being quickly dispersed.

Note on the attempt to capture the Faqir of Ipi, 21st June 1937.

In view of the efforts that had been made to ensure the success of the raid the results, at the time, were felt to be disappointing. It did not seem that the caves had been recently occupied to any great extent, and it was practically certain that no communal kitchen existed in the areas searched. The capture of Arsal Khan was of some importance, though, and the raid had demonstrated again the power of the military forces to move where and when they liked.

It was not until sometime later that it was learnt how near to complete success the operation had been. One report said that the Faqir had been at Gul Zamir Kot since the 17th or 18th of June, and had received information on the 20th that a raid on that place was likely to be made. (Confirmation of the latter part of this report was given by Arsal Khan when he was being interrogated.) The Faqir had, therefore, moved to Marsanzai that evening, and on the approach of the Scouts, was believed to have gone away eastwards, his head muffled in a sheet. Another report, perhaps not so reliable, stated that the Tochi Scouts when searching had missed the Faqir, who had his family with him, by a few hundred yards. The Mahsuds of his personal following offered to fight to save him, but he would not let them do so as he was afraid of the activity of the Scouts and of the aircraft to be seen overhead.

CHAPTER XVI.

Operations of the Waziristan Division to open the lines of communication from Wana to Jandola and Razmak, June 20th to July 6th.

The operations in the Shawali Algad had had a good effect on the local situation, and the breaking up of the lashkar there, with the raid to the Baramand area, enabled the attention of the 1st Division to be turned very largely to the construction of the roads.

The re-opening of the lines of communication with Wana and the punishment of the ringleaders among the Mahsuds west of the Central Waziristan Road still remained to be accomplished.

Instruction issued by Wazirforce H ad-quarters on June 15th for further opera-tions.*

On the 15th of June, Wazirforce Headquarters issued an instruction to the Commander Waziristan Division, stating that it was the intention to demonstrate to the Mahsuds at an early date the ability of the military forces to open the lines of communication to Wana from Razmak and Jandola. To carry out this intention, and to punish the hostile Mahsud ringleaders who had been in the field, the Commander, Waziristan Division was to despatch the Razmak and Bannu Brigade columns to Chalweshti (7901), Torwam (7292), and the Upper Baddar northwest of Chalweshti. The Wana Brigade column would visit Sarwekai (8973), Ispana Raghza (8885), and Tiarza (7287). The Jandola-Sarwekai road was to be opened on the 16th of June, and five days' supplies for the Wana Brigade column was to be put at the latter place. The programme of the operations was to be arranged to allow for the return of the Razmak and Bannu Brigade Columns to Razmak on the 6th of July.

The Commander Waziristan Division decided to concentrate his whole division at Torwam for one day.

*Moves of Brigades during these opera-tions.

The movements of the three Brigade columns in carrying out these orders were as follows:—

Date.	Razmak Brigade.†	Bannu Brigade†.	Wana Brigade.†
19 June	at Ladha	at Razmak	at Wana.
20 „		to Ladha	
21 „	to Chalweshti		
22 „		to Chalweshti	to Dargai Oba.

*[Ref. Sketch map A (in pocket), G 37 (Chap. XXI) and M. 37 (Chap. XVI).]
†For detail of the fighting troops of these Bdes. see pp. 26 & 27.

Date.	Razmak Brigade.	Bannu Brigade.	Wana Brigade.
23 June	to Torwam		to Sarwekai.
24 „		to Torwam	
25 „	road opening duties		
26 „		to Narai Raghza	to Imam Khan Kili. (8587).
27 „		to Torwam	to Tiarza.
28 „			to Torwam.
29 „	Operations west of Torwam Sharawangi Narai road.		
30 „	to Turabaz. (6601) and back to Torwam		to Tiarza.
1 July	to Chalweshti	to Chalweshti.	
2 „			to Wana.
4 „	to Pat Khel (7507) and	back to Chalweshti.	
5 „	to Asman Manza	to Ladha.	
6 „		to Razmak.	

Bannu Brigade Column joins the Razmak Brigade at Chalweshti Camp. The Bannu Brigade column, with the Headquarters Waziristan Division, marched out of Razmak on the 20th of June and joined the Razmak Brigade at Ladha Camp after an uneventful march. On 22nd June, the Waziristan Division, less the Wana Brigade column, was concentrated at Chalweshti Camp. There was no opposition during the marches on these two days, but during both nights there was considerable sniping at the camp from the surrounding scrub-covered hills.

Mullah Sher Ali's lashkar was reported to be in the hilly country between Chalweshti and Torwam, and to be in position about the Sharawangi Narai. It was said to number about two hundred and fifty, and

**1937
June 23rd.** to be composed of Mahsuds from various sections, Malikshahi Utmanzai Wazirs, Ahmedzai Wazirs, Kabul Khel Wazirs from Birmal, and Ghilzais. They made no secret of the fact that they intended to resist the troops in this area.

Local Mahsud maliks and Khassadars were active in assisting the force. Under the instructions of the Political Officer, the maliks, on the 22nd, went to the lashkar to attempt to induce it to disperse, but met with no success.

On the 23rd of June, the intention was that the Razmak Brigade and the Divisional Headquarters should move to a camp at Torwam. In the course of this operation, to facilitate the protection of the line of communications with Razmak, a temporary camp was to be established near the Sharawangi Narai khassadar post for the eight platoons of the South Waziristan Scouts with the force. To give the Razmak Brigade an uninterrupted passage for the first part of the march and to cover the construction of the Scouts Camp, the Bannu Brigade was to secure the road as far as approximately the Tare Jhowar khassadar post, returning to Chalweshti Camp for the night. There had been no opportunity for reconnaissance forward from Chalweshti. The maps available were inaccurate, the new road alignment along which the advance was to take place being unmarked. The hill features in the area to be traversed were big and thickly wooded, the trees coming down to the road on either side. West of the road the hills were, generally, somewhat lower than on the east, and although the country was very broken, it was on the whole less thickly wooded on the west.

Divisional Headquarter and Razmak Brigade march to Torwam June 23rd.

Leaving the 2/4 G. R., prepared to move at one hour's notice, in charge of the defences of Chalweshti camp, the Bannu Brigade started at 05-30 hours. The 2/1 Punjab R. led the way and was responsible for securing the road up to but exclusive of the Sharawangi Narai. From that point, the 2/11 Sikh R. took over the duties of piqueting up to the forward limit of the Brigade's responsibility.

One section of the 9th Light Tank Company was under the command of the Bannu Brigade in the initial stages and was employed with the leading battalion. This section came under the Razmak Brigade when the latter passed through. The country generally was unfavourable for action by light tanks. They were unable to leave the road until Sholam was reached, but had opportunities when their machine-guns were used with good effect.

There was no opposition as far as the Sharawangi Narai, and Brigade Headquarters was established there at 07-35 hours, the 1/17 Dogra R. coming into brigade reserve.

The 2/11 Sikh R. advanced from the Narai at about 07-30 hours. At 0800 heavy firing broke out from the direction of the ridge (759995) west of it, and a few minutes later from the high and densely wooded feature to the east of the line of advance.

Enemy opposition begins south of the Sharawangi Narai.

It was anticipated by the Political Agent South Waziristan that the sound of heavy firing would cause hostile elements from the populous Baddar valley to flock to the scene of action. The Brigade Commander accordingly decided to protect the right flank and rear by detaching one company and one machine-gun platoon from the 1/17 Dogra R. in the direction marked "A" on the sketch map. This company was in position by 09-00 hours. The course of events showed the wisdom of this decision, and this detachment successfully held up tribal reinforcements that endeavoured to approach from the Baddar valley.

1987
June 23rd.

By this time the detachment of the South Waziristan Scouts had arrived at the Narai, the lorries were unloaded, and the stores and supplies for the post were being carried up the hill to the site. At about 09-45 hours, a platoon of the Scouts was ordered to occupy a feature (marked B on the sketch map M 37) west of the road in order to strengthen the protective troops in that area.

Opposition to the South Waziristan Scouts.

The platoon moved off, covered by a single machine-gun and by one platoon of the Scouts and by machine-gun and artillery fire from the column. The line of advance was by an undulating, fairly heavily wooded ridge, which dropped sharply from the camp site and rose again about seven hundred yards away to a knoll. The platoon, advancing steadily, occupied the nearest point of the rise, and the leading line was approaching the top of the hill when it was rushed from two sides by superior numbers of the tribesmen, who had lain concealed until that moment in the dense undergrowth. Fierce close fighting ensued below the summit and the Scouts, losing nine or ten casualties, were forced off the hill. As the Mahsuds charged over the hill top the column guns and machine-guns opened fire. Unfortunately, at least one casualty among the Scouts was caused by this fire.

The O. C. Scouts' detachment, seeing what had happened, immediately sent two more platoons of the Scouts, and a little later, a third, to help the first platoon to establish itself, arranging with the column artillery and the Scouts' machine-gun detachment for covering fire. The two platoons, advancing methodically and steadily, drove the enemy off the hill and established the piquet. In this short engagement, the Scouts, although they had suffered considerably in the first rush of the enemy, succeeded in inflicting several casualties on the enemy and saved all their own rifles except one.

The 2/11 Sikh R., which had taken over the duties of piqueting the main route and the Narai was making steady progress on the big and densely wooded feature which overlooked the road on the east. The approximate areas occupied are shown as "C" on the sketch map (M 37). The tribesmen took full advantage of the cover and held their fire until the troops were at close range. In consequence, the fighting was close and confused, bomb and bayonet were freely used, whilst the impossibility of determining the location of the troops prevented artillery support. At 08-30 hours the Battalion was astride the road about one thousand yards north of the Tare Jhowar Khassadar Post. Shortly after they left the Narai one rifle company of the 1/17 Dogra R. had been sent to occupy the northern end of a high feature to the east of the Narai. This was done without opposition. The remaining rifle company of the 1/17 Dogra R., consisting of two platoons only, was sent to reinforce the 2/11 Sikh R. when the latter

2/11 Sikh R. advance to final objective of Bannu Brigade.

1937
June 23rd.

had reached the positions shown on the sketch map. This was used to establish another piquet on the southern end of the feature on which the first company of the 1/17 Dogra R. was posted. Passing through the 2/11 Sikh R., it advanced towards its objective, but was held up by heavy fire. Eventually, at about 13-20 hours, an attack was made along the ridge by the company posted at the northern end, and the position was captured. Except for this action, enemy opposition had died down on this flank at about 09-00 hours, and they confined themselves to sniping at long range, the main portion of the lashkar withdrawing in a southwesterly direction.

When the 2/11 Sikh R. commenced its advance it was clear that the Bannu Brigade would need more troops, and at 08-30 hours the Commander had ordered up two rifle companies of the 2/4 G. R. from Chalweshti camp to the Sharawangi Narai. These arrived at 11-00 hours. Two platoons were sent to relieve the Scouts' platoon at "B" on the sketch map, the other company being ordered to assist the Scouts in the preparation of their camp.

Razmak Brigade passes through to Torwam.
The Razmak Brigade had left Chalweshti camp at 07-30 hours, and between 09-30 and 10-00 hours began to pass through the foremost limits of the area that was secured and protected for them by the Bannu Brigade. The opposition encountered by the Razmak Brigade was of a minor nature, consisting of intermittent and long-range sniping. It was sufficient however to slow up the advance of the Brigade, which did not reach its camp at Torwam until 17-20 hours. The sniping inflicted two casualties on the leading battalion, the 5/12 F. F. R., the Commanding officer, Lieut.-Colonel P. Grant being killed and one Viceroy's Commissioned officer wounded.

No further incident occurred until about 14-30 hours, when under cover of a heavy hailstorm the tribesmen made a determined attack on the Scouts who were engaged in establishing their camp near the Narai. The tribesmen approached to within seventy yards, but were beaten off by the fire of the Scouts assisted by the company of the 2/4 G. R. and by a platoon of the 3/7 Rajput R. which provided the permanent guard for Bannu Brigade Headquarters.

In order to allow as much time as possible for the Scouts to complete the defences of their camp, the Bannu Brigade remained in its positions till 16-30 hours. The Brigade then withdrew. It was not followed up, and reached Chalweshti camp by 19-00 hours.

R. A. F. Co-operation.
Throughout the operation No. 28 (A. C.) Squadron Royal Air Force had provided continuous close support and tactical reconnaissance for both brigades. The densely wooded country, however, militated against effective action, but as dusk was approaching casualties were inflicted by air action on parties of tribesmen seen approaching camp piquets at Chalweshti.

During the day the tribesmen offered good targets on occasions and it was estimated that their number of killed, alone, was twenty four. They left four bodies behind, including those of Paind, a notorious Mahsud leader, and his brother.

RAZMAK COLUMN CAMP, TORWAM, 1937.

Casualties.	The casualties in the force were:—		1937
			June
Killed	Lieut. Colonel P. Grant	5/12 F. F. R.	
	2/11th Sikh Regiment	4 Indian other ranks.	
	1/17th Dogra Regiment	1 Indian other rank.	
	South Waziristan Scouts	3 Indian other ranks.	
Wounded	Captain H. S. King, R.A.		
	5/12th Frontier Force Regiment.	1 Viceroy's Commissioned Officer.	
	2/11th Sikh Regiment	12 Indian other ranks.	
	1/17th Dogra Regiment	5 Indian other ranks.	
	2/4th Gurkha Rifles	1 Gurkha other rank.	
	South Waziristan Scouts	13 Indian other ranks.	

In addition 1 Mahsud Khassadar was killed and 4 wounded.

Bannu Brigade column marches to Torwam June 24th. On the 24th of June the Bannu Brigade column marched to Torwam. Although Sher Ali and his lashkar were still in the neighbourhood the opposition offered to the troops was not nearly so stiff as on the previous day. The advance of the Bannu Brigade was considerably assisted by three platoons of the South Waziristan Scouts who secured the high ground east of the Narai which had been occupied on the previous day by the 1/17 Dogra R. Moving out of their camp at 06-15 hours, they reached their objective before the arrival of the Brigade at the Narai, surprising a band of fifty or sixty tribesmen and inflicting a number of casualties on them at the cost of only two men wounded.

The Bannu Brigade had to find its own protection as far as the Tara Jhowar khassadar post. From there the Razmak Brigade secured the road. When the road was piqueted military convoys were passed both ways between Torwam and Razmak without any interruption. A lashkar of about six hundred tribesmen collected in the hills south of the Upper Baddar valley, but for some reason remained inactive. Many small parties of the enemy were engaged by the troops with effect. One piquet of the 2/11 Sikh R. seeing a party of enemy coming towards them, allowed them to come to within twenty yards and then opened fire, killing five of them. In trying to seize the rifles of the dead men they suffered two casualties themselves. The total casualties of the force during the day were one British Officer, Lieut. R. F. J. Anderson, R. A. one British other rank and four Indian other ranks wounded. The enemy casualties during this and the preceding two days amounted to at least 29 killed and 22 severely wounded.

Arrangements for maintaining the force until the return march to Razmak. The Commander Waziristan Division had been made responsible for the maintenance of that Division after it moved south of Razmak, and now that the force was established at Torwam, there were two major administrative problems to be settled, how it was to be maintained and how casualties and sick personnel were to be evacuated. Adequate protection for the section of the Razmak road between Torwam and Chalweshti could only be assured by using the troops of both Brigades, and if they were used on this duty, other operations then in contemplation could

1937
June

not be carried out. Mahsud lorries which could run without protection, were available for maintenance purposes, but they were unsuitable for use either as ambulances or for the evacuation of sick animals. It was decided, therefore, that after the 25th of June maintenance needs should be met wholly by Mahsud lorries, and that sick and wounded men whose evacuation was considered essential should be sent to Wana under an escort of light tanks or armoured cars. Accordingly, on the 25th of June the road would be "opened" for the last time until the force withdrew from Torwam, and it was hoped that in the process of doing so there would be further opportunities of inflicting losses on Mullah Sher Ali's lashkar. When this operation was carried out, opposition proved to be even less than before. There was some occasional sniping only, but the light tanks succeeded in obtaining some excellent targets and in inflicting some casualties.

Some apprehension had existed that the fighting on the 23rd and 24th of June might result in general hostilities with the Mahsuds, and on the 25th the Commander Waziristan force obtained the permission of the Government of India to impose punitive air action, after due warning, on villages in the Upper Baddar valley, the Main Toi, the Sang Toi, and the Shawali Algad, as information had come in that villages in these areas had either been harbouring individuals hostile to Government or had provided reinforcements for the lashkars recently engaged with the troops.

Sanction given to special punitive air action.

On the dropping of the warning notices, most of the Nana Khel and Aimal Khel Bahlolzai Mahsuds held meetings and decided in favour of peace.

Whilst the Razmak and Bannu Brigades were moving from their respective bases to Torwam, the Wana Brigade was also marching to that place. It left Wana on the 21st of June, and reached Sarwekai, on the 23rd, spending a night at Tanai and at Dargai Oba on the way. It halted at Sarwekai until the 26th, and on that day, with a detachment of South Waziristan Scouts attached, it marched northwards via Barwand Raghza and Ospana Raghza to camp (at 856866) near Imam Khan Kalai. The Bannu Brigade, also with a party of South Waziristan Scouts attached, marched the same day to Narai Raghza (7988) via the Khaisara valley and the Shrawanai Narai. The Razmak Brigade assisted the Bannu Brigade by piqueting the first part of the route. The only opposition offered to the columns was a few shots at a long range.

*Wana Brigade column moves to Torwam, 21st to 28th June.

On the 27th of June, the Wana Brigade, protected for part of its march by the Bannu Brigade, marched via the Tangai Toi and Shrawanai Narai to a camp near the Tiarza Scouts' Post. When the Wana Brigade had passed through, the Bannu Brigade withdrew to Torwam, the last part of its march being secured by the Razmak Brigade. There was no hostile activity during the day, although early the previous morning reports had come in that some recalcitrants of the Khaisara valley were trying to organize resistance and that Malik Khonia Khel with at least one hundred fighting men was waiting for the Wana Brigade in the Tangi Toi at a place where the river bed passes between high, steep features. It is probable that the arrival of the Bannu Brigade at Narai Raghza dissuaded the tribesmen from using this ground, favourable though it was.

* Sketch Map G. 37.

The next day, the Wana Brigade moved to Torwam. On the way it destroyed what was left by the air bombardment of Mullah Sher Ali's residence at Urmar Khel Kile.

1937
June

Mullah Sher Ali's following, in spite of the casualties inflicted on it during the fighting of the 23rd to the 25th of June, was estimated still to be about three hundred strong. On the evening of the 28th of June these tribesmen were reported to be in and about the Titanai Pal (7297, 7298) to the west and northwest of Sholam Khassadar Post, Mullah Sher Ali himself living in a cave in the upper reaches (7298).

Sher Ali's lashkar reported in Titanai Pal area.

The Commander Waziristan Division decided to attack them the next day. Surprise was essential for success, and at first sight a converging movement under cover of darkness appeared to offer the best prospect of attaining it. This plan was, however, abandoned, chiefly because Torwam Camp was surrounded by Khassadar piquets, and these would have to be given warning of any impending movement by night. It was decided, therefore, to advance up the road towards the Sharawangi Narai with a portion of the force in daylight, to give the impression that the road was to be "opened" in the normal manner for the passage of convoys. With the enemy's attention fixed in this direction, a column was to be passed unobtrusively up the Titanai Pal to take the enemy in flank. Mobile forces, moving wide up the Main Toi, were to prevent the tribesmen escaping in that direction, and their egress via the Lare Lar Narai was also to be blocked.

Plan for attack on June 29th.*

To give effect to this plan, tasks were allotted to formations as follows. Leaving camp at 05-00 hours the Wana Brigade column was to piquet the main road as far as the Sholam Khassadar post and to remain in position until troops operating forward of it had withdrawn under its protection after the conclusion of the attack. The Razmak Brigade column, starting an hour later, was to move off from the main road south of the Sholam Post, and with its right on that post, was to seize in succession the lower spurs of the ridge running in a south-westerly direction from Sharawangi Narai Khassadar Post, the lower spurs of the ridge running parallel to it from a short distance west of the Lare Lar Narai, and finally, the high ground in square 7399. The Bannu Brigade column with one section 9th Light Tank Company, one squadron Probyn's Horse and five platoons South Waziristan Scouts attached, was to start at 06-30 hours, and following the Main Toi for the first part of its advance, was to seize the high ground in squares 7198 and 7298, moving forward subsequently to the high ground in squares 7199 and 7299. These movements would bring the Razmak Brigade in operation to the east of the Titanai Pal, and the Bannu Brigade to its west with the northern limit of the advance an east and west line just south of Zargar Ghundakai. The Bannu Brigade was to find and destroy Sher Ali's caves. The South Waziristan Scouts from the Sharawangi Narai were to occupy by 07-00 hours the high ground running northwest from the Lare Lar Narai and to act as a block to escape in that direction.

Meeting with no resistance, the Wana Brigade reached its positions quickly, by previous arrangement with the Razmak Brigade piqueting well westward towards the Titanai Pal to protect the left flank of that formation as it went forward.

Wana Brigade secure main road.

* [Ref. Sketch map G. 37 (Chap. XXI) and N. 37 (Chap. XVI).]

1937

June 29th

Razmak Brigade advances to its objective.

In order to strengthen its right flank, the Razmak Brigade continued the piqueting of the main road with one battalion to the vicinity of the Tara Jhawar Khassadar Post. The remainder of the Brigade advanced from the Sholam Khassadar Post at 08-00 hours, and an hour later had secured their second objective, the lower spurs of the ridge running in a south-westerly direction from the Lare Lar Narai. As they advanced from this spur to their final objective, a number of tribesmen, trying to escape, moved off from their front to the Titanai Pal and to the eastern spur of Boya Ghundakai which had not yet been occupied by our troops and which was later attacked by the 2/4 G. R. of the Bannu Brigade.

Advance of Bannu Brigade.

The leading troops of the Bannu Brigade column, with the five platoons of the South Waziristan Scouts in the van, left Torwam at 06-00 hours, the main body following half an hour later in accordance with the orders. The task of the South Waziristan Scouts was to search the thickly wooded country west of the Titanai Pal as far as the 98 east and west grid line, and then to move up the Central spur towards Boya Ghundakai, having as their first objective on the spur a commanding feature (715988) about one-third of the way up, and as their final position another dominating hill about one thousand yards further north (714994). They reached the grid line at 07-15 hours without opposition. As they changed direction to the central spurs, they heard the usual alarm cry of the tribesmen. Shortly afterwards, Divisional Headquarters at Sholam Khassadar Post could see considerable numbers of the enemy rushing about in confusion in front of the Scouts and evidently completely surprised. Many of them streamed away northwards, offering good targets to the artillery and machine-guns, whilst others took shelter in the dense scrub. The Scouts pushed steadily on, seized their first objective, on which an unoccupied sangar was found, without difficulty, and by 08-10 hours were in their final position after slight opposition. As they arrived, they saw some fifty or sixty enemy moving off to the north and northwest. These were successfully engaged by the artillery, the fire being directed by an artillery forward observing officer who accompanied the Scouts.

The 2/1 Punjab R., who followed behind the South Waziristan Scouts, had by this time reached their forward limit, the 98 east and west grid line.

Attack by 2/4 G. R.

Here the 2/4 G. R. passed through them and advanced to capture the right of the Bannu Brigade's final objective, the high ground at 721995.

(References in the account of the action of the 2/4 G. R. are to the panorama sketch 'N' 37 at the end of this chapter.)

The intermediate and final objectives given to the Bannu Brigade entailed movement up two spurs towards Boya Ghundakai which were roughly parallel to each other and to the Titanai Pal. The South Waziristan Scouts had already advanced up the western of these spurs. The eastern one was the route for the 2/4 G. R. and their final objective was a little less than a mile away.

The Titanai Pal, which bounded this ridge on the east, flowed close to the reported hiding place of Mullah Sher Ali. The low spurs rising from the stream joined in a tangled mass of densely wooded ridges.

1937
June 29th

When the 2/4 G. R. advanced, the South Waziristan Scouts were on Brown Hill, about four hundred yards west of the leading position of the 2/1 Punjab R. on Helio Ridge. The Commanding Officer of the 2/4 G. R. decided to capture his final objective in three phases. One company was to capture Sangar Hill and Black Rocks, a second company would then take Middle Ridge, and finally, the third company, going through the second, would seize Far Ridge, the Brigade objective on this spur. A platoon of machine-guns was to follow close behind the left rear of the first company's forward troops and come into action on Gun Ridge to support the attack on Black Rocks in the first phase and the advance in the second and third phases. The initial stages of the first attack were to be supported by a platoon of machine-guns of the 2/1 Punjab R. One platoon of machine-guns of the 2/4 G. R. would remain in reserve.

As orders to this effect were being issued, heavy machine-gun, rifle, and artillery fire was heard on the right front, showing that the Razmak Brigade was in action.

Soon after the first company passed through the troops on Helio Ridge, fire was opened on the leading platoon from Sangar Hill and Black Rocks. The machine-gun platoon had reached Gun Ridge very rapidly, and covered by its fire and by that of the machine-guns of the 2/1 Punjab R., the company was able to seize Sangar Hill with the loss of only one man slightly wounded. From this hill the advance to Black Rocks was carried out with great speed, supported by the machine-guns on Gun Ridge which were firing at a range of only four hundred yards and by those of the North'n R. and of the 5/12 F. F. R., of the Razmak Brigade, from Razcol Ridge about eighteen hundred yards away on the right flank. Two men were wounded in this attack, and it was obvious from the large quantities of blood and clothing found on Black Rocks that the enemy had suffered severely.

Beyond Black Rocks, the ground fell steeply to the Basin, a pocket in the hills enclosed by a spur from Middle Ridge, the slopes of V Hill, and Black Rocks hill itself. Two or three enemy seen running across this basin were shot down, and grenades were thrown and fired into its bushes.

Battalion advanced headquarters now moved up to Black Rocks with the reserve machine-gun platoon, which came into action ready to support the further advance and to deal with the enemy believed trapped in the Basin and unable to get away.

As soon as the second company secured Middle Ridge, which was accomplished with only a little sniping from V Hill, its right platoon and a platoon from the first company moved down in to the Basin. Several enemy were met here most of whom were Afghans. Some of them feigned death as the troops advanced and shot them in the back when they had passed. Two men were killed and one wounded in this way. There was some close fighting, and twenty six enemy dead, killed principally with the bayonet, were counted when The Basin was cleared. Five enemy rifles, ammunition, knives, bandoliers, and bags of atta were brought in by these two platoons.

1937
June 29th

Whilst this was going on, the platoon of machine-guns on Gun Ridge had moved forward to Middle Ridge to support the advance of the third company. This company captured Far Ridge, the final objective, with little opposition, the only hostile fire being sniping from Flat Hill.

It was now 10-30 hours, the Battalion was fully expended and there were still many enemy in the area. A company of the 2/11 Sikh R. was sent up to the 2/4 G. R. with orders that as the hour for withdrawal, 12-30 hours, laid down by Divisional Headquarters the night previously, was approaching, they were not to be committed unless absolutely essential. In view of this order no further advance was made, and the positions captured were held until the withdrawal commenced.

Squadron Probyn's Horse and section 9th Light Tank Company fired on, slight opposition.
The Squadron Probyn's Horse and the section 9th Light Tank Company were in position at about 07-30 hours in the more open ground west of the Bannu Brigade final objective and about one thousand yards east of the Main Toi. The ground was unsuitable for tanks owing to the many nalas. Soon after their arrival fire was opened on them from the north. Two mounted attacks were made by the squadron and the enemy were driven back into the hills. No more enemy appeared in this area.

Sher Ali's caves destroyed.
When the 2/4 G. R. had reached their final objective, one company and one machine gun platoon of the 1/17 Dogra R., escorting a section of No. 12 Field Company, were sent to the Titanai Pal, about the nala junction 726985, to find and destroy Sher Ali's headquarters. The completeness of the surprise which had been effected was shown by the domestic scene at these caves which must have been interrupted by the arrival of the troops. Food was cooking, and all preparations for the making of tea were in train.

The detachment of South Waziristan Scouts from the Sharawangi Narai camp were in position by 07-00 hours, but did not come into contact with any enemy.

R. A. F. Co-operation.
During the day close support was provided by No. 28 (A. C.) Squadron Royal Air Force. A thick haze and a dust storm, which persisted for most of the morning, made flying conditions bad and robbed the Royal Air Force of most of their opportunities. After the first sortie, machines were unable to leave the ground at Manzai. One sortie was immediately despatched from Miranshah, but bad conditions prevented more than one sortie from leaving there. Aircraft which were in the area continued to operate, based on Wana, and one machine of the Squadron, which happened to be at Wana, also assisted.

Withdrawal commences 12-30 hours.
The withdrawal to Torwam camp, which began at 12-30 hours, was not seriously followed up and was completed without incident. The operations had been very successful and had resulted in the complete surprise and demoralisation of Sher Ali's lashkar. Sher Ali himself left the neighbourhood with a small following, and took refuge in the upper stretches of the Main Toi. The occasion was unique as all three Brigades of the Division were employed together.

The casualties in the force were 2 Gurkha other ranks killed and 5 wounded in the 2/4th Gurkha Rifles, and 1 Indian other rank wounded of the 6/13th Frontier Force Rifles. At this small cost, not less than 50 enemy had been killed and 20 severely wounded. The bulk of the enemy's casualties were Birmal Wazirs.

Wana Brigade starts return march to Wana on June 30th.
On the 30th of June the Wana Brigade column commenced its return journey to Wana. It spent that night at Tiarza, and on the 2nd of July moved on to Wana, the whole march being carried out without any incident.

Reconnaissance by Division, less Wana Brigade to Turabaz, June 30th.
On the same day, the Bannu and Razmak Brigades advanced up the Main Toi as far as Turabaz (6602), with the object of reconnoitring for a suitable camping ground with water and of showing the flag. The inhabitants were very friendly, and no signs of any enemy were seen. All the troops were back in Torwam camp by 15-00 hours.

Information came in on this day that strong reinforcements had started from Shawal and Birmal to oppose the Division. Evidently they turned back as they were not heard of again. It was learnt that the action on the 29th of June had produced an excellent effect in Shakai and the surrounding area.

Division, less Wana Brigade marches to Chalweshti camp July 1st.
On the 1st of July, the Waziristan Division, less the Wana Brigade, marched out of Torwam on its way back to Razmak. That night it camped at Chalweshti, the march being unmolested by tribesmen except for some long-range shooting at the rearguard.

The Commander Waziristan Division decided that the next operation should have as its object the destruction of the fortified residence of a Mahsud, Paind by name, who had gained notoriety for his hostility to Government, and who himself had actually been killed in the fighting of the 23rd of June. Before undertaking this, it was considered desirable to allow a couple of days to elapse in order to admit of influence being brought to bear by the Political Authorities on the Mahsud maliks of the region to be visited, in an effort to enhance their authority. The interval was used in ascertaining the exact location of and the best route to Paind's house and in reconnoitring for a suitable site for a camp at Asman Manza, (8304) just north of Kaniguram, in which place the Razmak Brigade was to remain when Headquarters Waziristan Division and the Bannu Brigade returned to Razmak.

*It was ascertained that Paind's house was at Pat Khel (7606) in the Tirkha Algad. The route to it from Chalweshti which was reconnoitred as far as Tangarai (7804) by the Division on the 3rd of July, led down the Baddar Algad, up the lower reaches of the Ame Zhawar Algad and to the Tirkha Algad.

Destruction of Paind's house, Pat Khel, July 4th.
The operation was carried out on the 4th of July. The route was protected by the Razmak Brigade and the detachment South Waziristan Scouts, the Bannu Brigade holding the area round Pat Khel. The first troops left camp at 05-30 hours, and the Division was back at Chalweshti by 18-00 hours not a shot having been fired during the operation. The country was, exceptionally "big" and the physical difficulties encountered were such that it was considered doubtful whether the operation could have been finished in one day if there had been any resistance. That no

* Ref. Sketch map O. 37 (Chap. XXI).]

1937
June-July

hostility was shown was due to the helpful co-operation of the Mahsud maliks under the direction of the Political Authorities. When they were first informed of the intention to visit the Tirkha Algad they did everything in their power to dissuade the Divisional Commander, but when they realized that this was of no avail their co-operation was both loyal and effective.

Razmak Brigade moves to Asman Manza and Bannu Brigade to Ladha, July 5th, Bannu Brigade marching to Razmak, July 6th.

The 5th of July saw the Razmak Brigade installed at Asman Manza, whilst Headquarters Waziristan Division returned to Razmak, the Bannu Brigade with the eight platoons of South Waziristan Scouts from Sharawangi Narai camp marching to Ladha. The Bannu Brigade moved to Razmak the following day.

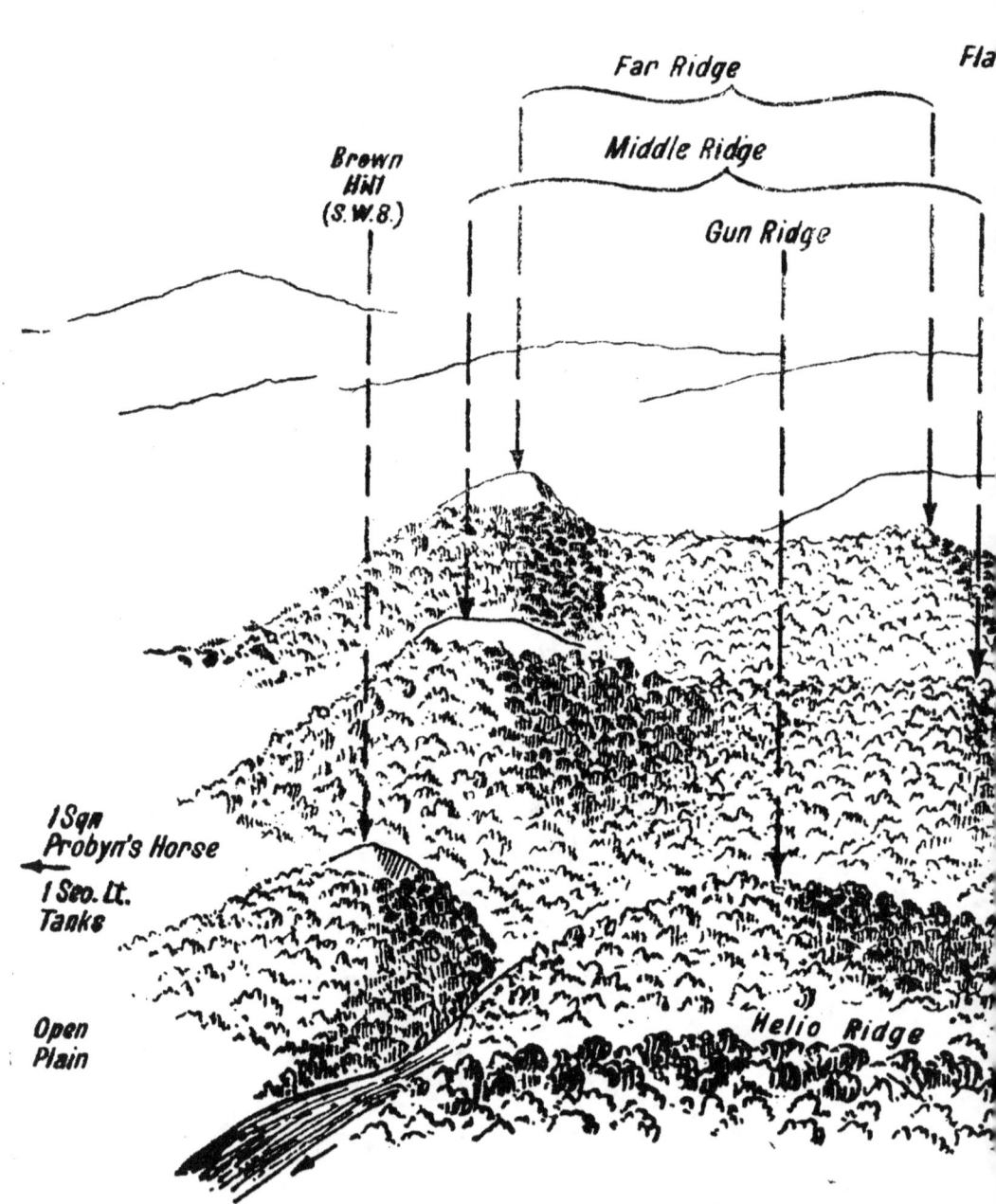

Sketch N. 37.

152A

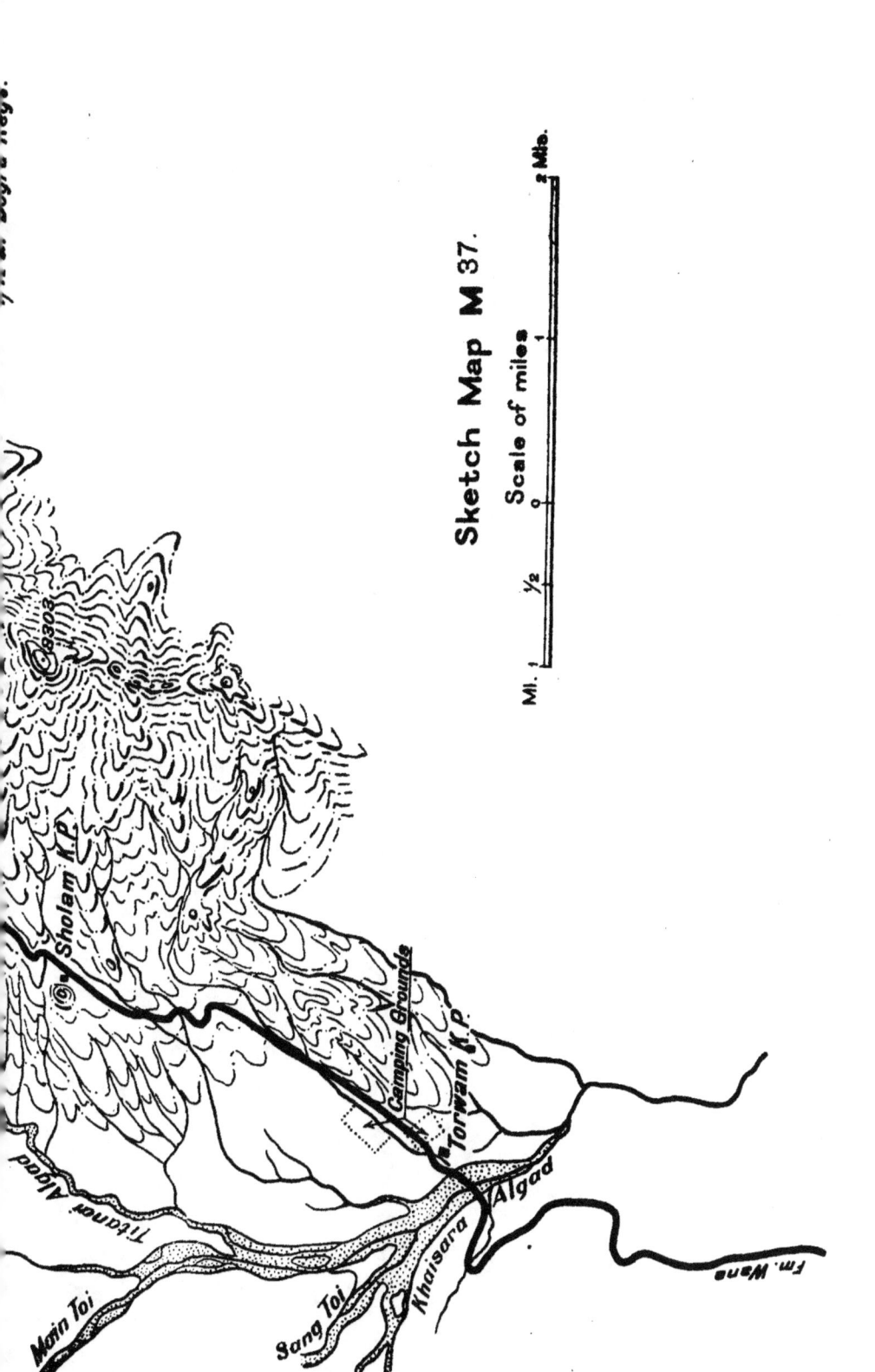

CHAPTER XVII.

Events in other areas from the 20th of June to the 8th of July 1937.

Sanction given for punitive air action against any village known to be harbouring the Faqir of Ipi or four of his followers.

One effect of the raid on the Baramand area was to make the Faqir of Ipi nervous of more attempts to capture him after this raid. He wandered about in Mahsud country accompanied by a small following of about one hundred individuals of various sections of the tribes, very seldom spending more than a night or two in the same place.

The difficulties of restricting the activities of the Faqir and his supporters, particularly his brother Sher Zaman, Malik Khonia Khel, Mullah Sher Ali, and the Din Faqir, had meanwhile prompted General Sir John Coleridge to ask the Government of India, on the 18th of June, to sanction the immediate dropping of warning notices imposing an air blockade on areas within a two-miles radius of certain places which, according to reports, were being constantly visited by these persons. General Coleridge's intention was that, after warning had been given, air action should be taken as soon as reliable information was received that any of the named individuals was in one of these specified places. A week later, he pointed out to the Government of India that the hostile leaders had moved to other localities outside the areas he had mentioned. In order to be able to deal with them wherever they went, he requested that he should be given authority to have warning notices dropped either imposing an air blockade in any area or as a preliminary step to taking punitive action against villages within a two-miles radius of localities reported to be the location of the individuals already named or of other prominent hostile leaders.

The Government of India, however, were unable to agree to the delegation of the control of the air arm to the extent implied by this request. At first they were disinclined to extend further the general sanction, already given in March 1937, to bomb, after due warning, any locality in which the Faqir was known to be harbouring.

General Sir John Coleridge explained that the principle he wished to establish was that the harbouring of the Faqir and other leaders would lead to punishment, and that it was necessary to deter villages and tribesmen from assisting or joining these leaders. Air blockade in these cases could not be fully effective, as was instanced by the fact that at Arsal Kot, although an air blockade was imposed within a three-miles radius of that place, tribesmen visited the Faqir without much difficulty. Still, the moral effect of an aerial bombardment of short duration of a limited selected area would certainly be of great assistance. He requested that he should be permitted to order at his discretion, after dropping a twenty-four hours' warning notice, the bombardment of villages or of areas in which leaders were known to be staying or which they were known to have been visiting recently. He again named the same five hostile leaders as those against whom he proposed to act in this manner, explaining that discretion would be used so as not to incite any of them who might be temporarily quiescent to further hostilities. He pointed out that as these individuals were outside the immediate reach of the

1937
June

troops he could not take direct action against them although they were the foci of hostile activities and that without authority of the nature asked for he could not even take indirect action against them.

The Government of India agreed that the Faqir of Ipi would lose prestige and influence if he was driven as a fugitive from the places in which he attempted to take refuge: moreover, if he were kept constantly on the move he would find it difficult to arrange meetings with actually or potentially hostile tribesmen. On the 1st of July they gave sanction for the bombing, after customary notice, of any village or locality in which from the information available it was reasonable to suppose that any one of the five enemy leaders named was actually located. If it was desired to take punitive action against any village or locality which had been harbouring any of these individuals but had since been vacated by that individual, application was to be made to the Government of India in each case. It was further suggested to General Sir John Coleridge that he should issue a general warning to the effect that any village or locality known to be sheltering or to have given refuge to the Faqir or to any of the other four leaders would be liable to punishment by air action.

Measures to quieten the Spinwam area*. Whilst the operations against the Mahsuds were taking place, there was a slight recrudescence of trouble among the Tori Khel. It had seemed that they would have no difficulty in the provision of tribal police but when all the details appeared to have been satisfactorily settled, dissensions broke out among them again, and on the day on which they were required to report for duty a number of the tribal police failed to appear. The chief opponent to the arrangements for producing these police was a malik of the Spinwam area, Gulla Jan. He had a certain number of followers, among them Gagu, the leader of one of the murder gangs organized by the Faqir of Ipi early in June. The pretext for this opposition was the refusal of Government to pay the tribal police for their services. To wreck the settlement of these arrangements various hostile acts were committed. An attempt was made to destroy the Olam bridge on the road to Thal-in-Kurram. The Assistant Political Officer, who was intending to visit the Spinwam area, was told that he would be obstructed and that his escort would be attacked. That officer, however, was not deterred and three-days' discussion was held with the Dreplarai Tori Khel maliks, which resulted in a meeting of the tribesmen at which they decided not to oppose the provision of tribal police. In spite of this, acts of hostility continued. More attempts were made to destroy bridges and culverts, and telephone and telegraph wires were cut and removed.

It was decided to take steps against them to prevent any further rapid deterioration of the situation.

On the 28th of June six platoons of Tochi Scouts moved to Spinwam escorted by one sub-section 11th Light Tank Company, to reinforce the four platoons already at Spinwam Scouts Post. No opposition was met. The Scouts travelled in lorries as far as the Sangasara Bridge. There they debussed and completed the remainder of the distance on foot. They found that two culverts had been badly damaged and two road blocks had been constructed of large boulders. Troops of the 9th

* [Ref. sketch map P. 37 (Chap. XXIV)]

Infantry Brigade were held ready at Mir Ali to support the Scouts if necessary. The role of the Scouts was to carry out reconnaissances with the object of gaining information, to take action, if opportunity permitted, against hostile gangs in that area, and to protect road-repair parties working on the Spinwam-Mir Ali Road.

The Dreplarai Tori Khel maliks at a jirga on the 30th of June, while producing security for the good behaviour of most of the bad characters in the neighbourhood, declined to do so in the case of Gulla Jan, Gagu, and one or two others. Accordingly, on the 1st of July, the Tochi Scouts, with one section of the 11th Light Tank Company, destroyed the house and tower of Gulla Jan. Opposition was slight, and there were no casualties in the force. This punitive action, combined with the jirga held on the 30th of June, had a steadying effect. Patrols of the Tochi Scouts moved freely about the area and there was cessation of minor offences and of attempts to interrupt road communications in the area.

Meanwhile, through the efforts of the Political Authorities, the Tori Khel tribal police, generally, had gradually been taking up their duties. They were all ex-Khassadars, and those in the Razmak and Spinwam areas were considered to have done well. For this reason, and because the behaviour of the Tori Khel as a whole since the 6th of June had been satisfactory, all kidnapped Hindus for whom they had been responsible having been surrendered, General Sir John Coleridge recommended to the Government of India on the 30th of June that half-pay from the 1st of July should be sanctioned as a temporary measure for all Tori Khel ex-Khassadars who reported for duty. He considered that if this was not granted as a recognition of encouragement for the effort the tribe was making, there might be a set-back after a certain period. The Government of India agreed, and the measure seemed to have a good effect, as by the 7th of July the tribe had produced three hundred and ninety-two out of the four hundred and sixty-seven men required for the effective discharge of their responsibility in the various areas.

Half-pay sanctioned for Tori Khel tribal police.

1937
June

During this time it was also necessary to take measures to maintain order in other areas.

The remnants of the lashkar which had been attacked in the Shawali Algad on the 16th of June had been joined by Azal Mir, a minor leader, seeking to do mischief wherever possible. As has been already described, sanction had been given on the 25th of June to warn villages in the Shawali Algad that punitive action might be taken against them. On that day, the inhabitants, who were Dreplarai Tori Khel, were told that they must either expel the remaining members of the lashkar before the 28th of June or they must evacuate the area by first light on that date. Meanwhile, in anticipation of their failure to comply with these orders, preparations were made to carry out punitive action. This was to consist of bombing by the Royal Air Force and of harassing fire by artillery. For the latter purpose the 4 Fd. Bty. (Howitzer) and a single gun of the 20th/21st Medium Battery were concentrated at Ghariom Camp.

Air and artillery bombardment of Shawali Algad area.*

As the orders of Government were not obeyed harassing fire was carried out by the artillery during the 28th of June, with air observation, against a number of selected targets in the Shawali Algad, two of them

* [Ref. sketch map H 37 (Chap. XVIII)]

1937
June-July

being the villages of Mir Ali and Lakan, the remainder being the junctions of various watercourses by which tribesmen travelled and places where tracks crossed watercourses. No. 20 (A. C.) Squadron Royal Air Force also carried out half-an-hour's intensive bombing on the 28th and intermittent bombing at other times during the day, repeating this on the 29th. The harassing fire was repeated during the nights of the 28th/29th and 29th/30th. Although little material damage was done, the action taken had satisfactory reactions. The Haibatai section of the Tori Khel came to the assistance of the Dreplarai in expelling fighting men of other areas from the Shawali Algad and some days later it was reported that only a few scattered gangs remained in the vicinity and that efforts by Azal Mir to increase his following had met with no success.

2nd Infantry Brigade visits Dinor villages.
It became known that the inhabitants of the Dinor villages, in the upper reaches of the Sre Mela Algad, east of Kach Manza, had been harbouring a number of hostile gangs. In order to remind them of their responsibilities, the 2nd Infantry Brigade at Coronation Camp carried out a demonstration march in that area on the 30th of June. A few shots were fired at the Brigade by hostile tribesmen. Otherwise, there was no opposition.

Other minor offences.
Minor offences by gangs of tribesmen continued. The water pipe line near Dosalli was cut. Piquets at Coronation camp, at Razmak, and in the Sham and Ghariom areas were attacked. Hostile parties fired on piquets in the vicinity of Nariwela Narai. A gang shot at a watering party of the 2/14 Punjab R. in the Shinki area. Razani camp and piquets were sniped and telephone wires in that area were cut. On the night of the 2nd/3rd of July a gang raided Pasanni village, about fifteen miles south of Bannu, kidnapping a Hindu boy and a girl.

Dredonai section of Wuzi Khel fined.
The section territorially responsible for the Razani area was the Dredonai section of the Wuzi Khel Mohmit Khel. As they had not prevented this damage they were fined twelve rifles. The Political Authorities also dealt with the Malikshahi Kabul Khel Wazirs dwelling in the upper portion of the Main Toi. These had allowed individuals to join in the recent fighting against the Waziristan Division. They were ordered to hand over a number of rifles and hostages as security for their future good behaviour.

Air action against Razin.
Another party which was reported to have taken an active part in the hostilities was composed of the Jalal Khel Mahsud inhabitants of Razin in the Dara Toi, seven miles west of Makin. Their maliks refused to present themselves at Razmak when ordered to do so, and sanction was obtained to punish them by air action. This was carried out on the 8th, 9th, and 10th of July by Nos. 27 and 60 (Bomber) Squadrons Royal Air Force. The first day's attack brought the leading malik of the place to Razmak to beg that the bombing might cease.

Progress of road construction.
The construction of the roads to the Sham Plain progressed rapidly. With the exception of a stretch of about one mile on the Iblanke ridge the road from Dosalli to the Shaktu river was through to Ghariom.

Work on the northern portion of the sector was being carried out by contract labour and by troops of the 2nd Infantry Brigade. South of

Ghariom to the Madamir Kalai in the Shaktu valley, construction was being carried out by units of the 1st and 3rd Infantry Brigades from Ghariom camp. To facilitate the work and its protection in the Shaktu area, the 3rd Infantry Brigade moved on the 8th of July to a new camp called Bahadur two miles above the junction of the Sham Algad with the Shaktu. A commencement had been made with Mahsud contract labour at the Sorarogha end on the road from Sorarogha to Madamir Kalai via the Barari Narai.

During the operations round Torwam of the Waziristan Division and in the Sham Plain area by the 1st Division, tactical reconnaissances and close support from the air were provided by Nos. 20 and 28 (A. C.) Squadrons Royal Air Force. R. A. F. officers and wireless personnel accompanied columns for liaison and inter-communication duties. In addition, daily reconnaissances were carried out in other areas and close support was provided daily for convoys and for road-protection troops on the lines of communication and for railway trains in the area of the Pezu Pass. Punitive action was also carried out. Flying conditions, generally, had been adverse owing to thick dust haze.

R. A. F. co-opera-tion.

Early in July, General Sir John Coleridge decided that the situation was sufficiently improved to justify a reduction in the strength of the Royal Air Force in the country. Accordingly, No. 28 (A. C.) Squadorn closed down at Manzai on the 5th of July. One of its Flights moved to Miranshah where it formed part of No. 20 (A. C.) Squadron. The Squadron, less this Flight, returned to Ambala, one Flight being kept ready to reinforce No. 20 (A. C.) Squadron at forty eight hours' notice, if required. No. 20 (A. C.) Squadron now consisted of Headquarters and three Flights, and came under the operational control of Wazirforce Headquarters from the 6th of July. If the tasks required were beyond the capacity of the sorties available, that Headquarters would decide the order of priority.

Reduction in strength of R. A. F.

1937
July

CHAPTER XVIII.

The road programme and movement of formations to protect the work of road construction.

Factors governing the selection of the alignment of the new roads.

The successful operations of the Waziristan Division in June and the early part of July had enabled the general attitude of the Mahsud tribes towards the policy of Government to be estimated and General Sir John Coleridge now pressed on the arrangements for the intensive programme of road construction which had been sanctioned by the Government of India on the 22nd of May. It would be necessary to retain the majority of the troops now in Waziristan until the new roads were nearing completion, to ensure the minimum of delays which, without the presence of an adequate number of troops, were almost certain to arise from interference by hostile tribal elements. At the same time, financial consideration made it necessary that the troops should be withdrawn as soon as practicable. It was essential, therefore, that no time should be lost in completing the programme.

The two main essentials in deciding on the specification of the roads and the types of labour to be employed were time and expense. To keep down the cost, military labour would have to be employed to the greatest extent possible. The existing unsettled conditions and the probability of the necessity of further military operations made it clear that the regular provision of military labour, apart from engineer units, was unlikely. For these reasons it was decided in the last week of June to raise four Road Construction Battalions. Three of these were composed of Indians each being commanded by a Royal Engineer Officer with another British officer to assist him and consisting of nine hundred and thirty Indian ranks. The fourth was raised in Waziristan and was recruited, for political reasons, from Mahsuds, to a strength of six hundred. All four battalions were ready to commence work about the 15th of August.

Although, for political reasons, the employment of local contractors and labour on those portions of the road for which military working parties were not available was desirable, the ruling factors of time and expense made it necessary to employ, in preference, experienced down-country contractors who had had experience of road construction under similar conditions. The political point of view, however, was met by arranging that the down-country contractors took on tribal labour through local contractors nominated by the Political Authorities.

The type of road to be made was "fairweather motor transport". The specifications laid down that they were to have a shingle surface, a normal minimum width of sixteen feet between side drains, reduced if necessary to twelve feet on short straight sections cut out of hard rock, and a ruling gradient of 1 in 15.

The total mileage of the roads sanctioned on the 22nd of May was eighty-seven and a half miles. For this an allotment of twenty-five lakhs was made. Later, it was agreed that a road should be made into the Bhitanni country. At first, the question of aligning this road along the water shed from the Barari Narai was considered, but subsequently it was thought preferable to build it from the east at Tajori, using the general alignment of the Rod Algad via Nunghar Tangi and taking the road to Kot in Gabbar. A further six lakhs was authorized for this, and the Government of India laid down that the total expenditure on road construction was not to exceed thirty-one lakhs.

As time went on it was found necessary to construct two small branch roads southwards from the Shaktu-Khaisora road to Ashwam Marsanzai and Karkanwam. Improvements to the Khaisora road built earlier in the year, to the road from Sarai Gambila to Tajori, in Bannu District to connect the latter place with the district road-system, and to a cart track connecting Jani Khel with the Karkanwam branch road were also necessary. The sum sanctioned covered the cost of these branch roads and improvements.

Military, political, and engineering requirements all governed the eventual alignment of the roads. Military considerations demanded that the roads should pass through or near those areas to which columns were most likely to require easy access. At the same time the road must be so sited that it could be as economically protected as possible. For the latter reason a trace along a watershed was preferable. This also met engineering requirements as damage to roads from rain would be reduced to a minimum and as a general rule such a line would be the shortest, thereby reducing expense. From the political point of view roads should pass within certain tribal boundaries, to facilitate subsequent responsibility for protection.

Alignments of roads.* After considering these different needs, the approximate alignments of the roads were settled as follows:—

Dosalli-Ahmedwam road—the Iblanke Ridge and Narai, the east side of the Sham Plain and Sham Algad, crossing the Shaktu Algad just north of Madamir Kalai, along the hills south west and passing to the east of the Barari Narai.

Razmak-Khaisora valley road—crossing the Engemal Narai, along the high ground south of the Shawal Algad, crossing the Shaktu Algad near Waladin, joining the Dosalli-Ahmedwam road near Ghariom Camp, from there following a course on the hills roughly parallel to the Dakai Algad and dropping into the Khaisora valley near the re-sited Bichhe Kashkai camp.

Method of fixing actual line of road. The only data available before the commencement of work, owing to the unsettled conditions, were what were contained in the ground reconnaissance reports prepared when columns were operating in areas through which there was a possibility that roads might be made, and in air photographs. From this information the approximate location of the road was fixed. Work was started from both ends of a road, and its general location thereafter was decided in the course of protected reconnaissances carried out up to a limit of five miles from road-head, the final location and marking cut being kept one mile ahead of the work.

* [Ref. sketch map T. 37 in pocket].

1937
July.

General Sir John Coleridge's intentions regarding the roads.

On the 7th of July General Sir John Coleridge announced his immediate intentions, which were that the northern portion of the Dosalli-Ahmedwam road should be opened to traffic as soon as possible, and that work should begin without delay from the Razmak end on the road from Razmak to the Shaktu valley. The former, work on which had started simultaneously on the 7th of June at Dosalli, Coronation Camp, and Ghariom Camp, was completed as far as Madamir Kalai by the 12th of August. The construction of the latter was begun from the Razmak end on the 10th of July and from Ghariom towards Razmak on the 29th of July, this section of the road being finished on the 15th of November 1937. Work on the southern portion of the road from Dosalli to Ahmedwam had begun on the 27th of June, but this section, which produced considerable engineering difficulties, was not completed until the 10th of December 1937. Work on the section of road from Ghariom eastwards to the Khaisora commenced as soon as the northern portion of the Dosalli-Ahmedwam road was completed, on the 14th of August from Ghariom and on the 4th of September from the other end, and was finished by the 17th of November. A branch was also made from it, about four and a half miles east of Ghariom Camp, south-eastwards to Ashwam Marsanzai (1628), to facilitate operations, when necessary, in the Shaktu Algad.

Interferences with construction.

Work did not go on entirely smoothly. Interruptions occurred, arising partly from agitation against the making of the roads and partly from inter-tribal jealousies and differences of opinion over the contracts and from the inefficiency and lack of application of local tribal contractors and labour. There was a certain amount of disinclination in certain quarters to accept contracts. The Mat Khel Galeshai, the Kikarai, and the Shabi Khel Mahsuds all at first refused to accept them, but were eventually prevailed on to do so. The Tori Khel, like the Mohmit Khel, would not take any. This led to some tension between them and the Mahsuds when the latter took over the construction of the portions originally offered to the Tori Khel, but through the efforts of the Political Authorities any serious trouble was avoided. Local tribal labour was employed for the whole of the twenty-three and a half miles northward from Ahmedwam and for portions of the Razmak-Khaisora Valley road, and the quality of the work undertaken wholly by local Contractors was frequently in question. There was a constant demand by them for advances of payment exceeding the total value of the contracts, and when these were refused, strikes and sabotage ensued. But although the Faqir of Ipi and his sympathisers did their best to organize resistance to the construction of roads, this did not prevent the tribesmen from accepting work on them. At the end of September seven thousand tribesmen, among them two thousand Mahsuds, were in employment. The Mahsuds, with the exception of the Shabi Khel who did not at first respond, also readily offered themselves as recruits for the Mahsud Road Construction Battalion, a unit in which they were better off than when working independently.

Location of troops protecting road construction.

The tasks of finding military labour and of protecting men working on the roads kept a large number of troops busy. The whole of the 1st Division was employed in connection with the roads from the Ghariom Camp area; the Bannu Brigade of the Waziristan Division was used on the Razmak-

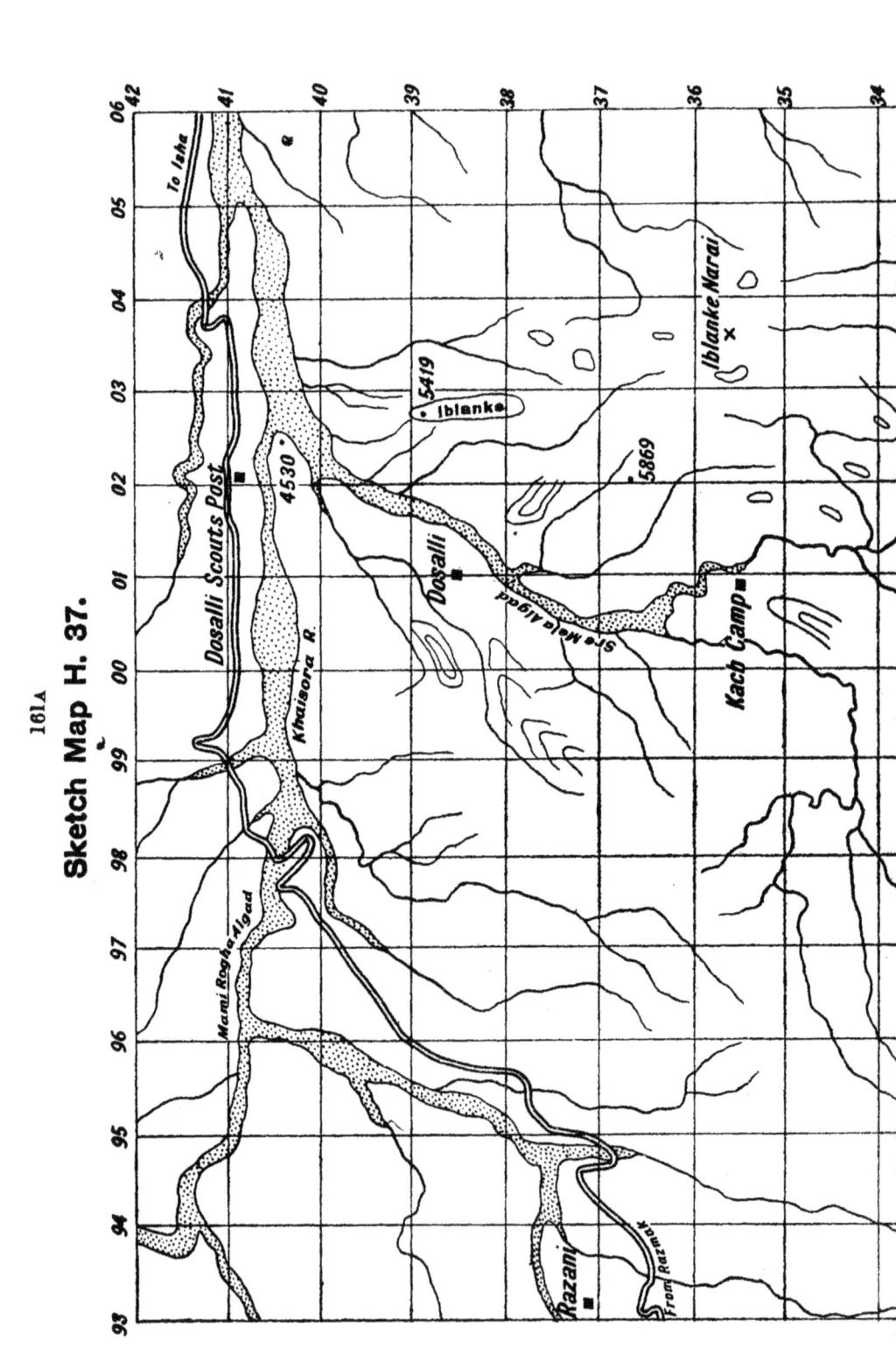

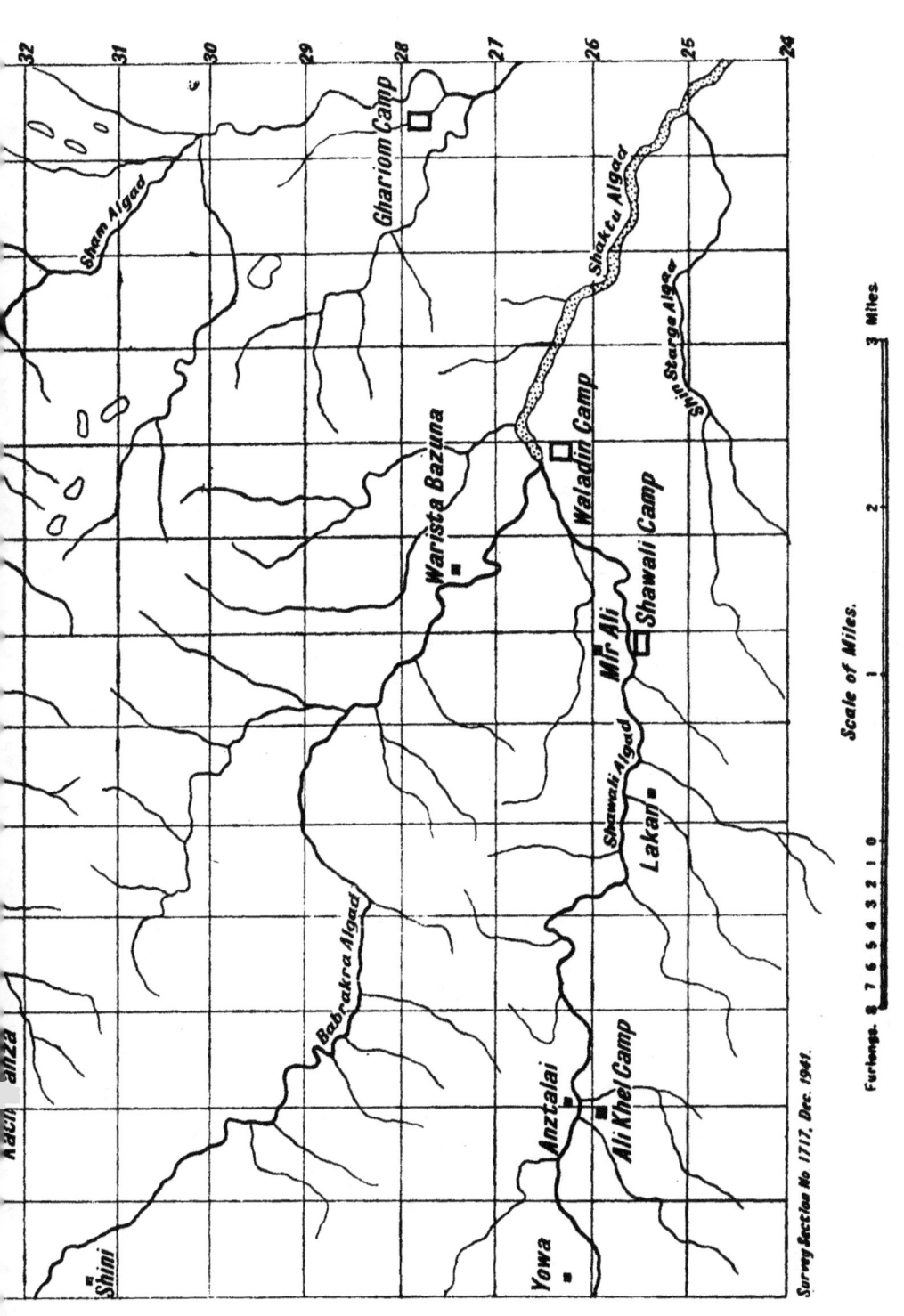

Ghariom road; and the Tochi Scouts and the South Waziristan Scouts also did a large share.

1937
July-Aug.

New camps were formed and old ones given up as the progress of the roads demanded.

*The 1st Infantry Brigade occupied Ghariom Camp until the 28th of October, when it left the Sham Plain for operations elsewhere. The 2nd Infantry Brigade which was concerned with the road from Ghariom to Razmak, evacuated Coronation Camp on the 14th of August, moving to Waladin Camp on that day. A fortnight later it moved to a new camp, Shawali, further west along the road. Here it remained until the 9th of October, when it was sent off to take part in other operations. Protection on this road was also provided by a detachment of eight platoons of the South Waziristan Scouts who formed a camp at Olai Narai on the 11th of August. The Razmak end of the road was dealt with by the Bannu Brigade, a detachment of which, known as "Lycol", went into camp at Ali Khel on the 8th of October, remaining there until the 2nd of December. The 3rd Infantry Brigade, which had occupied a new camp "Bahadur", on the 8th of July, on the road southward from Ghariom to Madamir Kalai, relieved the 2nd Infantry Brigade at Shawali camp on the 9th of October. It moved back to Ghariom camp in place of the 1st Infantry Brigade at the end of October and remained there until the 12th of December, when the roads were completed.

The protection of the roads from Ghariom to the Khaisora and from Ahmedwam towards Madamir Kalai was made the responsibility of the Tochi Scouts and South Waziristan Scouts respectively. On the Ghariom-Khaisora road twelve platoons of the Tochi Scouts looked after the Ghariom end whilst eight platoons were sent to the newly sited camp at Bichhe Kashkai.

In or close to the camps were accommodated all the Sapper and Miner units and Road Construction Battalions required for the work camps, for non-military labourers being established in their vicinity. Permanent piquets to facilitate road protection were built and garrisoned as required.

In order to make as many Sapper and Miner units available for road-construction duties as possible, work on the building of the new cantonment at Wana was stopped for the time being towards the end of July, and the majority of those units were concentrated in the road-making area.

Relief of certain Scouts' garrisons by regular troops.
The employment of the Scouts on road-protection in this area necessitated their relief in certain of the posts normally held by them. By the 26th of July troops of the Wana Brigade had replaced the garrisons of South Wadiristan Scouts at Tanai and Sarwekai, and, in part, the garrison of Jandola. The Tochi Scouts' posts at Miranshah and Spinwam were taken over wholly or in part by troops of the 9th Infantry Brigade on the 19th and the 24th of August, respectively. The Tochi Scouts' camp at Razmak Narai was evacuated on the 27th of July, and the protection of that sector of the Central Waziristan Road became the duty of troops of the **Waziristan Division.**

[Ref. sketch map H. 37 (Chap. XVII.)]

CHAPTER XIX.

Operations in the Spinwam area, July 11th—attempts by Mahsud Maliks to bring about peace in July—Sher Ali's activities—continued efforts of the Faqir of Ipi—Raid on Karkanwam July 24th—Conference in the Shawal in August—Expansion of area of L. of C. held by the 9th Infantry Brigade.

Operations in the Spinwam Area.

The arrival of the additional platoons of the Tochi Scouts at Spinwam towards the end of June and the destruction of Gulla Jan's house on the 1st of July had not resulted in the complete pacification of that area, and it was decided to carry out another small operation on the 12th of July. The objects were to round up hostile tribesmen who might be sheltering in the Datta Khel villages four miles southeast of Spinwam, to release a kidnapped Hindu reported to be held captive there, and to destroy the house of the outlaw Gagu, an associate of Malik Gulla Jan.

Eight platoons of the Tochi Scouts from Spinwam Post and four from Shewa Post started at 2300 hours on the 11th of July, and by 0430 hours the following morning had occupied positions on the hills forming a wide cordon round the villages, the Spinwam detachment south of the Kaitu river and the platoons from Shewa north of it. Another detachment of six platoons left Miranshah in lorries at 0230 hours, and escorted by six armoured cars of the 1st and 7th Light Tank Companies and by one section (tanks) of the 11th Light Tank Company from Mir Ali, moved towards Spinwam. A detachment of one company and one machine-gun platoon of the 3/7th Rajput Regiment from Mir Ali left that place in lorries at 0500 hours on the 12th and occupied positions on Tabai north and south of the Sarwek Algad to protect the eventual withdrawal of the Miranshah Scouts detachment. The latter, leaving one platoon on the high ground (4283) north of the Kandalai Narai, debussed on the road east of that ridge and moved *via* the Sarwek Narai to the Datta Khel villages, and at dawn commenced their search. During the operation armoured cars patrolled the road from Tabai Narai to Daulat Narai. The Light Tanks succeeded in reaching Datta Khel village moving by the Daulat Narai. The search was completed at 1000 hours and the withdrawal commenced, the line being along the banks of the Kaitu river. Coming as a surprise, the movements of the troops were not opposed. About twelve enemy followed up the withdrawal towards Kaitu bridge but caused no casualties. As a result of the operation, Gagu's house was destroyed and twenty-seven men were arrested. These were found to be of no importance. There was no sign of the kidnapped Hindu. Air-co-operation was provided by No. 3 (Indian) Wing, R. A. F.

Mahsud Maliks, at the instigation of the Resident, visit hostile leaders.

In order to bring further pressure to bear on the Mahsud maliks to persuade them to control the hostile leaders, on the 10th and 11th of July the Resident in Waziristan interviewed a number of leading maliks selected from all the Mahsud tribes. He impressed on them the danger of the existing situation, with special regard to the presence of the Faqir of Ipi in their country, to the unobtrusive hostility displayed by Mullah Fazal Din during the past eight months, and to the open opposition of Mullah Sher Ali and of other prominent leaders such as Malik Khonia Khel. He also told them that assurances were required about the attitude of Malik Musa Khan of Mandech, an Abdullai Mahsud, a determined and important opponent of the British from 1919 to 1923, who had of recent years been less hostile, but was known to have acted as host to parties of hostile Afghans passing through Mandech.

The Mahsud maliks readily admitted their responsibility for dealing with these problems, and appointed deputations to visit Musa Khan and the named leaders.

As was to be expected, the visit to the Faqir was unfruitful. He said he would only come to terms with the Government after he had consulted with his advisers and fellow leaders. These he refused to name, but asked for a truce of three weeks to enable him to confer with them. In view of his abuse of a similar concession made to him on a previous occasion this request was refused. Mullah Fazal Din seemed to have realized that the new roads were not necessarily a threat to himself and that his propaganda against the roads had had little effect. He sent emphatic assurances that he was not hostile to Government, and sent two of his brothers with the returning maliks, one of whom, it was arranged, should report at Razmak once a week. After this visit, his propaganda diminished and the following which he had gathered dispersed. The maliks had an interview with Khonia Khel, who said that he had linked his fortunes with the Faqir and could not make peace until his leader had done so. Musa Khan sent assurances of his friendly attitude; and explained that as an officer of the Afghan Government, (he was a senior Afghan allowance holder), with whom the British Government was on friendly terms, he would be the last to indulge in anti-British propaganda. He admitted having unwillingly entertained in the past various parties of Afghans at enmity with the Government, but insisted that he had done his best to dissuade them from taking part in the fighting and that in some cases he had succeeded in turning them back.

The party which went to see Sher Ali failed to find him, and achieved nothing except the surrender of two of the wanted Mahsud hostages. It was said, however, that at a jirga of the Upper Baddar tribes it had been decided that Sher Ali should either behave himself or be turned out of the tribe.

Activities of Sher Ali.

This threat if true appeared to have little effect on Sher Ali. On the 7th of July he had been reported with a small party in the Upper Baddar. He was again seen a few days later with a following of about thirty men in the area to the west of Sharawangi Narai. On the night of the 12th/13th of July his gang, or others instigated by him, made a surprise attack on a camp piquet of the Razmak Brigade at Asman Manza.

Attack on a camp piquet at Asman Manza*.

The post, situated about eight hundred yards from the camp, was garrisoned by seventeen other ranks of the 1/3 G. R. It was covered with a tent roof and had a wire fence round it about twenty yards from the piquet wall. Four sentries had been posted round the inside of the wall, but the first intimation of the presence of an enemy was the bursting of a bomb in the centre of the post, where men were lying asleep, at about

* See Map 'O 37' at end of Chapter.

1937
July

0330 hours. This bomb killed the signaller and wounded several other soldiers. The garrison, including some of the wounded, manned their alarm posts immediately, and the Havildar in command threw a bomb which burst in the wire fence. He was preparing another, when a second bomb from the enemy burst inside the piquet, killing or wounding all the survivors except one man. The havildar himself was badly wounded. Heavy rifle fire was then opened by the enemy from the wire and those of the piquet who could replied from the wall of the post. An attack was then made on the piquet by a knife and stone party who started to pull down the wall. A naik apparently realizing that the enemy were under cover close under the wall, and calling on two men to follow him, jumped over the wall. He was, later, found dead just outside the wall with a bomb in his hand. Another dead rifleman was found beside the Naik with several fired cartridge cases beside him. Others had also left the post to attack the enemy, as two other bodies were found nearby behind stones, with fired cases besides them. Near them was the havildar badly wounded in two places, still holding his rifle and just conscious.

Nine rifles, one light machine-gun and about eight grenades and fifteen hundred rounds of ammunition were taken by the tribesmen.

The casualties in the piquet were six killed, six seriously wounded, and four slightly wounded.

The noise of the firing was heard in the camp, but it was thought to come from the Baddar valley and to be due to local tribal quarrels as similar noises had been heard in that direction earlier in the afternoon. It was not until about twenty minutes after the firing, had stopped, when three or four wounded men arrived at the camp, that it became apparent that the piquet had met with a disaster.

It was at once decided to take action against the neighbouring villages.

Action taken against neighbouring villages. An hour or two later, troops of the Razmak Brigade and detachments of the South Waziristan Scouts left camp and surrounded, at dawn, the Shingi Khel Mahsud villages of Karon, Gudon, and Boi Khel. None of the missing weapons were discovered, but a number of men were detained for investigation and seventeen hostages were taken. Four days later, the maliks of the neighbourhood were told that Government held the people of Kaniguram and the residents of villages in the Murdar Algad responsible, and that the looted arms were to be produced and the identity of the gang disclosed by the end of the month, this period being extended later to the 20th of August when the maliks explained their difficulties in complying with the orders. Some time later, information was received that Sher Ali had possession of the rifles and was trying to dispose of them. A fine of twenty rifles and five hundred rupees was inflicted on Sher Ali's own tribal section for withholding information about the gang.

Trace of Sher Ali was lost for a week after this attack. He was then reported to be touring in Birmal, attempting to collect support for further hostilities. The news of his success at Asman Manza was received with great rejoicing in Shawal and Birmal, and resulted in a strengthening of hostile feeling in those areas.

The Faqir of Ipi, who, after he was driven out of the Arsal Kot area, was reported to be continually on the move, had by *Faqir of Ipi moves to Prekari Sar.* now settled down, and appeared to have given up the idea of continually changing his abode, and of seeking a safe asylum. He was located in a cave area on the north-western slopes of Prekari Sar in Shabi Khel Mahsud country some twenty miles south of Mir Ali (see map 'A'). This spot had been chosen with great foresight and care. It appeared to be safe from an unexpected raid by troops, and it was the most convenient centre for visits from his sympathisers, being within easy reach of the Tori Khel of the Lower Shaktu and its tributaries, of Bannu District, of Khonia Khel, and of the Din Faqir in Gabbar. Consisting of five natural caves, four of which were used as mosques and guest houses whilst the fifth housed his family, with grass huts and a walled compound near by, the Faqir's abode was in an area naturally strong for defence. It was approached from the Walo Tangi, near the junction of the Shaktu and Karesta Algads. A very rough and narrow path led up to it crossing four narais on the way. The last of these narais was very steep and narrow, there being room for only one man to pass at a time. Piquets were maintained day and night, to guard against surprise and it was reported that he had made arrangements with the Jalal Khel Mahsuds and the Bhitannis to oppose any possible advance from the southeast and southwest.

Faqir continues attempts to rouse opposition.

From this centre the Faqir continued his attempts to arouse opposition to Government. One of his chief original reasons for revolt had been the handing over of the girl in the "Islam Bibi" case to her Hindu relations. The fact that as a result of a further appeal in the Bannu courts this girl had recently been returned to the Muslim community, and that, thereby, this grievance had been removed, did not appear to have any effect on his attitude. He attempted to keep alive hostility in his own section of the Tori Khel by instructing them not to resume Khassadar duty and not to make peace with Government. He told those Tori Khel who were residing in Manzar Khel Wazir country not to take their families to the Razmak area and not to take up Khassadar duty again as he was going to send a lashkar shortly for attacks on the Razmak pipe line in the Sardar Algad. He renewed his appeals to sympathisers in the Afghan Southern Province, saying that he was going to start a fresh Jehad in two months' time "when the British will be occupied with a European war". He sent one emissary to visit Shakai and Shawal, where Tori Khel followers of his were already busy urging the tribesmen to take up arms against the Government, and another to the Wana area to ask for help. Endeavours were made to induce local tribal contractors, connected with the road-construction, to abandon work on the grounds that it was contrary to their religion, and to prolong the disputes taking place among the tribesmen about their contracts.

An increasing number of tribesmen, including many Mahsuds and sympathisers from administered territory as well as Afghan subjects, came to see the Faqir at Prekari Sar, induced perhaps partly by the fact that he opened a communal kitchen there about the 20th of July. Food supplies and money subscriptions were collected for him from a wide area, the gifts of cash being liberal and amounting to at least three thousand rupees a month. He now found it necessary to use two clerks to keep his ration and financial accounts, and it may have been this sudden affluence which led him to raise a body guard of forty Bhitannis on regular pay. His total immediate following amounted to some two hundred men. The Din Faqir, with whom he was in close touch, was appointed Commander-in-Chief of his forces and was given a red greatcoat bearing badges of rank.

1937
July.

He was known to have a cannon, made for him at Mamirogha. Several maunds of gunpowder had been sent to him from Birmal, and one hundred Krupp mountain gun shells, looted from Urgun during the revolt against King Amunullah,, were said to be available. The gun could be carried by two men and was intended for use against piquets and tanks. It played a prominent part in some of the Faqir's propaganda as an inducement to the tribesmen to resume hostilities.

Offences by hostile gangs. He issued instructions that hostile acts were to be committed whenever an opportunity occurred, and small wandering gangs became active at widely separated points. Sniping fire was carried on at road protection troops and piquets, particularly in the sector between Damdil camp and Dosalli. A piquet at Saidgi was attacked in the early hours of the 20th of July. Two days later, near Razmak between forty and fifty enemy, hidden in thick scrub, attacked a party of protective troops of the 4/8 Punjab R. Fire continued for about an hour, and was renewed again when the troops began to withdraw to Razmak. The enemy succeeded in wounding one British officer and two other ranks. A gang remained in this area for some days, shooting at the troops engaged in protecting the construction of the road. Although never of any great strength, it was favoured by the close nature of the country, and proved a source of some annoyance, selecting the moment to open fire and often causing one or two casualties, sometimes following up a withdrawal, but never staying to meet an attack by the troops. Towards the end of the month there was a certain amount of sniping activity in the Razmak area and at the camps and near the Sham Plain.

The Din Faqir. The Din Faqir, who with Khonia Khel had been active in propaganda against road-making, made use of the arrest by the Political Authorities of a man of the Aka Khel to stir up trouble. This arrest had caused some resentment among the Bhitannis, and the Din Faqir threatened unless the man was released, to raise a lashkar for renewed raiding on a big scale. Alternatively, he proposed an attack on Sorarogha or on Jandola Scouts' Post as he considered that the tribal artillery could be used successfully in either of these cases. The arrival of a detachment of the 3/6 Raj. Rif. at Jandola Scouts Post sent there to release Scouts for duties elsewhere, led the Bhitannis to anticipate that further action was to be taken against them, and at once made them apprehensive of an advance into their country from that direction.

Sher Zaman, brother of the Faqir of Ipi visited the Orakzai tribes in the Tirah, but his efforts there to gain support had no result.

Attempts to enlist the help of Mullah Fazal Din and the Faqir of Shewa. Attempts were made by the Faqir of Ipi to persuade Mullah Fazal Din, because of his known hostility to the road scheme, to join him openly. The latter however, though nervous of the threat to his own safety from a road so near to his home at Lataka, was not prepared to go to such lengths. Further efforts, also, were made by means of Mullah Sher Ali and other supporters of the Faqir of Ipi to induce the Faqir of Shewa, then in Shawal on his lawful occasions, to join in hostilities against the Government. These met with no success.

In spite of his failure to persuade the Faqir of Shewa and Mullah Fazal Din to help him, the Faqir of Ipi at the end of July was more hopeful of renewing hostilities on a large scale than he had been for some time, and urged the Mahsud mullahs, especially those of the Makin area, to send him reinforcements at once.

Reliable information was received in the middle of July that the Faqir was keeping a large stock of supplies at Karkanwam, a village on the south bank of the Shaktu river about two miles north of the junction of that river with the Karesta Algad. Wazirforce Headquarters issued instructions on the 21st of July to the Commander 9th Infantry Brigade at Mir Ali to carry out a raid on that place three days later with the object of destroying the supplies and arresting individuals wanted by the Political Authorities. The village was about six miles from the nearest point on the Dreghundai-Khaisora road, four miles from the Faqir's cave residence, and two miles from what was believed to be the position of his nearest piquet. The direct route from the road to the village was flanked to the west by a ridge rising to a height of three thousand feet at a point fifteen hundred yards west of the village. To the east, the country was open but intersected by numerous small nalas.

Raid by the 9th Infantry Brigade on Karkanwam*

1937
July

The force which it was decided to employ for the operation consisted of Headquarters 9th Infantry Brigade, detachment 9th Infantry Brigade Signal Section, 66 Fd. Bty., one sub-section 1st Light Tank Company and 7th Light Tank Company less two sections (armoured cars), one section 11th Light Tank Company, (tanks), 3/7 Rajput R. less one machine-gun platoon, 2/17 Dogra R. less one rifle company and one machine-gun platoon, twelve platoons of the Tochi Scouts, and six platoons of the Frontier Constabulary. Of these, the 2/17 Dogra R. and the Frontier Constabulary came from Bannu and the Tochi Scouts from Miranshah, being placed under the command of the 9th Infantry Brigade Commander for the operation. Sufficient motor transport was made available to carry all the infantry of the force.

The actual raid was to be carried out by the Tochi Scouts and the Frontier Constabulary, while the rest of the force supported them.

The plan was as follows:—

The debussing point selected (4346) was about two miles east of the eastern end of the Sein gorge on the Dregundhai-Khaisora road (map 'T' 37) immediately north of the Khaisora river.

The Tochi Scouts, starting from Miranshah at 2015 hours on the 23rd, were to be in position round Karkanwam by 0430 hours on the 24th, to prevent any tribesmen entering or leaving the village. The Frontier Constabulary, fixing their own time of starting from Bannu, were to carry out the search of the village, commencing at 0445 hours or as soon after as the state of the light permitted. They were to destroy the supplies and collect and remove the persons whose arrest was required. The Tochi Scouts' Commander was made responsible for ordering the time of withdrawal from the village, and it was impressed on him that the retirement was to begin as soon as possible after arrival and that speed was essential. The 9th Brigade Headquarters and Signal Section with a reconnaissance party of the 66 Fd. Bty. and the 3/7 Rajput R. were to leave Mir Ali at 0100 hours, escorted by the armoured cars. On the arrival at the debussing point, 3/7 Rajput R., to cover the eventual withdrawal of the Scouts and Constabulary, was to place piquets on the right flank to prevent

* See Map 'A' (in pocket).

interference from the hilly country to the west and to take up a general position about one mile north of the Shaktu river astride the line of withdrawal. The 66 Fd. Bty., with one sub-section 11th Light Tank Company (tanks) as escort was to start from Mir Ali at 0115 hours. On arrival it was to come into action near the road to cover the withdrawal. The 2/17 Dogra R., leaving Bannu at 0230 hours, was to take up positions of the hills overlooking the debussing point north and south of the river to protect the motor vehicles parked in this area ready for withdrawal. Its machine-guns were to be disposed for the close support of the transport, and one rifle company was to be kept as brigade reserve.

The two battalions of infantry were to retire on the orders of Brigade Headquarters.

After arrival at the debussing point, as soon as it was light enough, the armoured cars were to patrol the road in the area occupied by the 2/17 Dogra R., to prevent tribesmen coming down from the hills to the west and to ensure that there was no interference with the road where it debouched into the plain east of the debussing point.

The section of the 11th Light Tank Company (Tanks) was given two tasks. The section less one sub-section, moving from Mir Ali *via* Bannu, was to leave Bannu, in time to arrive at Jani Khel Post, about nine miles, east of Karkanwam by 0445 hours on the 24th, and as soon as there was sufficient light, was to advance towards Karkanwam to assist the withdrawal and to prevent the inhabitants of villages east of Karkanwam from taking part in any fighting. They were to return via Jani Khel as soon as the Scouts and Constabulary were north of the river Shaktu. The other sub-section, having escorted the 66th Fd. Bty., to the debussing point, was to cross the Khaisora river and advance as far as the Shaktu river towards Karkanwam, to assist the withdrawal north of that river. The Royal Air Force were to maintain three sorties in the air from 0530 hours on the 24th until the completion of the operation, to assist in the location of any enemy, to give close support if the withdrawal was pressed, and to give information of the progress of the operation.

The 24th of July had been selected for this operation in order to get the advantage of the full moon on the night of the 23rd/24th of July, as lorries and vehicles would have to drive without lights.

The Tochi Scouts reached the neighbourhood of Karkanwam by 0230 hours. Half an hour later, they moved forward to their covering position, four platoons occupying the hills west and north west of the village near the west bank of the Shaktu river, five platoons establishing themselves on the hills from the south to the east, about fifteen hundred yards from Karkanwam, and three platoons being kept in reserve about half a mile south of the village. The Frontier Constabulary, who had left Bannu at 2215 hours, moved into the village at 0500 hours, having left one platoon in a Khassadar post on the lower ground about two and a half miles east of Karkanwam. The village was found to be empty except for twenty sacks of flour, These were set alight, and at 0550 hours the Frontier Constabulary withdrew, followed by the Scouts A few shots were fired at the Scouts as the withdrawal commenced, but tribesmen who attempted to follow up were beaten by the speed of the withdrawal. Owing to the difficulty of the ground, the Scouts west of the river took some time in getting off the hills, but these platoons worked back along the ridges and eventually came in behind the Frontier Constabulary when the latter had taken up a temporary position near the Shaktu river. The two parties of Light Tanks both succeeded in getting well forward over very difficult ground. They withdrew, in accordance with their orders, by the routes by which they had advanced. The rest of the force, falling back on to the road where the lorries were parked, returned to their respective bases by Dreghundai. Embussment began at 0800 hours, and the rear parties were ready to leave the embussment area two hours later. There was then some delay, as it became necessary to search for some men of the Frontier Constabulary who had been overcome by the intense heat. The tribesmen did not interfere in any way, and the men were found. The rear of the force reached Mir Ali at 1330 hours.

The material gain of the operation had been slight. The Tochi Scouts and the Frontier Constabulary had had a trying time, a long march with the temperature particularly high. The enemy probably expected an attack further south than Karkanwam. The Faqir's piquets had been posted as far north as the left bank of the Shaktu river just west of its junction with the Karesta Algad, and it was noticed that sangars had been built on the hills some distance south of Karkanwam. It was from this latter area that the few tribesmen who did attempt to follow up the Tochi Scouts, emerged. During the search of the village signs were found that a large amount of supplies had been stored there. These had probably been removed when the communal Kitchen was started. The absence of any life in the village was due to the fact that there was no water in the Shaktu river The inhabitants had moved, in accordance with their usual custom, to small hamlets in the hills two or three miles away, where water was available and the heat less fierce.

The effect of the raid, however, on the Faqir of Ipi was quite considerable. It increased his fear of being captured by a raid of this kind, and before long combined with other causes to impel him once again to change his residence.

To put a check on hostile activities at Prekari Sar, General Sir John Coleridge now decided to proscribe an area round the Faqir's Headquarters.

Air action against the Faqir of Ipi's headquarters.

After the usual warning notices had been dropped, attacks by aircraft of No. 1 (Indian) Wing, Royal Air Force, began on the morning of the 1st of August. A few delay-action bombs were also used, to cover the night periods. Very little movement was observed in the area and as it was reported on the 3rd of August that the Faqir had left that part of the country the proscription was lifted from the 9th of August.

The report about the move of the Faqir stated that he was going to an unknown destination to confer with various hostile leaders. It was thought that he might be moving northwards to a refuge in Madda Khel country. If this were so, there was a possibility that he would cross the Central Waziristan Road near Idak Post that night, and arrangements were made to ambush his party if he did so. Actually, he had arrived during that day at Almanzai Sar in Madda Khel country on the western slopes of Shuidar some eight miles north west of Razmak.

Faqir of Ipi reported to have left Prekari Sar.

1937
Aug.

Faqir of Ipi goes to Mandech at the invitation of Malik Musa Khan to attend a conference.

On the following day he moved to Mandech (8021) in the Dara Algad about six miles S. W. of Razmak (see Map A) at the invitation of Malik Musa Khan, the leading Afghan allowance holder among the Mahsuds. Malik Musa Khan informed the Political Authorities that he had invited the Faqir of Ipi and other important tribal leaders to a conference in the hope of arriving at some agreement by which peace could be restored.

Whether fresh uneasiness at the Karkanwam raid or dislike of the air offensive were the causes of the Faqir's departure from Prekari Sar cannot be stated, but it seems that he was in any case content to accept the Malik's invitation, not because he contemplated in any way making peace, but with the idea of taking full advantage of such a gathering to further his own aims, and because he hoped he might even gain the support of the Afghan Government.

Initiative for calling the conference.

The initiative for the calling of this conference had been taken by the Afghan Government's representative at Urgun, an action which incurred the displeasure of, and later was disowned by the Afghan Government, but the orders of this official were, nevertheless, effective and the leaders invited by Malik Musa Khan began to assemble. On arrival at Mandech, the Faqir immediately began to receive a large number of visitors among whom were included almost all the hostile Tori Khel leaders and several Mahsud mullahs from various areas. He carried out no hostile propaganda at Mandech, but his meetings were viewed with suspicion, particularly as strong Mahsud and Wazir fractions were hostile to this attempt at arriving at a settlement.

Meeting of members of conference transferred to the Shawal.

Malik Musa Khan was now ordered by the Afghan representative at Urgun to put a stop to the Faqir of Ipi's meetings by taking selected tribal leaders into Shawal and holding the conference there. In accordance with these orders a meeting was held near Mana (6426) seven miles N.-W. of Mandech, on the 16th of August. The Faqir, who had left Mandech on the 10th, moved slowly down to Oblen about 2 miles east of Mana. Tribesmen were assembling in the area in some numbers, to hear what was going on. After Friday prayers at Oblen on the 14th, the Faqir preached a sermon in favour of a religious war to an audience of about 1,000. By the 16th, the gathering had increased to about 6 times as many. The leaders present were the Faqir of Ipi, the Faqir of Shewa, a steadying influence, Musa Khan and Sadde Khan, both Afghan allowance holders, and Fazal Din. Tribesmen had arrived from all over Waziristan, and there were many from the Afghan Southern Province.

Conference held on 16th of August.

At the meeting on the 16th the leaders took part in the discussion only three maliks being present, a Madda Khel, a Nazar Khel, and a Kabul Khel, and the results were not made known to the tribesmen. Finally, a letter was drafted and despatched to the Afghan authorities. This letter not only set-forth the terms, such as the cessation of road-making and the withdrawal of troops from areas where there had not previously been garrisons, on which the hostile leaders were prepared to make peace, but also made an appeal to the Afghan Government for official help in any future hostilities.

1937
Aug.

Faqir of Ipi addresses tribesmen after the conference.

When the discussions were ended, the Faqir mounted a horse and addressed the tribesmen. He said that peace could only be made if Government was prepared to conduct its dealings with the tribes in accordance with the Muslim religion and law, otherwise, he, being a Muslim, would continue to oppose Government, and that if the reply of the Afghan Government to the letter was unfavourable he would renew hostilities on his own initiative. He asked his audience if they would support him in a religious war, and was given enthusiastic promises of help. The majority of the Mahsud contingent particularly the Bahlolzai section, led by Mullah Fazal Din, the chief opponent of the road-construction, was in favour of following the Faqir whatever course he took, but the Wazirs for the most part were against war. The Faqir then told the tribesmen to go to their homes and remain quiet as he could not give them fresh orders until a reply, which could not be expected for three weeks, was received from the Afghan Government.

Extension of area of 9th Infantry Brigade on lines of communication.

In order to free the Waziristan Division, which, as affairs were now shaping, might be required in the near future for further operations, from its responsibility for the security of part of the Central Waziristan Road, other arrangements were now made for that portion, and on the 12th of August the 9th Infantry Brigade Area was expanded to include up to the vicinity of milestone 65 about one mile north of the Razmak Narai. Meanwhile as an encouragement to the Tori Khel in their improving conduct and to strengthen their resistance to the Faqir's propaganda, full pay had been admitted to their Khassadars from the 1st of August. The responsibilities of the Khassadars were also increased, and on the 2nd of August with the support of patrols of armoured fighting vehicles they were entrusted with the protection of the road from Razmak to the Razmak Narai. A fortnight later they also relieved the road piquets of the 9th Infantry Brigade from Khajuri to Isha. On the opening to motor traffic of the road from Dosalli via the Sham Plain to Madamir Kalai the 2nd Infantry Brigade moved from Coronation Camp to Waladin. In addition to its extended area on the main road, the 9th Infantry Brigade was also made responsible for the security of the road from Dosalli as far as the Iblanke Narai. On the 18th of August piquets on this road from the Iblanke Narai for about three miles to the north were occupied by Mohmit Khel Khassadars.

Extra units were allotted to the 9th Infantry Brigade Area, bringing the total of fighting troops under the Brigade Headquarters to two field batteries and one section including a post group, three sections and one sub-section of armoured cars or light tanks, one British Infantry Battalion, six Indian Infantry Battalions, and detachments of Tochi Scouts. The distribution of this force in the middle of August 1937 is given at the end of this chapter.

1937
Aug.

Distribution of the fighting troops in the 9th Infantry Brigade Area in the middle of August 1937:—

Mir Ali	Headquarters 9 Inf. Bde.
	7th Light Tank Company (armoured cars) less two sections.
	One sub-section 1st Light Tank Company (armoured cars).
	One section 11th Light Tank Company (tanks).
	3/7 Rajput R. (less detachments).
	2/14 Punjab R.
Spinwam Post	One rifle company and one machine gun platoon less one section, 3/7 Rajput R.
Khajuri Post	Post group (one section) R. A. 4·5" howitzers.
	Detachment 3/7 Rajput R.
Miranshah	One rifle company and one section, machine gun platoon, 4/6 Raj. Rif.
	Detachment Tochi Scouts.
Tal-in-Tochi	4/6 Raj. Rif. less detachment.
Damdil	Headquarters 4th Fd. Bde.
	4 Fd. Bty.
	One section 7th Light Tank Company.
	3/1 Punjab R.
	3/15 Punjab R.
Dosalli	1 R. Norfolk R.
	Seven platoons Tochi Scouts.
Razani	7 Fd. Bty.
	1/2 G. R.

In addition, one section 8th Light Tank Company at Razmak came under the orders of the Commander 9th Infantry Brigade.

The organization of the lines of communications in the 9th Infantry Brigade Area was by sectors. There were six sectors, headquarters being at Mir Ali, Miranshah, Tal-in-Tochi, Damdil, Dosalli, and Razani. A large proportion of the infantry in the sector was posted in permanent camp and road piquets. The armoured fighting vehicles were employed on the normal patrolling and escort duties.

CHAPTER XX.

Rumours of evacuation of Waziristan—Question of disarmament considered—Terms announced to Mahsuds at the end of August and to Tori Khel Wazirs, on September 10th, 1937.

1937
Aug.

Rumours and their effects on the tribesmen.

At the recent meeting held in the Shawal area strong rumours were circulating that Government intended to evacuate Waziristan. These were based partly on hopes, partly on the fact that work on the new construction at Wana had stopped, and partly on the fact that Scouts' garrisons had been withdrawn from certain posts. The result of these rumours, combined, with the Faqir of Ipi's appeals to their religious sentiments, was to cause considerable excitement and speculation in tribal areas, particularly among the Mahsuds. In spite of previous announcements, the Maliks of that tribe were doubtful about the intentions of Government. The tribesmen who got no share of the Government allowances were ready to follow anyone who held out any prospects of gain. The presence of a brigade at Asman Manza undoubtedly had had a calming effect, particularly on the inhabitants of the Baddar Valley, but it was felt that the announcement of Government's terms to all the Mahsud tribes would now do more than anything else to allay the general excitement.

Consideration of disarmament of tribes.

In considering the orders to be issued to the Mahsuds and the Tori Khel, which had now been receiving attention for some time, the Government of India had been of the opinion that the opportunity should be taken, if possible, of bringing about some measure of disarmament of the tribes. It was thought desirable not to hold the jirgas until the practicability of this step had been fully investigated, so that, if it were found feasible, the conditions could be published at the same time as the other orders of Government. The problem of disarmament was, therefore, most carefully examined by the Political and Military Authorities. The conclusion arrived at was that no scheme of even partial disarmament by direct action would be successful at this stage without disproportionate difficulty and expense. It was considered, however, that the same object might be reached, though more slowly, by extending the political system of protected areas which had already produced good results in certain frontier tracts such as the Tochi Valley and the Wana Plain.

The decision concerning disarmament having been made, jirgas of the Bahlolzai, Alizai, and Shaman Khel Mahsuds were ordered to appear at Ladha on the 24th, 25th, and 26th of August respectively. On the first day the Commander Wazirforce, General Sir John Coleridge, was himself present. On the other two days he was represented by the Commander Waziristan Division and by the Commander 1st Division.

Terms announced.

The Mahsud representatives were told that the Government had no intention of evacuating Waziristan, that it had not been interfering with their religious affairs and had no wish to do so, nor did it intend to alter the existing maliki and Khassadar systems or to increase the number of Khassadars. The reasons for the construction of new roads were explained, and the tribesmen were told that this policy would be continued in the case of any other tribes giving trouble. The fact that the Government was the ruler of Waziristan was emphasized. At the same time it was pointed out that Government wished the country

1937
Aug.

to be peaceful and prosperous. The institution of a Mahsud "Protected Area" was announced. This area was defined to be all Mahsud country which drains into the Shora and Spinkamar Algads (west and north-west of Razmak) and all country north of Shakakot Khassadar Post (8817) (4 miles south of Razmak) which drains into the Tauda China Algad. The vicinity of all Government roads and Posts would also be treated as "Protected Areas".

The meaning of a "Protected Area" was defined as follows:—

1. The Political Agent, assisted by a tribal jirga, will decide disputes according to "tribal custom" or "religious law". Cases concerning women or concerning Government will be excluded. The latter will be tried under the Frontier Crimes Regulations, with the help of a jirga.

2. Government will assume responsibility for protection of the area from outside aggression.

3. In present circumstances land revenues and regular administration would not be introduced. Misbehaviour may reverse this decision.

4. Special attention will be paid to improving the lot of inhabitants in "Protected Areas".

Fines were then announced, the Bahlolzai being ordered to pay Rs. 16,000 and 400 rifles, the Alizai, Rs. 16,000 and 450 rifles and the Shaman Khel, Rs. 8,000 and 150 rifles.

In addition to these fines, the Urmur Khel section were ordered to pay Rs. 500 and 20 rifles, in connection with the recent attack on a piquet at Asman Manza.

Ten days were given for the deposit of rifles.

It was also laid down that, except for Khassadars on duty, any person carrying a rifle on a Government road must have the rifle sheathed in cloth.

The jirgas were then warned that they must continue their efforts to arrest certain named men who were still hostile, and that any tribe harbouring them will be liable to punishment. When any of these men made his submission, the terms of the Government concerning him will be explained to the jirga. They were advised to return any property looted during the past year as such property was always liable to recovery and its possessors to punishment. They were also told that until the Faqir of Ipi made his submission, any tribe harbouring him would be liable to punishment.

In conclusion, it was announced that the Government, which was not forgetful of good services rendered, would consider the grant of rewards to certain individuals in due course.

The announcement of the terms was received quietly, and the Mahsuds immediately began to hold meetings to discuss the terms themselves and the method of compliance. Some of the younger men refused to assist in the payment of the fines, saying that this should be done by the individuals who received allowances. The tribes as a whole, however, agreed to comply with the orders given, and quickly commenced the collection of the rifles. These were handed in by the appointed date, but on examination, it was found that about 10 per cent. of them were of no value. These useless

Tribes agree to comply with terms.

weapons were then given back and a fine of Rs. 7,980 was levied instead. The Bahlolzai showed some reluctance to comply by the date given and a threat of air action was necessary to force them to conform.

It was not to be expected, however, that all excitement amongst the Mahsuds would die out at once. The maliks and elder men were anxious for peace, and in normal times, could exercise a measure of control over the younger element by persuasion or by threats of Government action. These younger men, having to rely on their own resources for a livelihood, had little to lose, and were prone to follow any personality who could play on their fanaticism and cupidity, and cared little if the leaders of their tribe suffered punishment for their misdeeds or not.

Terms announced to Tori Khel Maliks.
The Tori Khel maliks were summoned to Miranshah on the 10th of September to hear the orders of Government. The behaviour of the tribe had continued to improve, their refusal to take up road-making contracts because Government declined to agree to the exorbitant rates demanded had not led to fresh hostile demonstrations, and they appeared to be making steady progress towards a return to normal conditions. In recognition of this, the proscription of the Shinki defile, which had been imposed on the 12th of April, was lifted on the 9th of September.

The orders issued to the jirga, except for the details of a "protected area" and of fines and for a reference to contracts, were the same as those given to the Mahsuds. The "protected area" comprised all Wazir territory in the Razmak area the water of which drains eventually into the Tauda China Algad, all Wazir territory the water of which drains eventually into the Khaisora Algad, and all Wazir and Daur country from the village of Drewasta northeast of Datta Khel to the District boundary, the water of which drains eventually into the Tochi from the south. In addition, the vicinity of all Government roads and posts was to be treated as a "protected area". Fines of Rs. 20,000 and 420 rifles were inflicted and a period of ten days was allowed for the deposit of the rifles. With reference to contracts, they were told that many petitions for the restoration of their Razmak contracts had been received, and that, provided that they accepted the orders just announced and made a genuine effort to carry out their responsibilities, these contracts would be given back to them when the periods of the present holders terminated.

Attitude of jirga satisfactory.
The attitude of the jirga was satisfactory, several of the hostiles came to Miranshah three days later to make their submission, and the full number of rifles was deposited by the 19th of September. As had happened in the case of the Mahsuds, a number of these rifles were useless. A further fine of Rs. 5,600 was imposed in place of them.

CHAPTER XXI.

1937
Aug.

Hostile activities during August—Raids into administered territory—Raid on Chaudhwan September 6th—Action taken against Sher Ali's Lashkar and other hostiles from September 10.

Tribesmen at meeting near Mana disperse.
After the meeting near Mana on the 16th of August (see p. 170) the majority of the tribesmen who had collected there dispersed. There was a good deal of excitement among the younger men, induced by the rumours of the evacuation of Waziristan, of possible support by the Afghan Government, and of further hostile activity by the Faqir, but the general effect on the tribes was at the moment slight.

The Faqir of Ipi himself moved from place to place in the near neighbourhood for a few days, and on the 22nd of August took up his residence in some caves at Gumbakai (732361) N. E. of Mana in the Khina Algad near its junction with the Koreza Algad at a spot where overhanging cliffs provided some protection against air action. (See Map A).

Activities of hostile gangs during August.
During the month of August hostile activities by various gangs had continued. Sniping at camps, at troops protecting the lines of communications, and at parties working on the new roads was of almost daily occurrence. A party of about twenty-five enemy fired at Saidgi post and some of its piquets on two nights in succession in the first week of the month without doing any damage. Another small gang of about forty tribesmen followed up the withdrawal of troops in the Engamal area on the 2nd, 4th, and 10th of August, inflicting one or two casualties and themselves suffering some losses. A piquet overlooking the Mami Rogha Algad (963411) of the 1/2 G. R. who were protecting the Razani Sector of the main road was twice attacked, on the 18th and 27th of August. On the first occasion a small regimental mobile column left Razani camp in pursuit of the enemy but did not succeed in establishing contact with them. On the 27th of August the Battalion, supported by artillery, came up with the enemy and an action resulted which lasted all day. The 1/2 G. R. lost two Gurkha other ranks killed and three wounded. From signs seen later the enemy suffered some casualties.

It was known that many of the inhabitants of the Manzar Khel Wazir village of Mami Rogha (9041), about three miles north of Razani, had taken part in the numerous hostile acts in this area, and on the 28th of August a jirga of the Manzar Khel Wazirs was interviewed. They were ordered to deposit twenty magazine rifles within the ensuing week as a security for future good behaviour and to produce certain suspected individuals for trial. They handed in the rifles, but said they were unable to surrender the men as they were with the Faqir of Ipi in Shawal.

It had been decided to relieve the Razmak Brigade at Asman Manza by the Bannu Brigade from Razmak early in the month. The Bannu Brigade reached Asman Manza without incident. The Razmak Brigade on its march from Ladha to Razmak on the 8th of August was opposed by a gang of about forty enemy, who were holding the high ground north of Tauda China and the hill Pakkalita Sar* 3 miles south of Razmak. The lower features of Pakkalita Sar were under continuous

---

*N. B.—Not to be confused with Pakkalita north of Wana.

sniping fire, and, consequently, progress was slow. Troops came out of Razmak to piquet the last portion of the route, and the Brigade was in Razmak by 1930 hours. Casualties during the day amounted to one Indian other rank killed, one British officer, Lieut. P. W. P. Green, 1 North'n R., and three Indian other ranks wounded.

1937
Aug.

Move of formations in connection with road protection.*
The construction of the roads proceeded rapidly. On the 12th of August the new motor road from Dosalli to Ghariom camp was opened for all traffic. To facilitate work on the other roads from Ghariom formations were moved to new camps. On the 11th, eight platoons of South Waziristan Scouts from Razmak moved to Olai camp (936243) on the Razmak-Ghariom road escorted by the Razmak Brigade, on the 12th, twelve platoons of the Tochi Scouts with No. 3 Field Company and No. 1 Road Construction Battalion were installed in Bromhead camp (075282) on the Ghariom-Khaisora road by the 3rd Infantry Brigade, and on the 21st, eight platoons of the Tochi Scouts occupied Madamir Kalai camp. During the first operation, whilst troops were building piquets round the camp there was some slight sniping fire which caused two casualties. On the 12th, and 21st there was no opposition. On the 11th, the 2nd Infantry Brigade evacuated Coronation Camp, and assisted by the 1st Infantry Brigade, Light Tanks, and the Royal Air Force, moved to camp at Waladin (019266). On the 23rd, the 2nd Infantry Brigade, with a detachment of the Tochi Scouts, surrounded Warista Bazuna (0027) at dawn. Some suspects were arrested and some government property recovered. On the 19th, one company and one machine-gun section of the 3/7 Rajput R. moved from Mir Ali to Miranshah to take over duties at that place from the Tochi Scouts. On the 24th, another detachment of one company and one machine-gun section of the same Regiment escorted by a sub-section of Light Tanks relieved the Tochi Scouts in Spinwam Fort. The march from Mir Ali to Spinwam was slightly opposed by about thirty hostiles and troops had to debuss. Reinforcements of more light tanks arrived and the enemy were driven off. These moves had become necessary owing to the extended use of Scouts' detachments in connection with the new roads.

Attempt to capture Khonia Khel.
At one time in the month there seemed to be a reasonable hope of capturing Malik Khonia Khel. A report, believed to be quite reliable, was received on the 15th that he was at Badawi Kalai near Janata (Map L at end of Chap. XIV). The South Waziristan Scouts surrounded this village at dawn the following day, but either the information had been false, or if true had been given too late to be of any value, and Khonia Khel was not there.

Increased raiding into administered territory.
There was an increase in raiding activity into administered territory during the month also, half a dozen villages being visited on different dates. A considerable amount of property was destroyed or looted, and one Hindu was killed and nine kidnapped. Troops and Frontier Constabulary turned out to try to intercept the raiders, but only established contact on one occasion, at Khairu Khel, on the 4th of August. Information was received from the Frontier Constabulary on the 3rd that a gang was collecting to attack Probyn's Horse at Khairu Khel. Cavalry patrols were sent out at dawn on the 4th. After searching the country for about two

---

* See Map 'H' 37 at end of Chap. XVIII.

hours, enemy were seen and fire was opened on the Cavalry from some hills. The Cavalry withdrew further into the plain, hoping to entice the tribesmen to follow them to ground suitable for shock action. The enemy remained in the hills however, and eventually disappeared. The Cavalry wounded two enemy in the course of this encounter, having no losses themselves.

In consequence of these raids in Bhitanni country, a Bhitanni jirga was summoned to Tank on the 17th of August. It was announced that the Dhanna Bhitannis and four sections of the Tatta Bhitannis were forbidden access to British territory, that their crops in British territory were confiscated, and that any of them found in British territory after the 20th of August would be liable to arrest. Further, on the 20th of August a warning was issued that unless all kidnapped persons were returned by the 27th of August air action would be taken in the Bhitanni area. The kidnapped persons were not handed over, and air action was begun on the 30th of August. The task of proscribing this area was allotted to No. 1 (Indian) Wing, R. A. F., and one flight was moved to Manzai on the 30th of August for this purpose. In conjunction with the proscriptive air action, punitive air action against certain selected targets was undertaken at the same time.

Punishment for raids announced to Bhitanni jirga.

On the 2nd of September, on the orders of the Commander Wazirforce, air action was temporarily suspended in order to enable Maliks to move freely into Bhitanni country, to negotiate for the return of the kidnapped Hindus. As only two were returned, air action was resumed on the 9th of September.

On the 13th air action was again similarly suspended as it appeared possible that the Maliks, who were making further efforts, might now be successful in causing the remaining Hindus to be released. These attempts, however, again proved fruitless, and the area was once more proscribed from the 23rd of September.

On the 12th of October, the Bhitanni jirga was interviewed by the Commander, Wazirforce and the Resident. As a result of this jirga, General Sir John Coleridge ordered that air operations should again be suspended in order to allow deputations to enter the country to obtain the release of the four Hindus still in captivity.

The next day it was reported that all the kidnapped Hindus had been released and air action was stopped.

In these operations in the Bhitanni area operational flying had been carried out for seven hundred and ten hours, and fifty one tons of H. E. bombs, five hundred and fifty-five containers of incendiary bombs, and eighty thousand rounds of S. A. A. had been expended.

On the 23rd of August a demonstration flight was carried out over Waziristan by ten flights, each of three aircraft, in line astern. The area covered included the Shawal, Mahsud country from the Upper Baddar valley to the Tank Zam at Jandola; and the Bhitanni territory.

Demonstration flight by R. A. F.

This demonstration which was designed to impress the Faqir of Ipi and also to make a demonstration of force over the Mahsuds collecting to hear Government's orders caused some temporary alarm amongst the Faqir's immediate following, and led him to keep on the move for a few days. General Sir John Coleridge had had under consideration another attempt to capture the Faqir whilst he was at Gumbakai, but when the latter took alarm at this demonstration, the idea had to be abandoned.

On the 25th of August notices were dropped over the Shawal area warning the inhabitants that until the Faqir submitted to Government, any tribe sheltering him would be liable to punishment. As a result of this, the Faqir assured the Madda Khel that if and when he renewed hostilities he would leave their country.

Warning notices dropped on inhabitants of Shawal.

1937
Aug.-Sept.

General Sir John Coleridge now had everything in readiness for the proscription of a suitable area round the Faqir's headquarters in case tribesmen should again be summoned to a meeting.

Preparations for air action against Faqir of Ipi ready.

As however the Faqir did not issue such a summons the necessity for taking this air action did not arise for the moment. It was known that the Faqir had received a reply to his letter sent to the Afghan Government after the meeting on the 16th of August, and that this had made it quite clear that no help was to be expected from that quarter. Presumably for this reason he had not called the tribesmen to him, although they were waiting expectantly for the message. Many parties were ready to go, and some had actually set out but these latter dispersed as they received no sign from him. He was still receiving subscriptions in cash and kind, and he continued his propaganda, actively assisted by Khonia Khel and the Din Faqir. He tried to persuade the Mahsuds not to comply with the terms imposed on them and renewed his efforts to seduce maliks and Khassadars from their duty. He also decided to make a strong bid for the support of the Ahmedzai Wazirs, and summoned them and the Kabul Khel Wazirs of Birmal and the Ghilzais to meet him at Musa Nika on the 10th of September, giving them special instructions to bring ammunition instead of the usual money offerings.

By the end of August, having failed in his efforts to raise a really big lashkar, the Faqir decided to launch his new offensive with such of his followers as he could count on. The areas he selected were (a) southwest of Razmak, where under the leadership of Mullah Sher Ali, the Mahsuds of the Baddar valley and the Makin area might be expected to help, (b) Spinkamar, north of Razmak, the water supply of that place offering a good objective, (c) Razani where the local inhabitants had recently been active on his side, (d) Datta Khel in the Tochi valley and Spinwam, where he might hope for the support of the Madda Khel and of Afghan subjects from Khost, and (e) the line of communications between Jandola and Wana. In addition, raiding into the settled districts was to be intensified.

Faqir of Ipi decides to launch offensive with small parties.

*Mullah Sher Ali returned to the Upper Baddar valley after the conference near Mana (see page 183), assumed the title of "Khalifa", and established his headquarters and a communal kitchen at Laswandai (6908). To emphasize his importance he summoned the local Mahsuds and Wazirs to meet him. He succeeded in collecting a lashkar of over three hundred, the majority being Mahsuds of the Baddar and Main Toi valleys, and he commenced to have these instructed in drill and manoeuvres as practised by the Scouts. He began his offensive on the

Mullah Sher Ali starts an offensive— Raid on Chaudhwan, 6th September 1937.

---

* [Ref. sketch map Q 37 at end of Chapter].

1937
Sept. 6th

6th of September. A party of about one hundred and twenty of his men raided the village of Chaudhwan, near the administrative boarder about thirty miles southwest of Dera Ismail Khan, killing one Hindu and wounding two more, looting some shops, and carrying off some animals.

Regular troops, Frontier Constabulary, Civil Police, and village pursuit parties were all concerned in the attempt to intercept these raiders, and the following account of their efforts exemplifies the difficulties of conducting an operation of this kind.

News of the raid reached Manzai Area Headquarters at 0725 hours, 6th Sept. At 0730 hours one section of armoured cars was sent from Manzai to Daraban with orders to act according to the situation as known there. The Area Commander ordered a detachment of two rifle platoons of the 4/16 Punjab R., at Gumal to meet his mobile column at Surkamar Post on the road twenty-three miles north of Daraban, and directed that three platoons of the Frontier Constabulary at Manzai were to go to Zarkani (nine miles north of Daraban) and to await orders there. He asked the Royal Air Force to reconnoitre the area between Zam Post on the Khora river, eight miles west of Daraban, and the Chaudhwan Zam. At 0810 hours he left Manzai with the mobile column, four rifle platoons and one machine-gun platoon of the 4/16 Punjab R.

On his arrival at Surkamar Post at 0915 hours, the Area Commander found there the Civil Defence Officer and four platoons of Frontier Constabulary from Tank. He was informed that the raiders had been pursued by the civil armed police and the village pursuit parties into the hills of the Chaudhwan Zam near the administrative border. The Civil Defence Officer had heard that the District Officer, Frontier Constabulary, Drazinda, had moved his Constabulary platoons to various places. One platoon, from Mughal Kot, was going direct to Chaudhwan via Domanda; two more were piqueting the hills between Drazinda and Zam Post; two, from Zarkani, were to hold the Sheikh Haidar nala; one platoon and the Levies from New Luni had gone to Luni Post. The country between Domanda and Drazinda was being held by the village pursuit parties of the Sherannis, the inhabitants of the hilly area southeast of Drazinda.

At Surkamar Post the Area Commander sent orders to Tank that a rifle company of the 2/17 Dogra R. at that place was to come to Surkamar Post, escorted by a sub-section of armoured cars. The cars were to go on to Daraban.

The Area Commander then went on to Daraban with the Civil Defence officer, the Manzai Mobile Column, and the Tank detachment of Frontier Constabulary, arriving there at 1015 hours. It was now learnt that the armoured cars from Manzai had been sent on from Daraban to Chaudhwan by the Deputy Commissioner, Dera Ismail Khan, who had reached Daraban. It was decided to recall them, but it took some time to get them back as the cross-country track between these two places was very difficult.

Confirmation was received of the dispositions made by the District officer, and the Area Commander now made further arrangements. Two rifle platoons of the 4/16 Punjab R. under 2/Lieut. L. I. Jones, were to go in motor transport to the Chaudhwan Zam at the point where it issues from the hills. One rifle platoon and one machine-gun section was to occupy Daraban Post. The remaining three rifle platoons were to go to Shekh Mela, one taking up a position at the Shekh Mela defile, and another near the village of Landai. Of the two platoons Frontier Constabulary originally ordered by the District officer to piquet the hills between Drazinda and Zam Post and the one ordered to move to Chaudhwan, one was to occupy a knoll halfway between Daraban and Zam Post, one was to hold Zam Post, and the third was to cover a nala in that neighbourhood.

1937
Sept. 6th

The Area Commander and the Civil Defence Officer then took the remaining four platoons, Frontier Constabulary and the machine-gun section to Drazinda. On arrival there at 1215 hours, three of these platoons were sent to Dag, six miles southwest of Drazinda.

Meanwhile, the civil armed police and the village pursuit parties had withdrawn from the hills and had lost touch with the raiders. The former were met at a distance of two miles from the hills by a Frontier Constabulary platoon which was advancing to help them, and this detachment succeeded in regaining touch with the raiders shortly before 2/Lieut. Jones and his party reached their position.

At 1400 hours news reached Drazinda that this party was in touch with the Frontier Constabulary platoon, and that the latter, which in the course of the day lost three men killed and one wounded, was heavily engaged with the tribesmen.

Orders were sent immediately to Daraban that the platoon of the 4/16 Punjab R. there was to join 2/Lieut. Jones and that the Manzai section of armoured cars should follow it up as far as it could.

The District officer was ordered to take the three Frontier Constabulary platoons at Dag to Sheikh Mela, to pick up the detachment of the 4/16 Punjab R. at Sheikh Mela, and then move into the hills north of Domanda, turning eastward and coming in on the rear of the enemy opposing 2/Lieut. Jones and so cutting off their retreat to the south and west. To give him communication with Drazinda he was to leave a signal station at Dag. The whole of this party was carried in lorries, and the District officer was instructed to exercise great care with the vehicles and to take the troops out of the lorries and leave the lorries behind if the road became so bad that there was a chance of their not being able to travel along it.

The Area Commander also sent the sub-section of armoured cars from Tank, which had now come on to Drazinda, to patrol the road as far as Sheikh Mela.

From the information received it was clear that the force would have to remain out for the night. The intention of the Area Commander was to keep the raiders trapped for the night, and to finish off the action the next morning. If the raiders succeeded under cover of darkness in getting through the close cordon formed by the parties under 2/Lieut. Jones and the District officer, he intended to block their escape by an outer ring, preventing movement into the hills to the west or along the east side of the foothills.

With these objects, he ordered the detachment of the 2/17 Dogra R. at Surkamar Post to join him at Drazinda and sent two of the Frontier Constabulary platoons at Zarkani to Daraban. Two platoons of the 2/17 Dogra R. were sent to the defile near Pir Ghundi, and the other two with

1937 Sept.

the one remaining platoon of Frontier Constabulary took up a position covering a track leading through the hills to the southeast of Drazinda. The two platoons of Frontier Constabulary from Zarkani were intended to strengthen the cordon between Zam Post and the detachment located at the knoll halfway between Zam Post and Daraban, while armoured cars patrolled the road in the area. All other dispositions were to remain as they were.

At 1500 hours information had been received that 2/Lieut. Jones detachment had moved into the hills and was some distance to the north of the Chaudhwan Zam. After that hour until 1900 hours nothing more was heard of the forces which should have been closing in on the raiders. At 1900 hours a report arrived that the lorries which had conveyed the District Officer's party were stuck in the sand about three miles beyond Domanda, that they were being guarded by a platoon of the 4/16 Punjab R., and that the rest of the force under the District officer had gone down the Chaudhwan Zam. Efforts by 2/Lieut. Jones party to communicate with headquarters had failed, no messages had come through the signal station at Dag, and aircraft, which had been flying at some height, had seen no signs of either the raiders or our own troops. 2/Lieut. Jones' detachment had tried to outflank the raiders, but without success, and although it remained in its position during the night, the inner cordon was incomplete in the absence of the District officer's force. The outer cordon also was not closed, as the two Frontier Constabulary platoons from Zarkani, hearing on arrival at Daraban that a fight was in progress in the hills, waited for no further instructions and went off to take part in it.

The chances of preventing the escape of the raiders was therefore considerably reduced, and at 0930 hours on the 7th it was clear that they had got away. They had been forced, however, to leave a portion of their loot behind.

In the hope that they might be intercepted at a later stage in their withdrawal, a detachment of the 3/16 Punjab R. was sent from Wana to lay an ambush on a likely route passing near Tanai, but no more was seen of the raiders.

Sher Ali attacks Khassadar posts.*
Sher Ali followed up this raid by attacks on Khassadar posts in the Baddar Algad and Torwam areas on the 7th and 8th of September, two Khassadars being killed. Sharawangi (7600), Tara Jowar (7648) and Sholam (7396) Posts were seized and burnt. Posts at Shakai (7205) and Chalweshti (7701) were also attacked, but the enemy were driven off, in one case with the help of the local villagers.

Steps to be taken by Commander, Waziristan Division.
Instructions were immediately given to the Commander, Waziristan Division to despatch a force of a strength of not less than one brigade group to take punitive action against certain villages selected by the Political Agent, South Waziristan, in the Upper Baddar valley. He was also made responsible for the protection of the line of communications from Razmak to Asman Manza. In view of the possibility that the Faqir of Ipi would hold a jirga in Shawal and that, after that, a lashkar might move thence to interfere with the lines of communication,

---

* [Ref. sketch map G 37 at end of Chap.]

to counter such a threat, he was informed that the 3rd Infantry Brigade had been placed at twenty-four hours notice to be ready to reinforce the Waziristan Division, if required.

General Sir John Coleridge also decided to proscribe by air action all country drained by the Baddar Algad and Main Toi and their tributaries, down to, but exclusive of Sinetiza (7503) and of Daud (6501) respectively. The air offensive in these areas, in which action was to be taken against all tribesmen seen therein as well as against selected villages, was to begin on the 11th of September.

Air action against special areas.

The Commander, Waziristan Division decided to use the Bannu Brigade, which had been at Asman Manza for some time, for these operations, and in order to have more troops on the spot and to facilitate the protection of the line of communications, the Razmak Brigade was to move to Ladha.

Preliminary moves.

The 2/14 Punjab R., from the 9th Brigade was sent to Asman Manza to reinforce the Bannu Brigade and on the 9th of September Headquarters Waziristan Division also arrived there.

The Razmak Brigade group left Razmak on the 8th marching to Tauda China on that day. The column was slightly sniped when nearing the camp and in camp. During the night sniping was continuous and a piquet was attacked, unsuccessfully, with bombs. A jirga of the Abdullai Mahsuds was immediately summoned, and as a punishment for this incident, the Maliks' allowances were withheld and the tribe was fined Rs. 5,000. The next day the column marched on to Ladha. It met with a certain amount of opposition in the Marai Narai area. A platoon of the 1/North'n R. advancing to a piquet position just west of the Narai, came under heavy sniping fire. It was reinforced by another platoon of the same Battalion and by a platoon of the 4/8 Punjab R., before the piquet was established. Apart from this there was little opposition, and the withdrawal of piquets was carried out without any trouble. The casualties during the day were 2 British other ranks killed and 1 wounded of the 1/North'n R., 1 British other rank wounded, 9th Light Tank Company, 1 Viceroy's Commissioned officer killed, 7 Mtn. Bty., and 2 Indian other ranks wounded, 4/8 Punjab R.

Razmak Brigade column moves to Ladha.

On the 7th of September notices had been dropped warning the inhabitants of Laswandai (6908) that their village would be bombed, and action was taken by two flights of No. 2 (Indian) Wing on the 9th and 10th. It was stopped after the latter day in view of impending operations in the Baddar Algad, and because the village, situated on a high, narrow, and steep ridge, was found to be a particularly difficult target from the air.

Air action against Laswandai.

On the 10th, the Bannu Brigade began its task of administering punishment by destroying the houses of well-known Mahsud hostiles in the villages of Boi Khel (8206), Gudon (8205) and Pasham Din (8204) each within about one mile of Asman Manza Camp, without any opposition. The following day, a sub-section of the 21st Medium Battery, which had arrived at Asman Manza camp,

Bannu Brigade destroys towers and houses near Asman Manza.*

---

* Map 'O' 37 at end of Chapter.

1937
Sept.

shelled certain villages which had failed to produce hostages demanded by the Political authorities.

On the 11th and 12th of September, certain sections of Bahlolzai and Alizai Mahsuds, living in the Dara Toi (near Razin, where there had been signs of trouble in spite of the air action taken there in the previous July), the Dre Algad and the Dazhe Oba, were warned that unless they withdrew all their men now with Sher Ali and made their submission within three days their villages would be bombed. These sections complied immediately with the order and no air action was taken against them.

Certain Mahsuds warned to withdraw men from Sher Ali's lashkar.

On the 12th Sept. the Bannu Brigade column moved to the Upper Baddar valley, to deal with recalcitrants there. It camped near Abdur Rahman Khel (6908) having met with very slight opposition on the way. The following day it visited Kama Sperawunai (7405) and Sinetizha (7503) demolishing the houses of selected hostiles. This area was very peaceful, only two shots being fired at the column during the day. Returning to Abdur Rahman Khel for the night, the column returned to Asman Manza camp on the 14th, again finding no enemy on the way.

Bannu Brigade column moves to Upper Baddar.*

Whilst the Bannu Brigade was away, a section of the 9th Light Tank Company from Asman Manza camp carried out a road reconnaissance to Tara Jhawar Khassadar post on the Torwam road. Several road blocks were found, none of them serious, south of Chalweshti, and more were seen south of Tara Jhawar.

The air action and these operations of the Bannu Brigade column, so promptly undertaken, had a rapid and good effect on the inhabitants of the area. Sharawangi, Sholam, and Tara Jhawar Khassadar posts were re-occupied without any opposition, Sher Ali's lashkar melted away, and a jirga of the local maliks came in to Ladha. There they were ordered to hand in one hundred and twenty rifles as security for their good behaviour and to produce a number of hostages within the next three days. The Bahlolzai representatives displayed some truculence at first, but at a meeting on the next day they too decided to comply.

Results of air and ground operations.

Air action in the proscribed area was stopped from the 16th of September, when it was clear that the tribesmen were going to comply with the orders given.

The Razmak Brigade at Ladha was employed during these days, in conjunction with troops from Razmak, in protecting the road to Razmak for the passage of convoys. The only day on which any opposition was found was on the 15th, when, during the afternoon, an action developed against a small party of enemy in the Pakkalita Sar area (8919) The convoy was not checked, and troops withdrew, eventually, unpursued.

Certain villages in the Khaisara valley having contributed to the hostile contingents, it was decided that the Bannu Brigade Column should visit them also, the opportunity being taken to destroy crops near Urmar Khel Kile (7490) belonging to Sher Ali.

Bannu Brigade column visits villages in Khaisara valley†.

---

* [Ref. map O 37 at end of Chap.]
† [Ref. map G 37 at end of Chap.]

Map G. 37.

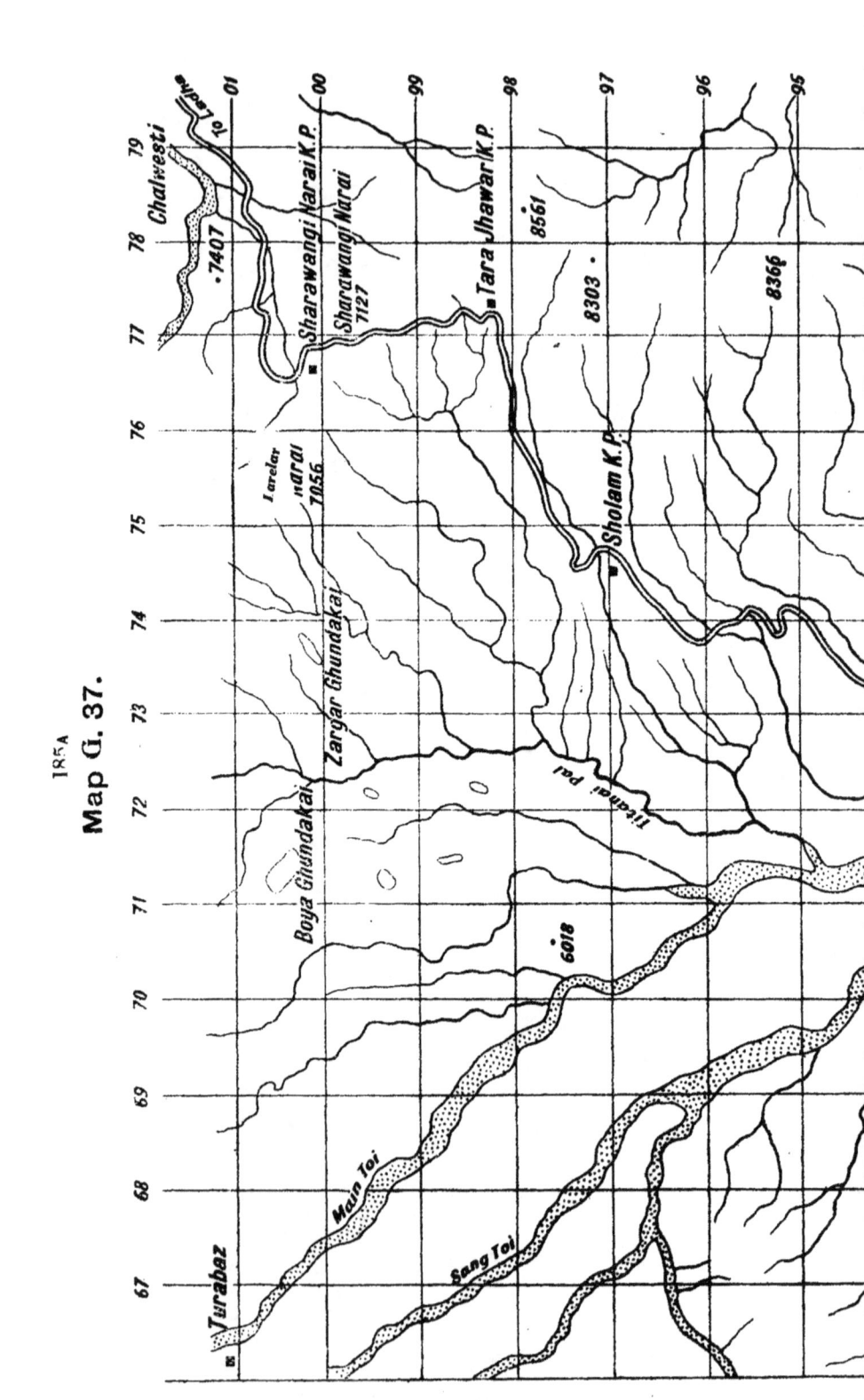

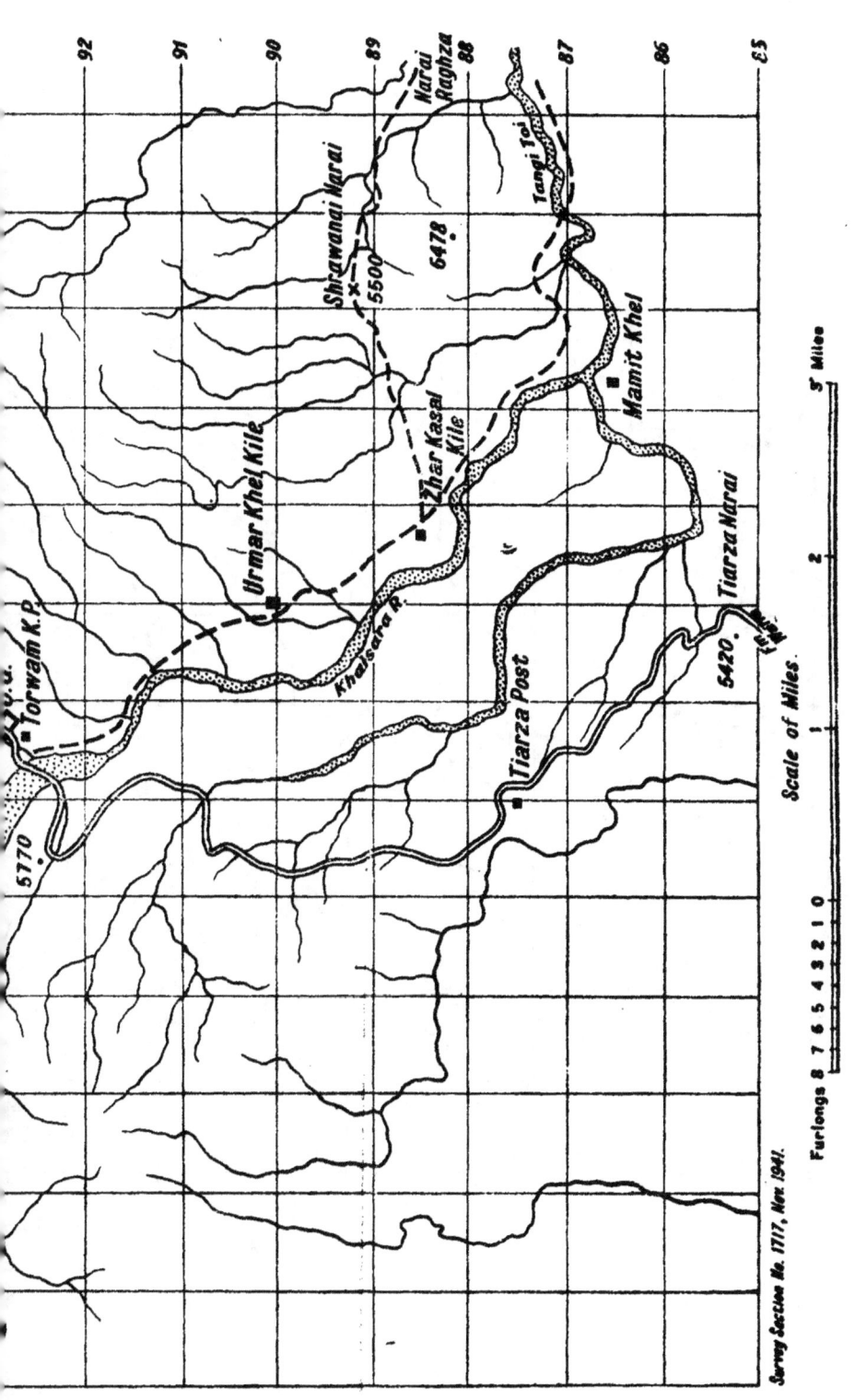

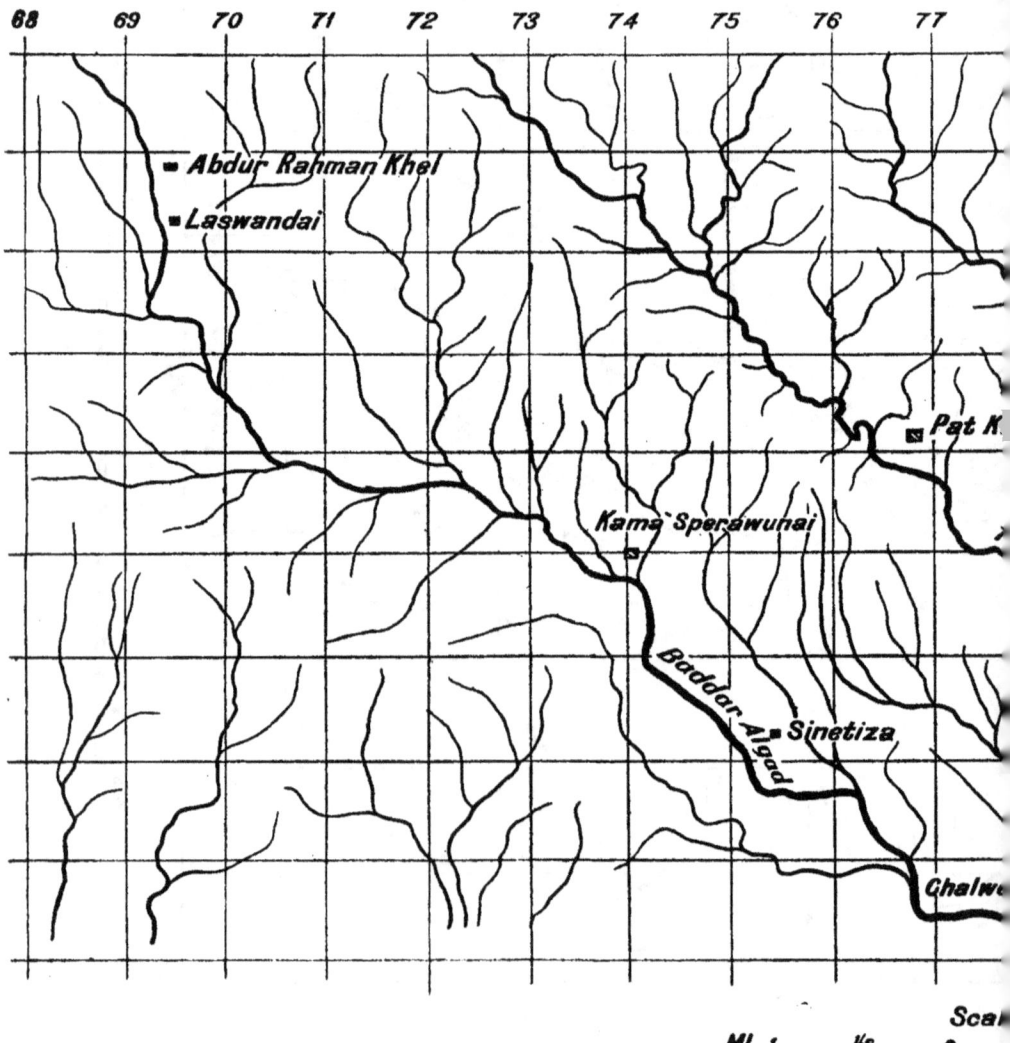

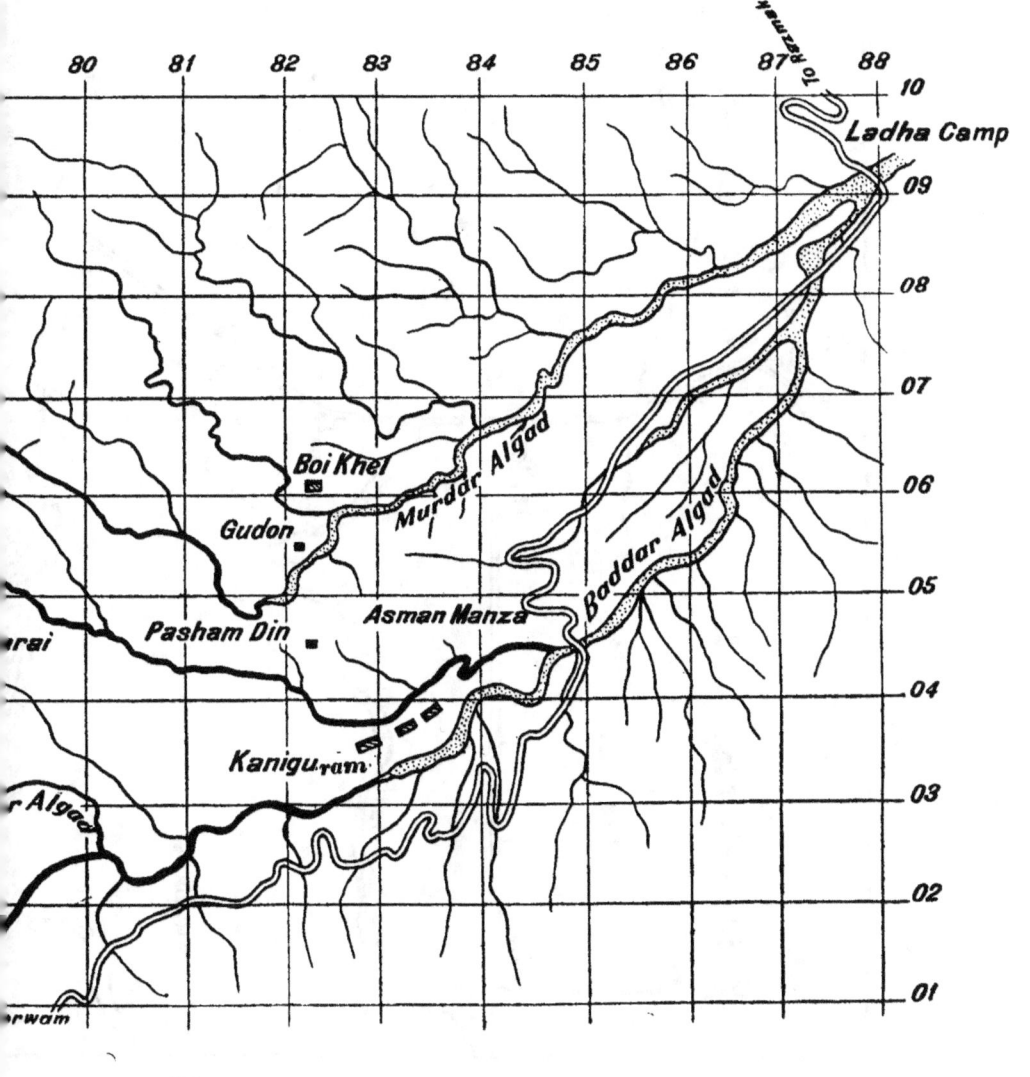

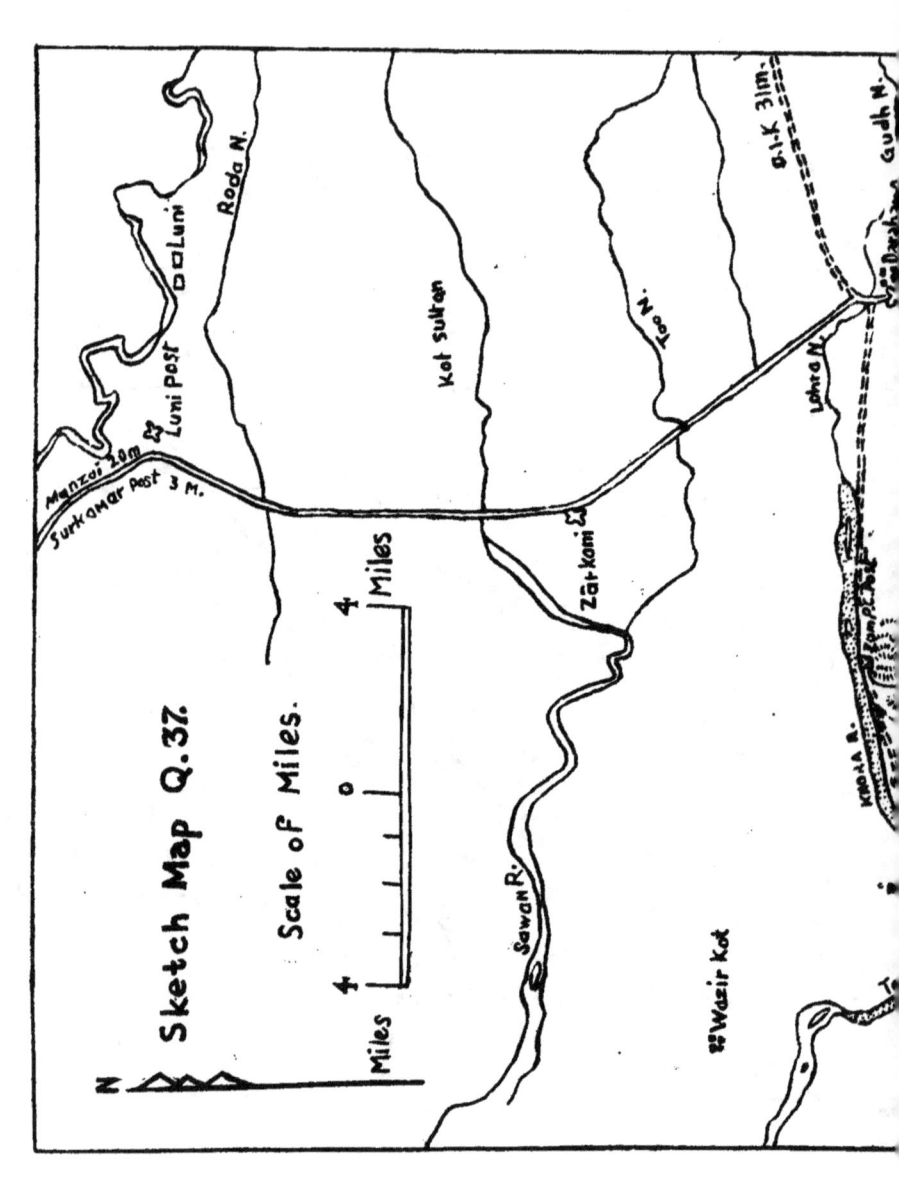

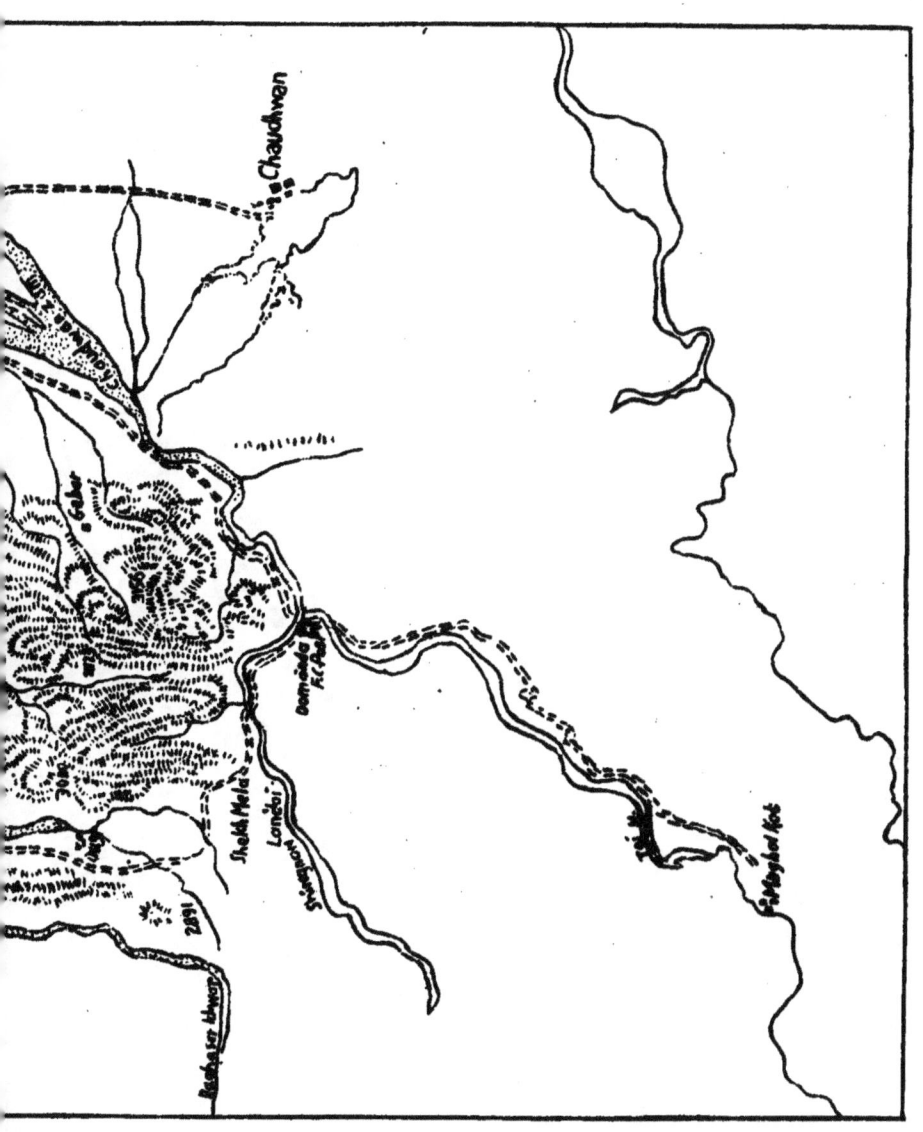

The 2/14 Punjab R. which had been attached to the Bannu Brigade to protect Asman Manza camp during the absence of the Brigade, being no longer needed for that purpose, was sent to Razmak, to enable work on the new road, which had been seriously interrupted by these operations, to be resumed. The Razmak Brigade column moved to Asman Manza camp.

1937

Sept.

On the 18th of September, the Bannu Brigade column, assisted by the Razmak Brigade which piqueted the road from Asman Manza via Kaniguram to the Sharawangi Narai, marched to Torwam, few enemy being seen during the march. The Bannu Brigade column spent the next two days destroying houses and towers in Mamit Khel (7686) and Zhar Kasal Kile (7488) and destroying Sher Ali's crops, and on the 21st, returned to Asman Manza camp, the Razmak Brigade again securing a portion of the road for them. No resistance was offered by the tribesmen during this period, and the fact that only a few long-range shots were fired at the Bannu Brigade when moving from Torwam to Asman Manza was taken as a definite indication that trouble on a large scale in this area need not now be anticipated.

There were now signs, however, of possible trouble in the area north of Razmak; and the Bannu Brigade column was sent back there, arriving in Razmak on the 24th Sept. having had a slight brush with some enemy at the Marai Narai on the way.

Bannu Brigade column returns to Razmak.

CHAPTER XXII.

Air action against Khonia Khel's habitation from September 18th—Faqir of Ipi holds a meeting at Musa Nika early in September—Faqir meets Mullah of Karbogha September 20th—Air action at Gumbakai from September 25th—Raid on Wana-Jandola Road September 24th.

Air action against Khonia Khel's abode.

After the unsuccessful attempt to capture Khonia Khel in August, he moved from place to place, trying to dissuade the Mahsuds from complying with Government's orders, and taking an active part with his gang in minor hostilities against the troops. His latest offence was the opposition to the troops protecting a convoy between Razmak and Ladha in the middle of September. Although he had not been very prominent as a hostile leader since April 1937, probably because he had not recovered completely from the wound received at the Shahur Tangi in April, he had long been due for punishment, and it was decided to take action against his residence. This consisted of two small buildings situated in the wild and sparsely populated area of the Saruna (see Map A, ten miles N. E. of Sorarogha Post).

Notices warning the inhabitants to evacuate the immediate danger area were dropped on the 16th of September, and bombing commenced on the 18th. This was carried out by two flights of No. 1 (Indian) Wing, R. A. F., stationed at Manzai. These attacks continued for eight days, when it was decided that sufficient damage had been effected. Eleven tons of high explosive bombs were dropped and seventy hours of flying time expended in this operation, and considerable damage was done; from the Royal Air Force point of view it was doubtful whether the material results justified the heavy expenditure, but the Political Authorities considered it well worth while.

Faqir of Ipi's meeting at Musa Nika.

In accordance with the summons he had issued for a meeting at Musa Nika, the Faqir of Ipi moved from Gumbakai to that place early in September. He held a large meeting on the 10th which was well attended by Ahmedzai Wazirs and tribesmen from Birmal and Shawal, in the course of which he made his usual appeals for support in the defence of Islam and urged the Kabul Khel and other migratory tribes to cancel their winter moves. After receiving sympathetic assurances from a number of those present, he returned to Shawal leaving an Ahmedzai Wazir Malik, Pirmullah Khan, a member of one of the leading Zilli Khel families, to raise a lashkar from that tribe, and Sher Zaman, his own brother, to do the same from the Ghilzais. In neither case was much success obtained.

Musa Khan arranges meeting between Mullah of Karbogha and Faqir of Ipi.

In the meantime, Musa Khan, continuing the efforts he had already been making for peace when he invited the Faqir to the Shawal, had called in the Mullah of Karbogha, religious mentor of the Faqir in his earlier youth, whose considerable influence was usually on the side of peace, to assist him. The Faqir had avoided meeting this Mullah by going to Musa Nika, and as on his return he still showed no desire for a conversation with him, the Mullah left the Shawal on the 12th and returned to the Tochi valley. He came back a few days later, and this time a meeting was arranged, and took place in Spinkamar on the 20th of September. Musa Khan and the Mullah pressed the Faqir to give up hostilities. The Faqir gave his usual evasive answer and said he would give a proper reply in two days' time. When the meeting between the leaders was over, Sher Ali, who had accompanied the Faqir, gave an address to the assembled tribesmen, about five hundred in all, producing the usual religious arguments in support of the Faqir and making fantastic claims about the Faqir's ability to give to the tribesmen everything they might expect from Government. The Faqir had, of course, no intention of making peace, and the Mullah of Karbogha again departed without having achieved his object. His efforts, however, combined with the persistently peaceful exhortations of the Faqir of Shewa, had a considerable effect on the attitude of many tribesmen.

After this meeting the Faqir returned to Gumbakai N. W. of Razmak and once more set himself to intensive propaganda, the objective this time being, principally, the sections of the Utmanzai Wazirs. Wild rumours of contemplated attacks in the Razmak, Datta Khel (Tochi) and Miranshah areas became widespread, and it was commonly reported that the Faqir had any thing from three to seven pieces of artillery and an ample supply of ammunition for them. Minor offences were common, particularly in Datta Khel area. Here, bridges and culverts were damaged, and the shopkeepers of Datta Khel itself packed up and moved to Bannu, always a sign of impending trouble. The Faqir's efforts to induce Khassadars to desert were again having some effect, particularly amongst the Manzar and Khaddar Khel and the Wuzi Mohmit Khel. The Madda Khel Khassadars, too, who were on half pay in order to settle a tribal fine, were becoming unsettled by the wide publicity given to the Faqir's offer of employment on regular pay with free rations and clothing. This form of propaganda led to some desertions, whilst other men left their duties owing to fear of hostile action which might involve them in blood feuds.

Faqir of Ipi continues his propaganda.

The general indications, however, gave the impression that the Faqir was not likely to obtain much support. Hostile tribesmen were pressing for an early start of an offensive on account of the approaching winter, but various factors were combining to counter this. The rapid suppression of Sher Ali's offensive had been discouraging. The Afghan authorities were taking stronger measures to prevent their tribesmen from going to the support of the Faqir. Crops were being cut and gathered. Movement to winter quarters was in progress. The Madda Khel maliks, too, were strongly opposed to any hostilities in their country. That tribe, in fact, held a meeting at which they decided that they would take part in no attack, although they would be unable to prevent one being made.

However, the Faqir still commanded a good deal of sympathy, and a number of discontented individuals were still prepared to give him assistance, and in the last ten days of September he had a following, not all of them armed, of about six hundred men at Gumbakai. Most of these he despatched to the various areas in which he intended to operate.

It was reported that the Faqir was now contemplating another meeting of the tribes in Shawal. In order to put a stop to this and to prevent the continuance of his activities at Gumbakai, it was decided to put into effect the general sanction received a month earlier by which the area of the Faqir's habitation could be proscribed when considered necessary. Notices were dropped on the 24th of September, and on the follow-

Air action against Faqir's temporary residence at Gumbakai.

1937
Sept.

1937 Sept.

ing day a flight of No. 1 (Indian) Wing R. A. F., based on Miranshah for the operation, commenced the air action. The areas proscribed were the country drained by the Korezai Algad and the Khina Algad down to but exclusive of their junction and the country drained by the Mana Algad and its tributaries which flow into the Bariala Algad south of the Shawal Tangi. Considerable movement was observed on the 25th and 26th of September, but after that practically no ground activity was seen. The bombing drove the Faqir into hiding and the area ceased to be used for hostile purposes. For these reasons and to allow the migratory tribes to use their customary route through the Shawal valley, the proscription was lifted on the 8th of October. In the course of the proscription the Royal Air Force had spent one hundred and nineteen hours in flying and had used twelve tons of high explosive bombs and sixteen thousand rounds of small arm ammunition.

Utmanzai Wazirs Warned—Orders issued to Daur jirga.

At the beginning of October, those sub-divisions of the Utmanzai Wazirs which had shown signs of being affected by the Faqir's propaganda were warned that action would be taken against them if they give any trouble, and they were ordered to recall all their fighting men serving the Faqir. About the same time the Kabul Khel Wazirs living in Waziristan were told that they would be held responsible for any offences committed in Waziristan by their brethen from Birmal. On this, they sent a deputation to the Birmal Kabul Khel, begging them to abstain from hostilities. It was understood, also, that the Afghan Government was taking steps to discountenance any activity on their part, and it was reported that they had been warned that the allowances given them by the Afghan Government would be suspended as long as they supported the Faqir. In addition, the Resident in Waziristan interviewed a fully representative jirga of the Daurs on the 5th of October and imposed on them fines of one hundred and fifty rifles and three thousand rupees for their participation, direct and indirect, in hostilities against Government since November 1936.

The effect of these measures was good, and made it even more difficult for the Faqir to get his much-needed support.

Raid on the Santala defile area of Wana-Jandola road led by Pirmullah Khan.

The envoys whom he had left behind at Musa Nika after the meeting there at the beginning of September had not succeeded in collecting much of a following. Pirmullah Khan had been trying to carry out the Faqir's instructions to raise a lashkar, but the Wana Wazirs, strongly influenced by the Bagdadi Pir, refused for the most part to have anything to do with him. He did succeed in getting together a gang of about one hundred and fifty Ahmedzai Wazirs and Afghan subjects and with these a raid on the Jandola-Wana road was carried out under the leadership of himself and one Ali Jan.

*During the night of the 23rd/24th of September his gang made attempts to destroy road bridges near Old Tiarzah Khula Khassadar post about three miles east of Wana. They tore down telephone lines along the roads in that neighbourhood, and attacked the Khassadar posts at Garu Kot (6972) and Karab Kot (7069) and were reported to be in position astride the Santala defile (7269, 7268). They had also looted and burnt a Mahsud

---

* [Ref. map R37 at end. of Chap.]

lorry on its way to Wana in the early hours of the 24th. News of this incursion was received at Wana Brigade Headquarters on the morning of the 24th, and a small mobile column was sent from Wana to engage and disperse this body. A rifle company and one machine-gun section of the 3/6 Raj. Rif. at Tanai post was ordered to co-operate by occupying the high ground at point 4365 (7168) west of the Wana-Jandola road. Khassadars from Tanai Post were sent to seize the high ground east of the road, their orders being not to move north of the track in squares 7368 and 7367.

The column from Wana, consisting of one section of the 2 Mtn. Bty., one sub-section of armoured cars, one rifle company and one machine-gun section 3/12 F. F. R., with ancillary troops and a detachment of Khassadars, left Wana at 11-25 hours, air co-operation being provided by one close-support aircraft.

The security of the road for the first three miles was ensured by the 3/16 Punjab R. who occupied the Ghiza Pezha Ridge, and by the remainder of the 3/12 F. F. R., and one squadron of Probyn's Horse, who took up positions to the north of Old Tiarza Khula Khassadar post.

The column moved at a fairly slow pace, testing bridges and culverts on the way. These were found to be intact, but telephone lines had been completely destroyed at intervals all along the road.

Piqueting with two platoons the high ground east of the road near 42 m.s. and immediately south of Rogha Kot (7071), the column halted just south of that place at about 12-45 hours. Here, news was received from Khassadars that the enemy were in the hills on both sides of the road about one and a half miles further on. Sounds of firing were heard in this area from the armoured cars which had advanced down the road and from the aircraft.

The rifle company, less the two platoons in piquets, covered by the artillery and by machine guns near the road just south of the Ghabargai nala near the 42nd milestone, was now sent to the southern end of the M. E. S. camping ground, overlooking the Santala Algad, with the object of cutting off any enemy retreating into the hills to the east. At the same time, the northernmost platoon in piquets was ordered to rejoin the company. A few enemy were seen escaping into the hills east of the Algad and were engaged with rifle fire. A little later, several parties of enemy showed themselves to the northeast and were heavily engaged by the artillery and machine guns.

The column commander now decided to replace the rifle company by Khassadars and to send it to a low plateau (about 723715) on the east bank of the Santala Algad to engage the enemy in that area. The company was ordered not to advance into the hills

The platoon recalled from piquet duty had now arrived, and the company, less one platoon, commenced its advance at 14-00 hours, its western flank being protected by Khassadars who moved to the high ground west of the Wana Toi opposite Karab Kot.

Shortly before this a certain amount of enemy fire was heard from the high ground to the northeast. Machine-gun fire had also begun from the Tanai detachment on the high ground above point 4365, but as it had not been possible to get into touch with those troops, no information was available about the enemy in their vicinity.

The advance of the company was not heavily opposed, and the enemy seemed to have been taken unawares. Several retreating parties were effectively engaged by the company and by the artillery and machine-guns. The close-support aircraft, also, found some opportunities of taking action.

After arrival at the plateau, the company commander reported the presence of a party of enemy about four hundred yards ahead of him, and asked for permission to advance to engage them, but firing had been heard to the northeast and the situation on this flank was obscure. It was necessary to protect the artillery and the lorries, and, moreover, an advance further into the hills with such a small force would have entailed serious risks, particularly in the withdrawal. For these reasons the permission sought was not given.

Lorries were sent back to the $43\frac{1}{2}$ milestone, and at about 16-00 hours the withdrawal began. A few tribesmen remained in the area and fired at the column as it went back, but the pursuit was only half-hearted.

The withdrawal was organized in two lay-backs, the lorries were reached without any difficulty and the column started back to Wana at about 17-50 hours.

The action had been very successful, as without any loss to troops, casualties amounting to at least 15 killed and 18 wounded had been inflicted on the enemy. This success was due to their being completely surprised by the rapidity of the move from Wana, and to the fact that the troops were on them before they had had time to take up any position.

Both Pirmullah Khan and Ali Jan, the latter a brother of a troublesome opponent of Government at the time under detention at Kabul, were residents of Nikaband, and the advisability of taking air action against this place was discussed. It was decided not to do so, however, since Musa Nika was on the frontier and the exact position of the frontier at this point was uncertain, and also as it was thought undesirable to run the risk of hitting a particularly important shrine located at Musa Nika.

A few days after this action, the Wana maliks surrendered some men suspected of having taken part in this attack, having taken reprisals against their property.

Dispersal of Pirmullah Khan's gang. Pirmullah Khan who was an Afghan allowance holder, (he was deprived eventually for continuing to make trouble), remained a source of anxiety for some time, striving to stir up the Ahmedzai Wazirs to hostility against the government. As time went on he became less of a danger as he found it increasingly difficult to get any result from his efforts. The feeling in favour of peace grew, the migratory tribes carried on steadily with their usual movements on the approach of winter, and those that did not leave were busily employed in gathering the autumn harvest.

The activities of his following were restricted to the occasional sniping of Wana camp, and finally, early in November, having received no assistance from the Faqir of Ipi, his gang broke up and dispersed.

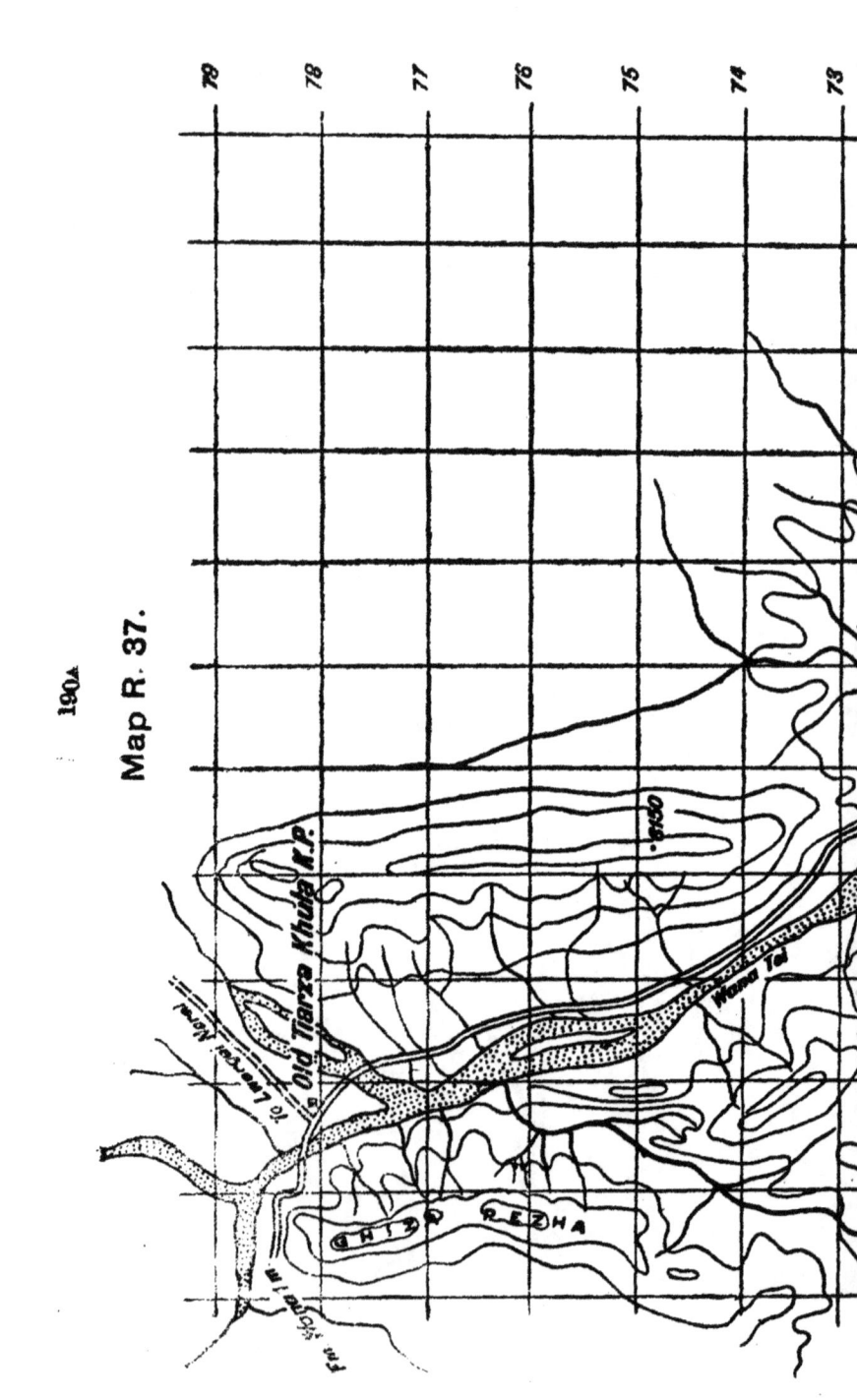

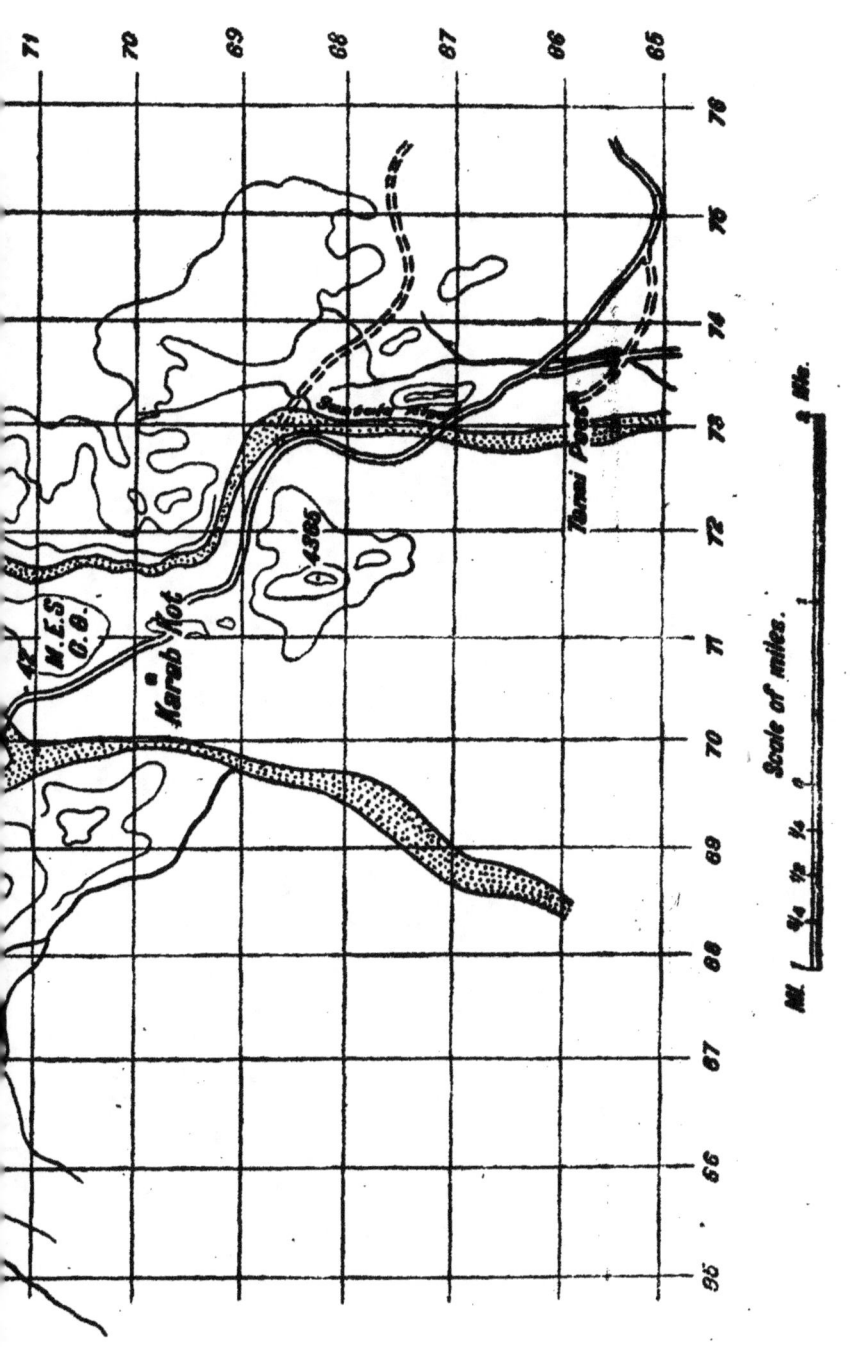

CHAPTER XXIII.

Attack on a hostile lashkar in the Sirdar Algad September 27th—Ambush by 1/2nd Gurkha Rifles near Razani September 25th—Mami Rogha village surrounded October 1st—Second attack on lashkar in the Sirdar Algad October 5th.

*Activities of hostile gang in Spinkamar area.

When the Faqir of Ipi decided at the end of August to carry on his offensive by means of gangs, one of the areas he had selected for the operations of these parties was Spinkamar, north of Razmak, where the Razmak water supply gave a good opportunity of giving trouble.

At first only a small party, of about thirty Wazirs, arrived in this neighbourhood. On the night of the 10th/11th of September, they made an attempt to damage the water supply in the Sirdar Algad, but were prevented from doing so by the Tori Khel Wazir Khassadar piquet guarding the spot. The size of the gang increased and on the night of the 21st/22nd of September it cut the pipe line. The Razmak Mobile Column was ordered out the next day to operate towards the water works at the head of the Sirdar Algad, in order to inflict as much damage as possible on the enemy if they were met and to encourage the Khassadars to remain at their posts. Contact was not established with the gang on this occasion. Two nights later, the gang, whose strength had increased to over sixty, mainly Tori Khel, surrounded the Khassadar post, turned out the garrison which surrendered without firing a shot, and did considerable damage to the water supply. The following morning a party of the Military Engineering Services, escorted by Light Tanks, attempted to repair the pipe line, but the attempt had to be given up owing to hostile fire. Another effort the next day, this time with an escort of Khassadars under the Assistant Political Officer, was no more successful.

It was clear that the enemy's strength was steadily increasing, and they were becoming daily more aggressive. On the 25th, a band of about eighty tribesmen was seen in the Salerai Shagga about one and a half miles west of Razmak and was shelled by artillery from Razmak.

By the 26th of September the lashkar was reported to be about three hundred strong, consisting of Madda Khel, Khaddar Khel, and Tori Khel Wazirs, and a party of about one hundred Kabul Khel Wazirs of Birmal led by a mullah who disagreed with the Faqir of Shewa's peaceful policy.

Although the presence of this lashkar in the Sirdar Algad was unwelcome to the majority of the Abdullai Mahsuds dwelling in Spinkamar who had informed the Faqir that they would not allow a lashkar to pass through their country, there was considerable tension here and also to the south of Razmak, particularly at Makin, as the result of recent propaganda. The attitude of the Wuzi Mohmit Khel and the Manzar Khel Wazirs inhabiting the country north of Razmak, who were answerable for many offences committed recently in the Razani sector of the line of communications, had been and still was unsatisfactory. It was appreciated that if Government forces could succeed now in inflicting heavy losses on this hostile party the effect on the general situation might be decisive and other small gangs still at large might be induced to disperse.

---

*[Ref. map K 37 at end of chapter and 'A' in pocket.]

1937
Sept. 27th

Attack on lashkar in Sirdar Algad area on 27th September.

It was decided, therefore, to attack this lashkar in the Sirdar Algad on the 27th of September, the primary object being to inflict all possible loss on it, repairs to the pipe line being carried out only if circumstances permitted.

Reconnaissance on the 25th of September, had shown that the enemy were occupying Babar Sar (8730) the ridge (857298 to 863307) eight hundred yards west of it, point 7590 (8527), and the feature (854287) one thousand yards north of this point. (The ridge, point, and feature were given the names "Gurkha Hill", "Black Rocks", and "Ridgeway Hill" respectively.)

As the Bannu Brigade had just returned to Razmak, the Commander Waziristan Division decided that the operation would be carried out by this Brigade, reinforced by one section 9th Light Tank Company, the 1/3 G. R., and the 5/12 F. F. R. In addition to the artillery of the Bannu Brigade Column, the 3 and 8 Mtn. Btys., one sub-section 20th/21st Medium Battery at Razmak was made available to strengthen the supporting fire. The Royal Air Force was to furnish continuous tactical reconnaissance and close support from first light.

The positions which were found to be held by the reconnaissance on the 25th were very exposed, and the Commander Waziristan Division thought it very improbable that the enemy would stay in them throughout the night. In his opinion it was most likely that during the hours of darkness the tribesmen would come down to the shelter of the nalas and of the deserted houses in the lower ground. Therefore, if full advantage were taken by the troops of night movement, there might be an excellent chance of inflicting heavy loss on the enemy. He considered that the most favourable plan would be to seize Babar Sar on the east and Black Rocks and Ridgeway Hill on the west by first light, using the 1/3 G. R. and the 5/12 F. F. R. respectively for this purpose, both of these units having been over the ground frequently, the rest of the force advancing up the Sirdar Algad between them. In his instructions to the Bannu Brigade Commander he pointed out that previous experience of fighting in this area showed that the tribesmen did not, as a general rule, offer much opposition during an advance, but that they invariably followed up the withdrawal, particularly from the west. Consequently, if the surprise in the early morning did not produce the desired results, it might be found possible to inflict loss on the enemy during the withdrawal by laying ambushes for them.

The plan adopted was briefly as follows. The 1/3 G. R., leaving Razmak at 0100 hours, were to move east of the Sirdar Algad and to seize and hold the general line point 7251 (8728)—Babar Sar. The 5/12 F. F. R., marching immediately after the 1/3 G. R., were to seize and hold the general line Black Rocks—Ridgeway Hill. No animals were to accompany these units except those carrying wireless sets. Their support companies were to move with the advanced guard. The advanced guard, which consisted of one section 9th Light Tank Company, the 2/1 Punjab R., and one rifle company, 1/17 Dogra R. was to piquet the route in daylight as far as the line of point 7251 and Black Rocks and was to seize and hold Ghuzak Khel Kalai (8629.) The 2/11 Sikh R. was to form the main body, leaving the 1/17 Dogra R. less one rifle company to carry out the task of rear guard.

The country in which the Brigade was to operate consisted of steep and, in places, precipitous hills, intersected by numerous small nalas, and covered with scrub and thick cover which changed to dense holly-oak forest near the summits. West of the Sirdar Algad the ground was dominated by Mamu Sar, but, as its main ridge was a considerable distance from the Algad, it was not necessary to piquet the mountain itself. Nevertheless, it was a potential source of difficulty as the under features about Ridgeway Hill were overlooked by it.

1937
Sept. 27th

The 1/3 G. R., moving round by Gaj Piquet, two and a half miles along the road north of Razmak, seized their objectives without opposition. The 5/12 F. F. R. also gained possession of Black Rocks without meeting any enemy. Between Black Rocks and Ridgeway Hill the way led along a narrow spur which met the latter at right angles. As the 5/12 F. F. R. approached Ridgeway Hill along this spur, three warning shots were fired by the enemy on the forward slopes of the hill, and shouting was then heard followed by firing by the enemy all along the face of the hill. It had been arranged that if the enemy were found in possession of any of the objectives laid down for the night advance, attack on them should be deferred until it was light enough for support to be given by artillery and machine-guns. The battalion, therefore, halted and proceeded to strengthen its positions and wait for daylight. It was now 0340 hours. Enemy in front of the battalion continued their firing, and at 0530 hours, when it began to get light, firing started from the slopes of Mamu Sar, whilst the volume of fire from Ridgeway Hill increased in intensity.

Meanwhile, a message had been sent to Brigade Headquarters to the effect that the attack would be launched as soon as the battalion's machine-guns arrived and there was enough light for observation, and asking for an additional rifle company.

The support company (machine guns) of the 5/12 F. F. R. arrived at about 0700 hours, and it was followed half an hour later by the company of the 1/17 Dogra R. which had been with the advanced guard. The support company came into action as soon as it reached the Battalion, and at about the same time the 1/3 G. R. opened fire on the rear of Ridgeway Hill from their positions east of the Algad. The artillery were all in action by 0700 hours, the mountain guns near Madai Ziarat (about 867275) and the 6-inch howitzer of the Medium Battery at Razmak.

The attack was timed to start at 0815 hours, all the artillery except one section of the 8 Mtn. Bty. which was with the 2/1 Punjab R. being used to support it. Whilst the artillery tasks were being registered several hostile parties were engaged by observation, with the result that the enemy's fire from Ridgeway Hill began to slacken.

At 0811 hours the artillery opened rapid fire on Ridgeway Hill, using both shrapnel and high explosive shells, and four minutes later, switched on to the enemy on Mamu Sar. Closely supported by the battalion machine-guns, one company advanced against the centre of Ridgeway Hill with orders to exploit westwards. A second company covered the left flank, and the company of the 1/17 Dogra R. moved up a nala on the right of the advance to attack the enemy's left flank. At the same time, the machine-guns of the 1/3 G. R., and of the 2/1 Punjab R. which was steadily advancing up the Sardar Algad, brought fire to bear on the reverse side of the objective. In twenty minutes the eastern half of the

1937
Sept. 27th

objective had been taken and the whole of it was captured by 0915 hours. The enemy fell back a short distance, but were then driven by heavy fire out of the positions, which they were attempting to hold. Caught at first by machine-gun fire, they offered good targets later to the artillery and the aircraft as they fled away to the north and northwest. The casualties in this attack were few, the company of the 1/17 Dogra R. losing one man killed and five wounded whilst in the 5/12 F. F. R. only three men were slightly wounded.

The enemy continued to offer targets for the rest of the morning particularly in the direction of Mamu Sar Narai of which due advantage was taken.

After the capture of Ridgeway Hill the advanced guard pushed on to the objective given it and the situation became stabilized. It was decided that there would not be enough time to carry out any effective repairs to the water supply, so arrangements were made for the withdrawal to Razmak, and ambushes were prepared to catch tribesmen who, it was hoped, would be induced to follow the troops.

The 2/1 Punjab R. began to move back at 1215 hours, the flanking battalions having been ordered to start their withdrawal half an hour later.

The 1/3 G. R. in their positions on Babar Sar had been subjected to desultory sniping fire all the morning. When the hour for withdrawal approached this fire became more intense. Some of the forward platoons were occupying a position from which the line of withdrawal led along a narrow ridge. These platoons had some casualties, and whilst these casualties were being evacuated and the platoons were retiring along the ridge more men were hit, the covering fire being unable to keep down the fire of the enemy. An immediate counter-attack had to be made and the vacated position re-occupied. Again, when the withdrawal from this spot was renewed, fresh casualties were incurred, and again the position had to be re-occupied. In all, three counter attacks had to be delivered before the troops could withdraw from this area.

The 5/12 F. F. R. on the western flank had had no difficulty in getting clear of Ridgeway Hill and Black Rocks, and was withdrawing steadily. Owing to the delay in getting the platoons of the 1/3 G. R. away, the withdrawal of the 5/12 F. F. R left their flank somewhat dangerously exposed. For this reason, and also because one of the light tanks on the right flank had broken down temporarily, the column Commander ordered the 5/12 F. F. R. to reoccupy Black Rocks, and the artillery to smother Black Rocks and Ridgeway Hill with fire. Pursuing tribesmen who had rushed up on to the top of Ridgeway Hill and had exposed themselves freely in doing so, were caught by this shelling.

As a company of the 5/12 F. F. R., having been replenished with ammunition and otherwise got ready, was advancing to retake Black Rocks, the 1/3 G. R. succeeded in extricating themselves from their position, and the damaged tank got on the move again. Orders were given cancelling the attack on Black Rocks and the withdrawal was resumed.

After this opposition to the early stages of the retirement, the enemy appeared to lose heart and the withdrawal was no longer followed up. The enemy's inactivity gave the ambushes no opportunities, and the parties were withdrawn without any opposition, covered by the section of light tanks. Throughout the day continuous support was provided by No. 5 (A. C.) Squadron R. A. F. and by a flight of No. 1 Squadron Indian Air Force, who took offensive action against parties of tribesmen.

The numbers of enemy actually opposing the Column had been at least one hundred and fifty. At one stage, tribesmen from Spinkamar began to move towards the battle, but the majority apparently thought better of it when they saw or heard of the casualties inflicted on the lashkar. It was noticeable throughout the action that some of the tribesmen were exposing themselves very freely, and there was evidence to show that those on the lower ground were mainly Afghan subjects. It appeared that the Wazirs, not for the first time, had put the Afghan tribesmen in the forefront of the battle, and that the latter, unacquainted with the ground and perhaps with the effect of modern weapons, had in their ignorance delayed their withdrawal from Ridgeway Hill too long and had not made proper use of the abundant cover available.

The enemy losses had been severe, the total being about 27 killed and 40 severely wounded. The casualties among the troops numbered 1 killed and 21 wounded, fifteen having been sustained during the withdrawal.

In the middle of September as it had been learnt that in addition to the Manzar Khel Wazirs of Mami Rogha whose section had been punished in August, the inhabitants of the Mohmit Khel village of Tamre Obo (9842) had been concerned in the offences in the Razani sector, action was taken also, against them. On the 14th of September the village was surrounded by a detachment of Tochi Scouts from Dosalli Post, and certain wanted men were arrested and their houses destroyed.

In spite of this, however, hostile acts, principally attempts to damage bridges and the destruction of telephone and telegraph wires, continued.

On the 25th of September a large gang was known to be somewhere between Razani and Datta Khel, and on the same day, the Officer Commanding at Razani was informed by the local political officer that there was another large lashkar in the Sirdar Algad area, whose object was either to attack piquets by night or to destroy the telegraph lines and culverts on the Central Waziristan Road.

*Ambush on Central Waziristan Road near Razani by 1/2 G. R.

On this information the Commander at Razani, considering that the enemy's strength was probably considerably exaggerated, that his piquets were sufficiently strong to resist attack, and that the easiest and, consequently, the most probable objective for the enemy was a culvert at the 65·4 milestone, decided to lay an ambush in the neighbourhood of that bridge.

The nearest piquet (Mussoorie Piquet, 922348) to that spot had a fighting patrol, but as it was possible that the piquet might be attacked it was inadvisable to use that patrol for the ambush. The Commander, therefore, detailed two platoons, under their Gurkha Officers, from Razani camp for the purpose.

There were five Khassadar or badragga posts in the area in which it was intended to operate, and khassadars were also accommodated near Razani camp itself.

It was considered important that these irregulars should have no knowledge of any movement of troops, and it would have been unwise for the two platoons to start before 2015 hours, by which time it might be expected that the khassadars at the camp would have retired to rest.

*[Ref. sketch map A in pocket.]

1937
Sept. 25th

Consequently, it was probable that the enemy would reach the culvert before the troops could get there, and would by then have their covering party in position. Accordingly, the platoons were directed to a point four hundred yards short of the probable enemy objective, in the expectation that the tribesmen would move north later in the night. This point was outside the Razani sector and had not been previously visited. The platoons, obviously, could not move along the road, the circuitous route selected instead of the main road had not been reconnoitred nor was any reconnaissance now possible.

The night was very dark until the moon rose at 2200 hours.

At 2015 hours the two platoons, under the command of the senior Gurkha Officer, a Jemadar, slipped out of camp. The men were bareheaded, and wore brown canvas rubber-soled shoes, and were equipped with rifles and kukris, bayonets being left behind.

They passed the Khassadar serai at the camp unobserved, and made for the main road near the 61st milestone. Crossing the road here, and keeping well east of the road for a while, they climbed up to Mussoorie piquet (922348), garrisoned by the Battalion, by the steep rocky spur from the north east. They then moved south, stopping short of and out of sight and hearing of piquet No. 80 (922347) where Khassadars were located, and turned westward towards the road, all the time in attack formation. Hearing enemy at work in the nala at the 65·4 milestone, they inclined northwards and reached the road at the 65·2 milestone.

As they reached the road, at 2230 hours, a hostile patrol came along but passed by without noticing anything.

In between the passing of enemy individuals along the road, the Gurkha Officer in command made his dispositions and put his two light-automatic weapons, wedged in by heavy rocks, on fixed lines directed on the road and on the spur below it. The greatest care had to be exercised in doing this on the steep stony hillside, as the position occupied was on the very edge of the road on a cliff six feet high and it had to be done so that enemy within three or four yards should have no inkling of its whereabouts. The enemy could be heard tearing down the telephone poles near the culvert, but the temptation to advance further south was resisted.

Parties of enemy moved up and down the road until the main body started to move north at about 0100 hours. As the leading party of about twenty men came abreast of the light automatics one of these opened on them and the rifle sections further south opened on the main body. The survivors of the leading party leapt off the road, to be caught by the second light automatic on its fixed line on the spur. Four dead lay on the road and more casualties were heard to fall into the bushes below. The main body was also driven off the road, but rallied and tried to drive in the rifle sections to the south. These were at once reinforced by the rifle sections from the north flank and moved forward to a low spur where they met and drove back the enemy three times by fire, inflicting more casualties.

The enemy fire was now completely silenced and the platoons withdrew to Mussoorie piquet, each platoon covering the other by stages during the withdrawal. From the piquet the commander of the party directed artillery fire on the culvert and on the road where the corpses were lying, to harass any enemy who might return to continue the work or to remove their dead.

There was only one casualty in the ambush party. The tribesmen were estimated to have numbered over two hundred and their casualties were believed to be between twenty and thirty, of whom at least six were killed and eleven seriously wounded. They had done little damage, and hampered by their casualties and by the difficult nature of the ground, had not progressed more than three miles from the scene of action by the next morning.

<small>Action decided on against Mami Rogha village.</small>
Whatever tribe it was that provided the members of the above gang, there was no doubt that the inhabitants of Mami Rogha had given it assistance in one form or another, and in view of their share in other offences as well, General Sir John Coleridge decided to follow up the blow given at the Sirdar Algad on the 27th of September by punitive action against Mami Rogha and other Wazir villages in that region. Mami Rogha had previously been punished for the misdemeanours of its inhabitants, but this had little apparent effect.

Notices were dropped on the 27th warning the leading men to recall their followers with the Faqir of Ipi at once if they wished to avoid punishment. Two days later the Resident in Waziristan interviewed the Manzar Khel jirga at Dosalli, and ordered them to hand over certain men from Mami Rogha who had taken part in hostile action. The attitude of the maliks was satisfactory, and although they explained that they had some difficulty in controlling those of their following who had hostile inclinations, they handed over two of the wanted men, one being an ex-subedar of Khassadars who had deserted his post and joined the Faqir.

Punitive action was to be taken against the houses of the other named individuals, and on the 29th of September, the Bannu Brigade marched from Razmak to Razani. On the way they destroyed towers, the property of certain hostile Mohmit Khel tribesmen in the village of Aziz Khel Kalai, whilst the Razmak Mobile Column carried out the same task in villages nearer Razmak.

On the 1st of October the Bannu Brigade moved up the Mami Rogha Algad to Mami Rogha village. Some slight opposition was encountered from a body of about one hundred and fifty tribesmen in occupation of some high ground about one mile south of the village, who opened fire on troops coming up towards this ground and succeeded in wounding one man.

They were promptly engaged by all the artillery, including a field battery at Razani, and by aircraft. They were evidently surprised by this fire, particularly from their rear at Razani, and withdrew from their positions. After demolishing the houses and towers of the wanted individuals who had not been surrendered by the maliks, the column camped for the night in the vicinity of the village. The withdrawal of the troops was not interfered with at all, but as it commenced, the high ground to the south was reoccupied by the party which had been driven off. They were again engaged by aircraft and artillery.

The night was peaceful, and the column marched back to Razani the next morning. It was fully expected that the enemy would follow up the troops on this march, but although they had received reinforcements they showed no enterprise. It was thought that the lashkar was the same one which had been ambushed by the 1/2 G. R. a few nights previously, and it was probable that the very severe handling they had received on that occasion, coupled with the losses they had undoubtedly suffered from the air and the artillery on the 1st of October, had quenched their ardour to a great extent.

The night was again peaceful and the Brigade marched back to Razmak on the 3rd of October.

*Second attack on hostile lashkar in Sirdar Algad area, on the 5th of October.

As a result of the successful action on the 27th of September, two-thirds of the lashkar in the Sirdar Algad, including Mullah Sher Ali and his following of Kabul Khel Wazirs, had dispersed, and the remainder had drawn off to the Shuidar area to await reinforcements. The Faqir, who was trying to keep this offensive going, sent more tribesmen and the lashkar, about two hundred strong, remained in the vicinity of Razmak, keeping widely dispersed through fear of bombing from the air.

A considerable moral effect, though small material damage was done, was produced on the inhabitants of this area by the shelling from Razmak on the 2nd of October, after due warning, of the village of Bahadur Khel Kalai, about four miles north west of Razmak, as a punishment for the participation of some of its inhabitants in the action of the 27th of September.

It had been seen on the 27th that the damage done to the water works in the Sirdar Algad had been considerable, but there had been no opportunity to make a thorough examination of it on that day. In order to do this, and also to inflict further loss on the re-assembled lashkar it was decided that the Bannu Brigade Column, increased by one section of the Light Tank Company, the 2/14 Punjab R. and the 1/3 G. R., should carry out a second operation in that area on the 5th of October.

The plan on this occasion was much the same as on the former one, but the Royal Engineer reconnaissance necessitated an advance further into the hills. The 2/14 Punjab R. took the place of the 2/1 Punjab R. as advanced guard battalion. The 1/3 Gurkha R. were right flanking battalion, as before, but the 1/17 Dogra R. replaced the 5/12 F. F. R. on the left flank.

The flanking battalions reached their positions before dawn without any difficulty, and the advanced guard piqueted up to the line point 7251 (8778)—Black Rocks in daylight. The 2/11 Sikh R. on the right and the 2/4 G. R. on the left then advanced between and beyond the flanking battalions to form a cordon on the hills from the flanking battalions round the water works (846295).

Up to this time there had been no opposition, but the tribesmen now opened heavy fire on the troops from the almost vertical face of a ridge running from high ground north west of the 2/11 Sikh R. to Mamu Sar. It was almost impossible to locate the enemy hidden as they were in thick woods and under enormous boulders, whilst to them every movement of the troops was visible.

---

*[Ref. sketch map K 37 at end of Chapter.]

Map K. 37.

Scale of Miles

Furlongs 8 7 6 5 4 3 2 1 0 1 2 Miles

Water pipe line......

Survey Section No. 1717, Dec. 1941.

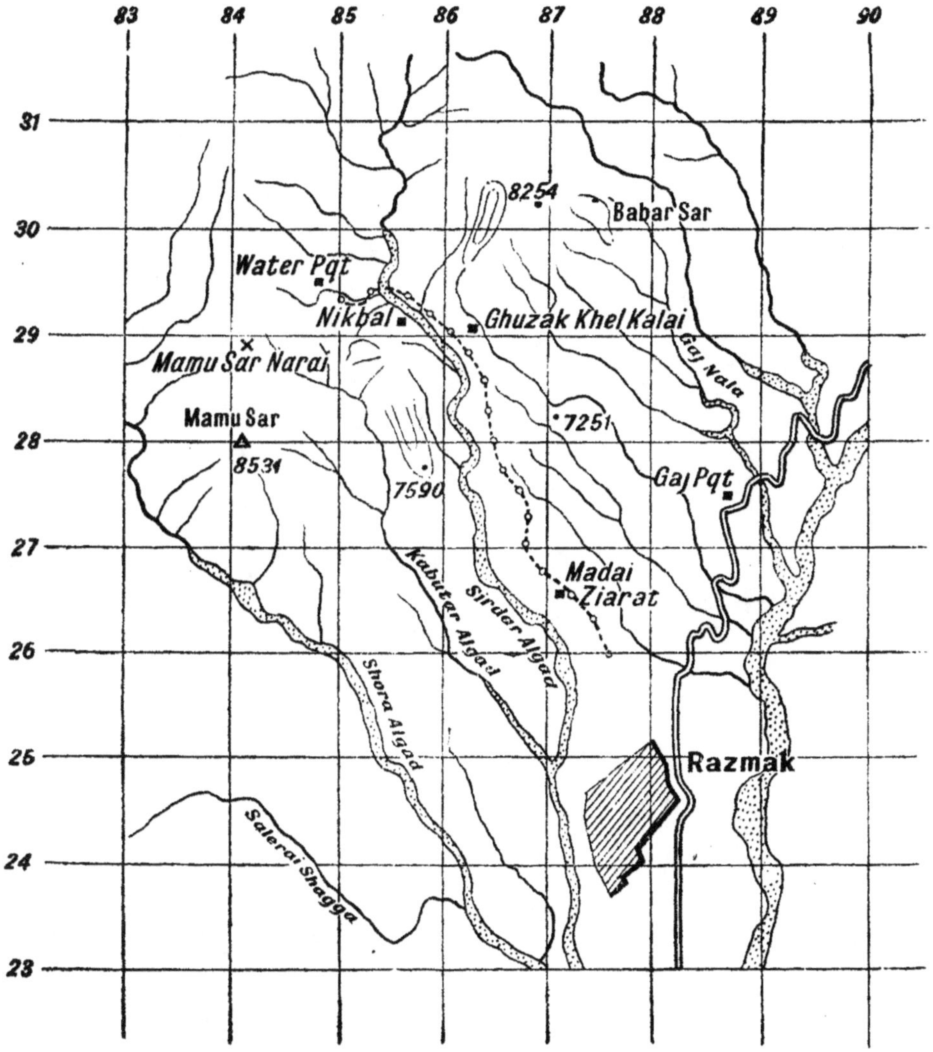

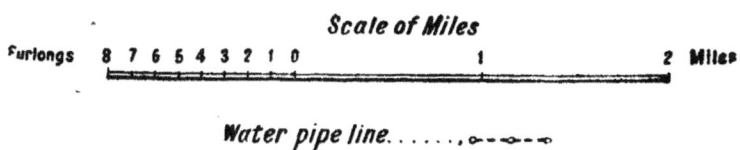

Although the enemy fire continued fairly persistently and their numbers increased, the artillery supporting the column fired freely and the losses in the Force were relatively light.

The withdrawal commenced at 1400 hours, and except in the Ridgeway Hill area was not seriously interfered with. Here, a piquet of the 1/17 Dogra R., which was in a somewhat exposed position, had two casualties as they withdrew, and a counter attack had to be delivered to get the wounded away. In the course of this, they suffered eight more casualties, a British officer, 2/Lieut. O. C. W. Bellamy, being killed whilst pointing out the situation to his Commanding Officer.

In the early part of the day only Tori Khel Wazirs were present, but as the day went on they were joined by Abdullai Mahsuds from the Spinkamar area and by other Mahsuds from Makin, who brought the total numbers of the opposing tribesmen up to eighty. They were careful to remain on the higher ground, and the ambush parties waiting for them during the withdrawal were again disappointed. The nature of the country made it difficult to observe the effects of the fire, but the total number of casualties to the enemy was later confirmed to be nine wounded. The casualties in the Column during the day were one British Officer and one Indian other rank killed and eight Indian and Gurkha other ranks wounded.

Besides establishing the fact that it would take five days' work to repair the water-supply arrangements, this action resulted in the final petering out of the Faqir's offensive in this area. He found himself unable to send any further reinforcements and withdrew from what was left a considerable number who were members of his own personal following. Signs that he was preparing to leave Gumbakai also greatly relieved the tension in the Spinkamar and Makin areas, and any enthusiasm which remained was damped by the increasing cold.

The situation in the Sirdar Algad remained peaceful, and when the Razmak Brigade, which stayed in Razmak for some time after its return there on the 21st of October, operated up the Sirdar Algad on the 12th of November to search the villages of Nikbal and Guzak Khel and the hills in the neighbourhood, the only opposition met was a little long range sniping.

CHAPTER XXIV.

Hostile ambush at Sarwekai, Sept. 27th—March of Razmak Brigade through Mahsud country, October 12th to 21st—Operations at Inzar Narai, October 19th and 20th—Operations in Spinwam area, October 15th to 23rd.

Early in August reports had been received of the formation of small Mahsud gangs in the Sarwekai area with the intention of doing mischief, attracted there, perhaps, by the news of the arrival of regular troops in relief of the Scouts at the Posts on that line.

*Hostile ambush at Sarwekai 27th September.

Nothing serious happened until towards the end of September, when on the 27th of that month a hostile gang was successful in ambushing a party of the 3/6 Raj. Rif. in the neighbourhood of the Sarwekai rifle range.

This range, which lies north of the post at Sarwekai, in country covered with scrub and broken by water courses, offered opportunities for hostile action to a skilful enemy, and the rule was that before any range practice took place, patrols of covering parties were sent out to search the area.

The range was to be used on the morning of the 27th, and as usual, a patrol, accompanied by the khassadars who happened to be a little behind when the fire started and supported by a section of machine guns in the Fort, was sent out. Its task was to search the nalas on the north side of the range furthest from the Fort, and having done so, to take up a position covering the firing party.

The patrol, which consisted of two sections, advanced in two parties, the commander at the time the incident occurred being with the leading section which was moving forward covered, as he thought, by the section in rear. At 0730 hours fire was opened on the leading section which had reached its bound at a moment when it was not in view of the support which was intended to cover it. The supporting section had taken up a faulty position from which it was unable to see the forward troops when they were lying down. Simultaneously, the rear section was pinned to its ground by fire. The enemy, about fifty or sixty strong, was organized in two main parties each subdivided into small groups and cleverly hidden in some of the many small nalas.

The whole of the forward party as well as some of the rear party became casualties, and the latter, immobilized by the hostile fire and unable to see what was happening in front, could do nothing to prevent the tribesmen from getting away with the arms and ammunition of the men of the leading party.

The losses in the patrol were five killed or died of wounds and three wounded, nearly all being incurred in the first burst of fire.

The ambush was a matter of minutes only, and the tribesmen hastened to withdraw under cover of the fire of some of their party. Although the ground favoured them considerably, in this retreat they presented fair targets to the machine guns in the Post and some casualties were inflicted.

An attempt to prevent them getting away was rapidly organized with such troops and khassadars as were available, but the withdrawal was too rapid for this attempt to succeed.

---

*[Ref. sketch map A in pocket.]

The gang had clearly made a careful study of the ground, with which they were perfectly familiar, and of the methods adopted to protect the firing party on the range. The position of the tribesmen was such that whatever route had been taken by the covering party one section at least must have come under fire. The success of the attack was facilitated by the dispositions of the covering party who, although they were in sight of the advancing section as long as they were moving were unable to see them when they lay down.

The gang concerned in this affair consisted mainly of Abdur Rahman Khel Mahsuds, but it included a sprinkling of Shaman Khel Mahsuds who had taken part in the raid on Chaudhwan.

The jirgas of these tribes were summoned immediately and they were given orders to return the looted rifles at once. By the 29th of September they had produced only one rifle, and were then ordered to hand in six British-made magazine rifles.

Air action again against tribes responsible for Sarwekai ambush. As these tribes seemed reluctant to comply with the orders, General Sir John Coleridge decided that it was necessary to proscribe an area in this country by air action until such time as all the rifles had been handed in. Notices were dropped on the 2nd of October warning the inhabitants to vacate an area of one mile on each side of the Splitoi Algad from Ghazgani (9189) to Splitoi Fort.

Air action commenced on the 5th of October, the task being undertaken by one flight of No. 1 (Indian) Wing, based on Manzai. It continued until the 15th of October, when all action was suspended to allow of a temporary visit of troops to the area. Further notices stating that air action would be resumed on the 19th of October were dropped on the 18th.

This and previous action resulted in complete capitulation and as by the 18th the tribesmen had complied with Government orders and had handed in the required rifles, air action was stopped.

In the course of this operation flying had been carried out for approximately one hundred and twenty hours, and about twelve tons of H. E. bombs and sixteen thousand rounds of small arm ammunition had been expended.

In addition to the inhabitants of the Splitoi Algad area, the Mahsuds of the region north of this, between the Razmak-Wana and Razmak-Kotkai roads and the Splitoi Algad, had also shown hostile intentions, a number of them having joined the Faqir's lashkars and taken part in various raids. The inhabitants of villages on the Dazhi Oba had only recently been warned that air action would be taken against them if they did not at once recall their men from Sher Ali's lashkar.

March of Razmak Brigade column through country from Asman Manza south east to Kotkai.

General Sir John Coleridge, considering that they should be reminded that they were not beyond the reach of military columns, instructed the Commander Waziristan Division to despatch a column to march through this area, visiting Karama (8800), and Ahmadwam (9695) on the Shinkai Toi.

The Razmak Brigade column, which was still at Asman Manza on the northern edge of their area, was selected for the task, and marched off on the 12th of October on the following itinerary.

---

*[Ref. sketch map A in pocket.]

1937 Oct.

October 12th—via the Karama Narai (8603) to camp on the north side of point 6154 (8900), (one mile east of Karama).

October 13th—via the Shinkai Toi to Umar Raghzai (0196).

October 14th—via the Inzar Algad, Inzar Toi, and Dargai Algad to Kotkai Post.

October 16th—via the Shinkai Toi to Isap (9988).

October 17th—via the Tsindai Narai and Shinkai Toi to Ahmadwam (9695).

October 18th—to Kotkai Post.

October 19th—to Sorarogha.

October 20th—to Piazha Raghza.

October 21st—to Razmak.

The column met with no hostile activity other than a few shots except when camping for the night at Piazha Raghza. Here sniping was continuous throughout the night, and as a punishment, the villages responsible were ordered to surrender twelve magazine rifles at short notice.

About this time there was a slight recrudescence of trouble in the Wana area. Mullah Sher Ali, after the meeting at Musa Nika which he had attended, returned to the upper reaches of the Main Toi and busied himself in attempts to raise another lashkar for an attack on the Razmak-Wana road. He met with a limited success in this, and on the 18th of October was reported to have a following of about one hundred men. On the 19th he attacked a party of the South Waziristan Scouts from Tiarzha Post.

Sher Ali active at the Iuzar Narai area.

This party, about one hundred and fifty rifles strong, was carrying out a patrol to Pakkalita (6688), leaving Tiarzha Post at 0800 hours, to search the Pakkalita area in which, according to reports received the previous evening, a small lashkar was present.

*Attack on patrol of South Waziristan Scouts.

Shortly after reaching the eastern slopes of Pakkalita heavy fire was opened on the Scouts. As the country in this area was difficult and the enemy, whose strength was unknown, had worked round the flanks and were firing on the patrol from three directions, further advance was considered inadvisable. The sound of a drum could be heard, indicating the likelihood that local inhabitants would reinforce the enemy.

After fighting for about two hours on the ground gained, the patrol, assisted by two more platoons of Scouts which had arrived from Sarwekai, withdrew successfully to Tiarzha Post, having lost only one man killed and one wounded. The enemy, whose strength had increased from forty at the beginning of the action to about one hundred and twenty during the day, had had two men killed and six wounded.

When news of this encounter reached Wana, a section of armoured cars and a rifle company of the 3/16 Punjab R. were sent to Tiarzha Post to support the Scouts in their retirement if necessary, arriving at the Post at 1415 hours. As events turned out, they were not called on to take any action.

*[Ref. sketch map A in pocket.]

The enemy remained for the night about Narai Oba and the Inzar Narai, and the following morning, the 20th, the Wana Brigade moved out to engage them. A rifle company of the 3/12 F. F. R. was sent independently at 0200 hours to be in position before daylight at Kotkum Range, a big feature to the north of Wana, its mission being to ambush any enemy who might follow up the withdrawal from Inzar Narai which was the Brigade's objective for the day. The Brigade itself marched out of Wana at 0800 hours.

Wana Brigade moves to Inzar Narai.

1937 Oct.

Contact was made at about 1100 hours with a party of enemy, about sixty strong, astride the Inzar Narai. Opposition was not strong and the Narai was secured by midday, the enemy offering good targets in the advance to and from the top of the Narai. The withdrawal commenced at 1400 hours, and was only half-heartedly followed up. What tribesmen there were in the pursuit came by the western flank and gave no opportunity to the company on the Kotkum Range.

The tribesmen's casualties were reported to be four killed and six wounded, whilst the losses in the Brigade amounted to two wounded only.

When the air action started against the Faqir's headquarters at Gumbakai (cf. chap. xxii), he decided to leave that area. It was thought that he might be going to Musatalbar, a village on the Afghan border fifteen miles north of Miranshah, and the maliks of the Titti Madda Khel Wazirs, living in that region, were warned to prevent their men from joining him.

*Move of Faqir of Ipi to Barman Sar.

Early in October it was found that he was touring the country to the north of the Shawal, inciting the Madda Khel and Afghan tribesmen living near the Afghan border to take up arms for the prosecution of his offensive in the Upper Tochi and about Spinwam. Establishing his headquarters in a cave at Kaurai near Barman Sar, about twenty one miles west of Miranshah, about the middle of October, he then visited the Kazha valley, where some of the migratory Wazirs were now arriving for the winter, the home of those Madda Khel who had sheltered the murderers of Lieutenant Beatty. It was reported that he had enlisted the leader of the murderers as one of his khassadars.

Meanwhile, his brother, Sher Zaman, disgusted at the lack of response from the Ahmedzai Wazirs, had left Musa Nika and was now assisting the Faqir.

In the Spinwam area, the Mullah Ghazi, Malik Gullajan and Gagu, who had previously been instrumental in creating trouble there, were touring the villages of that region as well as the villages on the Sheratala Plain between Spinwam Fort and Mir Ali, with the intention of enlisting recruits, the Tori Khel being told that the Government would take no further action in Waziristan for fear of the League of Nations.

The result of all these efforts was that the Faqir was joined by about three hundred Madda Khel tribesmen of various sections, and some Afghan tribesmen again appeared in North Waziristan, and trouble again broke out in the Spinwam area.

It was clear, however, that there was no general response to the Faqir's propaganda. The various measures taken to discourage the tribesmen from taking up arms, the quick suppression of Mullah Sher Ali's attack in the Torwam area, the relatively heavy losses inflicted on the enemy in

---

*[Ref. sketch map A in pocket.]

1937
Oct.

the raid on the Wana-Jandola road and in the actions in the Sirdar Algad, and the punitive operations in the Razani area had all produced a salutary effect. Mullah Fazal Din had now failed to support him, and many of the khassadars who had deserted or resigned as a result of his propaganda were now asking to be reinstated.

Nevertheless, the Faqir continued with his offensive. Having achieved nothing at Datta Khel in the Tochi Valley beyond slight damage to roads; he turned his attention to the Spinwam area, where Mullah Ghazi and Gagu were again meeting with some slight success in their efforts to arouse opposition to the Government.

*Offences committed in Spinwam area.

Spinwam, a post seventeen miles north of Mir Ali, is situated on a motor road which connects the Tochi valley with Thal in Kurram. The country in the vicinity of this road for the first four miles after leaving Mir Ali, consists of a series of low knife-edged ridges rising to between two and three hundred feet. These terminate somewhat abruptly in the Sheratala Plain, some ten miles in length and varying up to eight miles in breadth. Towards the north or Spinwam end of the Plain the high ground closes in on the west, and eventually, the road passes over a massif known as the Tabai Narai which rises about five hundred feet above the level of the surrounding country. The road then descends to the Kaitu valley, across which lies Spinwam Fort. The only water near the road, except at Mir Ali and Spinwam, is one small well.

The protection of the road from Mir Ali to Spinwam was entrusted to khassadars.

The hostile offensive began with the hold-up and looting of a civilian lorry on the road near the Tabai Narai. Shortly afterwards, in the early morning of the 15th of October, a lashkar about one hundred and fifty strong, consisting mainly of Tori Khel Wazirs from Datta Khel (near Spinwam), some Titti Madda Khel Wazirs, and Afghan tribesmen, attacked a khassadar post in the vicinity of Tabai Narai, some four miles south of Spinwam, turned out the garrison, and burnt the post. Culverts were demolished, making the road impassable, and the road itself was blocked in several places with large boulders. In the next day or two attempts were made to destroy the Olam bridge, on the road one mile north east of Spinwam Fort, and also the bridge over the Kaitu river near Spinwam. These attempts were defeated with the help of the Kabul Khel Wazir khassadars, who remained loyal. As a result of these offences several parties of Afghan tribesmen moved into the Spinwam area, some of the inhabitants of Datta Khel (Spinwam) evacuated their houses in anticipation of air action, and a Tori Khel khassadar jemadar with ten of his men deserted from Datta Khel and joined the enemy.

When the events of the morning of the 15th of October became known, it was decided that punitive action should be taken at once. The Wazirforce Headquarters issued instructions on the 17th of October to the Commander 9th Infantry Brigade at Mir Ali stating that the houses of certain individuals, known to have been implicated, were to be destroyed with all possible speed, and the greatest possible loss was to be inflicted on any lashkar opposing the troops.

Instructions issued to Commander 9th Infantry Brigade to undertake punitive operations.

---

*[Ref. sketch map P. 37 at end of Chapter.]

The Commander 9th Infantry Brigade, meanwhile, appreciated that the best chance of inflicting loss on the enemy was to encourage them to remain in the neighbourhood while sufficient troops were being concentrated to reopen the road to Spinwam and at the same time to engage the lashkars successfully in battle.

The 9th Infantry Brigade, with six battalions of Infantry under command, was responsible for protecting over fifty miles of road, from Saidgi to Razani, as well as for providing escorts, when required, for convoys from Mir Ali to Spinwam in the north and to Bichhe Kashkai in the south. The only troops available for immediate operations in the vicinity of Spinwam were one rifle company and one machine gun platoon of the 3/7 Rajput R., employed normally for the defence of Mir Ali, and one section of light tanks. Other sectors on the lines of communication had similar reserves, but these could only be moved away by day as they were needed for camp defence by night. (*For previous strength and distribution of 9th Inf. Bde. see pp. 184 and 185.*)

Steps to induce hostile lashkar to stay in the area.
To induce the lashkar to stay, the company and machine gun platoon were despatched in lorries on the morning of the 15th of October, escorted by the section light tanks, with instructions to reconnoitre the enemy's position. They were to withdraw if opposed. As the column approached the Tabai hills the tribesmen opened fire and it withdrew.

The following day, a rifle company of the 4/6 Raj. Rif. was brought in by lorry from Tal-in-Tochi and sent out along the Spinwam road towards the Tabai Narai with orders to ascertain the strength of the lashkar and where it had prepared a position. By drawing fire it was hoped to ascertain the enemy's dispositions so that some indication could be obtained as to his probable plan if attacked. In this the company was most successful. The men debussed and were engaged by the tribesmen in the foothills on the low ground. As they withdrew the enemy closed on their flanks, one piquet having difficulty in withdrawing. The day's operations confirmed the original estimate of about two hundred hostiles.

The operations of these two days apparently encouraged the enemy. They garrisoned two old khassadar posts near the Tabai Narai (at point 2695 and on the ridge west of this point), and followed this up by attacking and burning more khassadar posts on the Sheratala Plain and by threatening Tori Khel khassadar posts as far south as Mir Ali. News was received from local sources that they did not anticipate that more than one infantry battalion could be sent against them, and that they were full of confidence as they were convinced that they had already driven back that number during the operations of the 15th and 16th October.

Concentration of column at Mir Ali.
From the information now available and from previous reconnaissances it was decided that at least three battalions would be required to reach Spinwam, and a further additional battalion would be necessary for the subsequent operations in that neighbourhood. It was not convenient to take units of the Brigade from their duties on the lines of communication, but one battalion, the 3/15 Punjab R., was made available by placing the whole of another battalion in piquets. Headquarters Wazirforce placed two more battalions, the 2/11 Sikh R. and the 1/17 Dogra R., which were due to move from Razmak to Bannu in the course of ordinary reliefs, at the disposal of the Commander, 9th Infantry Brigade for the operations.

1937
Oct.

1937
Oct.

The fourth battalion was provided by keeping the company of the 4/6 Raj. Rif. at Mir Ali and by Headquarters Wazirforce detailing the 2/6 Raj. Rif., less one rifle company and one and a half machine gun platoons, from Kohat District. This unit, was to be lorried to Thal-in-Kurram, where, with one section 11th Light Tank Company which accompanied it from Kohat, it would be under the orders of the Commander 9th Infantry Brigade on the 19th of October. All the mechanized artillery in the 9th Infantry Brigade Area, as well as one and a half sections of armoured cars and one section light tanks were collected for the operation, Headquarters Wazirforce making available the ancillary services necessary to complete the column. The whole force was concentrated at Mir Ali by the 19th of October.

Other troops, of which a limited use could be made, were the 3/7 Rajput R., less two rifle companies and one machine gun platoon, at Mir Ali, and a rifle company, less one platoon, of this unit at Spinwam Fort, where there was also a single 4·5″ howitzer.

Destruction of houses at Kot Matagai south of Mir Ali, October 19th.

In order to distract the enemy's attention from the impending operations towards Spinwam and also to destroy the houses of several well-known hostiles at Kot Matagai, a village south of the Tochi river about four miles south of Mir Ali, in the vicinity of which the presence of some seventy armed tribesmen had been reported, the Commander 9th Infantry Brigade staged an operation with a small mixed force on the 19th of October. This was carried out without opposition early in the morning.

Advance to Spinwam, October 20th.

The force marched out of Mir Ali on the 20th of October, the objects of this day, as laid down in the 9th Infantry Brigade operation order, being to drive off and inflict as much loss as possible on the lashkar, to repair the road, to establish permanent piquets on or near the sites of the two old khassadar posts near the Tabai Narai, and to establish a camp at Spinwam as a base for further operations.

March to assembly position.

The first objective was a position of assembly about point (2119). To cover the route to this point, the 3/7 Rajput R. (less two companies) moved out from Mir Ali, and by 0300 hours had occupied piquets up to point 2047 at the Tarkhobai Bridge, the existing khassadar posts on the route being found deserted. This battalion withdrew to Mir Ali as soon as the section 66 Fd. Bty. had played its part in the battle and passed through on its return journey to Mir Ali.

The remainder of the troops moved to the assembly area in three columns.

(a) A marching column, comprising the 2/11 Sikh R., the 3/15 Punjab R., and a section No. 22 Fd. Coy., accompanied by all animal transport of the Brigade. This column left Mir Ali at 0230 hours and reached the assembly area about 0530 hours.

(b) A fast mechanized column, including the Headquarters 9th Infantry Brigade with artillery and infantry reconnaissance parties moving in lorries and escorted by one section 9th Light Tank Company. This left Mir Ali at 0530 hours, and arrived in the vicinity of the assembly area at 0610 hours, by which time it was beginning to get light.

(c) A slow mechanized column of the artillery and the 1/17 Dogra R., escorted by armoured cars of the 7th Light Tank Company. This reached the assembly area and had debussed by 0630 hours.

1937
Oct. 20th.

There was a bright moon and driving lights were not used on vehicles.

Attack on enemy position, October 20th.
The Brigade Commander carried out a short reconnaissance and decided to advance on a two-battalion front. On the right the 2/11 Sikh R. was allotted as its objective the ridge east of point 2695 to the khassadar post lying south west of that point, whilst on the left the 3/15 Punjab R. was to occupy the foothills about point 3130 and the ridge running thence north east to point 2800. When these objectives had been occupied, the 1/17 Dogra R. was to advance on the low ground between the battalions on the right and left flanks and seize the high ground about points 2703 and 2706.

The 4 Fd. Bty. (How.) was to support the advance of the 2/11 Sikh R. and the section 7 Fd. Bty. that of the 3/15 Punjab R. The 66 Fd. Bty. (How.) was to be prepared to support either flank as required.

The 9th Light Tank Company (less two sections) was in the first place to protect the deployment of the 3/15 Punjab R. and then to move to the right flank and patrol the area of the Zara Mela. It was anticipated that the ground in the east would prove unsuitable for tanks to move direct to Spinwam by that route.

Leaving the assembly area at 0700 hours, the 2/11 Sikh R. reached the nala north of Shamiri, where the commanding officer made his reconnaissance and issued his orders. At 0812 hours the attacking troops came under well-aimed fire from tribesmen who were estimated to number one hundred and fifty on this flank. They had occupied skilfully concealed positions on the sides of the hills, from which they could bring fire to bear on an advance by the main road and on the intervening spurs. Caves and boulders were utilized as cover, and fire positions were so well concealed in the shade and at the foot of cliffs that they provided practically no target to artillery or aircraft. The Battalion pushed up the ridges with great determination. By 0855 hours aircraft reported that tribesmen were withdrawing eastwards by the Sarwek Nala, and fifteen minutes later the Battalion reached its final objectives, with a loss of three killed and ten wounded. The tribesmen left twelve dead bodies and eight rifles on the ground passed over by the battalion, and during the mopping-up process two wounded tribesmen concealed in a cave were captured with their rifles.

The advance of the 3/15 Punjab R. on the left flank began simultaneously with that on the right. Shortly after it started fire was opened on the battalion by tribesmen dispersed in small groups on a hill feature about half way between the road and Tarakai. This feature was captured at the cost of one British officer, Major J. Moriarty, and three Indian other ranks wounded. During the rest of the advance to its final objective the battalion met with long-range sniping only.

By 0800 hours, the 2/6 Raj. Rif., less one company, and one section of the 11th Light Tank Company arrived at Spinwam from Thal-in-Kurram. The infantry built piquets on the high ground to the east of Kaitu bridge and began the construction of a motor track along the bed of the river from near this bridge south east towards Datta Khel. The light tanks then patrolled the road near Kaitu bridge and moved up the Kaitu river to Shadi Khel village. It was impracticable to use them towards the objectives of the troops from Mir Ali owing to the danger of their coming under the fire of our own artillery.

1937
Oct.

At about 0900 hours the 1/17 Dogra R. which was then at point 2140, advanced to its final objectives, reaching them without opposition by 1115 hours. Meanwhile, the company of the 4/6 Raj. Rif. working under sniping fire, had cleared the first road block and then set to work to assist the section No. 22 Fd. Coy. to repair the motor road.

There was now some delay owing to the difficulties presented by the ground on which the two permanent piquets were being established near point 2695. The site for the piquet at that point was on a cliff the only approach to which lay by a difficult track from the northern side. By 1415 hours, however, the work was completed and the piquets were established and provided with reserves of food and water.

Advance continued to Spinwam.
The advance of the main body to Spinwam was then resumed. Sniping at long range only was encountered, and all troops were in camp near Spinwam Post by 1800 hours.

The casualties in the column during the day amounted to three Indian other ranks killed and one British officer and fifteen Indian other ranks wounded. Tribal casualties included twelve dead left on the ground and two wounded prisoners. In addition, twenty five were estimated to have been seriously wounded.

Demolitions carried out on October 21st and 22nd.—Column returns to Mir Ali, October 23rd.
These operations had an excellent effect on the situation in the area, the bulk of the hostile lashkar dispersed, and efforts of the leaders to revive opposition met with no response. On the 21st and 22nd of October, the demolition of six towers and twenty nine houses was carried out in Spinwam and Datta Khel with no opposition other than some sniping fire. On the 23rd of October troops returned to Mir Ali without incident.

Air co-operation throughout the operations was provided by one flight No. 5 (A. C.) Squadron, R. A. F., one flight No. 20 (A. C.) Squadron R. A. F. and one flight No. 1 Squadron Indian Air Force, based on Miranshah.

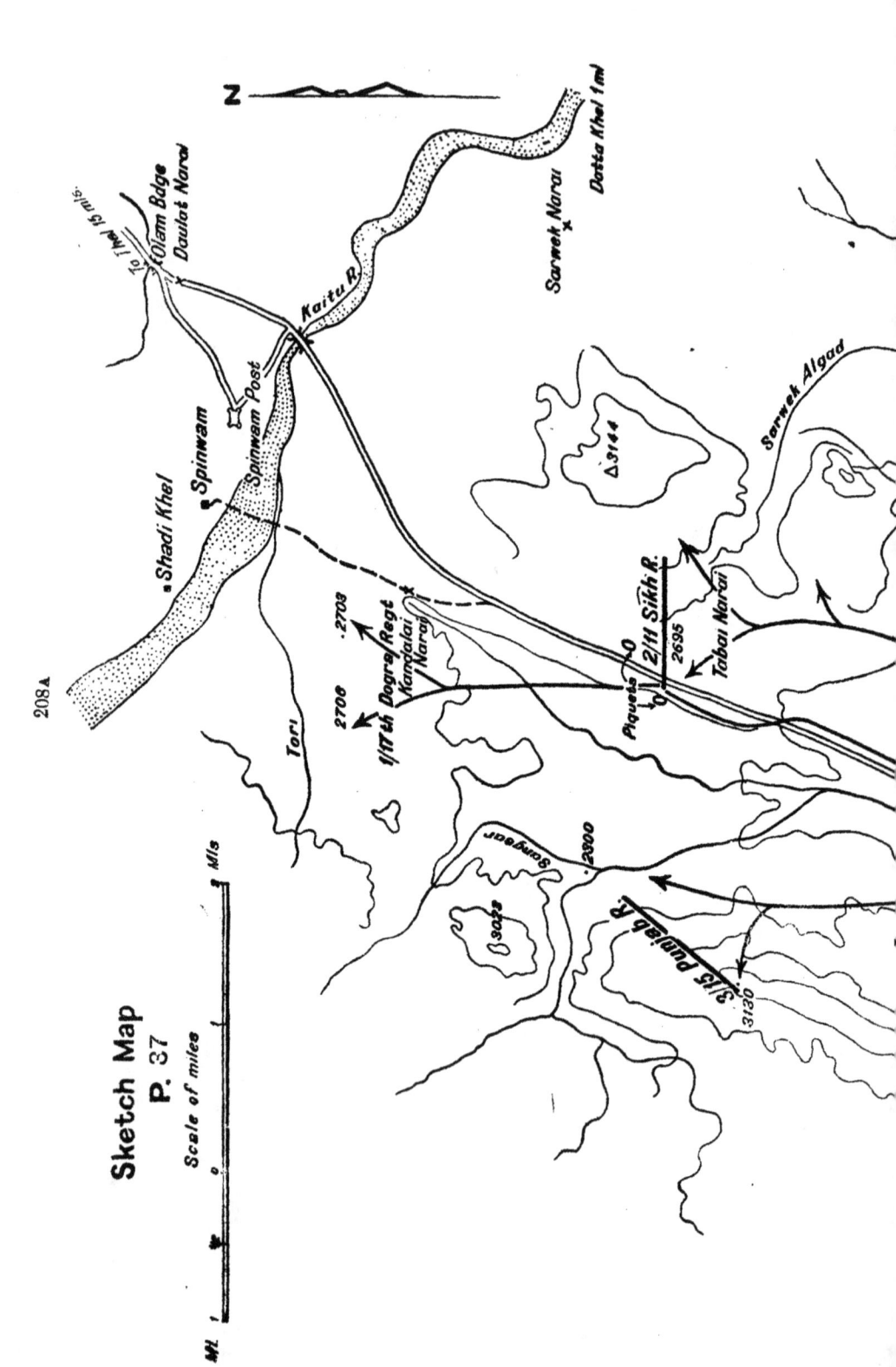

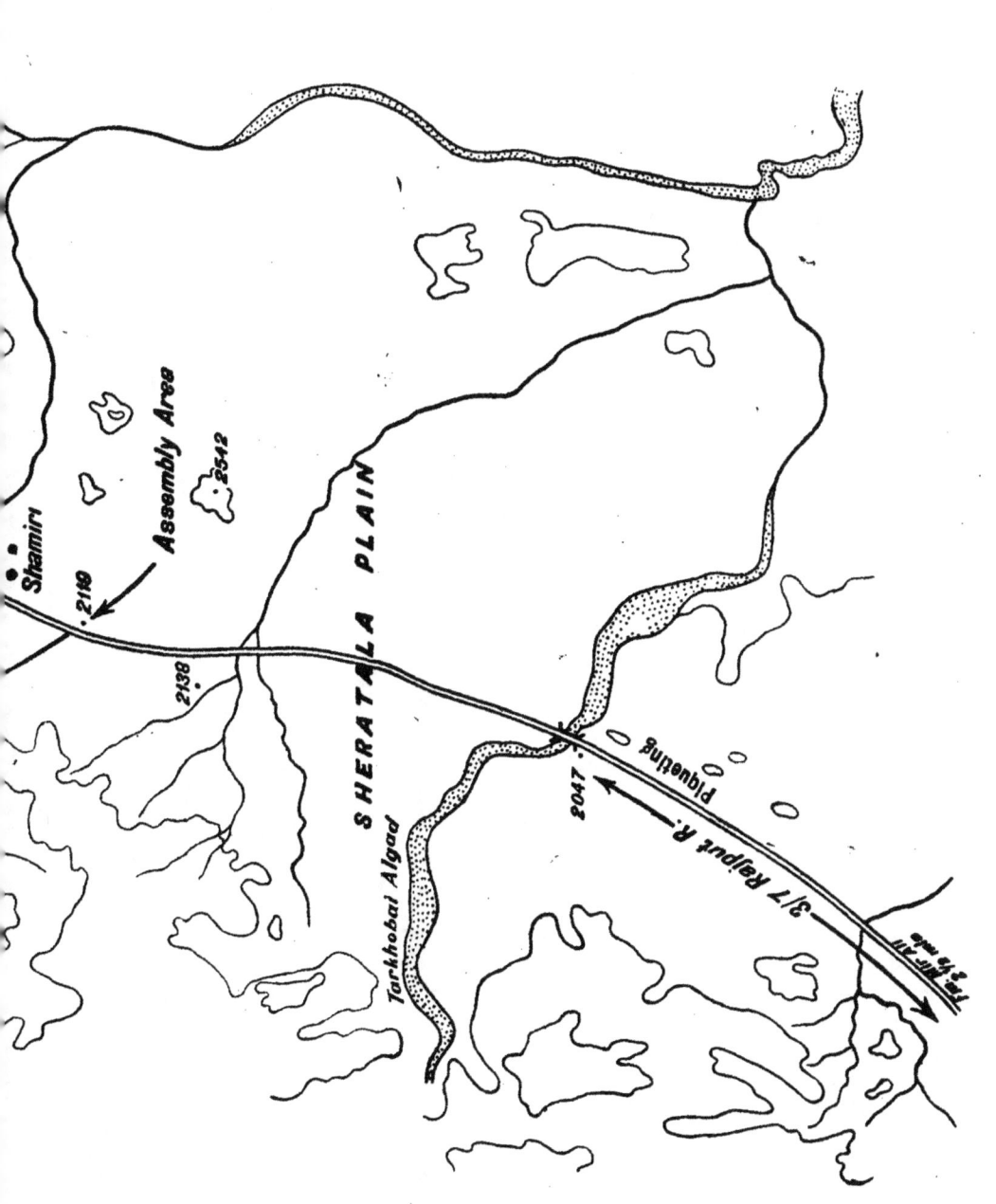

CHAPTER XXV.

Entry of troops into Bhitanni country in October, 1937.

1937
Oct.

For the past three months the Bhitannis, instigated by the Din Faqir, had been particularly troublesome. They had been implicated in several raids into administered territory with the resultant kidnappings of Hindus, and, stirred up by the Din Faqir's propaganda, a number of their khassadars had deserted or had had to be dismissed for unsatisfactory conduct. Their country had been proscribed from the air since the end of August and the political authorities had taken other measures against them. These measures did not have the desired effect, and the hostile attitude of the tribe continued, the general atmosphere of unrest in their country attracting gangs to the scene from other parts of Waziristan.

Bhitannis had been giving trouble for some time.

In the middle of September, the situation seemed sufficiently threatening to warrant the reinforcement of the counter-raiding troops in administered territory and the 8th Light Cavalry were ordered from Kohat to Tank, where they arrived on the 23rd of September, sending detachments a week later to Sur Kamar and Zarkani Frontier* Constabulary Posts

The net result, generally speaking, of the hostile efforts was small, owing to the watchfulness of the troops and of the civil forces in the Bannu and Manzai areas, which, since the counter-raiding precautions were first intensified, had prevented the commission of offences on a much larger scale. Considerable difficulty was experienced, though, in the endeavours to trace or intercept raiders after an offence had been committed. The whole problem was rendered more difficult by the enmity existing between the Hindu and Muslim communities in the villages, by their supineness, which showed itself in their lack of energy in attempting to defend themselves even when they were given weapons for the purpose, and by the vagueness of the information and the delay in sending it after a raid had been committed.

The Din Faqir.

The Din Faqir, although he had not attended the meeting assembled by the Faqir of Ipi in the Shawal in the middle of August, had paid a visit after that to the Mahsud country to forward the cause of the Faqir of Ipi. Subsequently, he had returned to the Bhitanni country and had busied himself in trying to persuade the Bhitannis to resist the invasion of their country, the imminence of which, according to him, was evidenced by the progress of the Tajori-Nunghar Tangi road, work on which had been started by the civil authorities on the 29th of August. At the same time he made known that his "terms" for making peace with the Government were that all cases against hostile Bhitanni tribesmen should be dropped, that all their hostages should be released, and that work on the Tajori road should cease. Attempts by the Bhitanni maliks to make him give up his hostile attitude met with no success.

These maliks had been striving to bring about the surrender of the kidnapped persons, but had not been completely successful, and on the 12th of October, although the majority of the captives had been returned, there were still four in the hands of the tribesmen.

---

*See sketch Map Q. 37 Chap. XXI.

1937
Oct.

Bhitanni jirga, October 12th. On this day, General Sir John Coleridge and the Resident in Waziristan interviewed a Bhitanni jirga. The jirga was informed that terms to the Bhitanni tribe for their part in recent hostilities and for their numerous offences of raiding and kidnapping would not be announced until troops had visited their country, and that a motorable road would be constructed to Kot in order to facilitate control of this area. The tribe was warned against the consequences of opposing the advance of the troops and was ordered to hand over the remaining Hindu captives. The maliks asked for an opportunity to hold a tribal meeting to arrange for the return of the four men and also to dissuade the tribesmen from opposing the troops. A suspension of the air-proscription was granted them, and they were successful in securing the release of the captives. As a result, the air proscription was stopped. They were not so successful, however, in their efforts to persuade the tribesmen to refrain from opposition to the troops.

Arrangements for advance into Bhitanni country.* Arrangements for the advance of land forces into Bhitanni country and for the construction of a road to Kot had been under consideration for some time. It had been intended to carry out this operation earlier, but the renewal of the Faqir's offensive in September had made a postponement advisable. It was now decided that the advance should begin when the road from Tajori to Nunghar Tangi was completed.

The Commander, 1st Division was made responsible for the conduct of the operations. The force was to consist, in the opening stages, of an infantry brigade group with additional troops, which would be made available by Wazirforce Headquarters. These consisted of one sabre squadron and one machine gun troop Probyn's Horse, the 25th Mtn. Bde. less one battery, and one section 9th Light Tank Company. For work on the road five Field Companies, Sappers and Miners (Nos. 2, 4, 5, 14 and 22), and four road construction battalions were attached to the force.

The first stage of the operations was to be a deliberate advance, during which the building of the road to Kot (4113) was to be pushed on with all possible speed. When Kot was reached, it was thought probable that an infantry brigade group would be required to visit certain places within three days' circuit of action of that place. Reinforcements for this purpose would be sent when the situation permitted of the withdrawal of another brigade from the Sham Plain area.

The concentration of the initial force at Sulaiman Khel, five miles east of the administrative border, and west of Sarai Gambila, was ordered for the 14th of October. From the 9th to the 12th of October a proportion of the technical troops, under protective arrangements made by Headquarters Bannu Area, worked on temporary improvements to the Frontier road between Jani Khel and Khairu Khel.

Operations to be carried out by 2nd Infantry Brigade and attached troops. The Commander 1st Division detailed the 2nd Infantry Brigade† for the operations, increasing the strength of the Brigade by one infantry battalion, the 2/5 R. G. R., from the 1st Infantry Brigade.

The fresh disposition of troops resulting from these new operations required a re-adjustment of the Divisional Areas. From the 12th of October, therefore, when Headquarters 1st Division left Dosalli, the Sham

---
*[Ref. sketch Map S. 37 at end of Chap. sketch Map A].
†For detail of units see p. 81.

THE FIRST M. T. THROUGH THE NUNGHAR TANGI INTO
BHITANNI COUNTRY, OCTOBER 1937.

Area was absorbed into the Razmak area under the control of the Commander Waziristan Division, and a new "Bhitanni Area", under the Commander 1st Division was formed. Roughly, the administrative boundary formed the easterly side and the Saraghar Range and the Shuza Algad formed the westerly side of this area, meeting at Wazirki Sar in the north and at the point where the Shuza Algad cuts the administrative boundary in the south. On the east side, the area included a stretch of country from Azad Khel *via* Sulaiman Khel to Sarai Gambila and back by Tajori to Khan Khelan. The Sham, Razmak, and Bannu areas were adjusted to exclude this Bhitanni Area.

On the 9th of October the 2nd Infantry Brigade marched from Shawali Camp on the Shawali Algad. They followed the new road from Ghariom to Bichhe Kashkai and on by River Camp to Jani Khel, arriving at Sulaiman Khel on the 14th of October. They were joined here on that day by Headquarters 1st Division. The Brigade halted at River Camp for a day, and the opportunity was taken of destroying the house of Agip, a known hostile, near Sein. A few sniping shots were fired at the troops between Ghariom and Bichhe Kashkai, but east of the latter there were no signs of enemy activity.

The Headquarters 1st Division also moved to Sarai Gambila, with advanced headquarters, later, at Masti Khel nearer the administrative border further west.

The force halted at Sulaiman Khel on the 15th, the day being spent in reconnaissances of the lines of advance to Spalvi, the next day's objective.

The Brigade Commander decided to enter the Bhitanni country by three routes, the Warmola, Nunghar and Khanda Tangis, each of these passes being secured by 0615 hours. The right and left columns each consisted of one infantry battalion with one sub-section of a mountain battery, the 2/8 Punjab R. taking the Warmola Tangi, and the 2/4 Bombay Grs. the Khanda Tangi. The centre column, consisting of the 1/11 Sikh R. and the 2/2 Punjab R. with the remainder of the Artillery, marched by the Nunghar Tangi.

Country entered October 16th.

Columns marched out of camp at 0130 hours on the 16th of October, and all three passes were occupied by the time laid down, 0615 hours. The right column, having established its piquets on the Warmola Tangi, turned southwards to Wazhai Wazar (5115), which had been given as the objective of the column. The country was found to be extremely difficult and it became impossible for mules to move with the troops. Under instructions from Brigade Headquarters these were sent back to enter through the Nunghar Tangi. Shortly after this, orders were received shortening the column objective to as far as the Marez Khwara, the left of their original objective being allotted to the 1/11th Sikh R. from the centre column. This objective was secured by 0945 hours.

The left column, after securing the Khanda Tangi, turned north west and by 1000 hours was in position on its objective a line south of the Rod Algad roughly north west and south east through Owobizhai Kile (5313).

The centre column advanced up the gap between the flanking columns and secured positions covering the camp site at Spalvi (5315), and all troops not employed in constructing or covering piquets withdrew to camp.

Column reaches Spalvi camp.

1937

Oct.

No opposition had been encountered during the day, but towards dusk a few shots were fired into the camp, slightly wounding one Indian other rank of a Road Construction Battalion.

Reports now received showed that with the exception of Khonia Khel and a small gang there were no hostile Mahsuds in Bhitanni country, but that some resistance was to be expected from the Bhitannis themselves to any further advance up the Rod Algad, although the attitude of the Din Faqir, who had been interviewed recently by the Political Naib Tehsildar at Jandola, was said to be more satisfactory.

Work on road commenced, October 18th.

The following day was spent in reconnoitring for the alignment of the road west of Nunghar Tangi, and on the 18th work on the new road was commenced. On neither day were there any signs of an enemy.

Reconnaissance up the Rod Algad, October 19th opposed.

On the 19th of October the Brigade reconnoitred up the Rod Algad. The original intention was to go as far as Qalandar Khel Kile (4612). Opposition was met, however, before the Brigade was two miles from camp, and it was decided not to go further than point 2020 (4813). Opposition started at the point where the Stara Wucha Khwara takes off from the Rod Algad. Enemy started firing from the northern flank and in a very short time from the south west and west also. As the advance continued, enemy parties were seen and engaged forward and on both flanks by air and ground troops. The enemy were estimated to number two hundred and seventy, mainly Bhitannis with a proportion of Tori Khel Wazirs and Mahsuds. A number of casualties were inflicted on them, but the exact numbers were not established as the local inhabitants were endeavouring to maintain that they were not implicated and would not divulge any figures. The troops lost one Indian other rank killed and three wounded.

That evening, information was received that eight hundred enemy were in the vicinity and that a fair proportion of these might be expected to oppose any fresh advance.

Reconnaissance repeated on October 20th, 21st and 22nd.

In view of the report and of the opposition already encountered, the Brigade Commander decided to advance in the same direction on the 20th, with the object of meeting the enemy and inflicting casualties. In order to give the Brigade a greater radius of action, work on the road was to be suspended for the day, thus obviating the necessity of employing a portion of the troops in providing protection for the construction parties.

The Brigade moved out of camp at 0700 hours and advanced as far as the line point 2308 (4714)—point 2020 (4813)—the high ground between the latter and Qalandar Khel Kile overlooking the Rod Algad. Parties of enemy were again seen and engaged with considerable success by aircraft and troops on the ground. Their casualties, as on the previous day, were difficult to trace, but 15 were known definitely to have been killed, and it may be assumed that the total list was a satisfactory one, comparing favourably with the loss of only one Indian other rank slightly wounded in the 2nd Infantry Brigade.

During the advance, a company headquarters of 1/11 Sikh R. at a point on the north bank of the Rod Algad were attacked by a party of five Bhitannis armed with knives. The ground was very broken and these men

SPALVI CAMP, 1ST INF. BRIGADE, 1937.

SPALVI TANGI.

TYPICAL COUNTRY NEAR SPALVI.

QALANDER CAMP.

had allowed the leading troops to pass them, waiting for a more favourable opportunity. They leapt from their cover and dashed in on the headquarters. The Sikhs, led by their company commander, at once charged them with the bayonet and killed them all.

The withdrawal started at 1330 hours. Neither on this occasion nor on the previous day was it followed up.

The operation was repeated on the 21st of October the Brigade advancing this time in two columns, in the hope of catching unawares any enemy who might intend to oppose an advance from the south bank of the Rod Algad. The left column advanced to Kuchia Wazar (4912) whilst the right one followed the Rod Algad. Very few enemy were seen and those only at a distance.

Another advance was made the next day as far as the west of Qalandar Khel Kile, again without opposition.

Road construction continues. Further reconnaissances were carried out during the next few days and the construction of the road continued. The 2nd Infantry Brigade moved freely about the area, meeting with no hostile activity. Work on the road went on rapidly, and the whole stretch to Kot was completed on the 3rd of December.

The lack of resistance by the Bhitannis may be attributed to the effect of air action taken over a considerable period in the proscribed area, to the casualties sustained in the early stages, and to the lack of support from the neighbouring Mahsuds, on whose help the hostile Bhitanni leaders had been reckoning.

On the 22nd of October the Bhitanni jirga was again interviewed, the Din Faqir himself being present. The recalcitrant Waruki section was ordered to produce its nine missing hostages within a week. The other sections were told that their hostages would be released on the deposit of two rifles as security for each hostage. They were also told that Khassadars who had deserted or had been suspended must either return to duty in seven days time or that one rifle must be produced as security for each man. The number of rifles to be given in amounted to eighty two on the former account and forty on the latter. They were also ordered to deposit at short notice another hundred rifles as first payment of a fine of rifles eventually to be imposed.

After a discussion, lasting two days, between the Resident in Waziristan, the Bhitanni maliks, and the Din Faqir. the last named agreed to bring in some close relative of his as a hostage and to use his influence in the tribe for making peace. He brought in his brother, publicly proclaimed that he was going to make peace with Government, and busied himself, with his followers, in deciding how the fine in rifles was to be made up. These rifles were all surrendered by the 4th of November.

The Faqir of Ipi and Mullah Sher Ali tried to dissuade the Din Faqir from coming to terms with Government. Considerably annoyed at the lack of support from the Faqir of Ipi and the Mahsuds, at first he rejected these advances, but soon there were indications that he was wavering.

1937
Oct.

Ali Khel and Kui villages punished, October 26th.

The inhabitants of the villages of Ali Khel and Kui, on the administrative border some ten miles north of where the 2nd Infantry Brigade had commenced its operations, had been known to harbour outlaws and to connive at raids into administered territory. It was decided that now was a suitable time for punishing them. On the 26th of October, Frontier Constabulary supported by the 1/13 F. F. Rif. and by a section of the 9th Light Tank Company, surrounded these villages. There was some opposition and the force sustained a few casualties, but several wanted men were arrested.

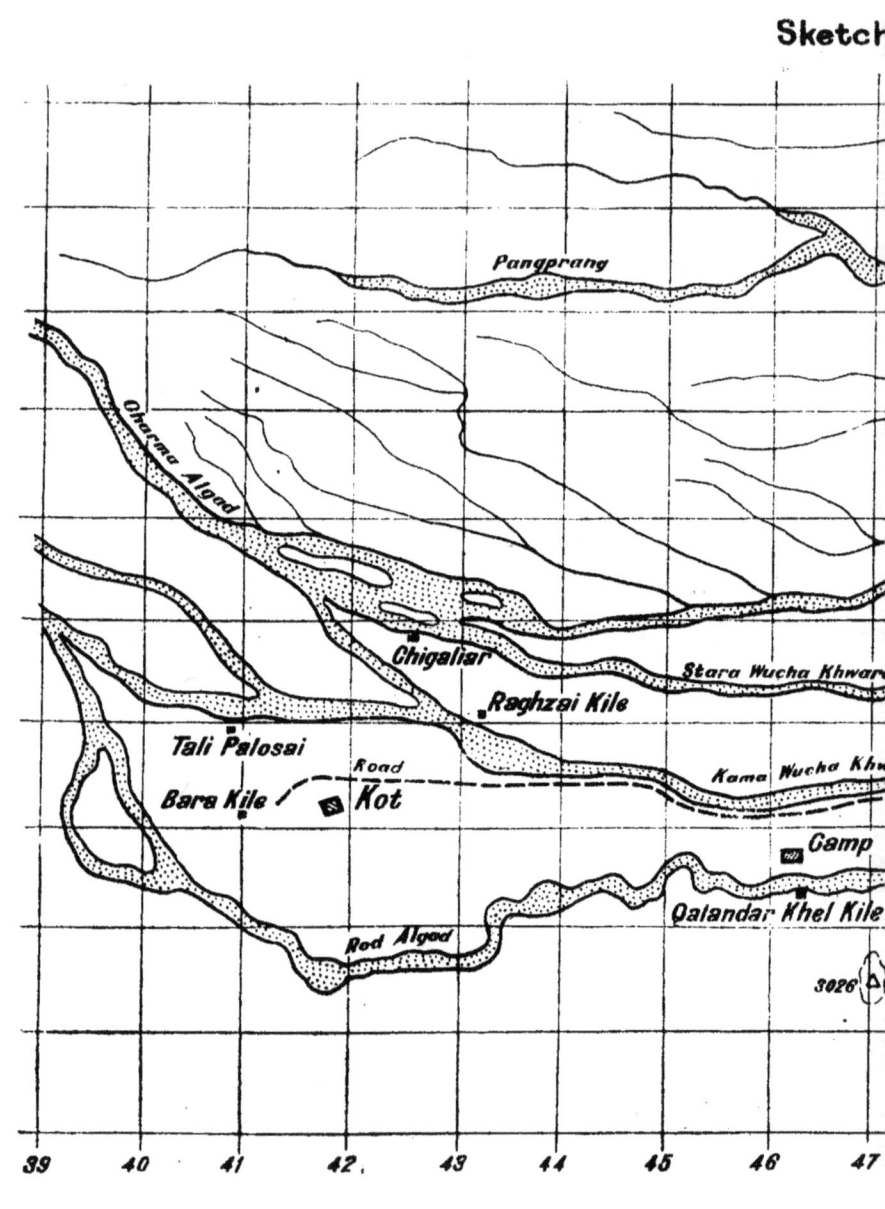

. 37.

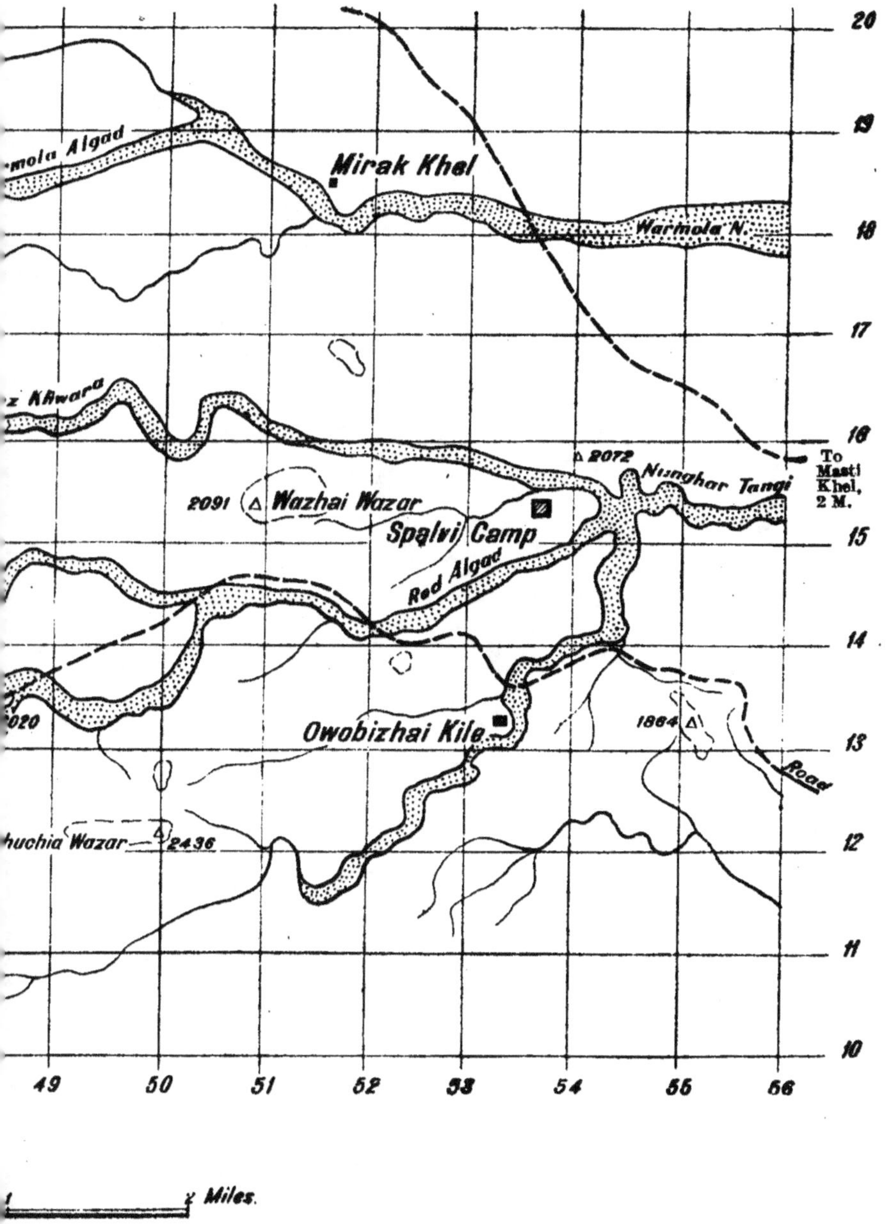

Mirak Khel
Warmola N.
Algad
z Khwara
2072
Nunghar Tangi
To
Masti
Khel,
2 M.
2091
Wazhai Wazar
Spalvi Camp
Red Algad
Owobizhai Kile
1864
Road
2020
huchia Wazar
2436
20
19
18
17
16
15
14
13
12
11
10
49
50
51
52
53
54
55
56
Miles.

CHAPTER XXVI.

Columns to deal with possible further offensives—Political summing up of the situation during second half of Oct. 1937—9th Infantry Brigade marches to Bichhe Kashkai *via* Boya and Damdil—1st Infantry Brigade marches to Masti Khel—Operations in the lower Shaktu Valley—Continuation of work on the road to Kot in Bhitanni country.

1937 Oct.

Columns located at Miranshah and Mir Ali.
It had been realized that the presence of the Faqir of Ipi so near to the Durand line—he had taken up his residence temporarily on or near the Khost border—might well lead to fresh incursions of Afghan tribesmen, excited by his propaganda, though much would depend on the amount of support and encouragement such incursions would receive from the tribes of Waziristan. The danger existed, though, and about the time when the Faqir's offensive in the Spinwam area was developing, measures were being considered to counter it and to ensure that if the situation did arise it should not interfere with the road construction which was progressing steadily or with the operations to be undertaken against the Bhitannis.

The solution arrived at was to locate mobile columns, each with a two-days' circuit of action on an "all-pack" basis, at Miranshah and Mir Ali. These, with the mobile column already in existence at Razmak, would attack and inflict the maximum possible loss on any hostile columns within reach of them. It was considered that these dispositions would afford the necessary protection for roadmaking and for the prosecution of the Bhitanni enterprise. The 1st and 9th Infantry Brigades were the nuclei of these columns at Mir Ali and Miranshah, and the concentration of the necessary troops at these places was completed by the 30th of October, the Brigades leaving Ghariom Camp and Mir Ali, respectively, two days' earlier.

Further adjustments to administrative areas.
These new dispositions necessitated further adjustments in administration areas which came into force on the 30th of October.

The Mir Ali Area, under the Commander, 9th Infantry Brigade, stretched from Thal-in-Kurram to the Sammal Narai, thence *via* Miranshah to the Dawe Manda where it reached the Durand Line. From this spot it followed the Durand Line to the boundary between the Waziristan and Kohat Districts.

The Bhitanni Area, the responsibility for which lay with the Commander 1st Division, remained largely as it was before. Its northern apex was now placed at the point where the Shaktu river crossed the Administrative boundary. On the north west the boundary was that of the Mir Ali area along the Shaktu and Karesti Algads, the south west side being from the Sammal Narai to the Shuza Algad immediately south of the Spin Ghar range.

The Razmak Area, under the Commander Waziristan Division, had a common boundary with the Mir Ali and Bhitanni Areas along the greater part of its easterly side. It included the Spin Ghar range and Jandola, met the Gumal river near Khuzma Post, followed the river to the Durand Line, and went along that Line to the Dawe Manda.

The Bannu Area, under Brigadier F. H. Maynard, C.B., M.C., comprised the rest of Waziristan District. By this reallotment the Manzai Area, which, owing to the decrease in raiding from tribal territory, was no

1937
Oct.—Nov.

longer really necessary, ceased to exist. For the same reason, the appointment of Civil Defence Officer was abolished from the 31st of October, the duty of co-ordinating the working and dispositions of the civil forces in the two civil districts and their collaboration with the regular troops falling to the Commander Bannu Area.

The incursion of Afghan tribesmen, which had appeared to be gathering momentum after the opening of the Faqir of Ipi's offensive in the Spinwam area, ceased abruptly after the successful action on the 20th of October against the lashkar in the Tabai hills. Although the possibility of its revival was always present, after a while there was every reason to believe that the prospect of its immediate renewal on any considerable scale was negligible. The series of defeats inflicted on the Faqir's lashkar and the other steps taken by the political and military authorities to make the tribesmen realize the power of Government had all had their effect.

At the end of October, in the course of a discussion on when the extra troops could be withdrawn from Waziristan, a matter which had to be kept constantly in mind, the situation was summed up by the Political Authorities as follows. All the tribes were tired of hostilities and were responding in an increasingly reduced manner to the efforts of the Faqir of Ipi to attract support. The Faqir, though still the focus of trouble, was losing his power. The morale of the khassadars throughout Waziristan had improved considerably and could now be said to be good. The danger in the coming cold weather would be only in comparatively small gangs. The necessity for the presence of these extra troops as long as the new roads were under construction was not in question, but the withdrawal of the majority of the extra troops would not only not cause any set-back in this improvement, it would probably have the opposite effect, as their presence forced some tribesmen to remain hostile on points of honour. Withdrawal therefore could begin as soon as the roads were completed and scouts were installed in the new posts of Ghariom and Bichhe Kashkai. The decision to establish these posts had been due to the increased responsibility which must fall on the Tochi Scouts for general control, following the construction of the new roads and the extension of the system of protected areas. By temporary reductions elsewhere and by postponing the re-occupation by Tochi Scouts' detachments of the posts at Khajuri and Shewa until twelve new platoons were fully trained, it would be possible for the Scouts to take over the posts at Ghariom and Bichhe Kashkai by the 1st of December. Until these extra platoons had been trained, that is to say until about May 1938, it was essential that a mobile column of some of the extra troops should remain in the Tochi Valley, based, preferably, on Mir Ali.

Political summing up of the situation.

In view of the greatly improved situation in the area north of the Tochi river, General Sir John Coleridge now decided that columns should visit certain other regions. These were to include marches from Boya to Damdil Camp via the Mot Narai and Lakki Khula, along the Jaler Algad from Sarobi to its junction with the Kiwa river, and from Mandawam to Karkanwam on the Shaktu river.

*Orders issued for further movements of 1st and 9th Infantry Brigades.

The task of conducting these operations was given to the Commander 1st Division, and the 1st and 9th Infantry Brigades were placed under his

---
* Ref. sketch map A in pocket.

command from the 11th of November for the purpose. For the operations between the Khaisora and Shaktu rivers seven platoons of the Tochi Scouts at Bichhe Kashkai Camp were placed at his disposal. As soon as the operations were concluded the 1st Infantry Brigade was to be sent on to Masti Khel, where it was to arrive by the 19th of November, for employment against the Bhitannis. The 9th Infantry Brigade was to be returned to Mir Ali by the same date.

The gang, to deal with which troops of the 9th Brigade had moved south of Mir Ali on the 19th October, was reported to be still in existence in the neighbourhood of Tarakai about two miles south of the Tochi river and six miles east of the Mir Ali—Bichhe Kashkai road. It was decided to disperse this party before the start of the operations now proposed, and the 1st Infantry Brigade, at Mir Ali, was ordered to attack it on the 3rd of November. Signs of military activity in this area, however, produced the required effect and on the 2nd of November the most important leader in the gang, an ex-subedar of Khassadars, surrendered unconditionally, the gang dispersing. The 1st Infantry Brigade operated in the area on the following day and found no signs of any enemy.

It was evident that the situation north of the Khaisora river had improved very considerably, and it was not expected that the early visit of troops to other parts of this area would meet with any opposition. The march down the Lower Shaktu might prove a more difficult proposition, though, as it had been suspected for some time that hostile tribesmen were using this area as a convenient harbourage.

9th Inf. Brigade (see pp. 184 & 185) marches via Boya, the Mot Narai, Damdil and Jaler Algad to Bichhe Kashkai.*

On the 12th of November the 9th Infantry Brigade marched from Miranshah to Boya. It moved on to Damdil via the Mot Narai and Lakki Maidan the next day, and on the 14th went to Bichhe Kashkai via the Jaler Algad. It was not molested during any part of the march except for a few shots fired at the Brigade when at Boya and Damdil. On the third day it was assisted in the last stages by the 1st Infantry Brigade, which moved to Bichhe Kashkai on the 12th. The march on this day was a slow one owing to the very difficult nature of the country, particularly between Damdil and the point where the route entered the Jaler Algad about half a mile north west of Saroli, where the movement of the animal transport was considerably impeded. The 1st Infantry Brigade had prepared a track from the Jaler Algad to Bichhe Kashkai, but even with this help their forward troops astride the Algad were not able to commence their withdrawal until it was getting dark.

1st Inf. Brigade (see p. 82) marches to Masti Khel via Karkanwam.**

The Advanced Headquarters 1st Division moved to Bichhe Kashkai on the 13th of November, preparatory to the advance to the Lower Shaktu, and three days later the 1st Infantry Brigade, to which formation the 3/15 Punjab R. had been attached, marched via the Pasta Algad to the Shaktu Algad and camped about one and a half miles to the east of Mandawam. The 9th Infantry Brigade with seven platoons of the Tochi Scouts protected the greater portion of the route for this march, returning to Bichhe Kashkai when the 1st Infantry Brigade had passed through them.

---
* [Ref. sketch map A in pocket.]
** [Ref. sketch map B 37 at end of chap.]

1937

Nov.

The local tribesmen had been warned that troops might be operating in the direction of Mandawam, and on arrival at the Shaktu river the 1st Infantry Brigade was met by a party of about seventy friendly inhabitants. There had been no opposition during the actual march except for a few shots fired at a piquet of the 9th Infantry Brigade, but whilst the 1st Infantry Brigade were preparing their camp piquets a company of the 3/15th came under fire and lost two men wounded and a solitary sniper killed one of a covering party of the 1/6 G. R. After dark this sniper continued his operations for over two hours, changing his position at frequent intervals and succeeding in hitting some of the mules.

The instructions issued by the Commander 1st Division for the operation laid down that on the 17th of November the 1st Infantry Brigade was to march to Karkanwam while the 9th Infantry Brigade went to River Camp so as to be within reasonable supporting distance of the former Brigade on the 18th. On the 18th the Brigades were to march to Jani Khel and Jaler Camp respectively, the objectives for the third day being Masti Khel and Mir Ali. The 3/15 Punjab R. and the 19 Mtn. Bty. were to leave the 1st Infantry Brigade on the third day and join the 9th Infantry Brigade at River Camp, moving northwards from the Shaktu river from a point about two miles north east of Karkanwam. When the 9th Infantry Brigade moved to River Camp on the 18th, Advanced Headquarters 1st Division was to return to Mir Ali.

The initial portion of the country traversed by the 1st Infantry Brigade on the 17th did not present any great obstacles, but the difficulties began at the big bend of the river round Arap Kot. The right bank here is dominated by the precipitous Babar Kunati range some eighteen hundred yards away. Beyond Arap Kot and a few hundred yards before the river turns east, the left bank becomes a precipice about one hundred feet high, and extending for about three quarters of a mile. From the top of this cliff the hill rises steeply for about one thousand feet from the nala bed. The difficulties then decrease until the Shaktu Tangi is reached. This Tangi is formed by the rivers breaking through the Babar Kunati range. On the south bank of the Tangi there are two distinct ranges. The west slope of the western range is difficult but not insuperable. The top is a knife-edge and the eastern slope a smooth rock face almost perpendicular and quite impracticable. The eastern range is not so difficult but can only be approached by a very wide detour to the south or by moving through the western end of the Tangi. The western range is higher than, and to some extent dominates the eastern one. The north bank of the Tangi is steep and difficult but not impracticable.

The immediate object of the 1st Infantry Brigade on the morning of the 17th was to discover whether it was possible to make a track across the Arap Kot peninsular and thereby avoid the big bend in the river and save piqueting. It had been intended to carry out a reconnaissance the afternoon before under cover of the piqueting party of the 3/15 Punjab R., but when the latter became involved with the enemy the reconnaissance had to be cancelled. The advanced guard and piqueting troops (1/6 G. R. and 3/15 Punjab R.), therefore, left camp before dawn to secure a position to cover a reconnaissance for this track. The position was secured by 0700 hours without opposition but the reconnaissance showed that it would take most of the day to make a track fit for mules or camels. Accordingly, the advanced guard moved forward and seized the right bank of the Shaktu river north of Arap Kot, while the 1 S. Wales

Bord., who were at the head of the main body, moved along the nala piqueting the right bank from the junction of the Shaktu river and the Sheramia Algad, to join up with the advanced guard. There were a number of people about who all seemed quite friendly. The piqueting therefore was confined to the lower features and troops were not sent to the top of the Babar Kunati. The transport and the rear guard followed the 1 S. Wales Bord. by the nala route and the latter cleared Arap Kot without incident.

In the meantime, however, the advanced guard had met opposition.

Advance opposed. The nature of the left bank where the river turns east was such that it could not be piqueted from the south or from the west. A company of the 3/15 Punjab R. moved forward under the cliff until they came to a climable spur. They seized this and then attacked the cliff from the east, securing a position which dominated the whole length of the cliff. This attack was opposed by enemy estimated at thirty men, but owing to good covering fire and use of ground, and, above all, to the speed with which the movement was carried out, no casualties were sustained.

Brigade Commander decides to camp where he is. The advance then continued until 1300 hours, when the leading troops had reached a point about one mile from the Tangi. Route piquets and the leading troops were now under fire from the south bank. The 1 S. Wales Bord. had already moved up to the advanced guard as piqueting troops and only three platoons were available for piqueting until other piquets withdrawn by the rear guard had rejoined. The Brigade Commander after a reconnaissance came to the conclusion that two battalions would be required to secure the Tangi. As these could not be made available it was obvious that the objective for the day, Karkanwam, could not be reached. Orders were issued for troops to camp in the nala bed about fifteen hundred yards from the west end of the Tangi, the site selected being defiladed from the high ridge on the south.

Work on camp piquets began at once, and the sniping soon became general on all sides, including long range fire on the camp site. It was directed particularly against the 1 S. Wales Bord. who were establishing piquets south of the camp. The enemy on this side were originally on top of the Babar Kunati range but were seen to be working forward closer to the covering parties. Work on piquets in this area was suspended for a time while an artillery and machine gun plan was prepared. Fire was then opened on the known enemy positions by one and a half batteries of artillery and eight machine guns, ably supported by the close support aircraft with bombs and machine guns. This had the desired effect. Several enemy were seen to be hit, and the sniping in this area ceased except for a few desultory long range shots. All camp piquets were successfully established. There was some slight sniping during the late evening but no shots were fired during the night.

Objective for the 18th Nov. altered to Rocha. On the 18th the destination of the 1st Infantry Brigade had been Jani Khel, but as opposition was anticipated at the Shaktu Tangi, it was altered to Rocha, which was some three and a half miles closer.

To assist the 1st Infantry Brigade the 9th Infantry Brigade was to move south from River Camp as far as Point 3007 and cover the left flank

1937
Oct. 18th

of the 1st Brigade from that point back to Rocha. This meant that once the Shaktu Tangi was secured little further opposition was to be anticipated.

The plan for the advance was in two phases. In the first phase the 2/6 G. R. on the right and the 3/15 Punjab R. on the left, each supported by one mountain battery, were to attack the Tangi. In the second phase the S. Wales Bord. with the 13 Mtn. Bty. in support, were to pass through the west end of the Tangi, seize the east end, and then piquet down the right bank of the Shaktu, while the 3/15 Punjab R. moved along the high ground on the left bank to meet the 9th Infantry Brigade. The 1/6 G. R. with the 19 Mtn. Bty. in support were to be the rear guard.

The first phase began at first light and all objectives were taken without opposition. The S. Wales Bord. then moved forward under cover to the west end of the Tangi, while the commanding officer carried out his reconnaissance. The right flank was still the dangerous one. The 2/6 G. R. had secured the western ridge of the two ridges south of the Tangi, but owing to the nature of the ground could not move forward to the eastern ridge, which had to be taken by the S. Wales Bord.

The entrance to the Tangi was only fifteen yards wide but it opened **Advance opposed.** up immediately to about fifty yards.

A platoon of the 1 S. Wales Bord. had moved forward into the Tangi, another platoon was on its way to piquet the eastern ridge on the right bank and another to the eastern ridge of the left bank, when the enemy opened fire. A few seconds before the fire began the intelligence officer of the S. Wales Bord. had reported the presence of some enemy. There were none to be seen but he had spotted a loophole through which he could see daylight, and whilst he was looking the light had been blotted out.

The first burst of fire caused casualties in the vanguard platoon and in the piquet moving out to the right. A platoon of machine guns in action just west of the Tangi opened fire on the enemy positions, firing through the entrance to the Tangi. A section of the 13 Mtn. Bty. was close behind. The Battery Commander, who was with the officer commanding the S. Wales Bord., realizing that he could best support the advance by direct fire over open sights, brought his guns into action under cover, ran them forward into the mouth of the Tangi which was still under fire, and opened rapid fire with shrapnel.

This prompt and efficient support enabled the platoon on the right to continue its advance which had been slowed up by the enemy fire though not completely stopped. Eventually it reached its objective having had one man killed and four wounded, including the platoon commander.

The action of the artillery and of this platoon undoubtedly saved what might have been a nasty situation. There were some thirty or forty enemy immediately opposite the leading troops of the S. Wales Bord. with as many more further along the ridge to the south. They were very strongly placed behind solid rock faces with narrow fissures which had been filled with stones to make loopholes. They must have been caught unprepared as they allowed the leading troops to move into the Tangi and

LOWER SHAKTU TANGI.

almost half-way to their objectives before opening fire. Had they shot immediately the first troops moved through the entrance casualties must have been much higher. As it was, when the platoon reached its objective on the right the enemy had to withdraw to the south or across the Karesti Algad.

1937

Nov. 18th

The S. Wales Bord. then continued their advance through the Tangi. The enemy again opened fire from the right bank of the Karesti but withdrew rapidly when attacked by one company of the S. Wales Bord. By this time the S. Wales Bord. had all been used up, but it was found possible to withdraw the 2/6 G. R., less one company, and to send them forward as advanced guard.

There was no further opposition to the advance, and interest became centred on the rear guard, the 1/6 G. R., which had been having an anxious time. No camp piquets could be withdrawn during the first phase as the two batteries of artillery were required to support the attack on the Tangi. In addition to the enemy opposing the advance through the Tangi there were between fifty and a hundred tribesmen in small parties engaged in sniping the camp piquets.

As soon as the 19 Mtn. Bty. was free to support the rear guard all camp piquets west of the camp site were withdrawn, at a cost of only two casualties. The rear guard then stood on a line through the camp site until transport was clear of the Tangi, when it continued the withdrawal. The 2/6 G. R. and the 3/15 Punjab R. had difficulty in withdrawing some of their piquets over the Tangi, partly because of the difficult nature of the ground and partly on account of heavy sniping. However, the enemy made no attempt to follow up closely, thanks possibly to two close support aircraft, which had no difficulty in spotting the enemy once he started to move forward and whose support during the withdrawal through the Tangi was invaluable.

9th Brigade in position to help.
The column was clear of the Tangi by 1310 hours, and from there onwards the tribesmen made no attempt to interfere with the march. The 9th Infantry Brigade was established on the hills from point 3007 to point 2754, and after the 1st Brigade had passed this area, it returned, joined by the 19 Mtn. Bty. and the 3/15 Punjab R., to River Camp. The camp site at Rocha had been secured by the Bannu mobile column and a prominent hill south of the Khaisora river some distance to the east of the camp by the 1/17 Dogra R. from Jani Khel. When the 1st Infantry Brigade reached Rocha camp, at about 1730 hours, the mobile column and the battalion withdrew.

During the operations from the 16th to the 18th of November the casualties in the 1st Infantry Brigade had totalled four killed and nineteen wounded. The enemy, who were estimated to have numbered about two hundred, mainly Shabi Khel and Jalal Khel Mahsuds, were believed to have sustained about fifty casualties. Most of the hostile leaders, including Sher Ali, Khonia Khel, Azal Mir and Gagu, had been present. They remained in the neighbourhood for some days, hoping to find other opportunities of attacking the troops.

On the 19th of November the 9th Infantry Brigade returned to Mir Ali. The 1st Infantry Brigade halted at Rocha Camp for the day, and continued its march to Masti Khel on the 20th, reaching that place on the following day, having left the 2/6 G. R. temporarily at Rocha camp.

1937
Nov.

Sanction given for the construction of a road from Rocha to Karkanwam.

General Sir John Coleridge now asked the Government of India for sanction to the construction of a fair-weather motor road from Rocha to Karkanwam. He explained that experiences throughout the operations of 1937, culminating with those of the 1st Infantry Brigade in the Lower Shaktu, had shown that Karkanwam should be made accessible for motor transport and for mechanized units and that the operation recently carried out to the villages of Kui and Ali Khel had demonstrated the difficulty of the country in this region. The Karkanwam area now formed part of the newly-proclaimed protected area, but control of it by the civil forces would be difficult unless the communications were improved.

This sanction was granted and a small force consisting of 4 Fd. Bty., and 2/6 G. R., and one road construction battalion was formed at Rocha Camp for the purpose. This force was placed under the orders of the Commander Bannu Area, who was made responsible for the protection of the line of communications from Bannu to Rocha camp.

Eventually, the road was taken to a point about two miles east of Karkanwam, and from there, to facilitate movement in the area by the Frontier Constabulary and to enable the Tochi Scouts to co-operate with them, it was linked up with Jani Khel by improving the old cart track, made in 1900, between that place and Karkanwam.

Work on road to Kot continues.

Work on the road in the Bhitanni country to Kot under the protection of the 2nd Infantry Brigade was progressing well in spite of local jealousies over labour contracts. Opposition to the troops, who moved about the area freely carrying out reconnaissances and protecting the work on the road, had ceased after the 20th of October except for a little long range sniping.

The difficulty of bringing individuals to book for offences.

The following incident, which followed an attempt at sniping some troops who were on road-protection duty in the area, illustrates the difficulty of bringing offenders to book in these circumstances and shows the results of patient endeavour to discover the culprits.

A company of the 1/11 Sikh R., whilst on road-protection duty on the 15th of November between Spalvi Camp and Masti Khel, came under sniping fire. Two platoons of the 1/13 F. F. Rif. were sent out to cut off the retreat of the snipers. They captured four men, all unarmed and although they were apparently harmless, a close examination showed that one at least had recently been wearing a bandolier. The ground in the neighbourhood was searched, but nothing was found. Still believing that arms and equipment were hidden somewhere near, the 1/13 F. F. Rif. laid an ambush that night to catch anyone returning to retrieve his property. The ambush saw and killed one man who turned out to be the father of one of the prisoners. The Political Authorities now took charge of the case and collected enough evidence to convict the son of the man killed in the ambush, but could find nothing to implicate the other three prisoners. A further search for the hidden arms was made by the 1/13 F. F. Rif. on the 17th, and this time a rifle, bandolier, and knife were discovered, which made it possible to take action against the remaining three men.

Orders of Government to Bhitannis. The Bhitanni maliks of Dera Ismail Khan district were assembled at Jandola on the 15th of November and of the Bannu district at Tajori on the 18th of November, to receive the orders of Government. The former were fined Rs. 3,350, thirty-four magazine rifles, and two hundred other rifles. In the case of the latter the fines were smaller being Rs. 1,650, sixteen magazine rifles, and one hundred other rifles. The jirgas were given ten days to produce the rifles and were informed that Bhitanni tribal territory to the south of the Shuza Algad was declared to be a protected area. The attitude of the jirgas was satisfactory and they left to arrange the settlement of the fines. Nearly all the rifles demanded were surrendered by the 6th of December, the most zealous in complying with the order being the Waruki section who had hitherto been foremost in supporting the Din Faqir. Warning was sent by the maliks to Sher Ali, Khonia Khel, and other leaders not to enter their country as the tribe was making their peace with the Government.

Din Faqir still showing hostile intentions. The Din Faqir went to Jandola to attend the jirga on the 15th of November, but left before the jirga took place. He was accompanied by a number of bad characters who apparently hoped that he would plead their cause with the Government. In this they were disappointed. He received a letter from Sher Ali and this, added to the efforts of the Faqir of Ipi and others to persuade him to re-open hostilities, upset his already undecided state of mind. He made an attempt to turn the jirga to his advantage in promoting his aspirations to recognition as leader of all the Bhitannis and made demands on the Political Authorities as to the method of conducting the jirga, including the right for himself and his followers to carry rifles. On being told that the jirga would be conducted according to the wishes of Government, he left in dudgeon for Mahsud territory, taking a few of his followers with him. There he got into touch with Sher Ali and Khonia Khel and summoned the hostile Bhitannis to join him.

The Bhitannis had evidently had enough of hostilities and their response to the Din Faqir's call was poor.

Not only had opposition to the troops in this country ceased, but the situation in the settled districts had been improving. To help to restore confidence there, the 8th Light Cavalry carried out a demonstration march from the 6th to the 11th of November, visiting Kulachi, Saggu, Daraban, Drazinda and Zarkani.

Road completed to Kot. 2nd Brigade leaves Bhitanni country, 2nd Dec. 1937. As conditions were returning so satisfactorily to normal, a process which may have been assisted by the presence of the 1st Infantry Brigade at Masti Khel and Spalvi in addition to the 2nd Infantry Brigade at Qalandar Khel Kile, the latter formation was not called on to traverse the surrounding country except to the extent required to

1937 | Nov.—Dec.

ascertain the water resources within a day's march of Kot. These reconnaissances continued until the 2nd of December, when the road to Kot was completed. The 2nd Infantry Brigade then left the Bhitanni country on its way back to its permanent peace stations.

Din Faqir goes to interview the Political Authorities.

The Din Faqir, finding that there was little prospect of any help from the Mahsuds, and having had it strongly impressed on him by the Bhitanni maliks that he would be very foolish to re-open hostilities in view of the improbability of his being supported by the Bhitanni tribe, now decided to take steps to make his submission, and on the 15th of December, went to Jandola to interview the Political Agent.

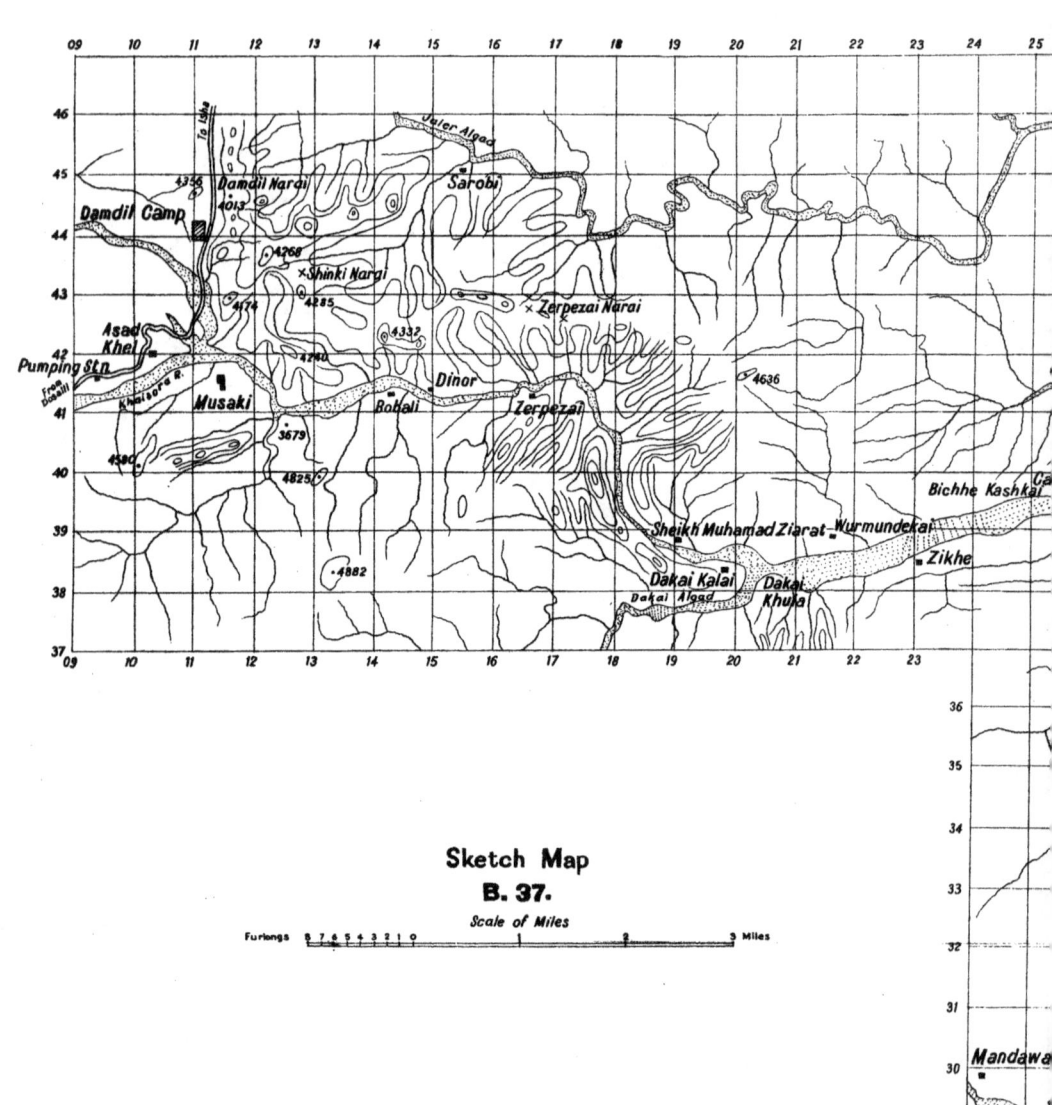

Sketch Map
B. 37.

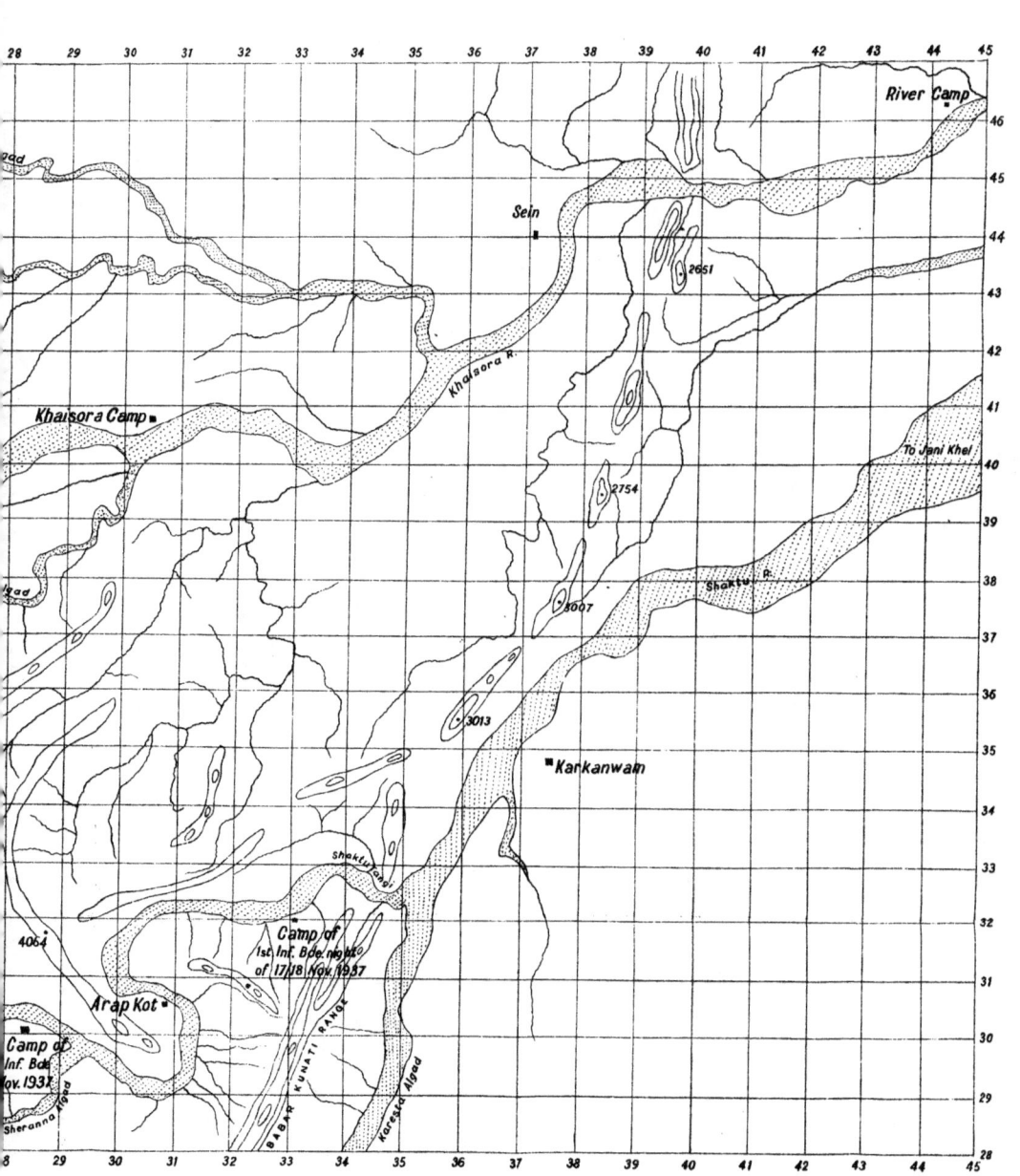

CHAPTER XXVII.

Further punishment in the Razmak—Dosalli Area in Nov.-Dec. 1937— Madda Khel ordered to expel the Faqir—the Faqir's efforts meet with little response—Government's Orders to Bakka Khel and Jani Khel Wazirs.

In the latter half of November, steps were taken to deal out punishment for the many minor offences that had been continually committed in the areas through which the Dosalli-Ahmedwam and Razmak-Bichhe Kashkai roads were being constructed. Sniping, though slight, had been constant, particularly at Ali Khel camp. Contractors' lorries had been held up and the occupants killed, kidnapped or robbed. The Dosalli pipe line had been cut on many occasions.

Further punishments carried out.

The tribesmen responsible for these offences were to a large extent the inhabitants of the local villages. Reprisals had been carried out by arresting suspected individuals, imposing fines of rifles, and destroying property, but it had been necessary to exercise continued vigilance to prevent a successful outrage.

It was now decided to inflict further punishments.

The Shabi Khel village of Shami Khel, two miles west of Razmak, whose inhabitants were known to have been participating freely in the sniping of Ali Khel camp, was surrounded on the 20th of November by troops from Razmak with a detachment of the Tochi Scouts. There was no opposition, and thirty-seven wanted men were arrested. The result of this was that the sniping of Ali Khel camp declined.

Shami Khel village surrounded.

The houses of certain hostile tribesmen of Dosalli were destroyed by maliks and khassadars under the supervision of the Political authorities, and troops of the 9th Infantry Brigade destroyed another house at Asad Khel. The inhabitants of Dosalli were fined ten rifles for their share in cutting the pipe line, and for numerous offences in the Engemal Narai area a section of the Shaman Khel was ordered to produce five rifles.

Houses at Dosalli destroyed.

The Shabi Khel's delinquencies attracted attention. They hoped that by keeping the local situation disturbed they might be able to avert the dismissal of their badraggas when Ali Khel camp was evacuated. These badraggas, who provided for the general security of the sections of the road for which the tribe was responsible, had not only contributed indirectly to the unsatisfactory state of affairs by their slackness and negligence but had themselves connived at some of the offences. A number of the tribe, too, had taken part in the recent fighting with the 1st Infantry Brigade in the Lower Shaktu. It was decided, therefore, to arrest a large number of them, and on the 2nd and 3rd of December, when the badraggas came into Razmak and other places for their pay, one hundred and forty arrests were made, in which number were included several persons of importance. The resulting excitement amongst the Shabi Khel was probably a measure of the effectiveness of the action taken.

Shabi Khel badraggas arrested.

1937
Nov.

Considerably annoyed by it, the tribe began to hold indignation meetings and to discuss what they could do against the Government. Mullah Fazal Din joined in these discussions but seemed to be more concerned for his own safety in case a raid should be made on his house at Lataka than for anything else. But Mullah Sher Ali and Malik Khonia Khel tried to foster the excitement amongst the Shabi Khel. The tribe became considerably heated over the affair, and there was a good deal of talk about buying arms and about the best way of carrying out hostilities, and threats were made if the arrested men were not released.

Wiser counsels prevailed, however, and by the 15th of December everything was in train for a settlement with Government by negotiation.

Faqir of Ipi at Kaurai.

During October and November 1937, the Faqir of Ipi moved his residence frequently, never stopping very long in any one place. In the middle of October he was at Kaurai near Barman Sar* in Madda Khel country. It was clear that at this time he had realized that his prospects of renewing the struggle at once with success were not bright as he advised the many visitors who came to see him at Kaurai to return home and await further orders unless they preferred to undertake active hostilities round Spinwam, where some of his supporters were collecting. He also told his brother, Sher Zaman, who was unceasing in his efforts to obtain help, not to raise another lashkar for the present but to send small parties to various areas. He tried to persuade the Madda Khel Zadrans and Tanis to settle their usual inter-tribal differences and to combine in the common cause. A large Zadran contingent offered their services, but the Faqir told them that he did not want them immediately.

It was rumoured that the Faqir intended to resume hostilities during the Ramzan or at its close in the first week of December. The arrival of troops at Miranshah on the 30th of October alarmed him.

Madda Khel ordered to expel the Faqir of Ipi.

His arrival at Kaurai in Madda Khel Territory had caused some stir among that tribe which resulted in a definite split. The leading men, with whom about half the tribe were in agreement, were not in favour of incurring the displeasure of Government, which was bound to happen if the Faqir was permitted to carry on his activities unchecked in their midst. The rest of the tribe followed the lead of two fanatical mullahs who considered it their religious duty to support the Faqir at all costs.

On the 1st of November the Madda Khel Jirga was interviewed at Datta Khel. The maliks were ordered to expel the Faqir from their country within two days and were told that failure to do so would result in punitive action. At the same time they were told that owing to the slow progress of the payment of the fines inflicted on them early in the year on account of the murder of Lieut. Beatty, one fourth of all timber exported by the tribe through Datta Khel would be confiscated by Government in part payment.

The attitude of the jirga was subdued, but after showing some reluctance the maliks accepted the responsibility of taking two Government officials with them to see that the order to expel the Faqir was obeyed. These officials traversed suitable portions of the country and found no trace of the Faqir, who had evidently departed for the time

* See Map 'A' in pocket.

being. The maliks, evidently uncertain as to how they stood with Government, failed to attend jirgas to which they were summoned on the 6th and 8th of November. They were then informed that Government was satisfied that the Faqir had left their country, but that it was rumoured that he would return soon and that if this happened the Government would hold themselves free to take any action considered necessary without further reference to the tribe. They were also told that if they wished to give the Faqir refuge they could do so provided that they gave security for him and reported his location and subsequent movements immediately. To this they gave no reply.

Faqir of Ipi moves to Afghanistan.
On the 10th of November the Faqir arrived at Pasta Mela, a Madda Khel village in Zadran territory in Afghanistan, where preparations had been made to receive him, it was said, by one of the gang that had murdered Lieut. Beatty.

Existing dispositions suitable for a further attempt to capture the Faqir should he return.
Although there was now no definite information as to where the Faqir intended to re-establish his headquarters, General Sir John Coleridge was confident that it would soon be located and thought it probable that it would be found at some place in Waziristan territory not far from the Durand Line adjacent to the border of Khost.

In these circumstances the existing dispositions of the troops, with the 1st Infantry Brigade at Mir Ali and the 9th Infantry Brigade at Miranshah, were very suitable for another attempt to capture the Faqir. Before putting such operations in train, however, General Sir John Coleridge consulted the Government of India about the advisability of such action. It was possible that operations near the Durand Line might result in the local tribes and, in their turn, Afghan tribesmen becoming involved in hostilities against the British Government, and further, that the Faqir might take refuge in Khost, stir up trouble there, and create difficulties for the Afghan Government. Limitations regarding the use of aircraft near the Afghan border might also reduce the amount of assistance which could be given to columns by the Royal Air Force.

After a full consideration of these factors, it was decided that the risks of stirring up a situation which was improving day by day were too great to justify military operations in an area near the Durand Line, and it was thought, also, that the odds against the capture of the Faqir were heavy.

The Faqir of Ipi and his brother continue attempts to enlist support with little success.
After his arrival at Pasta Mela the Faqir and Sher Zaman made propaganda tours on both sides of the Durand Line with the object of raising a lashkar for action at the end of Ramzan. As this time approached, he called on Fazal Din, Sher Ali, and his other lieutenants to prepare for hostilities in the immediate future, and organized meetings to take place in Maizar and Laswandai. He sent appeals to most of the tribes in Waziristan and across the border in Khost to join him and to collect supplies, and gave orders that representatives of all Mahsuds and Wazir tribes should report to him during December.

The appeal for supplies and subscriptions produced some result, but powerful factors were combining to prevent any open response to the Faqir's call to arms. The constant pressure applied by the Political authorities and the heavy blows which had been struck by the armed forces at the tribesmen whenever they had collected to offer resistance had produced a deep impression, and a number of the lesser hostile leaders and others had surrendered to Government unconditionally. The Faqir of Shewa, in spite of accusations that he was pro-British, had been frequently touring among the Madda Khel, preaching against war, and the Afghan Government had strengthened further their measures to prevent their tribesmen from joining in the hostilities.

As a result, the Id passed without incident, and a parade held in Madda Khel country during the Id celebrations to encourage recruiting for the Faqir of Ipi was a complete failure, only twelve men with arm bands appearing at the parade.

Sher Ali and Khonia Khel had had no success in their efforts to stir up the Shabi Khel, and their attempts to raise lashkars to oppose the troops in the Bhitanni country had met with no response. The Wana Wazirs, in spite of the blandishment of Pirmullah Khan, had already shown that they had no intention of taking any active steps to help the Faqir.

Faqir of Ipi back in Madda Khel territory.

The Faqir, after remaining in the neighbourhood of Pasta Mela long enough to give truth to the assurance given to Government that he was not in Madda Khel country returned to that territory still keeping close to the Durand Line. At the end of November he moved to Maizar. His presence in their area still continued to exercise the Madda Khel. They held many meetings to decide whether or not to admit openly that he was being sheltered by them and so regularize their position with Government and whether to expel him or not, but they were unable to come to a decision, the only point on which they were in unanimous agreement being that any tribesman who gave information to the authorities should be severely punished.

Bakka Khel and Jani Khel jirga.

On the 12th of November the last jirga of importance before the end of this period of operations in Waziristan was held, dealing with the Bakka Khel and Jani Khel Wazirs, who inhabit the country between Saidgi and Bannu stretching from some way north of the Central Waziristan Road to south of the Shaktu River.

The jirga was informed that they were to be punished for the participation by men of their tribes in the hostilities of the past year. The orders issued to them followed the lines of those given to the Mahsuds and Tori Khel about three months earlier. The Bakka Khel were fined Rs. 1,000 and had to surrender ten magazine rifles and fifty other rifles. The Jani Khel were fined the same amount of cash and had to hand in twenty magazine rifles and sixty other rifles. All tribal territory of these tribes situated to the south of the Bannu-Tochi road was declared to be a protected area.

The maliks protested that the terms were harsh but nevertheless they complied with them in full.

CHAPTER XXVIII.

Conclusion.

Additional troops withdraw from Waziristan in Dec. 1937 and those that remain come once again under the command of the G. O. C., Waziristan District.

From the end of September, when the situation in Waziristan began to appear easier a few units that could be spared returned to their normal peace stations.

By the middle of December conditions had returned almost to the normal and it was possible to withdraw the bulk of the remaining additional formations and troops. "Wazirforce" ceased to exist on the 15th of December, and all troops left in Waziristan came once more under the command of the G. O. C., Waziristan District.

For the time being the normal peace garrison was increased by one mountain battery, one light tank company, one infantry brigade with two extra battalions, and some additional transport and supply units.

The withdrawal of the troops marked the close of the active unrest, which, having its origin in April 1936, came to a head in November of that year, and with one brief interlude after the settlement of the 15th of January continued in degrees of fluctuating intensity for the ensuing twelve months. During this period casualties amounted to two hundred and forty-five killed and six hundred and eighty-four wounded, whilst there were seventy-three deaths from disease. Tribal casualties are of necessity difficult to assess, but confirmed figures were considerably in excess of these numbers; in addition, there had been the loss and dislocation occasioned by protracted operations and by air action in proscribed areas.

In the course of the year many districts had been visited by troops either for the first time or for the first time for a long period. Large areas of Mahsud and Wazir territory hitherto inaccessible had been opened up by motor roads, approximately one hundred and fourteen miles of which had been constructed. Considerable tracts were now classified as "protected areas", a development which must be gradual in its effects but which according to previous experience should eventually lead to more settled conditions of life.

These changes constituted the most comprehensive step forward in the history of Waziristan since, as a consequence of the campaigns of 1919-22, the decision was taken to occupy central Waziristan and to construct the Central Waziristan Road.

Two new Scouts' posts had been established in the "protected areas" at Bichhe Kashkai and Ghariom, the strength of the Scouts being proportionately increased. The strength of the Wana garrison had been augmented by one battalion to bring it up to a complete brigade and was to receive an additional battery. Certain Scouts' posts were for the future to be stocked with reserves of supplies in order that they might serve as temporary bases for mobile columns which would then be able to move with less transport and so have increased mobility. The construction of additional landing grounds and an increase in the numbers of bomber transport aircraft were matters under consideration to facilitate maintenance by air which played an important part during the recent operations.

No change in general policy in Waziristan had taken place other than the policy of extending "protected areas", which in itself marked a considerable advance. Disarmament would be desirable but there were many factors which made this more than a local problem. As it was, the fines of rifles that had been imposed on the tribes were greatly in excess of any previous forfeitures and the carrying of rifles on the main roads had been restricted.

The economic problem of Waziristan still remained to be solved. The military occupation and development of roads had brought money into the country and led to an improvement in conditions. But the chief need appeared to be that of finding employment for the young men, now deprived of their traditional occupation of raiding, if they were to develop into useful and peaceable members of society. A few Mahsuds were enlisted in the army and a considerable number of tribesmen found part-time employment as Khassadars, but the possibilities of economic development were limited and it is doubtful whether much more was possible in this direction than was being done. During the recent operations an experiment had been made by raising a road construction battalion of Mahsuds as a military unit. This had worked well. Other plans to increase the opportunities for education and to improve the chances of employment being found for the tribesmen were also being investigated.

The situation concerning the possibilities of further hostile activity, also, had shown very considerable improvement. The orders of the Government had been accepted by the jirgas of the various tribes and they were endeavouring to satisfy the terms. The policy of the Political authorities throughout had been to restore the power and influence of the Maliks and the effects were showing themselves appreciably. Most of the lesser leaders and some of the more important ones among the hostile groups had surrendered themselves. The Faqir of Ipi, who had been the focus of all the trouble from the beginning, was still at large, as were four or five of his most ardent lieutenants, but his and their power and prestige had been very considerably diminished, and they were finding it very difficult to obtain supporters.

CHAPTER XXIX.

Points for consideration.

1. Difficulties which arise when an operation which starts as a "peacetime" operation changes to an operation of war.

The General Situation in Waziristan in 1936, and the atmosphere in which troops were serving there, have been described in Chapter I (p. 2).

The advance into the Khaisora valley to Bichhe Kashkai from Damdil and Mir Ali on the 25th of November, 1936, was undertaken with the expectation that it would be practically a peace-time operation, that is to say that any opposition would be slight only and the difficulties of reaching the day's objective would be those that might be expected normally in a column march. As events showed, the opposition was considerable.

Owing to this expectation of peace-time conditions and of the rapid conclusion of the march, there was no organized line of communication along the route of the march, supplies for a very limited time only were taken, and there were no arrangements for increasing those supplies if necessary. This meant that the radius of action of the columns and the time they could stay away from their bases were strictly limited.

Had they been able to remain at the scene of the disturbance and to exact immediate retribution for the resistance offered, the effect on the tribesmen might have been considerable. As it was, the success which the tribesmen considered that they had gained led to the enhancement of the prestige of the Faqir of Ipi and to considerable unrest among the tribes.

2. The distances given to Razcol and Tocol to cover, in their advance into the Khaisora on 25th November, 1936.

"Frontier Warfare, India" in discussing the distances which can be covered by forces operating in hostile tribal territory, gives five miles or less in a day, for a force weaker than an Inf. Bde. Group. It gives also as a rough guide to the distance which an Inf. Bde. Group with artillery and other troops in proportion, can expect to cover in a day in reasonable security, a distance of not more than eight miles *even if unopposed*.

Previous official works and manuals on Frontier Warfare have always advised similar limitations.

On the 25th November, 1936, Razcol was a Brigade Group with artillery and other troops in proportion. Tocol was a force weaker than a Bde. Group and it had no artillery. (For composition of Razcol and Tocol, *see* p. 15). The march given to Razcol from Damdil to Bichhe Kashkai was approximately 12 miles. The march given to Tocol from Mir Ali to Bichhe Kashkai was approximately 14 miles.

As has been described (Chapter III) Razcol reached Bichhe Kashkai with difficulty. Tocol was benighted four miles short of its objective and suffered losses of kit and equipment. Although there were other contributory factors to the success the Faqir of Ipi was able to claim (*see* paras. 3 and 5 (b) below], the example is clearly one of a risk being taken in disregard of accepted principles. That the existing peaceful conditions and expectation that no serious opposition would be encountered influenced the decision to make such long marches is clear. Moreover, Razcol and Tocol frequently had covered similar distances.

On the other hand, the words "even if unopposed" are a noteworthy inclusion in the extract from the manual, quoted above. Moreover, the history of operations on the North Western Frontier abounds in instances of risks being habitually taken, and the price being paid in the end. In this instance, the actual loss suffered by the Columns was disproportionate to the gain of prestige to the Faqir of Ipi who up to that date had been a figure of comparatively little consequence.

3. Influence of the Supply Problem on Frontier Operations.

Frontier Warfare, India, states "when planning for an offensive in tribal territory, due allowances must be made for the necessity arising for advancing by phases to admit of the accumulation of supplies at selected points before each forward move".

The effect of this is to slow up the advance into areas in which it is intended that troops shall enter. In some cases, e.g., the operations in the Lower Khaisora valley in November and December, 1936, and in the further advances from the Sham Plain from June, 1937, the collection of supplies had to await the construction of motor roads, so entailing appreciable delay in further movement forward.

4. The advantages of a converging attack.

Frontier Warfare states "a converging attack by two or more routes against the objective may have much to recommend it. The advantages of a converging advance are that it is likely to divide the tribesmen and to threaten their lines of retreat for the safety of which they are usually much concerned".

This is demonstrated by the advances of the 1st Infantry Brigade and the Bannu Brigade to the Sham Plain on the 12th of May, 1937. The 1st Infantry Brigade moved up the Sre Mela Algad whilst the Bannu Bde., climbed the Iblanke spur on the east flank. The result was, as envisaged in the extract quoted, that the enemy, finding their line of retreat threatened, left their positions.

5. The value of night operations and advances and dangers of their misuse.

(a) "Frontier Warfare—India" states that "valuable hours of daylight may be saved by a night advance to secure the necessary covering positions before dawn", and, again ,"there is no doubt that night operations, provided they are not allowed to become habitual or stereotyped, can be of great value in frontier fighting". In another place it says, "the saving of time which may be effected by a resort to night operations is of particular importance in frontier warfare, in which, owing to the need of constant all round protection, all daylight operations are likely to be slow and prolonged".

This was exemplified many times during the operations of 1937.

The first, and perhaps the most outstanding example was the advance by the Bannu Brigade up the Iblanke Spur on the night of the 11th/12th of May during the advance to the Sham Plain. The object of this advance was to secure positions outflanking the enemy who had established themselves in the upper reaches of the Sre Mela Algad in an area which presented many difficulties to the attackers. By dawn on the 12th of May the Bannu Brigade had secured the high ground of the Iblanke with very little opposition, in spite of enormous physical difficulties, with the result that the enemy, finding their rear threatened, abandoned the areas in which they were prepared to resist, and the Sham Plain was occupied without much trouble.

Later, when operations were commenced on the 27th of May from Ghariom Camp and from Bichhe Kashkai to destroy Arsal Kot on the Shaktu river, the first part of the route from Ghariom Camp was secured before dawn by a detachment of the Tochi Scouts. The 2nd Infantry Brigade, from Bichhe Kashkai, as their march was a long one through difficult and unreconnoitred country, also moved off in the dark in order to get as far as possible by daylight so as to complete the march in time to finish camp arrangements before dark that evening.

Another example is found in the attempt made by detachments of the Tochi Scouts and South Waziristan Scouts supported by the 1st Infantry Brigade to capture the Faqir of Ipi near Gul Zamir Kot on the Shaktu river on the 21st of June. An advance by day would certainly have resulted in the flight of the Faqir if he was actually there. The detachments of Scouts moved to their positions successfully, during the night of the 20th/21st of June.

Further examples are the advance of the Bannu Brigade up the Sirdar Algad on the 27th of September and again on the 5th of October and of the 9th Infantry Brigade to Spinwam on the 20th of October. In each of these cases darkness was used to cover the movement of the leading troops to secure commanding features of the first part of the advance and in each case this was done without opposition.

(b) The danger of continuing movement after dark with a force which has been engaged during daylight with tribesmen.

Frontier Warfare, India, says in this connection, "to attempt after dark to continue movement with a force which has been engaged during daylight with tribesmen, who have been able to acquaint themselves thoroughly with its dispositions, is to court disaster".

It is a matter for consideration whether the Bannu Brigade on the evening of the 25th of November 1936, should not have halted and gone into camp before dark near the Jaler Algad instead of attempting to continue its march to Bichhe Kashkai. When it marched on after dark it suffered several casualties and owing to the stampeding of horses and mules lost several loads of ammunition and stores, the bolting animals causing much confusion in the column. This was in no way a disaster, but a decision to camp before dark would have avoided this loss. The factors which chiefly influenced the decision to go on were the impression which, based on misleading reports and failure of inter-communication, was incorrect, that the Razmak Brigade was held up some way from Bichhe Kashkai, and the knowledge of the encouraging effect it would have on the tribesmen if no part of the force reached Bichhe Kashkai that night.

(c) The essentials to success in a night advance.

In Frontier Warfare, India, is the following statement. "Valuable in frontier warfare as advances by night may be, they cannot safely be attempted unless secrecy is maintained and surprise effected. The making of a plan for movement by night demands great foresight, the most careful attention to detail and the close observation of the principles defined in Field Service Regulations for the conduct of night operations".

It lays down the following as essentials, secrecy as regards intention, simplicity of plan, strict limitation of the objective, thorough prior reconnaissance, mystification of the enemy, close control and supervision, and an ample margin of time.

The operations in 1937 which best bring out the steps taken to produce these essentials are the advance to the Sham Plain in May 1937 and the attempt to capture the Faqir of Ipi in June.

Secrecy as regards intention.

Written orders and instructions were not issued until the last possible moment. The minimum of responsible officers were informed beforehand of the intention. Troops were not told until after night arrangements were in force or before the actual start of the march. Plans which were either misleading and consequently cancelled before the commencement of the operation or were so framed that with very slight alterations they could apply to the intended operation were made public. False reports were spread about as to the destination of the movement.

Simplicity of plan.

In both cases the plan was quite straight forward, involving a march over very difficult country, certainly, but with no great difficulties of direction.

Strict limitation of the objective.

The final objective was clearly defined. In the case of the advance by the Iblanke spur there were intermediate objectives, but the country over which the advance was taking place was very narrow and these objectives were not difficult to locate when reached.

Thorough prior reconnaissance.

For the capture of the Faqir of Ipi the country over which the Scouts had to move had already been traversed by some of them on the previous occasion when a force had moved to the Shaktu to destroy Arsal Kot.

In the case of the Iblanke advance, as will happen frequently in operations of this nature, reconnaissance of the actual ground, owing to the needs of secrecy, was not possible. Full use was made of field glasses and of air photographs, but owing to the dense scrub cover on the spur these means did not reveal as much as was desired.

Mystification of the enemy.

Before the advance up the Iblanke, in addition to the spreading of reports that the force was moving to Razani and to the issue of orders, later cancelled, to the Razmak Brigade to go there, a reconnaissance of the water supply at Razani was carried out on the 10th of May. That this effort was successful was shown by the presence of a lashkar numbering about four hundred in the Razani area on the 12th of May.

Close control and supervision.

The need for and the difficulties of supervision and control increase with the numbers in the column concerned and with the nature of the country over which the advance is being made. In the case of the Scouts going to the Shaktu river, their numbers were by comparison small and they consisted of infantry men only, having no other arms or animals with them.

In the Bannu Brigade on the Iblanke were some thousands of men, mountain batteries with their mules and other transport animals.

A strict control was kept on the number of animals with the column by Brigade Headquarters laying down precisely what animals were to be taken. Control of the animals themselves was dealt with by increasing the numbers of mule leaders and detailing special guards.

Control of the column generally was arranged for by placing W/T sets with the advanced guard, and at the head, centre and rear of the column also by the use of liaison officers, and by giving intermediate objectives on which the column could close itself up.

Protection of the column during the night was ensured by very careful and detailed arrangements by the officer commanding the battalion detailed to provide piquets.

(d) Remaining on the battlefield throughout the night.

Frontier Warfare, India states "unexpectedly strong opposition may make it impossible for the attacking troops to secure their final objectives before nightfall. In this contingency, it will probably be preferable for them to remain throughout the night in occupation of the ground won instead of withdrawing to bivouac".

There was one occasion in particular in this campaign when such a step, had it been possible, would in all probability have produced considerable results.

This was when the 1st Infantry Brigade fought an action near Asad Khel on the 29th of March, 1937.

There were about one thousand enemy opposing the brigade, located in lower ground in a valley. The brigade with units at minimum strength and still further depleted by camp protection and duties had with considerable difficulty established itself on the greater part of the three sides of the higher ground of the valley. The Brigade was very strung out, one battalion had had many casualties, and there was still a large area which it had not been possible to reach, by which, unless it was occupied, the enemy could get away without difficulty. More troops would have been required to block this exit. Troops were not available and the exit could not be closed. Consequently, to stay out for the night on this occasion with the troops where they were, would not have attained the desired object of keeping the enemy in the ground they were occupying and might have given them the opportunity of attacking the weakly defended camp. It is for consideration, however, what the results would have been, if battalions had been at full strength or if it had been possible to find the extra troops. Fighting during the night would, certainly, have been fierce, but the prospects of inflicting very large losses on the enemy would have been good, and the further effect of such a defeat on the recalcitrant tribesmen would have been considerable.

6. The use of detachments of the Frontier Corps with regular troops.

Frontier Warfare, India, lays down that owing to their speed, activity and freedom from impediment, they may be usefully employed in co-operation with regular troops to cover the advance of a column acting in the capacity of "advanced guard mounted troops", to effect surprise, particularly by night, and in the attack to protect the flanks of the attacking troops, threaten the flanks and rear of the enemy, and to exploit success.

1937
Dec.

In the operations of 1936-37 they were used in all these ways.

During the advance of the Razmak and Bannu Brigades to Bichhe Kashkai on the 25th of November, 1936, they were employed in protecting the flanks. When the Bannu Brigades advanced to the Sham Plain on the night of the 11th and during the 12th of May and during the march to Arsal Kot on the 27th of May, they acted as advanced guard mounted troops. During the action against Sher Ali's lashkar near Torwam on the 29th of June, the detachment with the Bannu Brigade first carried out the tasks of advanced guard mounted troops and then protected the left flank of the Brigade. Another detachment on the same day moved to the north of the area in which the enemy were known to be, to cut off any men leaving the area in that direction. There were many occasions during which they were used with the object of effecting surprise, the main examples being the attempt to capture the Faqir of Ipi on the 21st of June, 1937, and the operation to destroy the Faqir's supplies at Karkanwam on the 24th of July, 1937.

Why they are particularly suitable for these tasks is because they are very mobile, being much more lightly clad and equipped than the regular forces, and they have continuous practice in long and rapid marches over the hills, and from their normal employment they have an intimate knowledge of the country. Their organization and equipment are not such as to enable them to overcome serious opposition without the support of regular troops and by using them in these roles, economy of the better equipped regulars for tasks more suited to them is ensured.

7. The necessary ingredients of a successful ambush.

Frontier Warfare, India, Chapter XI, Section 43 (18) gives these ingredients.

Ambushes are common incidents in Frontier Campaigns, and were of frequent occurrence in the campaign of 1936-37. One of the most successful was that carried out by a party of the 1/2nd Gurkha Rifles on the Central Waziristan Road near Razani on the 25th of September, 1937.

In this case, secrecy was ensured by fixing the time of start of the party so that the night was still dark and individuals who might reveal the movement to the enemy were likely to be asleep. Detailed preliminary reconnaissance was not possible owing to the necessity for secrecy. Special care was taken to ensure that the party passed the places where irregulars and civilians were encamped without being noticed. Men were as lightly equipped as possible and wore rubber-soled shoes.

It is to be noted how the observance of the principle of the maintenance of the objective was followed in this case. The party started with the intention of laying an ambush at a certain place on the road with the object of catching the raiders as they left the scene of their labours. On arrival at this spot, the enemy could be heard a little way away. The idea of shooting at them whilst at work was tempting. By sticking to the original plan, there is no doubt that greater damage was inflicted.

8. The use of cavalry.

Frontier Warfare, India, states, "mounted troops may be used to accelerate the advance of the forward infantry".

For the most part, the country through which troops moved during this campaign did not lend itself to the use of cavalry. When it is possible to use them, occasions will always arise when a mounted attack, boldly delivered, will enable the infantry to get on when they have been held up. An example of this was the use of the squadron of Probyn's Horse with the Bannu Brigade when advancing towards Bichhe Kashkai on the afternoon of the 25th of November, 1936. The 3/7th Rajput Regiment had been ordered to drive off some enemy on the right front of the column. Opposition was strong and the battalion was unable to reach its objective. The country was comparatively flat. The squadron was ordered to carry out a mounted attack. They galloped the position in four or five minutes, suffering only two casualties.

9. The possibilities of surprising and misleading the enemy.

The most common method of doing this was by movement by night. This has been considered in a previous paragraph. Very successful efforts were also made in this campaign to mislead him by day and so to entice him to attack or await attack in circumstances which gave good prospects of inflicting heavy losses on him.

One example of this is to be found in the action fought by the 2nd Infantry Brigade from Bichhe Kashkai towards Mazai Raghza on the 29th of April, 1937. The enemy were in a strong position in the hills west of Bichhe Kashkai north of the Khaisora river. It was intended to bring them to action with the object of inflicting as heavy losses as possible on them, and to do this the commander decided that the most likely plan was to advance up the hills south of the river, thereby enticing the tribesmen to cross the river. At the same time he did not wish them to start crossing the river until his troops had reached positions on the south side favourable to his purpose. For the success of his plan it was essential that the enemy should continue in the belief that he was going to attack to the north. The steps he took to bring this about were as follows. The political authorities instituted enquiries about the water supply at a village on the north bank. Two days before the action, the Commander's pennant was conspicuously displayed by troops covering the occupation of camp piquets on the north bank. On the morning of the action as soon as it was light, one battalion and a light battery made a limited but ostentatious advance up the north bank.

These steps met with complete success and the enemy did not attempt to cross the river until the troops of the main column were some distance up the hills on the south bank.

Another example is afforded by the preparations of the 9th Infantry Brigade for their attack on an enemy lashkar in the Tabai area between Mir Ali and Spinwam on the 20th of October, 1937.

In this instance the primary object of the Commander was to keep the lashkar in its position until the force was collected to attack it. The lashkar was not a very large one and there was the possibility that if it realized that a large force was collecting it would depart.

He succeeded in attaining this object by sending small forces on two occasions to reconnoitre the hostile position, the columns withdrawing as soon as any opposition was shown, and by using a large part of his force, when it was collected, the day before his intended attack on the Tabai position in carrying out a small operation in the opposite direction.

10. The advantages arising from a successful counterattack during a withdrawal.

Frontier Warfare, India, states, "a swift, vigorous and boldly planned local counter-attack may often have the effect of completely checking the enemy".

It is necessary at times in a withdrawal to deliver a counter-attack in order to enable a piquet to get away from its position. Such action frequently results in dissuading the enemy from further pursuit. An example of this is found in the counter-attack delivered by the 2/11th Sikh Regiment during the withdrawal of the 2nd Infantry Brigade down the Khaisora river on the afternoon of the 22nd of December, 1936. The forward company of the 2/2nd Punjab Regiment found itself unable to withdraw, and the reserve in the hands of the battalion commander had not been sufficient to extricate it. The Brigade Commander ordered the 2/11th Sikh Regiment to counter-attack, supported by two batteries and by close-support action from the air. The counter-attack was carried out with great speed and dash and was completely successful, the further withdrawal of the Brigade meeting with very little opposition.

11. The disadvantages of siting a piquet on a forward slope.

Frontier Warfare, India, states, "owing to the difficulty likely to be experienced in withdrawing from such positions, the siting of piquets on the forward slopes of hills is to be avoided".

The difficulties arising from such a position were exemplified on two occasions during the advance to and withdrawal from Arsal Kot in May, 1937. On both occasions the piquet suffered heavy casualties and a counter-attack was necessary to enable it to withdraw.

12. The advisability of using strong fire power to cover the withdrawal of a piquet from a dangerous position.

This is exemplified by the arrangements made on the 30th of May, 1936, during the withdrawal from Pasal to Ghariom camp to cover the withdrawal of a piquet of the 2/4th Gurkha Rifles. This piquet in its withdrawal had to cross some very exposed ground, and it was probable that the enemy, who were pressing the withdrawal of the rearguard closely, would find an opportunity of inflicting loss on the piquet by rushing on to the vacated position and shooting at the piquet on the exposed ground. To counter this, arrangements were made for the fire of ten 3.7" howitzers to come down on the reverse slope as soon as the position was vacated whilst twelve machine guns fired at the crest line. The enemy attempted to rush the position but gave up the effort when they saw the amount of fire, and the piquet got away without a shot being fired at it.

13. The value of artillery in Frontier Warfare.

"Frontier Warfare, India" states that "the moral effect on tribesmen of well directed artillery fire is usually great; and when the country permits, medium and field artillery should always form part of a Force operating in Tribal territory. It will generally be found however that except where roads exist or the country is unusually flat and open, mountain artillery alone can be used in Frontier Warfare".

The only occasion on which a Column of any importance during the operations of 1936/37, moved without any artillery, was the initial march of Tocol into the Khaisora on November 25th, 1936. Tocol consisted (*vide* p. 15) of a mixed force less than a Bde. in strength, and it had no guns. As has been seen in the description of the operations, the column was in difficulties throughout the day. The main effort of the tribesmen was against Tocol, and this was probably due to the fact that its weakness was known to them.

As cavalry formed part of Tocol on this occasion, it is possible that field artillery might have accompanied it also, had the guns been available. Mountain artillery could certainly have accompanied it. It is for consideration to what extent the operations would have been influenced in our favour, had there been artillery with Tocol on this occasion.

APPENDIX I

SYSTEM OF PROTECTION USED IN THE RAZANI SECTOR OF THE L. OF C. DURING WAZIRISTAN OPERATIONS 1937.

The system used for the protection of this sector of the L. of C. was one that probably had not been tried before in quite this form.

The sector (a rough sketch of the area is given at the end of the Appendix) extended along the Central Waziristan Road on both sides of Razani Camp and village, from the 55th to the 65th milestone a defensive front of twenty miles.

The situation which presented itself to the Commander of the sector garrison when his Battalion marched in to take over was this. The Faqir of Ipi, having been driven out of his refuges near the Shaktu river, had gone to the Shawal plain west and northwest of Razmak, where he stayed until late in October. Supplies and reinforcements for him from the Shaktu valley area had to go round by the north or south of Razmak. Through the sector ran four of the favourite and most used routes from the Shaktu area, all four converging to the west of the main road on to the Manzar Khel village of Mami Rogha, a hotbed of wickedness throughout the operations.

These routes were, (a) by Dosalli to Tamre Obo, one thousand yards north of the 56th milestone, northwest of which village it joined a track from the Tochi river to Mami Rogha, three and a half miles northwest of Razani camp (b) by the Shishan Algad to the Mami Rogha Algad, (c) by the Matinghai Algad to the Mami Rogha Algad or to Wuche Faqiran one mile north of Razani Camp, and (d) by the Shini Algad to the Mami Rogha Algad or to Razani and Wuche Faqiran.

Supplies and reinforcements had for a long time been passing backwards and forwards across this sector unimpeded. The system of permanent piquets had not yet been put into practice in this sector, and the road had been opened every day solely by columns operating from Razani. Consequently there had been no activity by the troops between the hour when the road was closed, about 1500 hours, and the time, about 0700 hours, when it was opened again the next morning. Thus, the sector belonged to the enemy for a large part of each day and for the whole of each night.

It was obvious that by stopping all hostile movement across and along the sector, the garrison could exert a pressure on the Faqir far away up in the Shawal, which might well have a big effect on the course of the operations. It was certain that the garrison in trying to attain this object, would set out on an offensive policy that would protect this part of the road better than even the strongest of defensive systems.

The local situation had been bad for a considerable time. Razmak had been cut off from access by road from Bannu for some weeks, the road had been torn up, bridges and culverts destroyed, and telegraph wire and poles torn down over great stretches. A small force had moved into Razani in the early summer and had, with Sappers, begun to repair the road. Sniping of the camp at Razani had been frequent, in spite of active steps taken to discourage it, and camp piquets had been shot at by day and small hostile parties had fired on the road protection troops as they went out from Razani to open the road. With no permanent piquets, the system in this type of country of opening the road daily by road protection troops gave many advantages to the enemy such as the time, direction, method and destination of the daily movement. It was even obvious that there were certain points to which piquets must go. The local villagers were giving all possible help to the enemy, and the loyalty of the Khassadars was very much open to suspicion. The result was that the troops had been able to get no help or information from any tribesmen in the area.

As a first step, the garrison set themselves to deal with the local hostiles and to prevent a single man from moving by day or by night without their knowledge, and except at the peril of his life if he were armed. As the country to the south of the road was big and thickly covered with scrub, this task was no small one.

To attain their objects the troops had to have effective offensive forces at short notice at any spot in the sector and to know the country far better than the enemy. They set to work to build and man four strong piquets, each of which held in it a striking force of about one platoon and a minimum garrison of one machine-gun section or one machine-gun detachment. These piquets were heavily wired with two double aprons each and trip wires between.

At thirty-five paces, out of bombing distance from the piquet, was the outer double apron. In addition to these were two "pinpoint" piquets of fifteen men each and the usual camp piquets. Three of the camp piquets had a machine gun and two gun numbers in them.

Before describing the system any further, it is desirable to make a few remarks about piquets. A piquet, with its garrison inside, is only effective at night up to the distance it can see to shoot—on a dark night, perhaps twenty yards, on a bright moonlight one up to one hundred and fifty or two hundred yards. For the purposes of this system, such small piquets were termed "pinpoint piquets". A piquet without a good wire fence, unless it is situated on a precipice, can, on any dark night, be bombed, rushed and overwhelmed by superior numbers with the greatest ease, provided the attack is a sudden one. With sufficient wire the attack can be checked and beaten off. But piquets should, normally, in any case only be regarded as places of temporary rest. They should be looked on as bases for offensive patrol which creep out and sit up for attackers or snipers, kill and return to rest. Piquets located specially for this purpose may be termed "fighting piquets". They may be wired but must have more than one defiladed exit. "Pinpoint piquets" *must* be properly wired, even if the stay is only for one night. "Fighting piquets" must be active. Theirs is the hard, strenuous and enterprising life which alone leads to success against the tribesmen.

All the machine guns were placed in piquets, none being kept in Razani camp. They were given their night lines to sweep away any attack on the camp and to settle any snipers whom the patrols might conceivably miss. Thus the camp was defended directly by fixed line weapons enfilading its perimeter from the camp piquets, whilst the camp defence made little attempt to defend these piquets with small arms fire from the camp. The whole system of night defence in the sector was locked in by machine-gun fixed lines and by light machine guns wedged into ammunition boxes to give them their fixed lines. In fact, the sector was, as would seem essential since the tribesmen obtained small bore rifles and bombs, one big defensive locality.

Machine guns very seldom left their piquets. From the piquets they could help to cover the day movements of offensive patrols. If they had moved they would only have hindered the very mobile patrols and the central mobile column.

In the camp at Razani was Battalion Headquarters, a rifle company as mobile column with mechanized transport, and a mechanized field battery which was invaluable, and the hospital and supplies. It should be noted that most of the strength was on the hills.

In the hills the piquets actually occupied the ground from which the enemy could shoot at the road. Thus, the road was at all times secure during the day without the necessity of moving a single man. An occasional patrol downwards to comb out the low wooded slopes by the road was all that might be required. The piquets started with a sense of security and comfort that no other system could have given them, and in this way were always ready for offensive action.

In addition to the troops in the Razani sector, a section of armoured cars ran in from Razmak daily and operated in the area. To give these mobility, tracks were levelled out from the main road to overlook all nalas on each side and for half a mile along the bushy Shini Algad plain. Thus, all offensive patrols could be covered when moving up these concealed lines of advance by day, and the rationing and relief of all piquets could be watched by armoured cars. Oneway motor roads for 30-cwt lorries were made up to the bigger piquets so that all watering, rationing and delivery and removal of stores and kits could be done by M. T., saving many men—and mule—hours of work. The cutting of such rough roads was not so difficult nor did it call for such skill as was expected. Rocks were broken up by heating them, sluicing cold water over them, and attacking them with sledge hammers.

The Battalion, with a strength of about six hundred, operated with three sections in a platoon instead of four which was then the normal organisation. In this way the section commanders had good strong effective sections with plenty of manoeuvring and hitting power, whilst the light machine gun sections were strong enough to carry their ammunition and their guns quickly over great distances.

The whole sector was split into two sub-sectors, each under a company commander, the action of the whole being co-ordinated and directed by a daily instruction issued by the sector commander. Piquets opened the road at all hours, often by night, remaining in concealed positions to catch any enemy party that might approach either before or just after dawn to worry the convoys. They frequently patrolled at night, evacuating their piquets and lying up in dead ground to hit any one who might try to attack their piquet. They put out ambushes all over the area, sometimes combining and sometimes acting separately, by day and by night.

Snipers were only of interest for the first week, as on the second night, a patrol followed up a party of them to one of the villages, and then having got the evidence asked for, shot up the stragglers. Two more episodes of this kind with snipers, a few rounds from the guns, three graves dug in a near-by graveyard, and sniping ceased, at no cost in life to the garrison. Later on, the Faqir sent a party down by night to get a message through to his friends. The party was caught by an ambush dropped "on spec" by a daylight patrol, the messenger was killed and his letter taken. Still later, sixty men of the garrison lying up at night smashed up a Lashkar of two to three hundred bent on mischief, inflicted many casualties, drove them off and themselves withdrew at the cost of one man wounded. In this way the garrison got complete control by night of the sector and of the area round so that no tribesman could move for fear of his life. But, above all this, was the very high morale engendered by surprising the enemy and by small successful affairs, and the initiative and efficiency born in junior leaders.

The system was one of dispersion to create the situation which would allow the troops to concentrate about the enemy to fight him at his disadvantage. At short notice three hundred rifles could be collected at any part of the sector. Thus, one fairly large gang which shot at a light machine gun section protecting the road was set on by the nearest fighting patrol and pinned until reinforcements came up and, slipping round behind by a big detour, fell upon the gang from the higher ground. Had the movement come from one place the enemy could have watched the concentrated effort. As it was, it fell "from the blue" upon him although the country held very little cover, and created such an impression that no further attempt was made to meddle with the road by day.

The principle of the protection of the area was for the garrison to cast its net wide, so wide that it could always place some of its men behind the enemy and utterly surprise him.

Thus the whole policy of this sector was aggressive. The system was one of strong little fighting patrols sitting in piquets here and there on the enemy's ground, getting about by day and by night at odd times, occupying his pet positions before he could get to them, and knowing the hills and valleys far better than he knew them, with the valley floors patrolled by armoured cars. Behind all these, to extend their control and by sharp unexpected movements to make the enemy fear to move, a rifle company with its M. T. was located centrally at Razani Camp. In fire support of the whole sector was a mechanized field battery, and the whole system was one long defensive locality, locked in by fixed line machine guns and light machine guns which had registered with indicator bullets. Main infantry and artillery arteries ran along the whole length with spurs off to all piquets, and lines were laid to the routes along the Algad bottoms from the nearest piquet for listening posts to tap in on at night and to report movement to the fighting patrols above them.

This system of securing the safety of the lines of communication is, it is pointed out, completely in accordance with the principles laid down in the training pamphlets for modern war, and complies in miniature with the requirements of the offensive.

The following is an extract from Army in India Training Memorandum No. 2, War Series, 1940, dealing with the Offensive in Modern War, which, though written for warfare where all the most modern types of armament are employed on a large scale, has its direct application to circumstances such as those that exist in warfare in Waziristan. "The framework will consist of securely held bases, in effect 'keeps' of varying size. Formations, pivoting on keeps can manœuvre and attack the flanks of enemy forces. These formations will be supported as necessary by infantry transported in mechanized vehicles, whose role will vary according to the nature of the terrain".

Again, in Army in India Training Memorandum No. 6, 1941, with reference to Modern Warfare in Mountainous and Forest countries, we find the following :—

    (a) The following conditions will govern modern warfare in the extensive theatres in which we may expect to fight, whenever armoured forces can move freely :—

        (i) The predominance of the Mobile Arms,

        (ii) The existence of open flanks.

        (iii) Adequate means of supply for the Mobile Arms.

Sketc

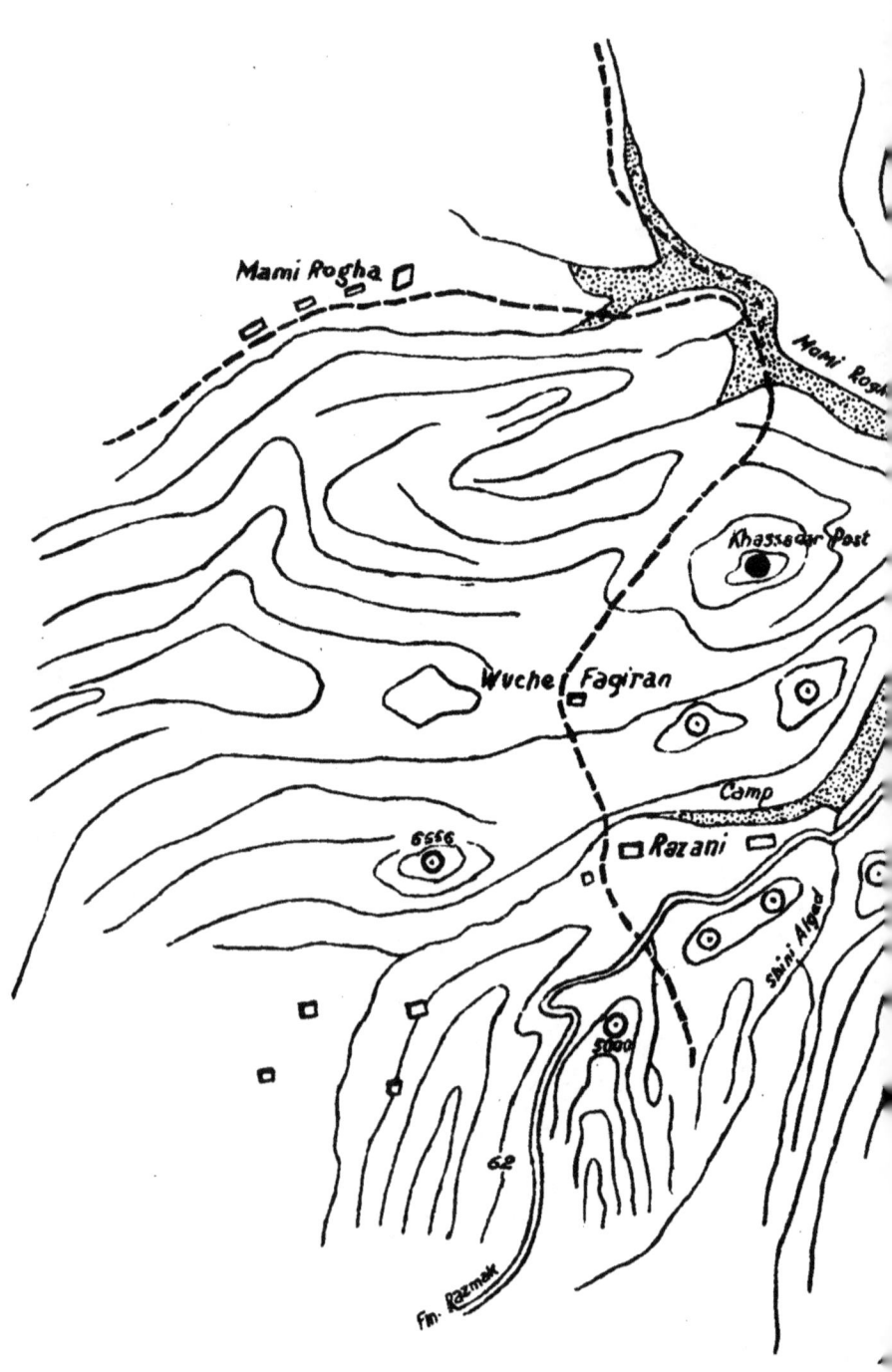

"Fighting" Piquets .....
"Pin Point" and Camp
Armoured Car Tracks

V. 37

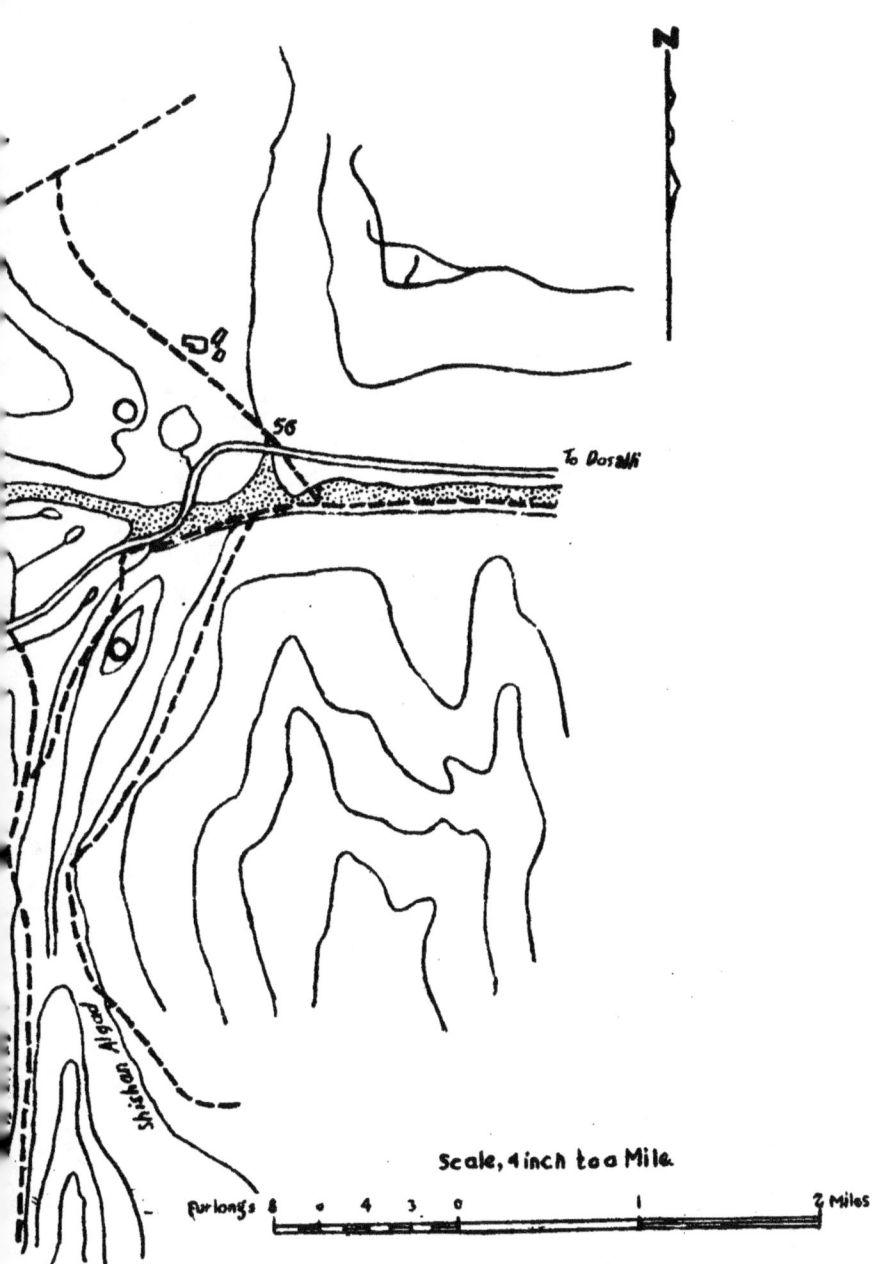

(b) Mobility is relative. That is, whereas infantry on foot is comparatively immobile in country where M. T. can move freely it is the most mobile arm in mountainous and forest country.

If it is possible to keep infantry easily supplied and thereby to maintain its mobility and effectiveness in these countries, then the three conditions above will have come about and the same methods of fighting will be the best. That is to say, we will establish well-defended, well-sited, well-provided bases at strategic points over a wide area. From these, our mobile infantry columns can move and strike rapidly in any direction and the consequent scope of offensive action will paralyse the enemy's mobility.

(c) The same methods can be applied with properly trained infantry to the defence of a sector of L. of C. against both a modern and a tribal enemy.

In the system just described we have our well-defended, well-sited, well-provided bases with small columns pivoting on these bases and using their mobility to enable them to attack any enemy at any time in this area, and if these small columns are not enough themselves to deal with the enemy they are supported by a larger body transported in mechanized vehicles.

APPENDIX II

The Employment of the Engineer Units.

During the course of 1937, between March and December, nine Field Companies, one Divisional Headquarters Company, and four Road Construction Battalions were employed in Waziristan. Three Commanders, Royal Engineers, were appointed, with Wazirforce, Waziristan Division and 1 Division, and later, a Deputy Chief Engineer became part of the Wazirforce staff.

In the early stages of the campaign the main works to be undertaken, apart from normal Engineer work with columns, were the repair of culverts and the construction of piquets and pill boxes for bridge defence, these being among the principal objects of hostile attack. Landing grounds, also, had to be made or enlarged, ice factories erected, and the chapparing of tents taken in hand.

The next operation of the troops, was to advance by the Sham Plain to Arsal Kot on the Shaktu road, the headquarters of the Faqir of Ipi, with the object of demolishing his stronghold there.

A piped water supply and water supply points were constructed at Dosalli for the concentration of the troops. On the 6th of May a motor transport track was begun along the Sre Mela Algad, thence rising one thousand feet to the Sham Plain and crossing the Plain to Ghariom, a total distance of thirteen miles. This was completed by Sappers and Miners supplemented by Infantry working parties in seventeen days. Five camps on the line of advance, involving normal water supply arrangements were established during May. Engineer assistance was also given to units in the construction of camp piquets and tracks to them. The advance to Arsal Kot culminated in the most important demolitions of the operations, the destruction of the Faqir of Ipi's caves where his headquarters had been established, and the completion of the destruction of Arsal Kot, already begun by the Royal Air Force.

On the 22nd of May the Government of India authorized the construction of roads from Dosalli and Ahmedwam to Madamir Kalai and from Razmak and Bichhe Kashkai to Ghariom, a total of $87\frac{1}{2}$ miles.

Work on the Dosalli-Madamir Kalai road was started simultaneously at Dosalli, Coronation Camp, and Ghariom, on the 7th of June. Both down-country contractors and troops were employed at the Dosalli end, but at Coronation Camp and Ghariom the labour was exclusively Sappers and Miners and troops from 1 Division aided by machinery.

On the 27th and 29th of July, Field Engineers and Staffs from the Military Engineer Services started work at Madamir Kalai and Ahmedwam respectively with tribal contractors and local tribal labour under protection of the Scouts. The Razmak-Bichhe Kashkai road was started from Razmak by troops of Waziristan Division on the 10th of July, and from Ghariom towards Razmak by 1 Division on the 29th of July. The portion from Ghariom towards Bichhe Kashkai was commenced by Sappers & Miners and Road Construction Battalions with Scouts' protection on the 14th of August, and Field Engineers with Military Engineer Services staffs and down-country contractors started work at Bichhe Kashkai and Forward Camp (some three miles east of Ghariom) on the 4th of September and the 29th of August respectively.

All these roads were completed to full specification by the middle of December, except for parts of the sector Madamir Kalai-Ahmedwam, where, owing to the influence of hostile propaganda on tribal contractors, the shingling was not fully completed.

Between June and October, in addition to the work on these roads, punitive demolitions were carried out, and a piped water supply, ten miles in length, from Ghariom towards Bichhe Kashkai, with a pumping installation at Ghariom and reservoirs *en route*, for the supply of water to four road construction camps, was laid down by Sappers & Miners, and some nine other special water projects were undertaken.

On the 16th of October, 1 Division began operations in the Bhitanni country and constructed a road from the existing roadhead at the eastern entrance to the Nunghar Tangi to Kot, which was completed on the 14th of December.

The work as far as Spalvi was done by down-country contractors under the C. R. E. Wazirforce. From Spalvi to Kot it was carried out by 1 Division reinforced by an extra Field Company, three Road Construction Battalions, and road

THE NEW ROAD TO THE SHAM PLAIN.

THE " MONSTER " AT WORK.

MEN OF THE 1st Bn. THE SOUTH WALES BORDERERS ROAD MAKING NEAR GHARIOM.

THE 1st. Bn. THE SOUTH WALES BORDERERS MARCHING DOWN THE SHAM PLAIN ROAD.

machinery. At the same time, work was carried out on the improvement of lateral communications, and one Field Company and one Road Construction Battalion made the track from Khairu Khel to Masti Khel passable to regular motor transport. A track from Rocha to Karkanwam was also constructed.

At the beginning of November work on two semi-permanent Scouts' posts, at Ghariom and Bichhe Kashkai, was started by Sappers & Miners supplemented by a Road Construction Battalion and Infantry working parties. This reached completion in the second week of December 1937. Each post contained accommodation for twelve platoons of Tochi Scouts and a magazine of supplies for an Infantry Brigade for three days.

Bridge defences.—At the commencement of the operations there were no special protective arrangements for important bridges other than the normal permanent piquets built for road protection, from one or more of which the bridges were under long range fire by day.

After the first attempts on them with explosives, temporary piquets were constructed overlooking the bridges, but it was found that they were not close enough to keep all vulnerable parts of the bridge under observation or fire.

Pill boxes, therefore, from which it was possible to bring fire to bear on any vulnerable portion of the bridge, were built on the piers. They were provided with electric spot lights run from batteries and were garrisoned normally by one N. C. O. and six men.

The design consisted of a two-storey pill box on the pier or, where space was insufficient, cantilevered from it, with living room for the remainder of the garrison constructed between the main girders under the roadway. The posts were held at night, normally, the garrison being found from the nearest permanent piquet.

Scouts' Posts.—Two posts were constructed, each to accommodate twelve platoons of Tochi Scouts, at Bichhe Kashkai and Ghariom. They were both built to one general specification consisting of a boulder perimeter wall 6 feet high, two corner towers, two belts of double apron wire fence, a permanent water supply with a reservoir to hold 48,000 gallons, a magazine for stores and supplies for one infantry brigade for three days, an approach motor transport road, and camp piquets as necessary.

The post at Bichhe Kashkai was begun on the 11th of November and completed on the 8th of December, the work being carried out by two Field Companies and one Road Construction Battalion. At Ghariom two Field Companies and an average infantry working party of four hundred men started the work on the 1st of November and finished it on the 4th of December.

Demolitions.—Extensive punitive demolitions were carried out during the operations.

The commonest task was the destruction of a tribesman's "kot" consisting of a fortified tower with adjoining buildings surrounded by a courtyard. Loads were organized so that the detachment of Sappers & Miners could be divided easily into two or more self-contained parties, each party taking with it four made-up charges of twentyfour guncotton slabs in addition to about one hundred and fifty slabs in tins. Concussion charges were used in all cases in which the building was sound and was to be entirely destroyed. One made-up charge of twentyfour slabs was used for towers standing alone, and fortyeight slabs for towers which had rooms adjoining, the two made-up charges being connected with instantaneous detonating fuse Cutting charges were used to demolish towers the roofs of which had previously been destroyed by fire. A charge of five pounds placed in one corner was enough to bring the whole tower down if the walls had been sufficiently weakened by digging.

The largest demolition was the destruction of the Faqir of Ipi's headquarters in the caves of Arsal Kot.

Two Field Companies accompanied the Force which marched from Ghariom camp.

From intelligence reports and air photos it was known that there were two groups of caves, one to the north east of the village and one to the south west, the latter containing the Faqir's own cave. Before the start of the march, therefore, explosives were divided equally, each company having in addition to its own company load of explosives two self-contained groups of additional necessities.

One Field Company was allotted for each group, and orders were given that as far as possible charges should be placed in chambers recessed into the haunches of the roof of cave chambers, and that all charges in caves were to be ready, provisionally, for firing two and a half hours after arrival at Arsal Kot.

Each Company sent a reconnaissance party with the Advanced Guard to ascertain the extent of the demolitions in its allotted area and thereby to save time in the allotment of explosives to the various tasks when the main body arrived.

Eight caves in all were prepared for demolition, five in the south west group and three in the north east, and permission to blow them up was given at about 1245 hours, about four hours after the arrival of the Field Companies.

Water Supply.—During the operations in addition to the normal water supply necessitated by the moves of troops and carried out by the Field Companies with them, storage and supply of a semi-permanent nature had to be arranged at practically all the camps at which troops and Road Construction Battalions had to stay for any length of time. Except in one case where water was brought in tanks, carried by lorries, pipe line was laid down and the supply was delivered either by pumping or by gravity.

The largest installations were one at Dosalli camp and one in connection with the Ghariom-Bichhe Kashkai road.

The existing supply at Dosalli was from a well in Dosalli Scouts' Post from which an electric pump delivered 23,000 gallons daily to two reservoirs. To increase the amount of water available a 4" victualic pipe line was laid direct from the water supply channel at Dosalli village down the bed of the Sre Mela Algad and up the Khaisora to the storage reservoir at the water point. The line had to be laid complete in one day during road open hours, and gave a supply, by gravity, of 6000 gallons an hour. Two and half miles of piping were laid, the labour being provided by one hundred and eighty Sappers, two hundred infantry soldiers, and fifty coolies, the time taken being ten hours.

At a later date the line was extended a further sixteen hundred yards to the spring feeding the irrigation cut, and at the same time the whole pipe was relaid so as to be proof against spate.

Stand posts were provided in Dosalli camp, each with two steps, so that no unit had to walk more than fifty yards for its water.

On the line of camps from Ghariom to Bichhe Kashkai a piped water supply was arranged to the first four camps, Bromhead, Forward, Middle and Next. The total length of pipe was twelve thousand yards. For each of the first two camps fifty Sappers and one hundred and fifty infantry soldiers or coolies were employed for three days. The amount of labour was increased by ten Sappers & fifty other men for the last two camps, the distances to be covered being greater. These tasks were completed in two and three days respectively.

Water was pumped from the Sham nala at Ghariom camp to two high level reservoirs immediately south of the camp and about one mile away. All distribution forward, other than local distribution in camps, was by gravity. Reservoirs of tarpaulin or concrete were erected in the camps.

On the completion of the road the pipe line was dismantled and back loaded, half via Dosalli and the other half via Bichhe Kashkai.

Motor transport tracks.—For operational purposes fourteen motor transport tracks totalling 42 miles were constructed in addition to the new roads. Both troop and local labour was employed. It was found that for tracks of this nature, likely to be used for a short time only and in fine weather, much steeper gradients could be used than had been customary, and a ruling gradient of 1 in 15 was found possible.

The longest continuous track made was that from Dosalli to the Sham Plain. Its total length was thirteen miles. From Dosalli it descended into the Khaisora river, and then followed the nala bed of the Sre Mela Algad, a rise of 1 in 25, for about three and a half miles. Leaving the nala bed it climbed to the top of the Sham Plain, about seven and a half miles, and then descended a gradual slope, to Ghariom camp. The track was completed in eighteen days, involving 23500 man-hours of Sapper and 24500 man-hours of Infantry labour. In the later stages a road-builder and a grader were employed.

Bridge and culvert reconstruction.—At the beginning of the hostilities the enemy carried out a number of demolitions. Against well built bridges these were never successful, but where bridges and culverts of indifferent masonry and low specification were attacked, the damage was sometimes enough to interrupt traffic. Altogether eleven culverts and six bridges had to be repaired.

Miscellaneous works.—In addition to Field Works, much semi-permanent work for the comfort and accommodation of the troops in the hot weather was undertaken. Amongst this the most important items were the chapparing of over five hundred E. P. tents, the erection of three ice factories, the installation of six cold storages for meat and of two hundred and fifty electric fans, the building of two large scale disinfectors, and the construction of sixty additional bath houses and cook shelters.

Road construction.—A total length of one hundred and fifteen miles of new road was constructed and improvement to fifteen miles of existing road was carried out between the 7th of June and the 15th of December, at a cost of thirty-one lakhs.

Owing to the presence of enemy lashkars, the normal peace time methods of reconnaissance and location could not be adopted. Prior to commencement of work the approximate location had to be decided by means of air photographs, air reconnaissance, and the limited reconnaissance carried out by Royal Engineer officers, with mobile columns operating in areas through which roads might eventually pass. On the data so obtained work was started at one or both ends of the road, and the general location was decided by protected reconnaissance going out in advance of roadhead up to a limit of five miles, the detailed location and marking out keeping one mile ahead of the work.

With regard to the alignment, military, political and engineering considerations had all to be taken into account. Military needs demanded that the roads should pass through or be adjacent to specified hostile areas. The road alignment should also be the one which could most economically be protected. For this reason the alignment of the roads along watersheds rather than in valleys was preferable. The political requirements were that roads should be within certain tribal boundaries in order to facilitate subsequent responsibility for protection. From the engineering point of view, owing to the fact that the roads were to be gravel ones with a minimum of culverts, (to reduce the possibility of enemy damage), and as it was unlikely that efficient maintenance could be carried out for a long time, it was desirable to locate the roads as far as possible on actual water sheds so as to reduce the damage from rain to a minimum. In addition, as a general rule a shorter line could be found on the water shed than in the valleys.

The type of road to be constructed was a fair-weather motor transport road. The gradient was not to exceed 1 in 15, and the width was not to be less than sixteen feet except on short straight sections cut out of hard rock where it could be reduced to twelve feet. The centre twelve feet of the surface was to be shingle. Retaining walls and culverts were to be reduced to a minimum, scuppers being largely used in place of the latter.

Although the construction of culverts was avoided as far as possible, it was found necessary to build two bridges and three large reinforced concrete culverts.

Extensive use was made of road making machinery. A small portion of this was already available in Waziristan. Further requirements were either purchased or brought in to Waziristan from other places outside. It was all staffed by the M. E. S. and administered by the Staff Captain (E. & M.) who also maintained a small central staff of mechanists and fitters for inspection and running repairs in the field.

Waziristan Base Engineer Park.—During the Khaisora operations in the winter of 1936-37 a small dump of engineer stores had been formed at Mir Ali. The organization was unsatisfactory, but as the stores required were few, no serious complaints were made at the time.

For the 1937 operations an advanced section of the Waziristan Base Engineer Park, then situated at Mari Indus, was opened at Bannu. Subsequently, the Waziristan Base Engineer Park was transferred to Bannu and this section was absorbed. The site of the Park was an area of one and a quarter acres of railway land opposite the railway station. In June it was decided to construct a second and semi-permanent park in Bannu on a new site close to the Kohat gate. The total area of this site was three and a half acres, and it was found to be only just sufficient for the stores backloaded at the conclusion of the operations.

The Officer Commanding Waziristan Base Engineer Park, who was also Officer Commanding M. E. S. Workshops and M. E. S. Depot, was placed directly under the orders of the Chief Engineer Northern Command.

Some of the staff were obtained from the Mir Ali Park, but the majority were posted specially by the Chief Engineer, Northern Command. The total reached, which was found to be only just enough, was two officers, one S.D.O., two Supervisors, four storekeepers, two store munshis, and eleven clerks.

Labour was found from local coolies and these were very successful once they had got the knack of handling the heavy stores. During the summer it was found necessary to stop all work between 1300 and 1700 hours, the stores becoming too hot to touch and there being no sheds.

A large number of forward dumps were formed, of two types, Wazirforce Dumps and Field Company's or Field Engineer's Dumps. Wazirforce Dumps, to which alone the Base Engineer Park made issues, were formed at Mir Ali, Manzai, Dosalli, Ghariom, Razmak and Masti Khel. Field Engineers formed small dumps of their own, based on Wazirforce Dumps.

APPENDIX III.

The Ordnance Service in Waziristan, 1937.

These operations did not involve fighting on the large scale of the 1919-21 operations in Waziristan, but give an indication of what is required for fighting on even a moderate scale.

The strength of the forces in Waziristan varied from time to time, but in round figures the average number of personnel, for whose maintenance the Indian Army Ordnance Corps was responsible, amounted to 54,000.

The main units which comprised the force were 2 cavalry regiments, 5 field batteries, 11 mountain batteries, 6 light tank companies, 36 infantry battalions, 12 companies Sappers & Miners, 7 signal units, 2 motor transport companies, 9 independent motor transport sections, 15 animal transport companies, 46 supply units, 7 field ambulances, 2 labour companies, and 4 road construction battalions

The Assistant Director of Ordnance Services, Wazirforce, was responsible for all the Ordnance arrangements in the Forces. There was a Deputy Assistant Director of Ordnance Services (D. A. D. O. S.) with each division and a brigade ordnance warrant officer with each brigade. In addition, it was found necessary to appoint a D. A. D. O. S. Lines of Communication to deal with units which did not form an integral part of a division.

Until the 1937 operations, the Ordnance field organization, apart from mobile workshops, consisted of railhead ammunition depots, railhead ordnance officers detachments, and tent repair units. This organization was found to be rigid and uneconomical in personnel, and a new organization based on the Home one was tried out successfully during the operations. This consisted of a number of ordnance field companies, each of which had a company headquarters and a number of sections. The company headquarters co-ordinated the working of the whole company and operated the main field depot. Sections were of three types, general duties, tent repair, and oil cooker repair. General duties sections carried out the main duties connected with stores, ammunition, and salvage; they assisted in the main depot and operated subsidiary depots. The duties of the other sections were as their names implied. Sections were sent forward from Arsenals as required, and the organization was thus elastic and capable of adjustment according to the situation.

All Ordnance installations in the field were called Ordnance field depots. In 1937 the main Ordnance field depot was at Bannu (railhead), and all stores despatched to the theatre of operations passed through this depot. Small field depots were established at Dosalli and Razmak, where a number of important stores were held for rapid issue to troops.

The system of supply of ordnance stores and clothing was as follows. Divisional units submitted indents through the Brigade ordnance warrant officer, one of whose main duties was to assist units in the preparation of indents. The indents were approved by the D. A. D. O. S. and were then passed to the Ordnance field depot for compliance. In the case of units on the Lines of Communication, the indents were approved by the D. A. D. O. S. Lines of Communication. Stores were despatched with supply columns and were normally received by the units within a week of the submission of the indent. The supply of ammunition was automatically carried out as laid down in Field Service Regulations.

Articles rendered unserviceable or no longer required by units were returned to the nearest ordnance field depot or to the Brigade ordnance warrant officer, empty returning transport being used for the purpose. On receipt by the depot returned stores were immediately sorted into three categories. unserviceable, repairable, and serviceable. Unserviceable stores were broken down. the serviceable and repairable components being salvaged. Repairable stores were either repaired in Ordnance mobile workshops or sent back to Arsenals. Serviceable stores were absorbed into the stocks of the depot.

All equipment and clothing taken into the field must be serviceable and have a remaining life of at least three months under field service conditions. The replacement issues, therefore, in the early stages of a campaign may be few, but will increase rapidly after two months. In peace, the Indian Army Ordnance Corps provided for a total of some 3,50,000 personnel. This total includes the Royal Air Force in India, Indian State Forces, certain militias, military police and other auxiliary corps, in addition to the regular army. It is interesting to compare the average issue of certain articles in peace to 54,000 men for six and a half months with the issues made to a force of the same number under active service conditions in Waziristan over the same period.

Article.	Peace issues.	Issues in Waziristan
Water bottles	2000	4679
Web equipment belts	1800	4931
Haversacks	1150	4024
Mess tins	1050	3857
Nosebags	3600	8892
Collars	750	1083
Girths	700	1318
Helves for pick axes.	1050	4065
Ground sheets	4350	3806
Khaki drill shorts	13000	50804
Worsted socks, pairs	60700	111100
Boots	8000	14612
Flannel shirts	10250	47102

From the above figures it will be seen that there is no uniform relation between issues in peace and issues under war conditions. The difficulties, therefore, of calculating extra requirements for mobilization and for minor operations will be appreciated.

The actual supply of stores and the assessing of the cost of the extra equipment required were, moreover, complicated in 1937 by certain factors. During minor operations pressure cannot be brought on the trade to give precedence to military needs to the same extent as would be possible after mobilization. In 1937 firms were approaching normal conditions after years of depression and civil demands were increasing. This not only affected the time taken by the trade to supply but accounted for considerable fluctuations in price.

With regard to ammunition, the expenditure in operations on the North-West Frontier is always small in comparison with a campaign against an organised enemy. The following details may be of interest (numbers of guns and rifles are shown in brackets).

6-inch howitzer (2) . . . . . 88 rounds.
3·7 inch howitzer (49) . . . . 11086 rounds.
4·5 inch howitzer (14) . . . . 1218 rounds.
Vickers guns (484) . . . . ⎫
Light automatics (469) . . . ⎬ 759723 rounds.
Rifles (25073) . . . . . ⎭
Grenades . . . . . . 1079.
Gun cotton . . . . . . 8548 slabs.

Altogether 2357 tons of Ordnance stores and clothing and 696 tons of ammunition, including R. A. F. bombs, were forwarded from Arsenals and passed through the Ordnance field depot at Bannu.

To carry out all the duties in connection with the maintenance of the Force in equipment, clothing, and ammunition, the personnel of the Indian Army Ordnance Corps employed in the theatre of operations consisted of seven officers, forty British other ranks, thirty-four Indian clerks and storekeepers, and seventeen followers, a total of ninety-eight persons in all. These figures include officers and clerical establishments employed at Force and Divisional Headquarters but do not include the personnel of Ordnance mobile workshops. In addition, personnel of labour companies were attached to depots for loading and other duties.

The Ordnance mobile workshop, the total establishment of which was forty-eight, carried out all second line repairs, that is to say, those repairs which units with their hand tools could not effect and which did not merit being sent back to Arsenals for a major overhaul. The workshop has two technical lorries on its establishment and required three 3-ton lorries to move its personnel, tents, and stores. Some details of the items repaired by the Ordnance mobile workshops are, artillery equipments, rifles and pistols, machine guns, range-finders, dial sights, binoculars, visual line and wireless signalling equipment, oil cookers, stretchers, water stores, and saddlery.

An Ordnance mechanical engineer from the mobile workshop visited regularly all units in the war area, inspecting equipment and so obtaining early information of defects in design. It was his duty to devise means to overcome such defects quickly and to report to Army Headquarters through departmental channels the nature of the defects and his recommendations to overcome them. If new items of equipment were considered by the General Staff to be urgently necessary experimental items were made up in Ordnance mobile workshops and put into use, pending their production in numbers by Ordnance establishments in rear.

During the 1937 operations the Ordnance mobile workshop was situated at Bannu. A few fitters were sent forward to Dosalli and Razmak to carry out repairs to oil cookers and small arms. From a departmental point of view the location of the workshop at Bannu was unsound, as time and transport was wasted bringing repairable stores back to Bannu and sending them forward again after repair. It was decided, however, by the General Staff that space in perimeter camps was too restricted to allow of the workshop being moved forward.

APPENDIX IV.

THE ORGANIZATION OF THE L. OF C. AND THE PROTECTION OF CONVOYS.

At the commencement of the operations the system adopted was that all vehicles were collected in one convoy for each destination and that convoy ran through to its destination and back to its starting point as one convoy. The Central Waziristan Road was divided into sectors, the responsibility for each sector being allotted to a particular commander.

There were very few permanent piquets for road protection. At first light troops patrolled the road and the country in its immediate vicinity, making a close search of all culverts, small nullahs and other likely hostile hiding places. These troops then occupied supporting positions in their Sectors and remained out until all convoys had passed through, when they returned to camp.

Convoys were commanded by R.I.A.S.C. (M.T.) officers, and were provided with close infantry and Sapper and Miner escorts, found from the station in which the convoy originated. One section of armoured cars also accompanied each convoy as close escort, remaining with the convoy for the round trip, their dispositions in the convoy being varied daily. Other sub-sections of armoured cars patrolled each of the following areas—

(a) Saidgi—Khajuri, both inclusive.

(b) Exclusive Damdil to inclusive Dosalli.

These patrols remained in their Sectors until returning convoys had all passed through.

Close support R. A. F. sorties operated continually over the road during convoy hours and also for half an hour before convoys left their starting point.

In order to show protecting troops when the complete convoy had passed, the last lorry of each convoy carried a red flag.

During the first phase, the sectors and their commanders were as follows :—

(a) Commander Bannu—Bannu to inclusive 14½ milestones.

(b) Commander Khajuri—exclusive 14½ M. S. to exclusive 21½ M. S.

(c) Commander 1st Division (L. of C. troops)—inclusive 21½ M. S. to inclusive 23½ M. S.

(d) Commander Idak—exclusive 23½ M. S. to inclusive 32 M. S.

(e) Commander Bannu Brigade—inclusive Isha to inclusive Miranshah to inclusive Thal to inclusive 41 M. S.

(f) Commander 1st Inf. Brigade—inclusive 41 M. S. to inclusive Damdil to exclusive 42 M. S.

(g) Commander Waziristan Division—inclusive 52 M. S. to inclusive Dosalli.

Convoys ran daily except on road closed days, as under :—

(a) Bannu—Damdil—Bannu.

Timings.

Up { Bannu—0800 hrs.
Mir Ali—0930 hrs.
Damdil—1100 hrs.

Down. { Damdil—1300 hrs.
Mir Ali—1400 hrs.
Bannu—1530 hrs.

The convoys consisted of fast lorries only and did not exceed eighty vehicles in number.

(b) Bannu—Mir Ali—Miranshah—Bannu.

Timings.

Up { Bannu—0930 hrs.
Mir Ali—1100 hrs.
(Mir Ali portion detached)
Miranshah—1200 hrs.

Down. { Miranshah—1400 hrs.
Mir Ali—1500 hrs.
(Mir Ali portion detached).
Bannu—1630 hrs.

The combined Bannu—Mir Ali and Bannu—Miranshah convoy did not exceed 80 lorries.

(c) Mir Ali—Dosalli—Mir Ali.

Timings.

Up { Mir Ali—0830 hrs.
Damdil—0930 hrs.
Dosalli—1000 hrs.

Down { Dosalli—1200 hrs.
Damdil=1230 hrs.
Mir Ali=1400 hrs.

II. This method continued in force until the beginning of May 1937, when certain modifications were introduced.

The infantry and Sapper and Miner close escorts were abolished as it was considered that they were likely to prove more of a lure, inciting tribesmen to attack in the hope of acquiring rifles, than a safeguard to the convoys they were escorting.

Permanent piquets were constructed for the road protection troops.

Convoys were run in sections, each of about twenty-five vehicles, starting at intervals of twenty minutes. Control stations were installed all the way along the road and the sections ran to a definite time table.

Close escort armoured cars were abolished and all armoured cars were employed as patrols. The road was divided into Sectors, one section of armoured cars being allotted to each sector. Armoured cars patrolled their sectors before convoys arrived and in the intervals between convoy sections. During the actual passing of convoys they took up tactical positions on the road, guarding nalas and other dangerous localities.

III. On June 7th convoys commenced running to Razmak, and from this date onwards sectors of responsibility were allotted as follows :—

(a) Commander Bannu—Bannu to inclusive 14½ M. S.

(b) Commander 9th Inf. Bde.—exclusive 14½ M. S. to exclusive 51½ M. S.

(c) Commander 1st Division—inclusive 51½ M. S. to inclusive 54 M. S.

(d) Commander Waziristan Division—exclusive 54 M. S. to Razmak.

The same system of permanent piquets with floating supports by day continued to operate in areas (a) (b) and (c). In area (d) there were no permanent road piquets other than camp piquets, until sometime later. Temporary day piquets were occupied every morning by troops or scouts, with supporting troops and patrolling armoured cars at tactical points along the road. Khassadars were also employed in this sector in increasing numbers, as the political situation improved.

IV. A few days later, initially as an experimental measure, with the object of reducing the numbers of hours for which road protection troops were on duty, the convoy system was abolished and the following introduced.

(i) Lorries were organized into blocks of five running at 2½ minutes interval between blocks. The use of the red flag on the last lorry was discontinued.

(ii) Control stations were established at Bannu, Saidgi, Razani and Razmak. A time table was issued showing the hours between which traffic was permitted to pass each control station on both the Up and Down journeys. No traffic was allowed to leave a control station before the prescribed hours, and traffic arriving at a control station after the prescribed hour was impounded for the night.

Cars containing officers or other ranks were made to adhere to these road open hours. In cases of extreme urgency, Area Commanders were permitted to allow officers to travel during road closed hours, but were responsible for making suitable escort arrangements for them.

(iii) Armoured cars worked as before, patrolling sectors. In addition, a complete patrol of their sectors was made before road open hours. Another complete patrol was made after road closed hours, to ensure that no break downs were left on the road.

(iv) Breakdown lorries patrolled each sector, and M. T. officers in Ford Vans patrolled the roads to ensure strict adherence to march discipline.

(v) Air reconnaissance of and close support to the road was continued, the number of sorties being reduced as conditions became more settled.

This system remained in force for the remainder of the operations in 1937 and worked very smoothly.

APPENDIX V.

THE SUPPLY SERVICE AND THE TRANSPORT SERVICE IN WAZIRISTAN IN 1937.

The Supply Service.

From the 8th of March 1937 the peace supply organization in Waziristan ceased to exist and peace units and installations were transformed into units of the R. I. A. S. C. War Organization. In addition, the number of Supply Depot and Supply Issue sections were largely increased by the importation of these units from Northern Command with one or two from Eastern Command.

The administration of the supply services in the Force was controlled, under the orders of the Force Commander, by a Supply Directorate at Force Headquarters, comprising the A.D.S. & T., D.A.D.S., and Staff Captain (S), and administration and control were carried out through No. 3 Supply Personnel Company, Cs. R.I.A.S.C., and directly to Field Supply Depots in an emergency.

The most important link in the chain of supply was No. 3 S. P. Company, the number of units administered by the officer commanding this company rising from twenty-five to fifty-five. The necessity for a second S. P. company soon became apparent, but the difficulty of finding officers to form the Headquarters of an additional company precluded the formation of such a unit. In August 1937, Cs. R.I.A.S.C. were made responsible for certain items of general and local administration in their areas, so relieving the officer commanding No. 3 S. P. Company of the duties of inspection of the majority of the Supply Units in Divisional Areas. He still retained the work in connection with the personnel of such units and his responsibilities in connection with the regularization of the stocks of supplies to be held in the Force. Briefly, his duties were as follows. He worked under the command of the A.D.S. & T. Supply units of the Force worked under his administrative command, except as and when delegated to Cs. R.I.A.S.C. and he was responsible to the A. D. S. & T. for the general co-ordination and administration of these units. He established Supply Depots as ordered by the A. D. S. & T. He was responsible to the A. D. S. & T. for the maintenance of stocks in Supply Depots as laid down from time to time except when this duty was delegated to Cs. R. I. A. S. C. He was responsible to the A. D. S. & T. for the placing of demands for supplies for the whole Force on the D. D. S. & T. Northern Command and the D. S. & T. Army Headquarters.

Immediately prior to the operations Headquarters, Northern Command laid down the number of days reserves of supplies to be maintained in Waziristan. Headquarters Wazirforce ordered the distribution of these reserves to Advanced Base Supply Depots and Field Supply Depots in the area of operations. Changes in the distribution owing to the closing of certain Depots and the opening of other new ones being published as necessary.

The system of demand for supplies followed accepted principles, modified to meet the special conditions of the Force. Up to the end of May, Field Supply Depots submitted daily demands, but as by then stocks had been accumulated in Depots, the daily demand was altered to a weekly one.

As was to be expected in operations involving a Force of this size, difficulties of supplies which had to be surmounted were many.

One of the chief ones was the delivery of fresh meat to the British troops. The closing of the L. of C. to Razmak and Wana stopped the normal peace system by which cattle were killed in R. I. A. S. C. butcheries at these two places and meat issued locally. The supply was maintained successfully by using Mahsud and other lorry contractors who were able to run their lorries unprotected. For all posts, excluding Razmak, on the Bannu-Razmak line meat was prepared at Bannu and transported to the posts in the daily convoy. As the L. of C. extended it became necessary towards the end of May to establish another butchery forward of Bannu. This was placed at Dosalli and all troops of the garrison and in the Sham Plain were then maintained from that place.

The provision of meat for Indian troops did not present the same difficulties. Arrangements were made to supply it "on hoof" to units, delivery being made to Supply Issue Sections and to Field Supply Depots by Government or hired M. T. in the early stages and by meat contractors' own lorries later.

In peace time Government bakeries existed at Wana, Razmak and Bannu. Owing to the closing of the L. of C. the task of supplying bread for the greater part of the Force fell on the bakery at Bannu. As the bakery there was small and space for expansion did not exist, a new bakery was built which would meet the requirements of the peace garrison and were capable of expansion in war. Later, when the L. of C. was firmly established as far as Dosalli a field bakery was established there to supply the garrison and the troops in the Sham Plain.

Considerable use was made of refrigerating equipment during the hot season of 1937. At the start of the operations only two mechanically refrigerated vehicles were available. It was obvious that more would be required as soon as possible. A third was in process of construction at Chaklala. Two more were obtained from Calcutta and five others were put in hand at Chaklala. In the meantime the situation was helped out by the use at Bannu of eight insulated containers cooled by small electrically driven compressors, supplied by a Calcutta firm. Eventually, arrangements for chilling meat were made at Dosalli, and at Razmak. In addition to meat, vegetables were carried in cooling containers with very good results. Fresh milk was also transported in the same way.

The Transport Service.

The administration and operation of the Transport Service throughout the Force were controlled by the A. D. S. & T. who had a D. A. D. T. as a member of his headquarters staff.

For L. of C. transport this control was exercised through Staff Captain (T) and Station Transport Officers working directly under the Transport Directorate. Cs.R.I.A.S.C., acting under the orders of Formation Commanders, controlled transport allotted to Formations. Officers Commanding Field M. T. Workshops and M. T. Companies dealt with 2nd line Repair Organization, 3rd Line Repair Organization coming under the Officer Commanding Heavy Repair Shop (M. T.) Class III.

A considerable increase in the number of A. T. and M. T. units was necessary when the operations were started, and nine A. T. companies, 2 M. T. companies, four Independent M. T. Sections, 1 M. A. Section, and two L. of C. Workshop Sections were brought in to the country. A considerable amount of hired transport was also taken into use.

The M. T. with the Force rarely functioned as 2nd line M. T. The immediate establishment of "dumps" of supplies and ammunition in the vicinity of the troops as they moved forward meant that the M. T. used to maintain the troops became in effect L. of C. transport. "Daily Availability" states, showing the availability of M. T. at 0900 hours on the following day, were sent by Staff Captains (T) and Station Transport Officers to reach Force Headquarters by 2200 hours daily. By this means the distribution of the M. T. as required by the Transport Directorate was controlled.

The 2nd Line R.I.A.S.C. Repair Organization consisted of Field Workshops (M. T.) capable of throwing out detachments as required and of the workshops of the M. T. Companies located in the theatre of operations.

The artificer personnel of the Field Workshops (M. T.) was formed from those belonging to Independent M. T. Sections, L. of C. Workshop Sections and the personnel of units not responsible for their own 2nd line maintenance. M. T. Companies carried out their own 2nd line repairs as self-contained units.

Animal transport (mule and camel) was allocated to subordinate formations as necessary by Force Headquarters. The Force reserve of 2nd line transport once allotted normally remained under the administration of subordinate formations until required for work with another formation, when Force Headquarters ordered the necessary re-distribution.

Throughout the campaign animal transport was extensively used. The nature of the country to be traversed necessitated the reorganization of the animal transport with the Force on an "all-pack" basis, and except when formations or units moved along the central Waziristan Road carts were rarely used. Carts could not be kept in forward camps owing to the possibility of sudden movements or of the evacuation of such camps, and they were kept parked in some central camp on the main L. of C.

Camel companies proved invaluable in carrying 2nd line loads and for the stocking of forward Field Supply Depots. These camels also carried the khajawahs used for the evacuation of casualties.

The condition of the animals generally throughout the campaign was satisfactory. There were a certain number of casualties from enemy action, nearly all being the result of sniping fire into camps.

At the commencement of the operations there were a few M. T. vehicles fitted with Berridge equipment for the carriage of horses and mules. As these could transport one animal only, experiments were carried out to produce a more suitable means of transport for animals. The final results of these experiments were the conversion of a 3-ton lorry so that while still capable of carrying a three-ton supply load, it could, if required, carry four horses or six mules or two camels. Ultimately ten 3-ton lorries were converted in this way, providing enough M. T. to move the 1st line unit transport and chargers of a full battalion.

Sketch Map A
OF
WAZIRISTAN

Scale of Miles.

Administrative Boundary
Boundary of Afghanistan
Railways, Narrow Gauge
M.T. Roads in existence on 1.12.36
Cart Tracks

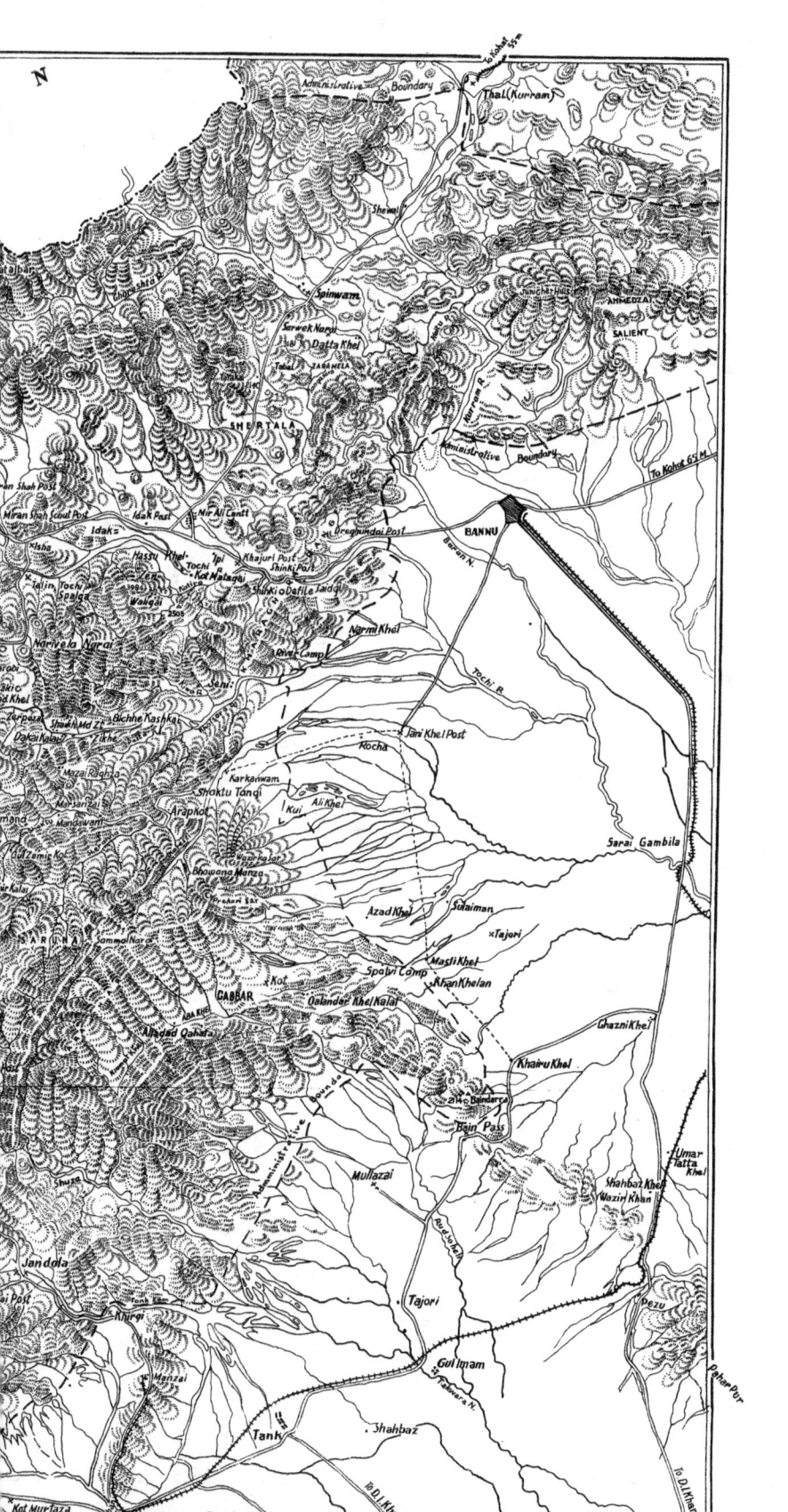

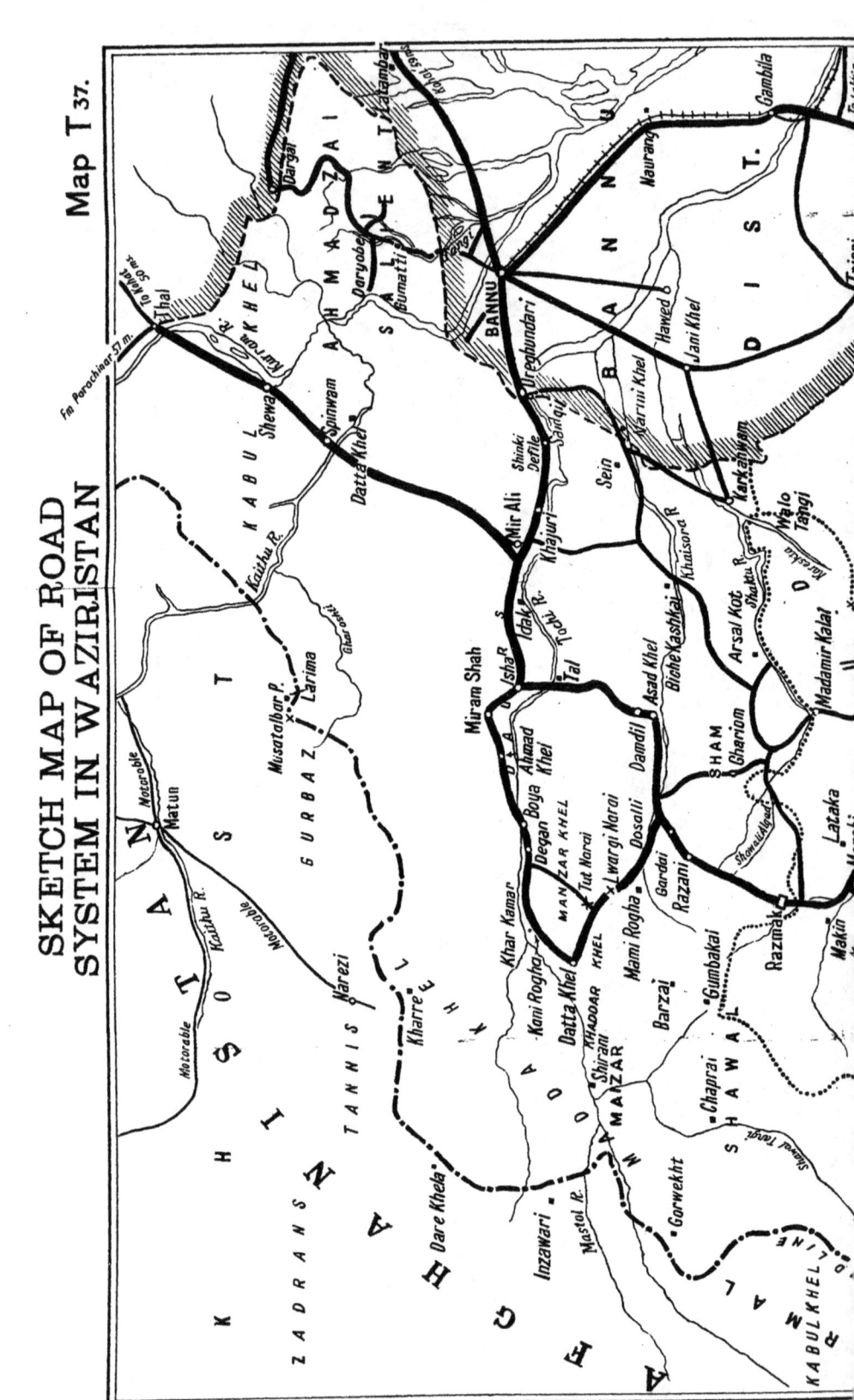

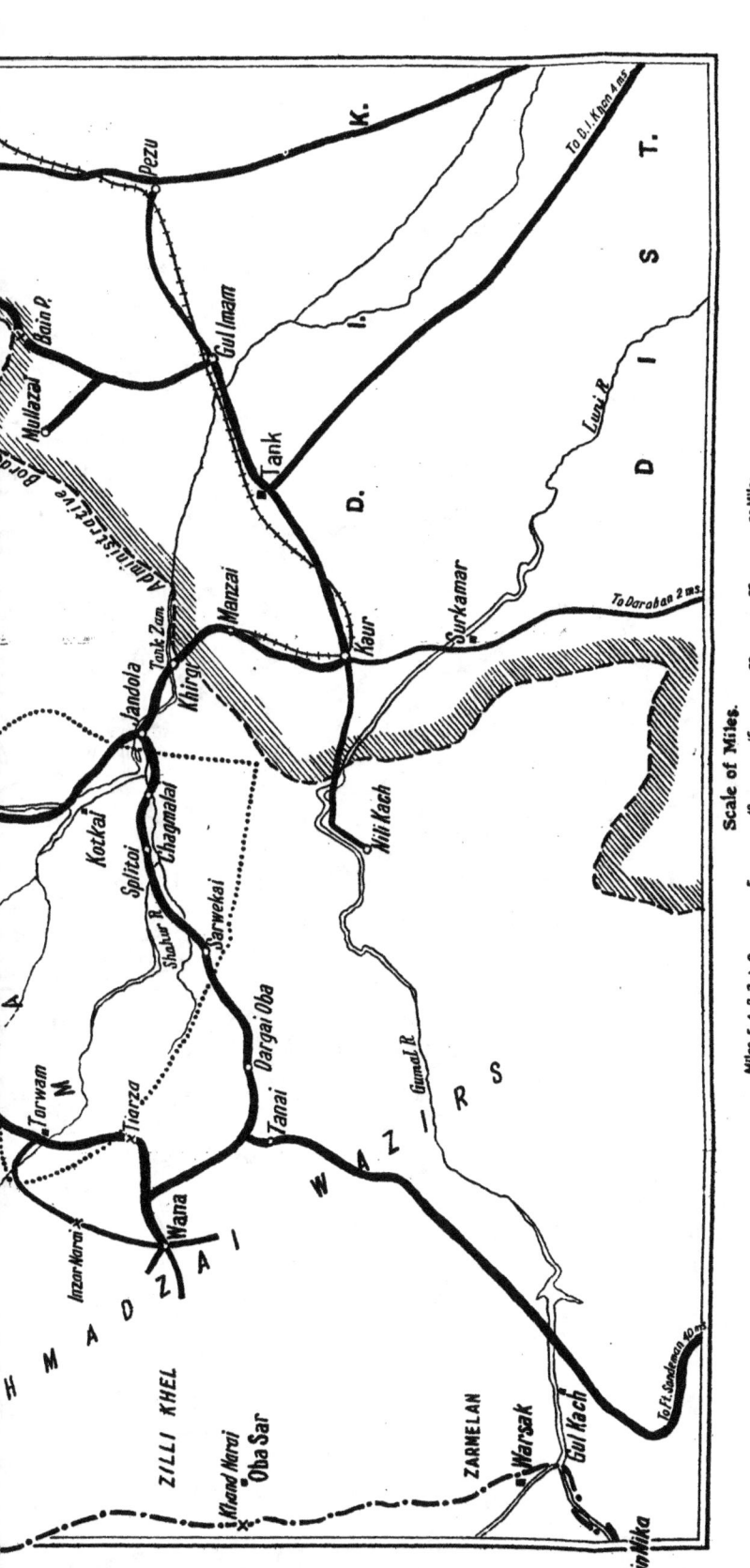

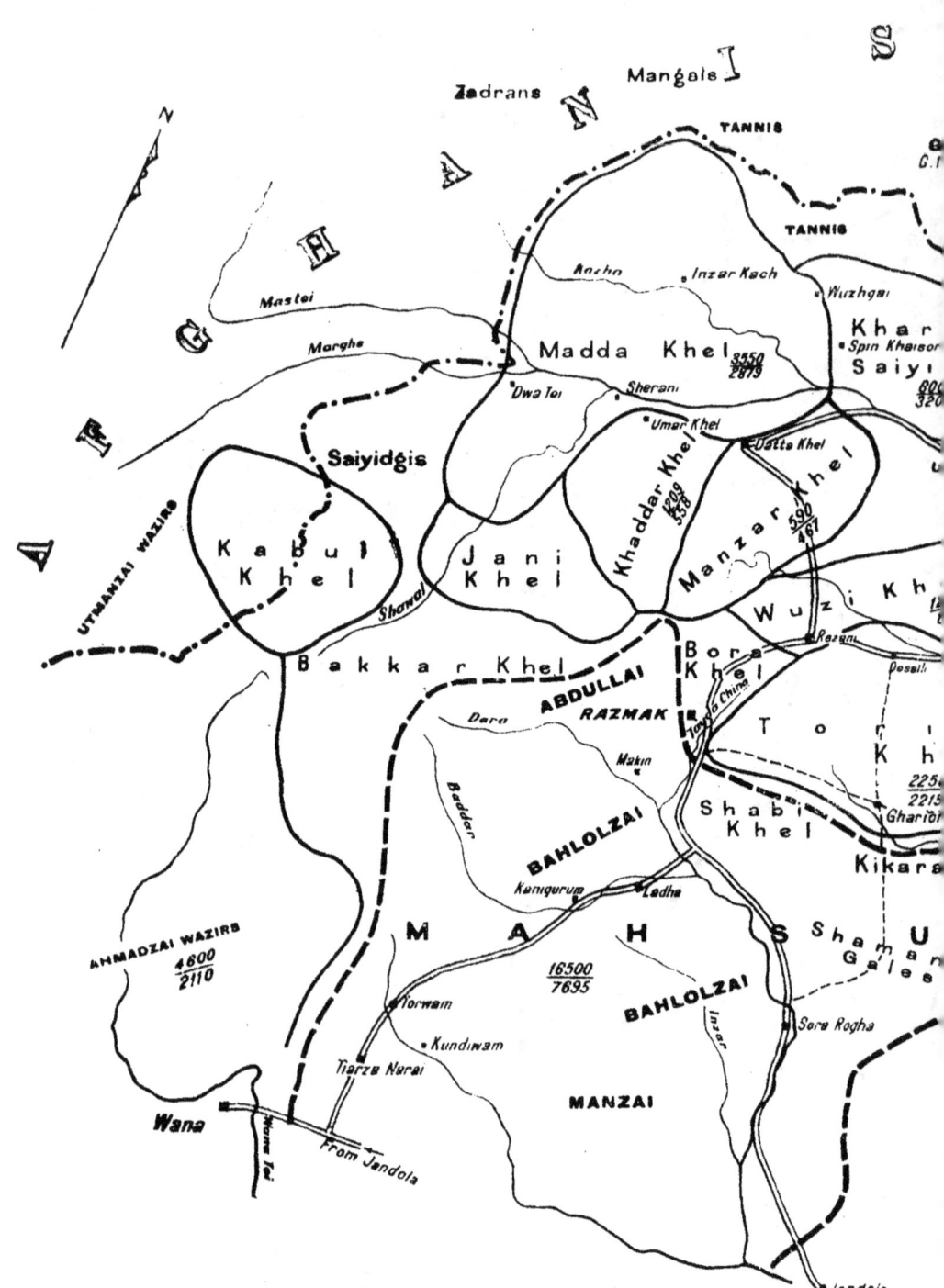

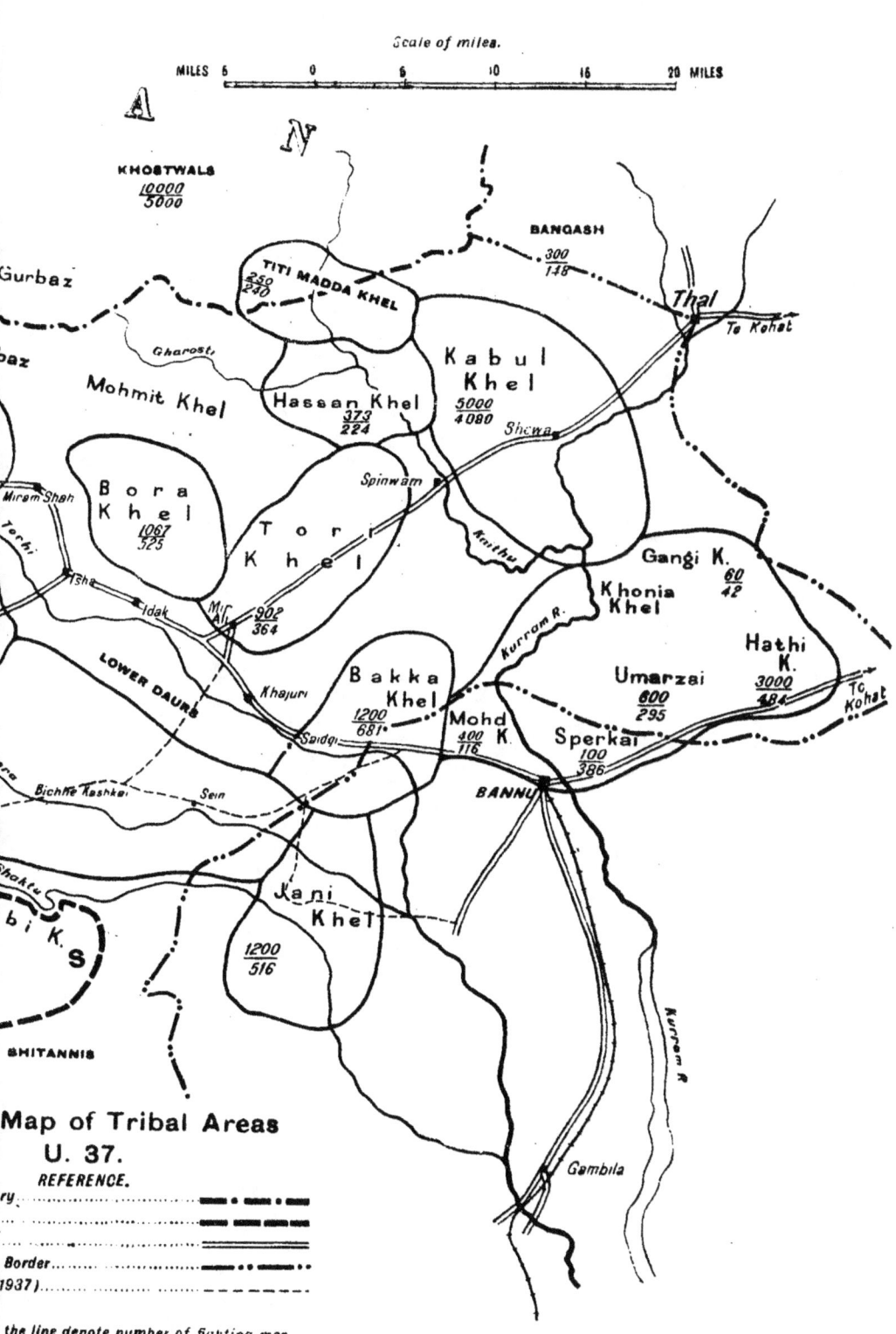

www.ingramcontent.com/pod-product-compliance
Lightning Source LLC
Chambersburg PA
CBHW050330230426
43663CB00010B/1800